Story and Art by Arina Tanemura

SAKURA HIME

The Legend of Princess Sakura

8

Characters

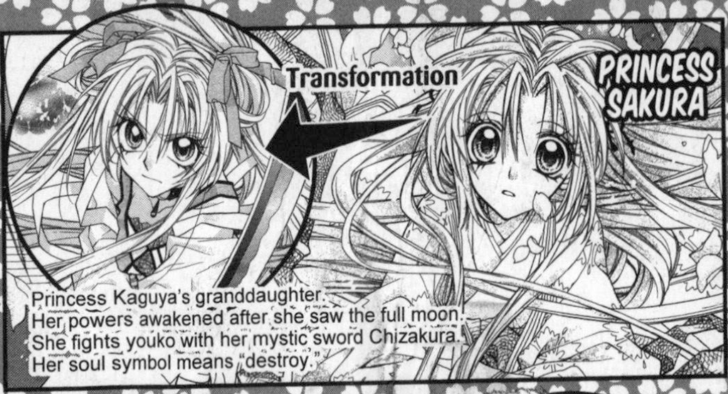
PRINCESS SAKURA
Transformation
Princess Kaguya's granddaughter. Her powers awakened after she saw the full moon. She fights youko with her mystic sword Chizakura. Her soul symbol means "destroy."

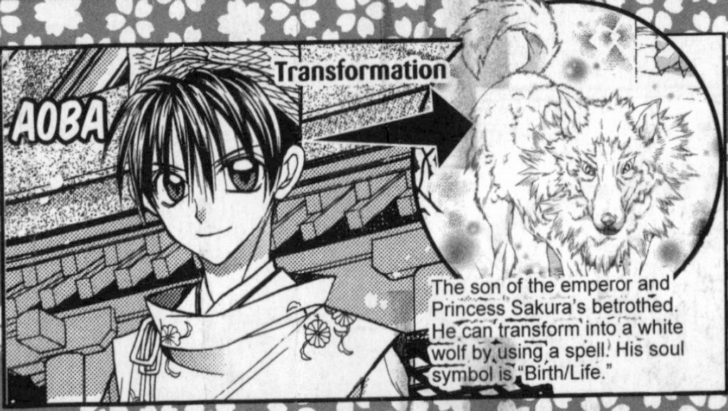
AOBA
Transformation
The son of the emperor and Princess Sakura's betrothed. He can transform into a white wolf by using a spell. His soul symbol is "Birth/Life."

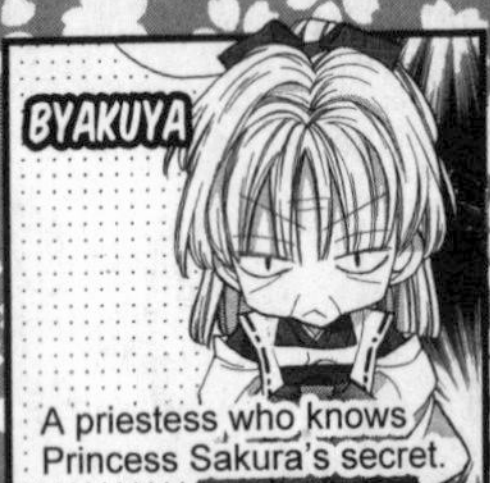
BYAKUYA
A priestess who knows Princess Sakura's secret.

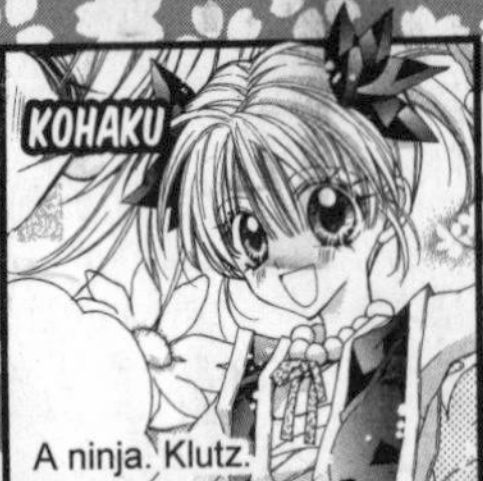
KOHAKU
A ninja. Klutz.

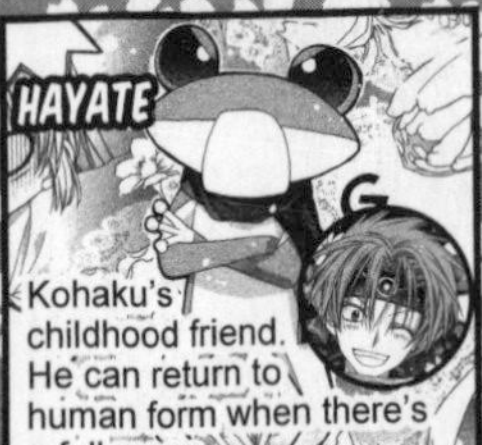
HAYATE
Kohaku's childhood friend. He can return to human form when there's a full moon.

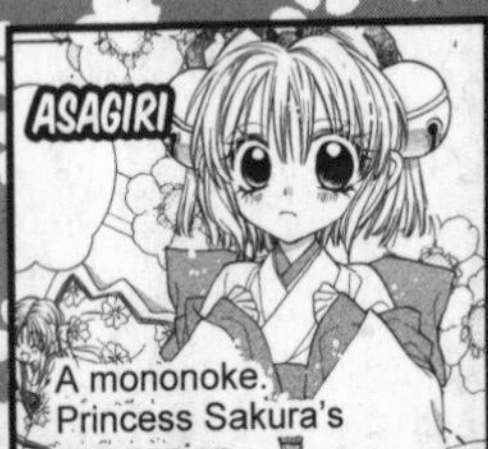
ASAGIRI
A mononoke. Princess Sakura's companion.

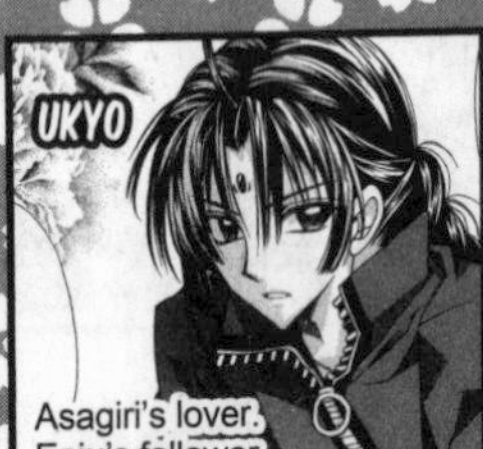
UKYO
Asagiri's lover. Enju's follower.

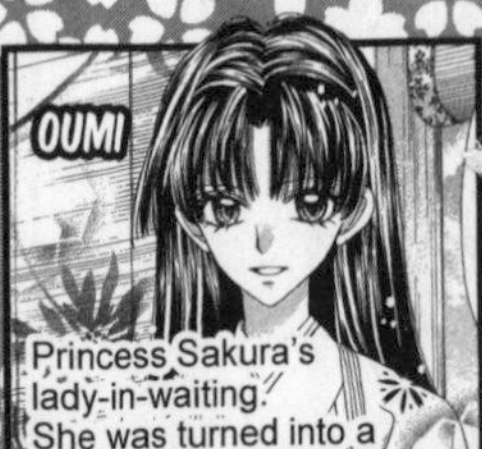
OUMI
Princess Sakura's lady-in-waiting. She was turned into a youko by Enju.

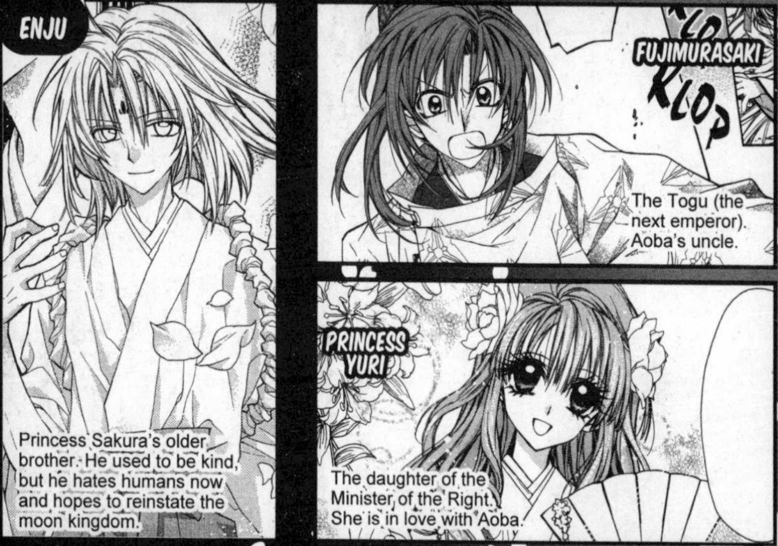
FUJIMURASAKI
KLOP
The Togu (the next emperor). Aoba's uncle.
PRINCESS YURI
The daughter of the Minister of the Right. She is in love with Aoba.
ENJU
Princess Sakura's older brother. He used to be kind, but he hates humans now and hopes to reinstate the moon kingdom.

Sakura Hime: The Legend of Princess Sakura

Story Thus Far

Heian era. Fourteen-year-old Princess Sakura travels to the capital to marry Prince Oura, her betrothed. But Aoba, the emissary who has come to pick her up, is actually the prince.

Sakura finds out that she is the granddaughter of Princess Kaguya and has the power to wield the mystic sword Chizakura. Sakura is given orders from the emperor to hunt down a youko in Uji.

There she meets a mysterious man named Enju. He is her older brother Kai whom she thought dead. Enju despises humans, and he kidnaps Sakura with the help of his followers...

Aoba and Sakura's friends attack Enju's hideout, Shura Yugenden, defeating Enju's followers to save Sakura.

But Enju erases Sakura's consciousness to control her, and he forces her to use Chizakura to kill Ukyo, who had betrayed him. Sakura learns about Enju's plan to revive Princess Kaguya and makes up her mind to part ways with Enju once and for all.

Fujimurasaki arrives to rescue Sakura and her friends, and Shura Yugenden goes up in flames. Enju and his followers are now missing...

SAKURA HIME
The Legend of Princess Sakura

....

CONTENTS

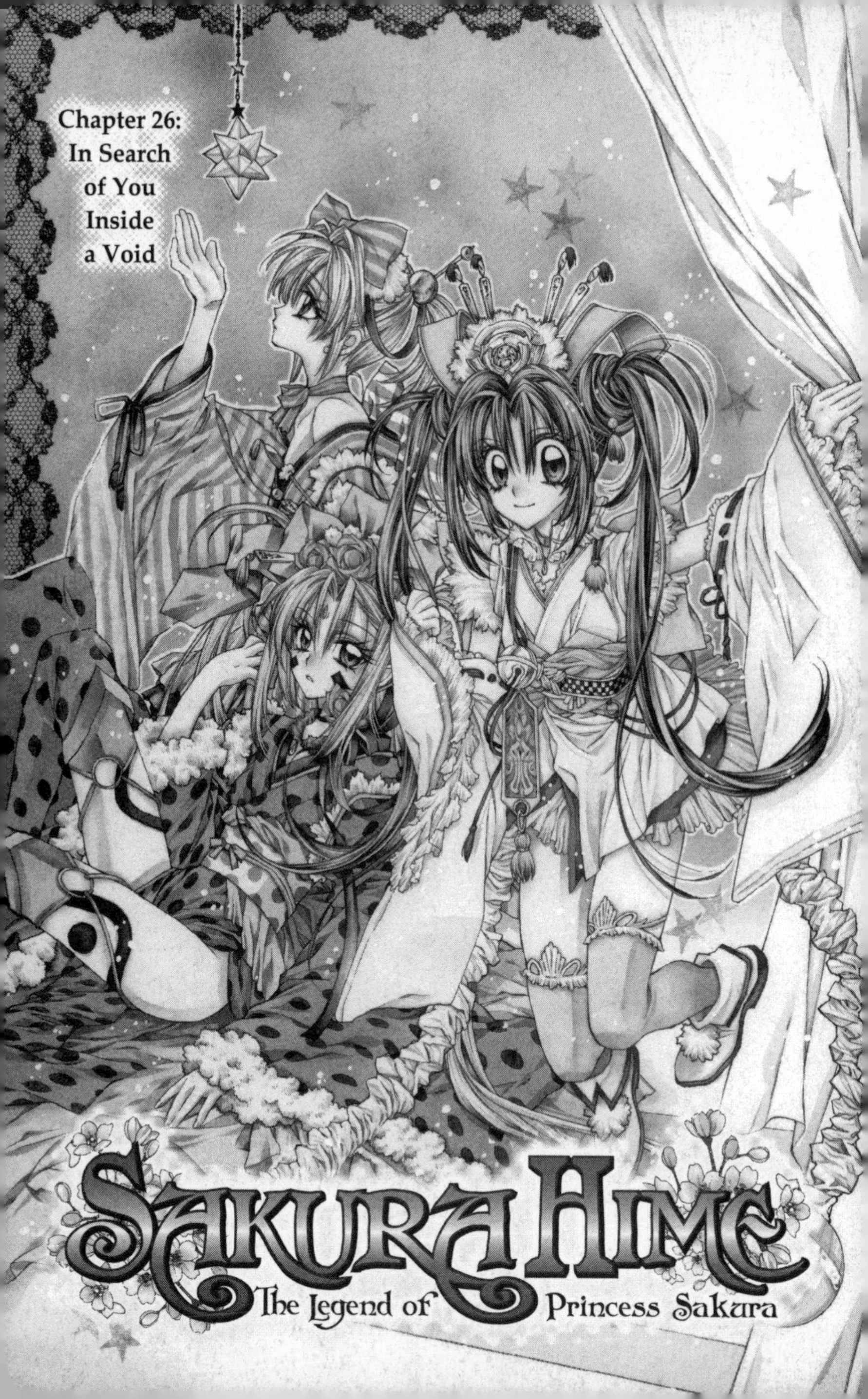
Chapter 26: In Search of You Inside a Void
SAKURA HIME
The Legend of Princess Sakura

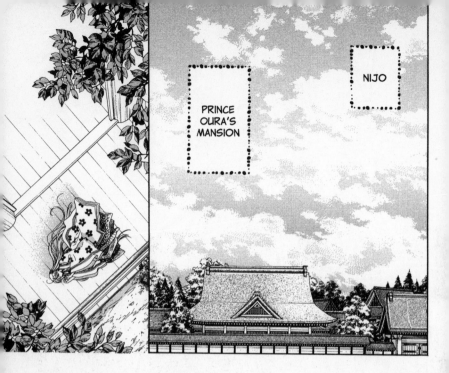

In the image: PRINCE OURA'S MANSION, NIJO

Chapter 26: In Search of You Inside a Void

✻ I'm giving away the story.

Now the story takes a new turn, and a new character will appear too. The feel of the Heian era seems watered down in the story arcs centered around battles (because I lack the sufficient skills... ♥), so I wanted to reset the story. Anyhow, I created Princess Yuri without much thought, but she seems to have many secrets hidden up her sleeve. I have a feeling you will be seeing her quite often from now on.

The emperor clearly seems to dislike Sakura. Maybe he's the kind of man who can't accept people outside his inner circle, or maybe he just can't trust other people? He feels the need to control Sakura, but he also schemes because he dislikes her. But maybe an emperor who rules over a country has to be this cautious? I was thinking of doing a side story about Sakura's kimono featuring Asagiri, but I decided to use it here as a way to introduce Princess Yuri. (In the Heian era, it took a lot of formal procedures for noble families to become acquainted, so I had to come up with some way for the princesses to meet quickly. ﹤▲﹥)

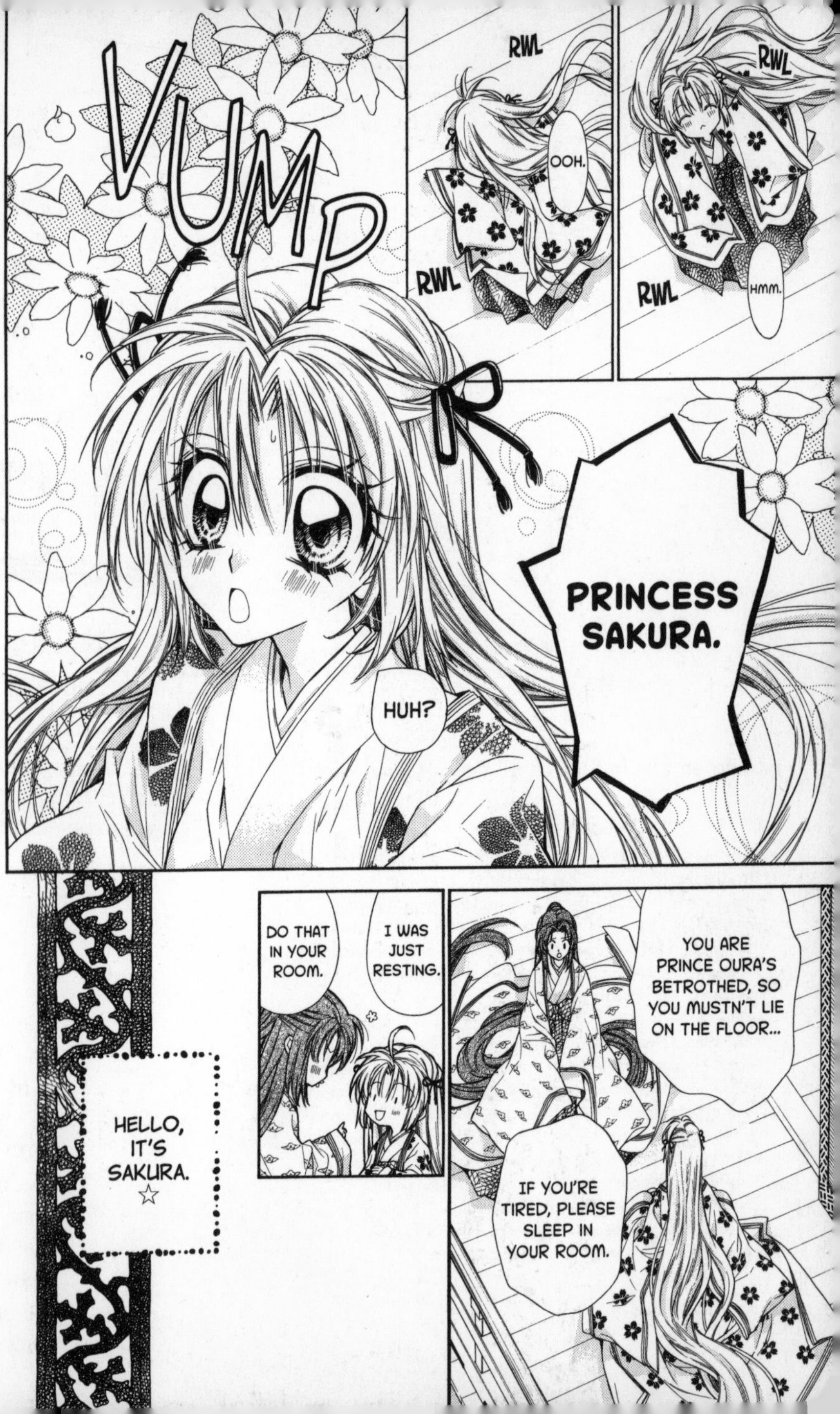
RWL
RWL
HMM.
RWL
OOH.
RWL
VUMP
PRINCESS SAKURA.
HUH?
YOU ARE PRINCE OURA'S BETROTHED, SO YOU MUSTN'T LIE ON THE FLOOR...
IF YOU'RE TIRED, PLEASE SLEEP IN YOUR ROOM.
I WAS JUST RESTING.
DO THAT IN YOUR ROOM.
HELLO, IT'S SAKURA. ☆

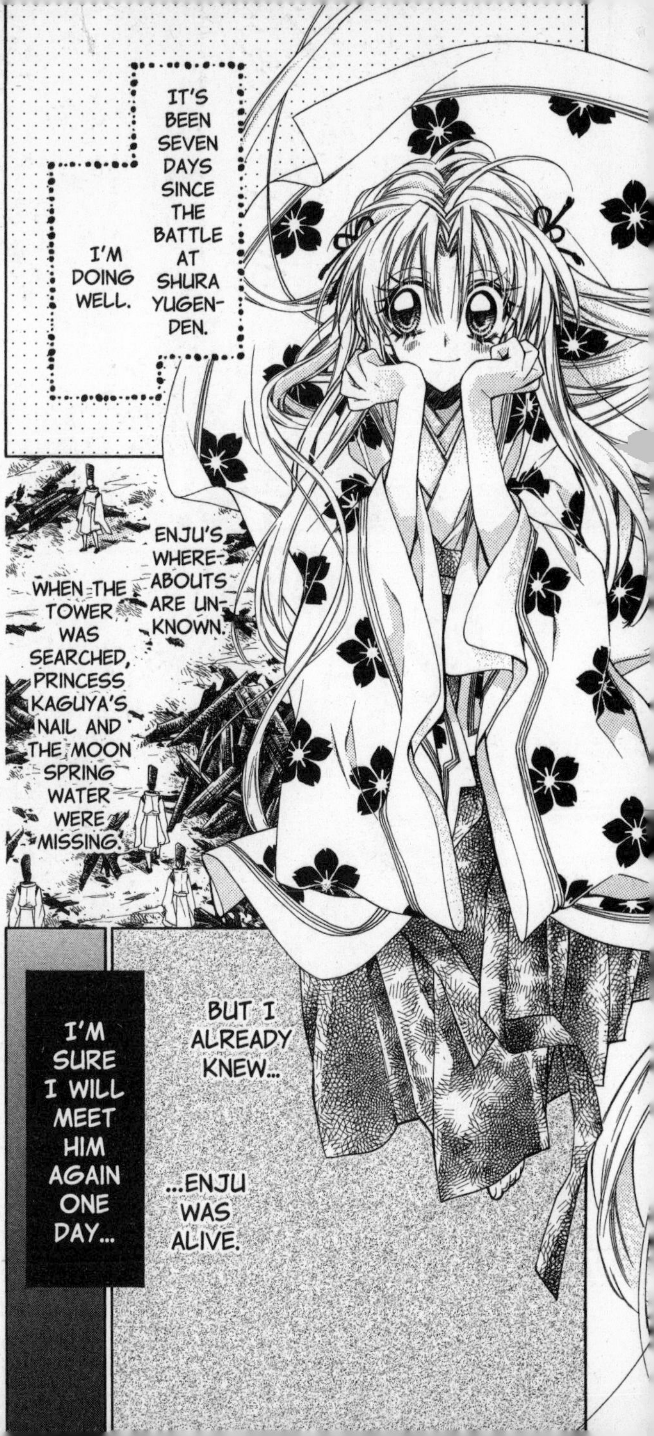
IT'S BEEN SEVEN DAYS SINCE THE BATTLE AT SHURA YUGEN-DEN.
I'M DOING WELL.
ENJU'S WHEREABOUTS ARE UNKNOWN.
WHEN THE TOWER WAS SEARCHED, PRINCESS KAGUYA'S NAIL AND THE MOON SPRING WATER WERE MISSING.
BUT I ALREADY KNEW...
...ENJU WAS ALIVE.
I'M SURE I WILL MEET HIM AGAIN ONE DAY...

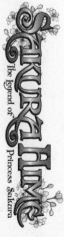

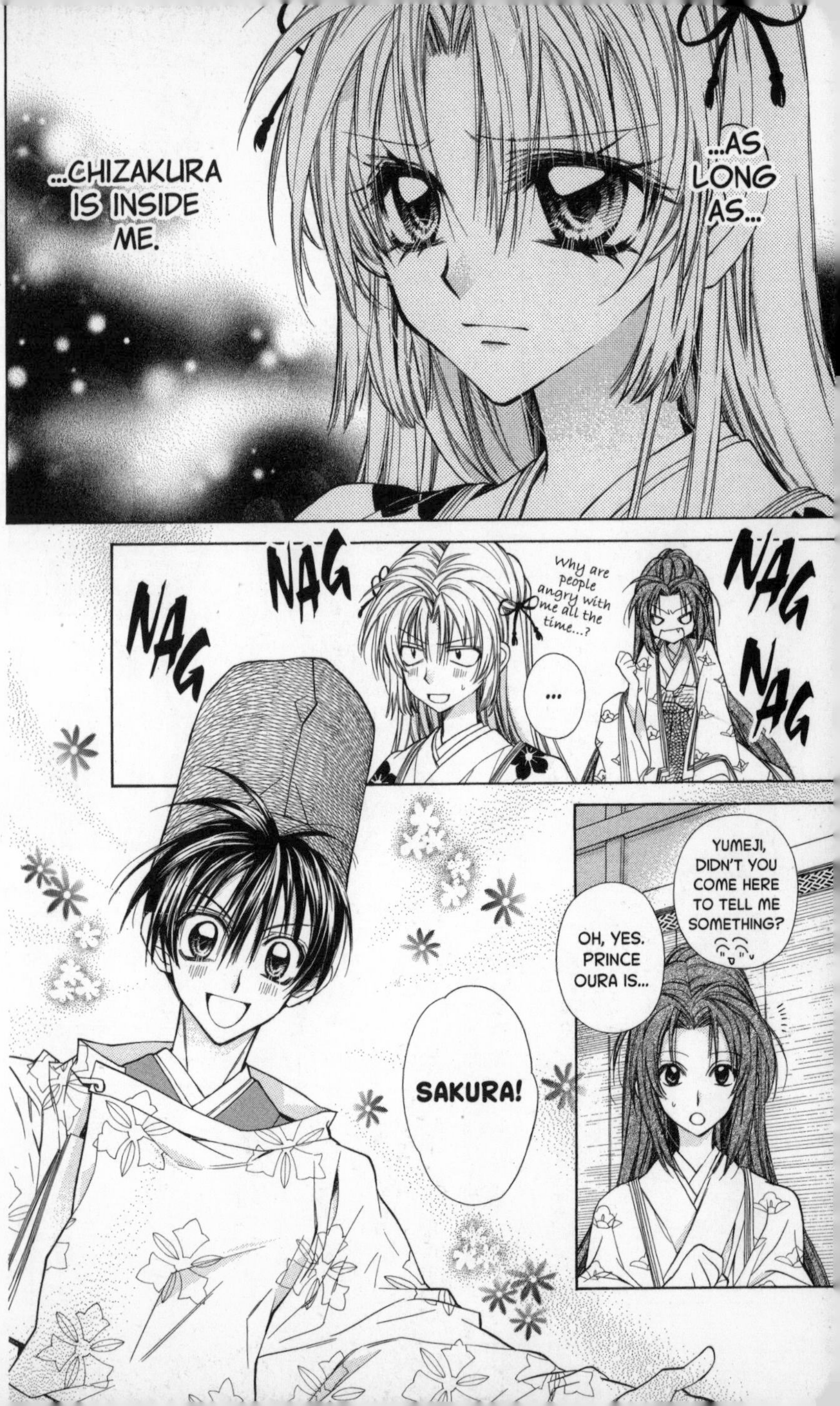
...AS LONG AS...
...CHIZAKURA IS INSIDE ME.
NAG NAG NAG
Why are people angry with me all the time...?
...
NAG NAG
YUMEJI, DIDN'T YOU COME HERE TO TELL ME SOMETHING?
OH, YES. PRINCE OURA IS...
SAKURA!

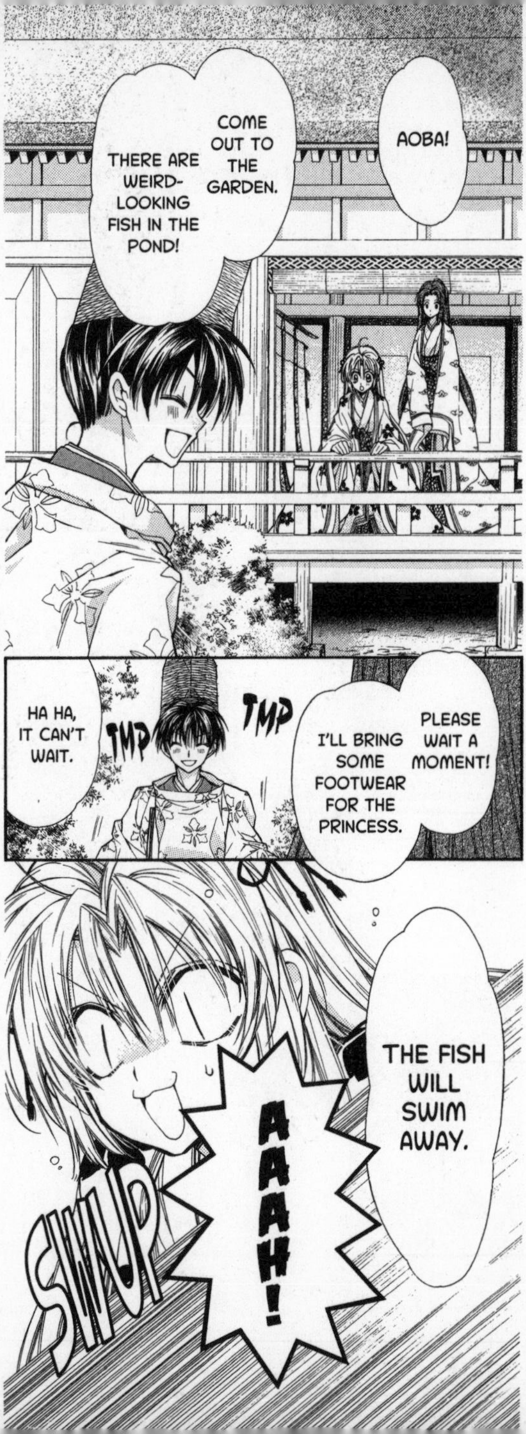
AOBA!
COME OUT TO THE GARDEN.
THERE ARE WEIRD-LOOKING FISH IN THE POND!
PLEASE WAIT A MOMENT!
I'LL BRING SOME FOOTWEAR FOR THE PRINCESS.
TMP
TMP
HA HA, IT CAN'T WAIT.
THE FISH WILL SWIM AWAY.
AAAAH!
SWUP

Hello ✿

Long time no see. Arina Tanemura here. I bring you volume 8 of *Sakura Hime: The Legend of Princess Sakura.*

The illustration on the cover is Princess Sakura and Princess Yuri. You may be surprised to see how different the atmosphere of the story is compared to the last volume. I tried to make it more cheery, but maybe it turned out too comedic? (laugh) Nevertheless, I don't think all the characters will be able to escape their fates... (mystery)

The story had been rather heavy going until now, so it would be great if you would read this volume with a light heart.

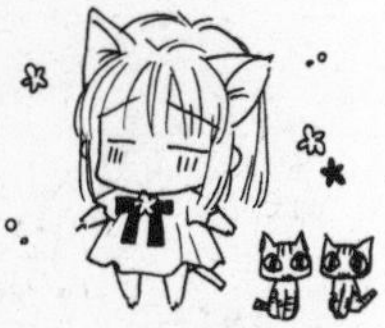

Spring has come...

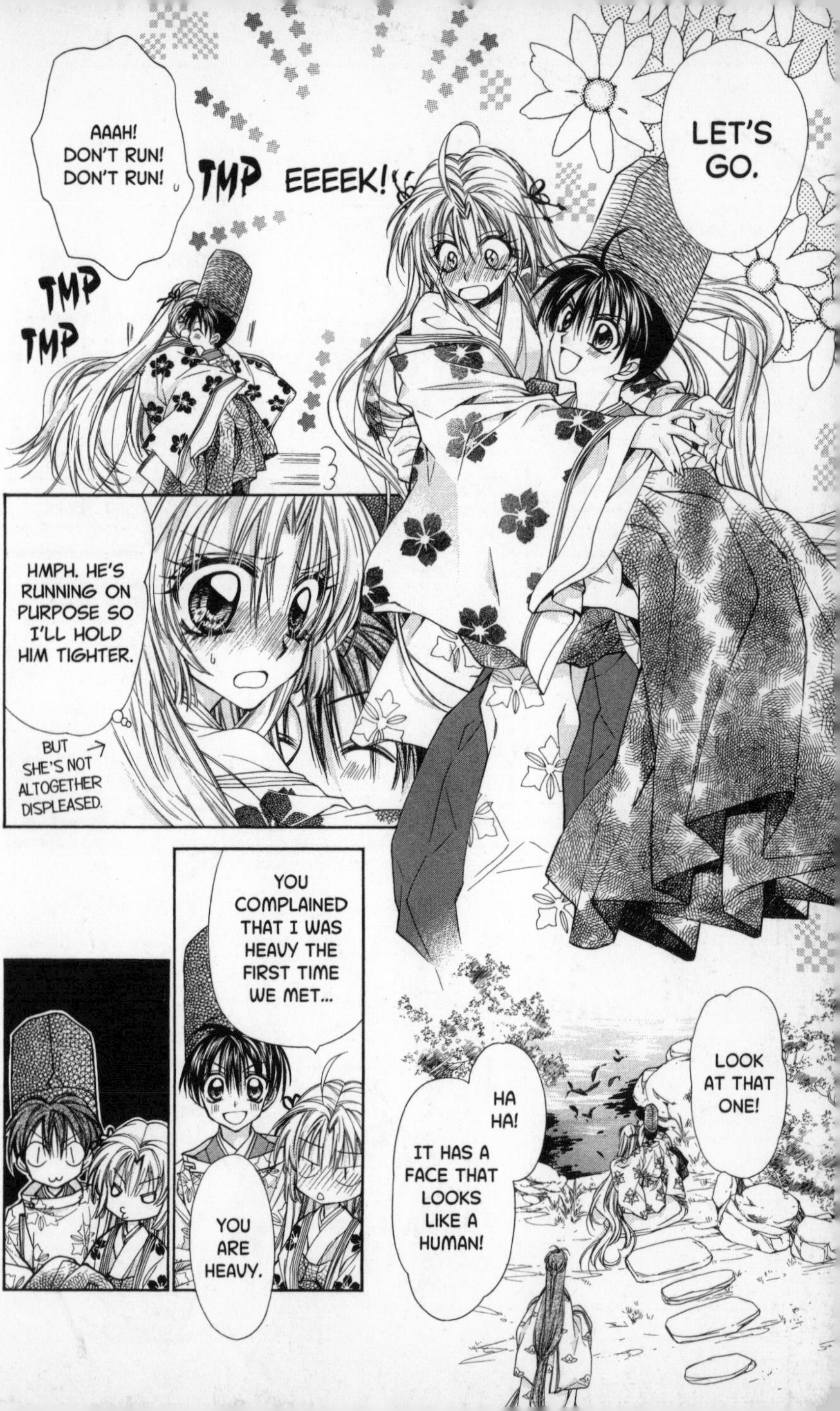
LET'S GO.
EEEEK!
TMP
AAAH! DON'T RUN! DON'T RUN!
TMP TMP
HMPH. HE'S RUNNING ON PURPOSE SO I'LL HOLD HIM TIGHTER.
BUT SHE'S NOT ALTOGETHER DISPLEASED.
LOOK AT THAT ONE!
HA HA!
IT HAS A FACE THAT LOOKS LIKE A HUMAN!
YOU COMPLAINED THAT I WAS HEAVY THE FIRST TIME WE MET...
YOU ARE HEAVY.

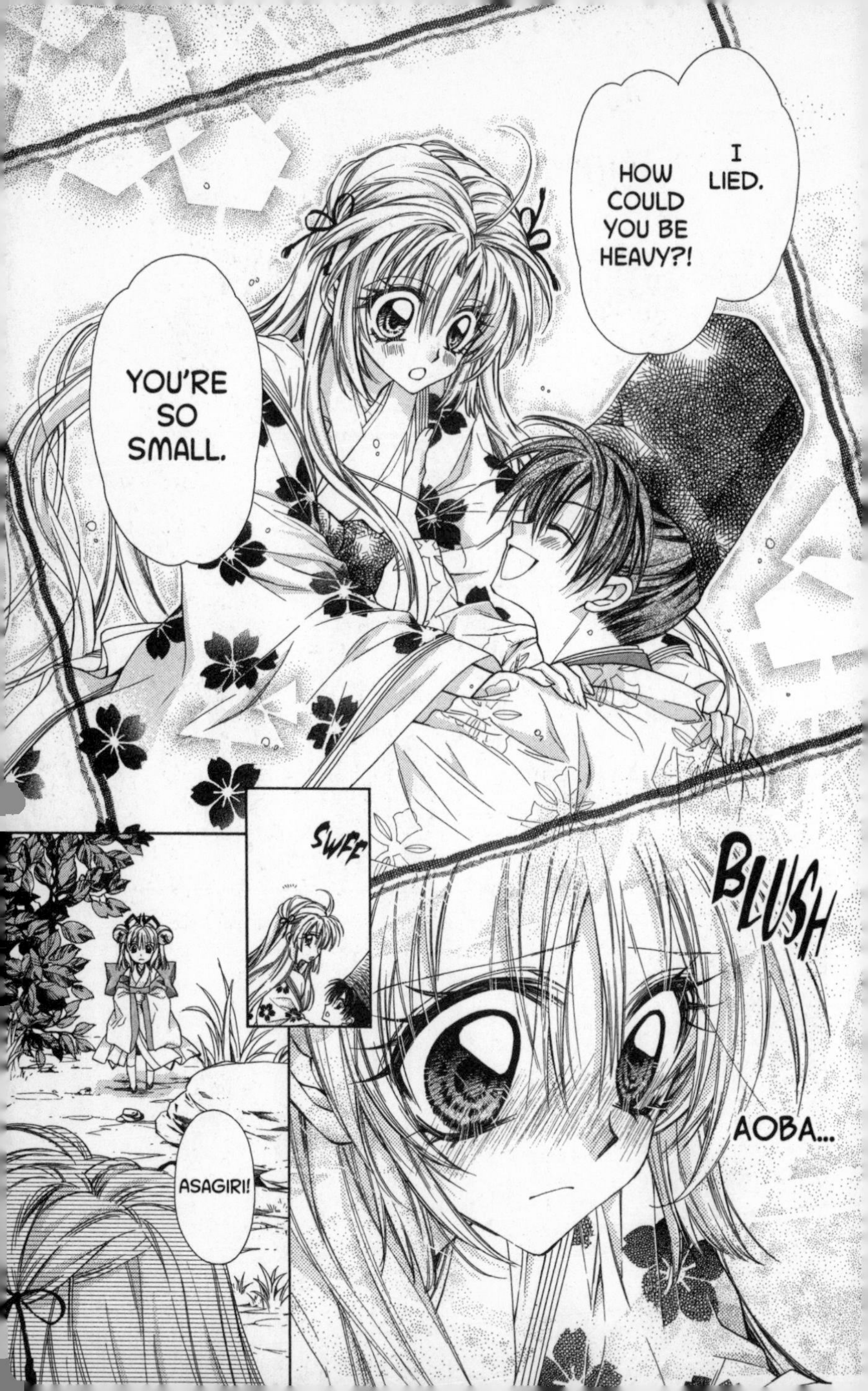
I LIED. HOW COULD YOU BE HEAVY?!
YOU'RE SO SMALL.
BLUSH
AOBA...
SWFF
ASAGIRI!

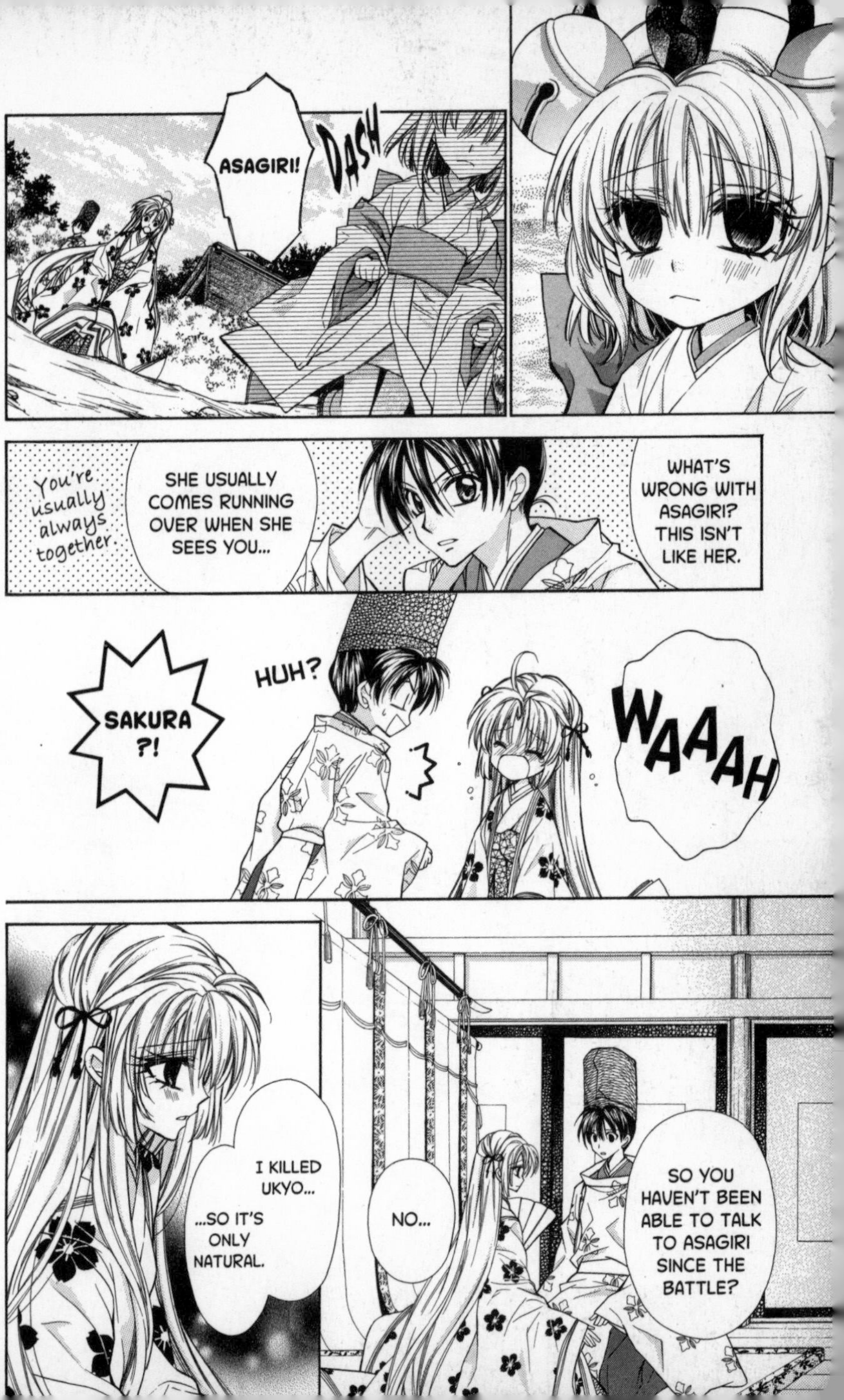
ASAGIRI!
DASH
WHAT'S WRONG WITH ASAGIRI? THIS ISN'T LIKE HER.
SHE USUALLY COMES RUNNING OVER WHEN SHE SEES YOU...
You're usually always together
WAAAH
HUH?
SAKURA ?!
SO YOU HAVEN'T BEEN ABLE TO TALK TO ASAGIRI SINCE THE BATTLE?
NO...
I KILLED UKYO...
...SO IT'S ONLY NATURAL.

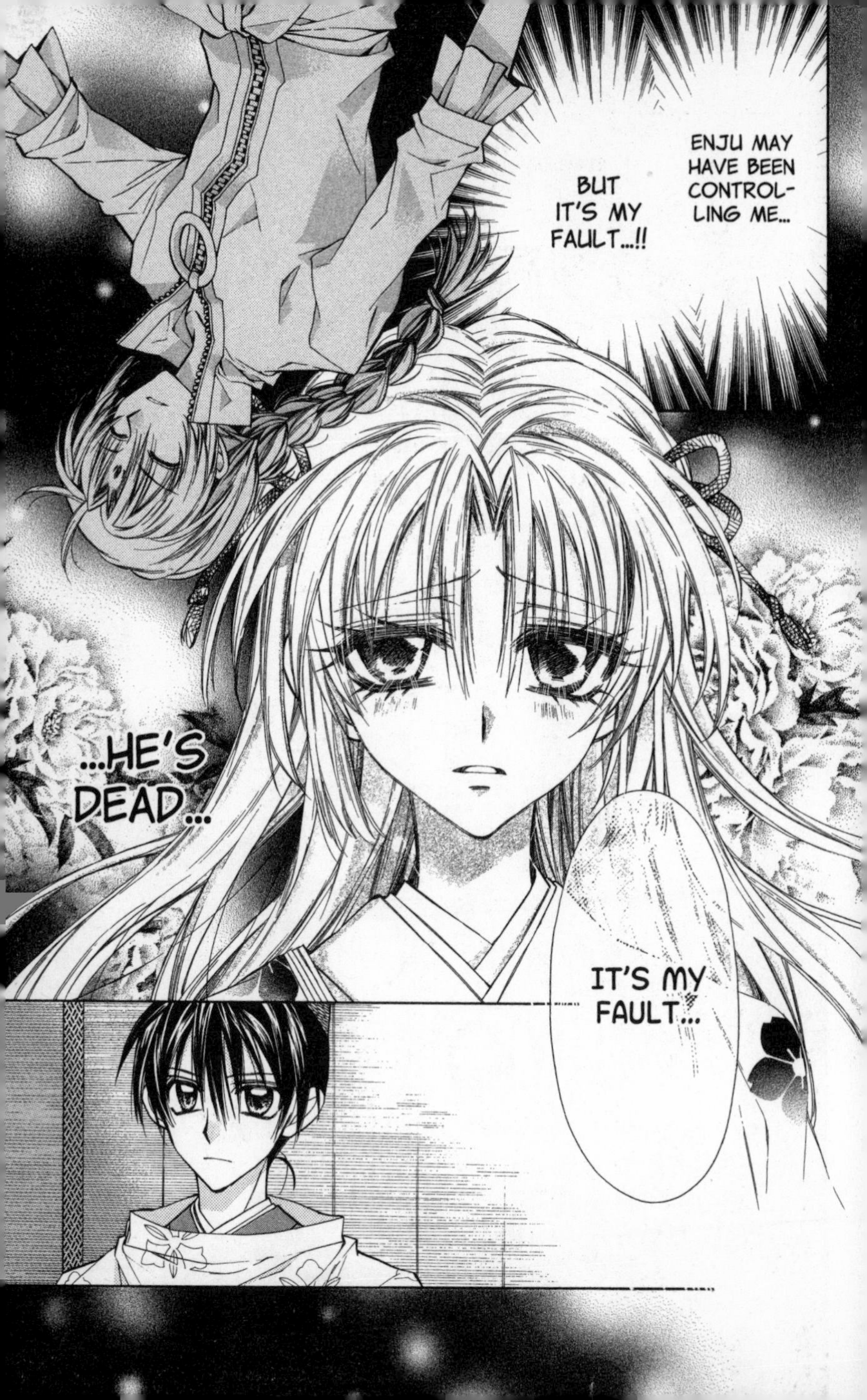
ENJU MAY HAVE BEEN CONTROL-LING ME...
BUT IT'S MY FAULT...!!
...HE'S DEAD...
IT'S MY FAULT...

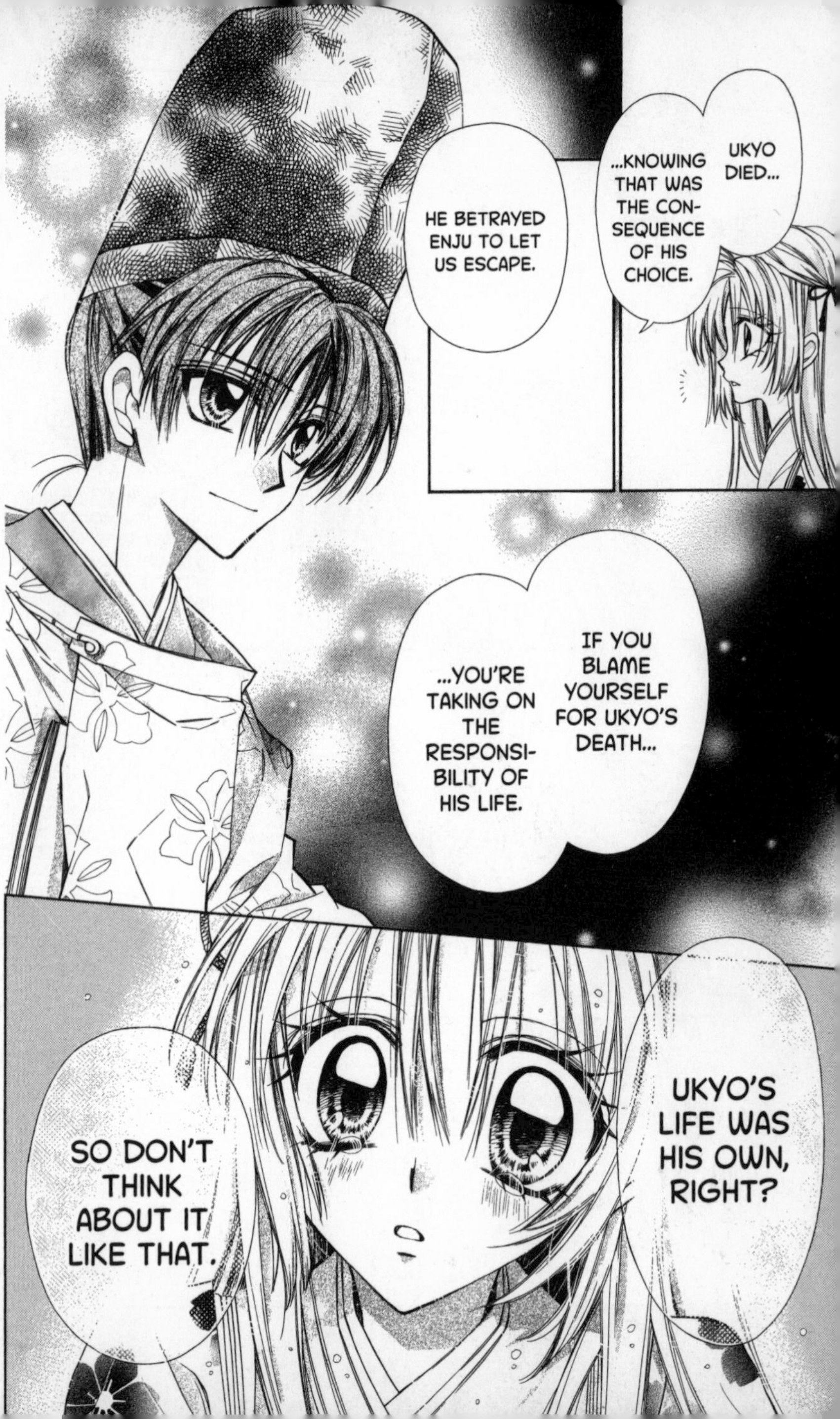
UKYO DIED...
...KNOWING THAT WAS THE CON-SEQUENCE OF HIS CHOICE.
HE BETRAYED ENJU TO LET US ESCAPE.
IF YOU BLAME YOURSELF FOR UKYO'S DEATH...
...YOU'RE TAKING ON THE RESPONSI-BILITY OF HIS LIFE.
UKYO'S LIFE WAS HIS OWN, RIGHT?
SO DON'T THINK ABOUT IT LIKE THAT.

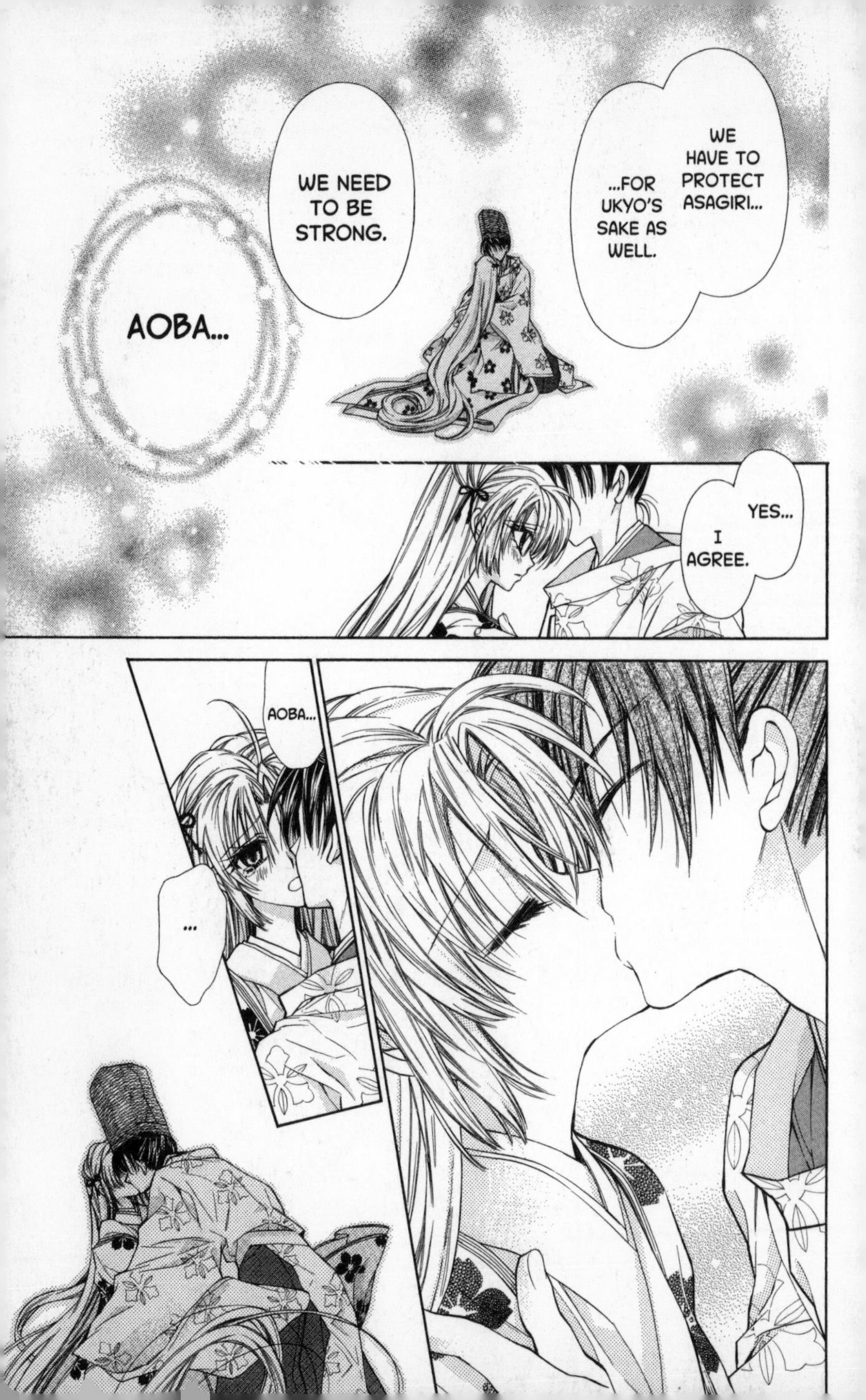
WE HAVE TO PROTECT ASAGIRI...
...FOR UKYO'S SAKE AS WELL.
WE NEED TO BE STRONG.
AOBA...
YES... I AGREE.
AOBA...
...

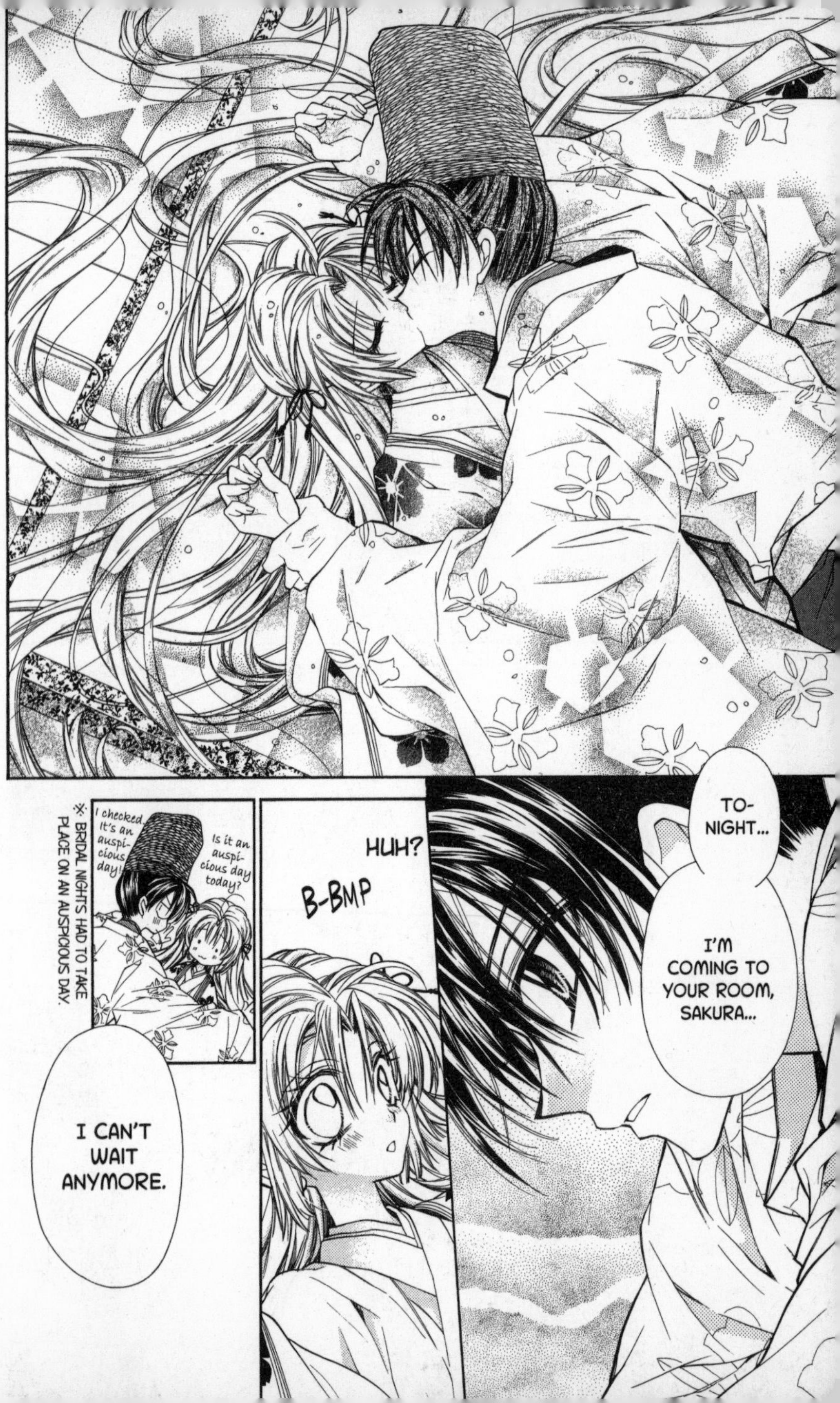
TO-NIGHT...
I'M COMING TO YOUR ROOM, SAKURA...
HUH?
B-BMP
Is it an auspicious day today?
I checked. It's an auspicious day!
※ BRIDAL NIGHTS HAD TO TAKE PLACE ON AN AUSPICIOUS DAY.
I CAN'T WAIT ANYMORE.

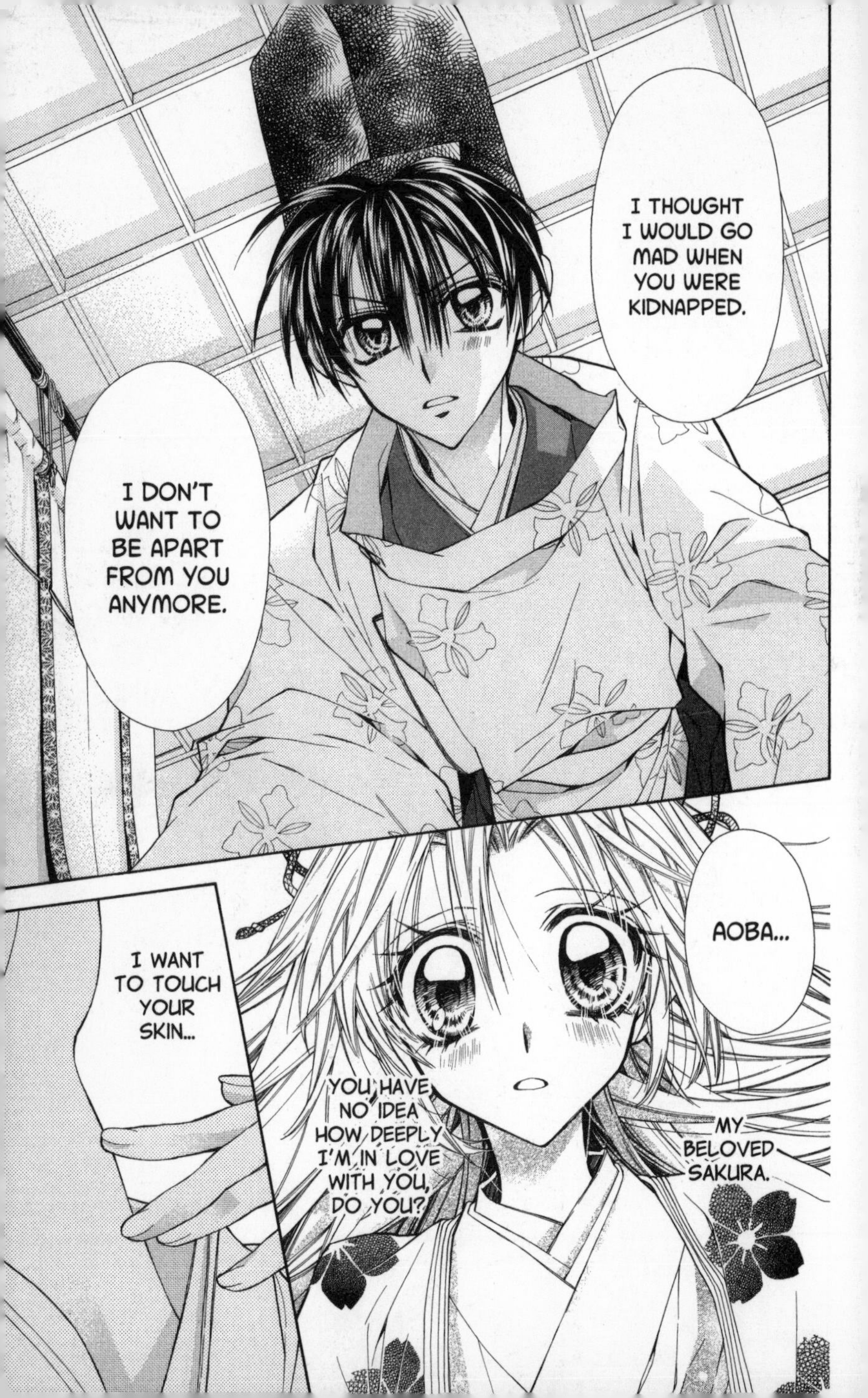
I THOUGHT I WOULD GO MAD WHEN YOU WERE KIDNAPPED.
I DON'T WANT TO BE APART FROM YOU ANYMORE.
AOBA...
I WANT TO TOUCH YOUR SKIN...
MY BELOVED SAKURA.
YOU HAVE NO IDEA HOW DEEPLY I'M IN LOVE WITH YOU, DO YOU?

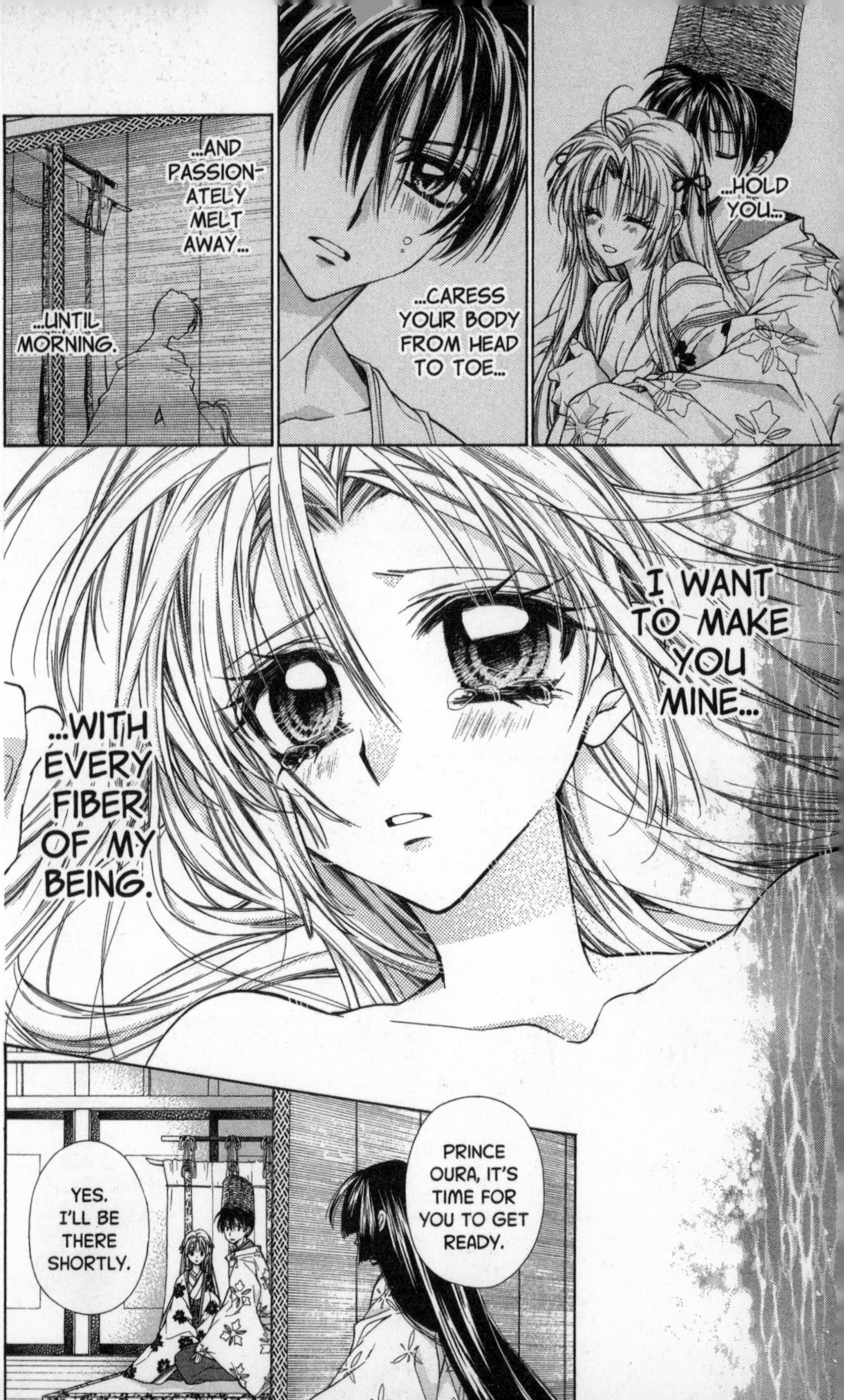
...HOLD YOU...
...CARESS YOUR BODY FROM HEAD TO TOE...
...AND PASSION-ATELY MELT AWAY...
...UNTIL MORNING.
I WANT TO MAKE YOU MINE...
...WITH EVERY FIBER OF MY BEING.
PRINCE OURA, IT'S TIME FOR YOU TO GET READY.
YES. I'LL BE THERE SHORTLY.

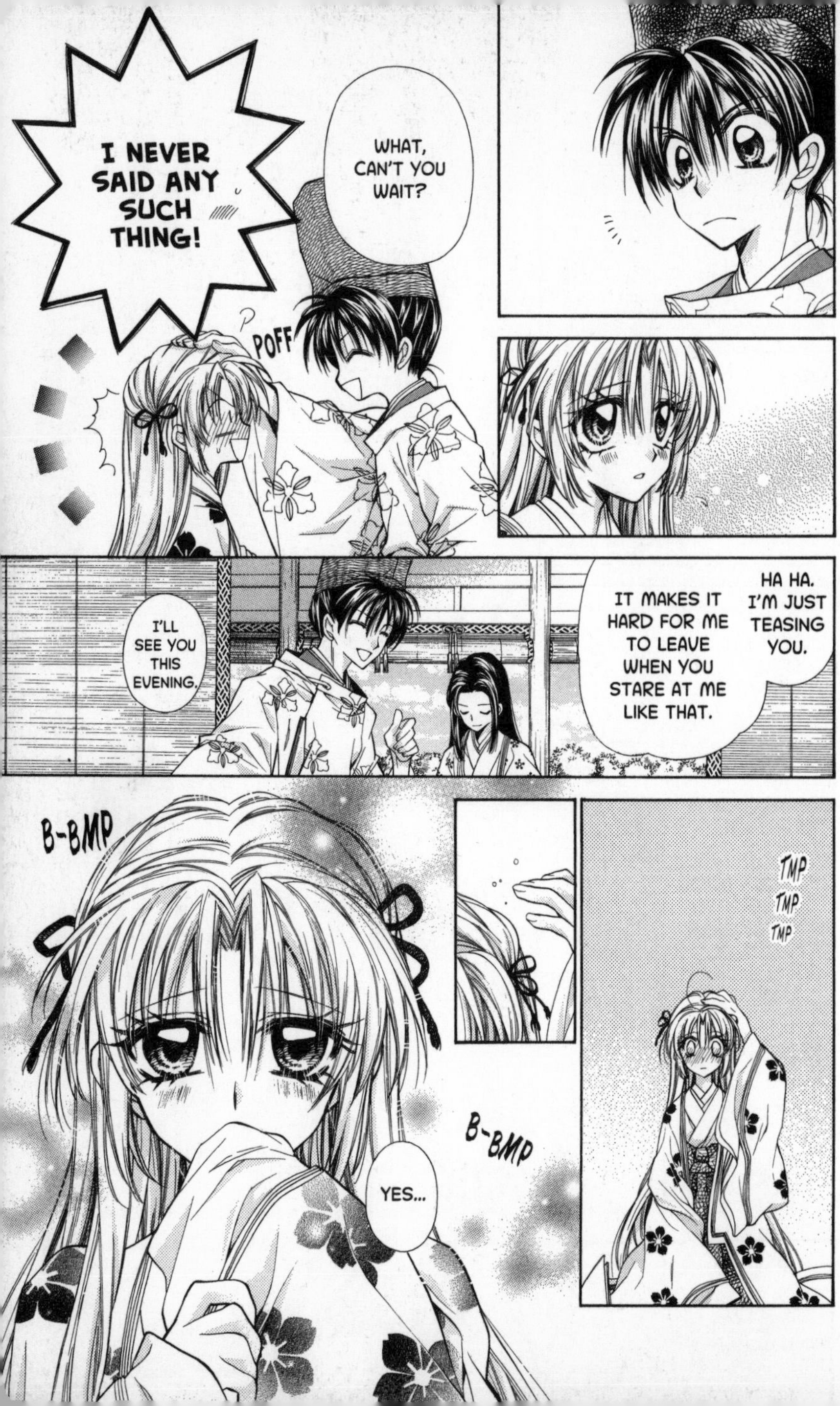
WHAT, CAN'T YOU WAIT?
I NEVER SAID ANY SUCH THING!
POFF
HA HA. I'M JUST TEASING YOU.
IT MAKES IT HARD FOR ME TO LEAVE WHEN YOU STARE AT ME LIKE THAT.
I'LL SEE YOU THIS EVENING.
TMP TMP TMP
B-BMP
B-BMP
YES...

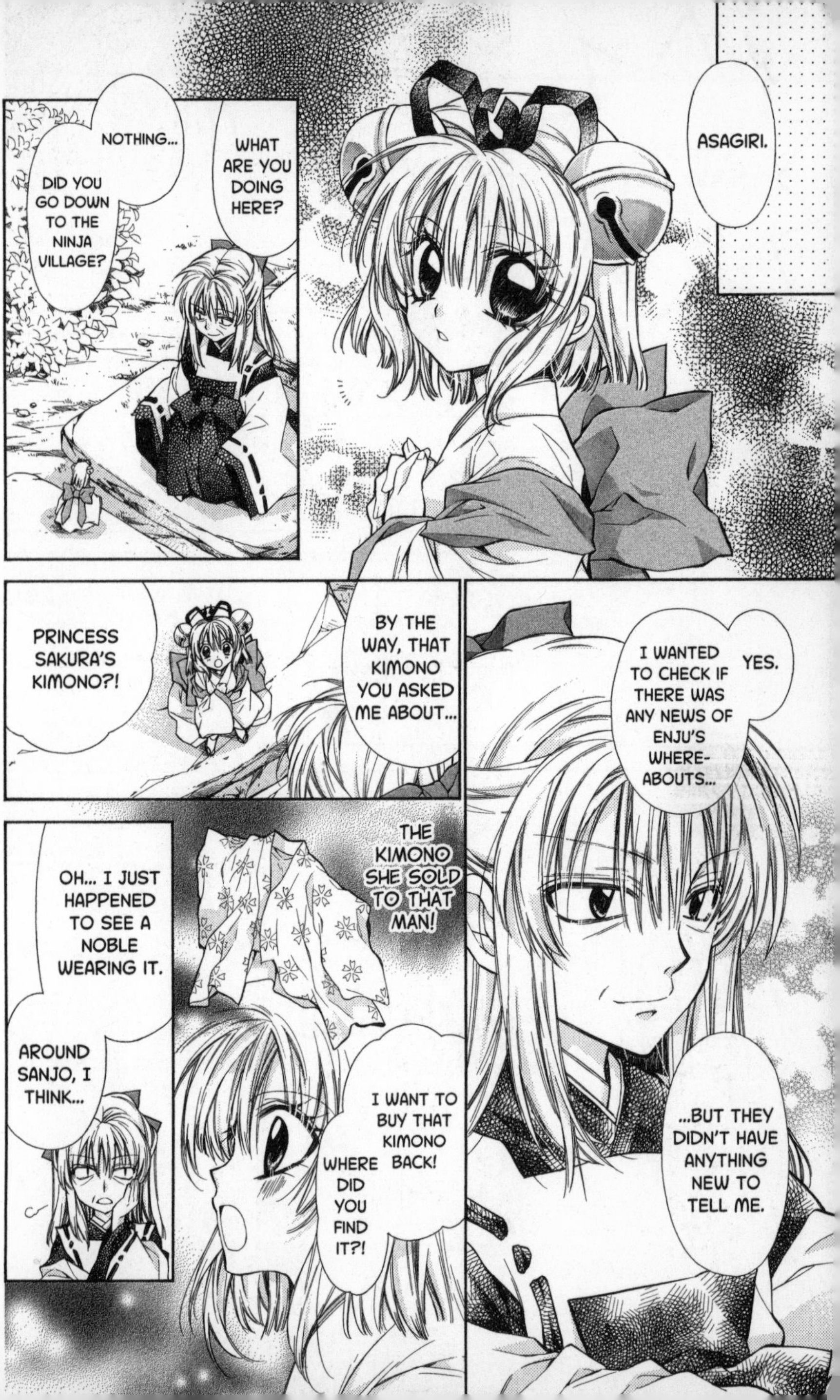
ASAGIRI.
WHAT ARE YOU DOING HERE?
NOTHING...
DID YOU GO DOWN TO THE NINJA VILLAGE?
YES.
I WANTED TO CHECK IF THERE WAS ANY NEWS OF ENJU'S WHEREABOUTS...
...BUT THEY DIDN'T HAVE ANYTHING NEW TO TELL ME.
BY THE WAY, THAT KIMONO YOU ASKED ME ABOUT...
PRINCESS SAKURA'S KIMONO?!
THE KIMONO SHE SOLD TO THAT MAN!
I WANT TO BUY THAT KIMONO BACK!
WHERE DID YOU FIND IT?!
OH... I JUST HAPPENED TO SEE A NOBLE WEARING IT.
AROUND SANJO, I THINK...

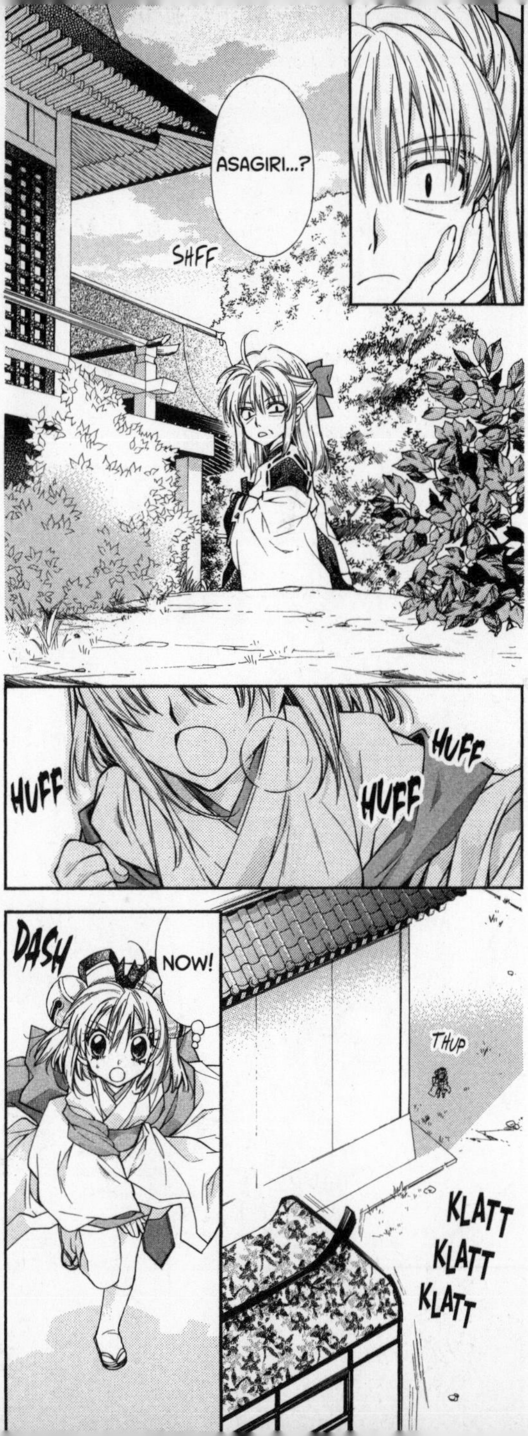
ASAGIRI...?
SHFF
HUFF
HUFF
HUFF
THUP
KLATT
KLATT
KLATT
DASH
NOW!

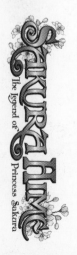

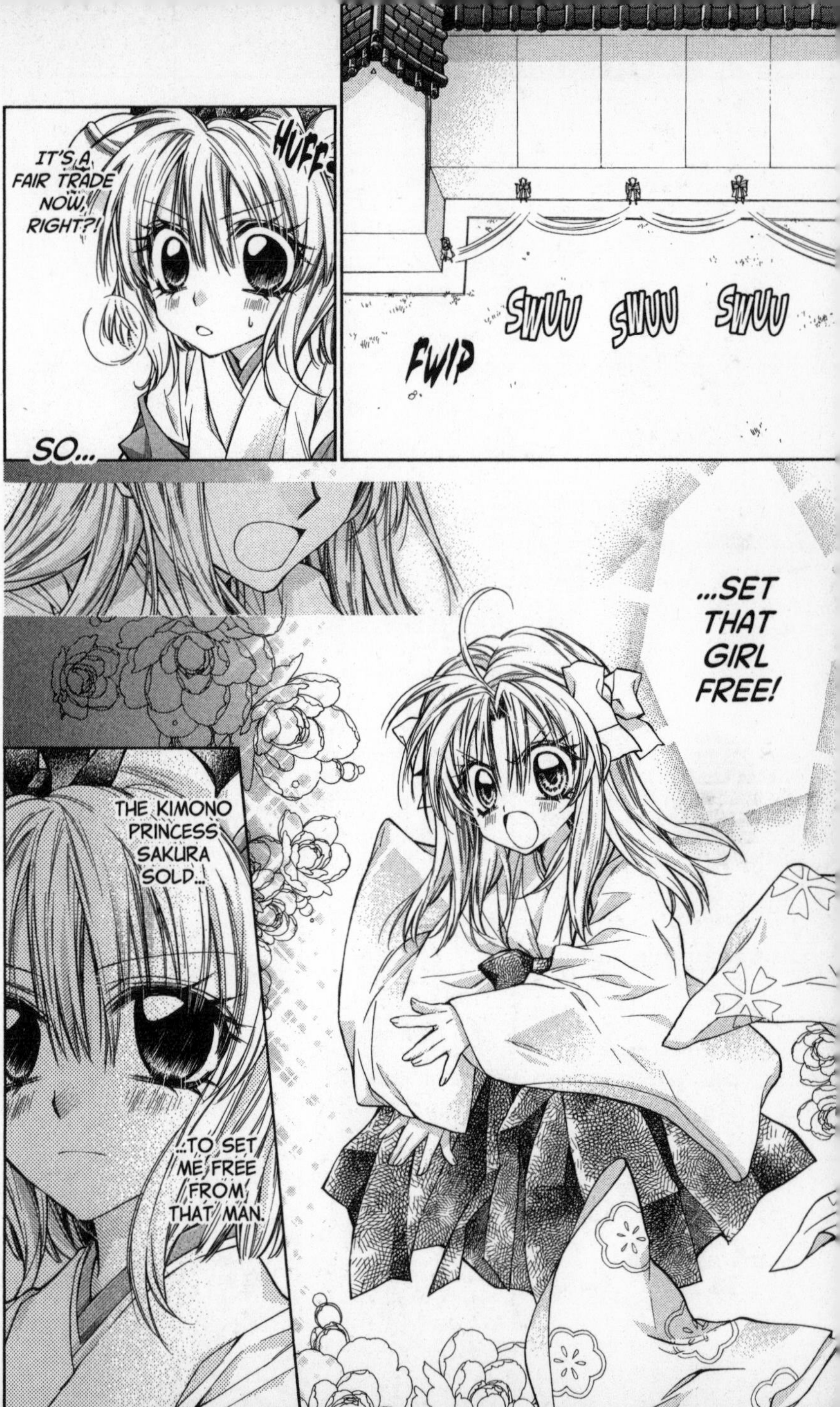
SWUU
SWUU
SWUU
FWIP
HUFF
IT'S A FAIR TRADE NOW, RIGHT?!
SO...
...SET THAT GIRL FREE!
THE KIMONO PRINCESS SAKURA SOLD...
...TO SET ME FREE FROM THAT MAN.

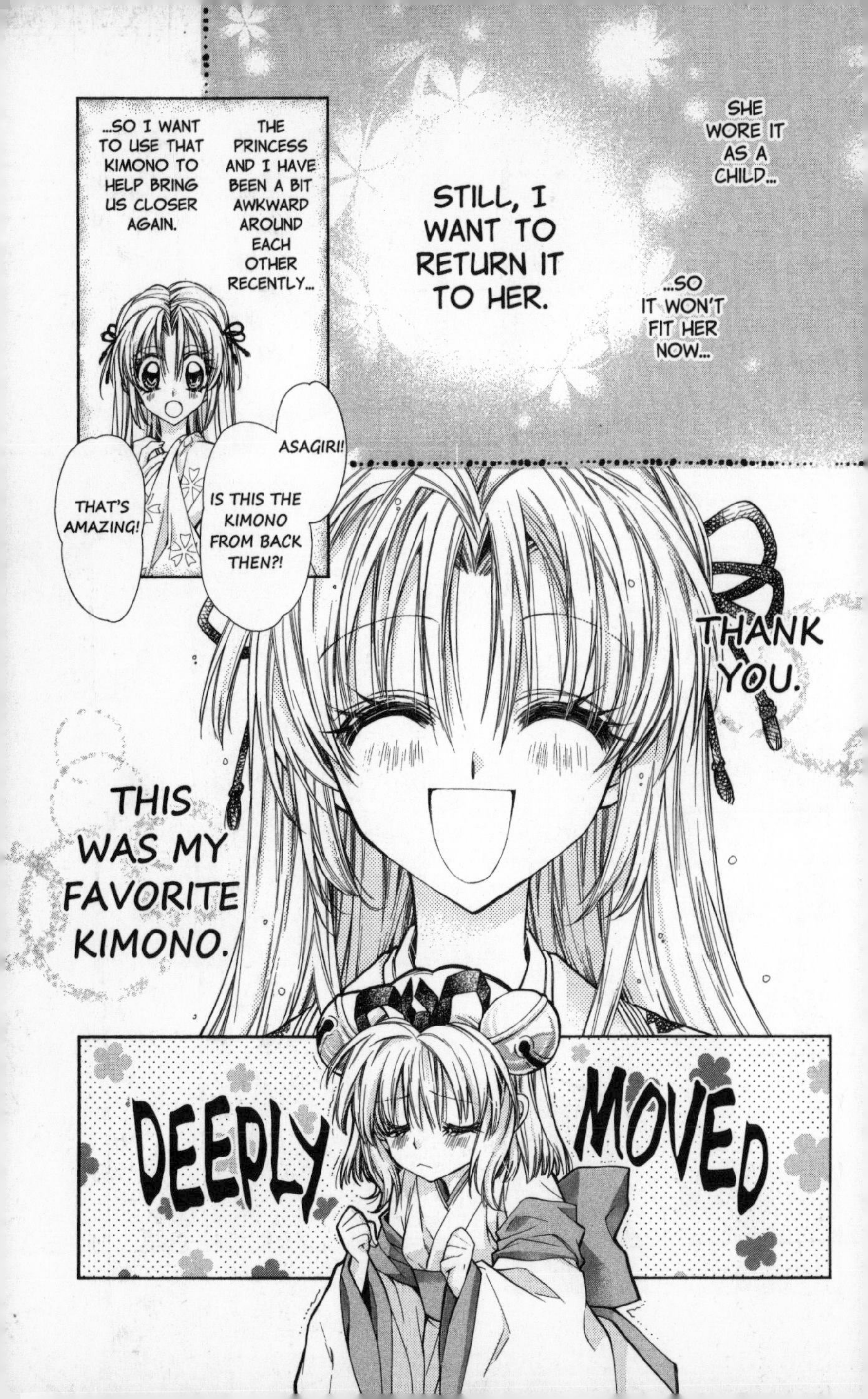
SHE WORE IT AS A CHILD...
...SO IT WON'T FIT HER NOW...
STILL, I WANT TO RETURN IT TO HER.
THE PRINCESS AND I HAVE BEEN A BIT AWKWARD AROUND EACH OTHER RECENTLY...
...SO I WANT TO USE THAT KIMONO TO HELP BRING US CLOSER AGAIN.
ASAGIRI!
IS THIS THE KIMONO FROM BACK THEN?!
THAT'S AMAZING!
THANK YOU.
THIS WAS MY FAVORITE KIMONO.
DEEPLY MOVED

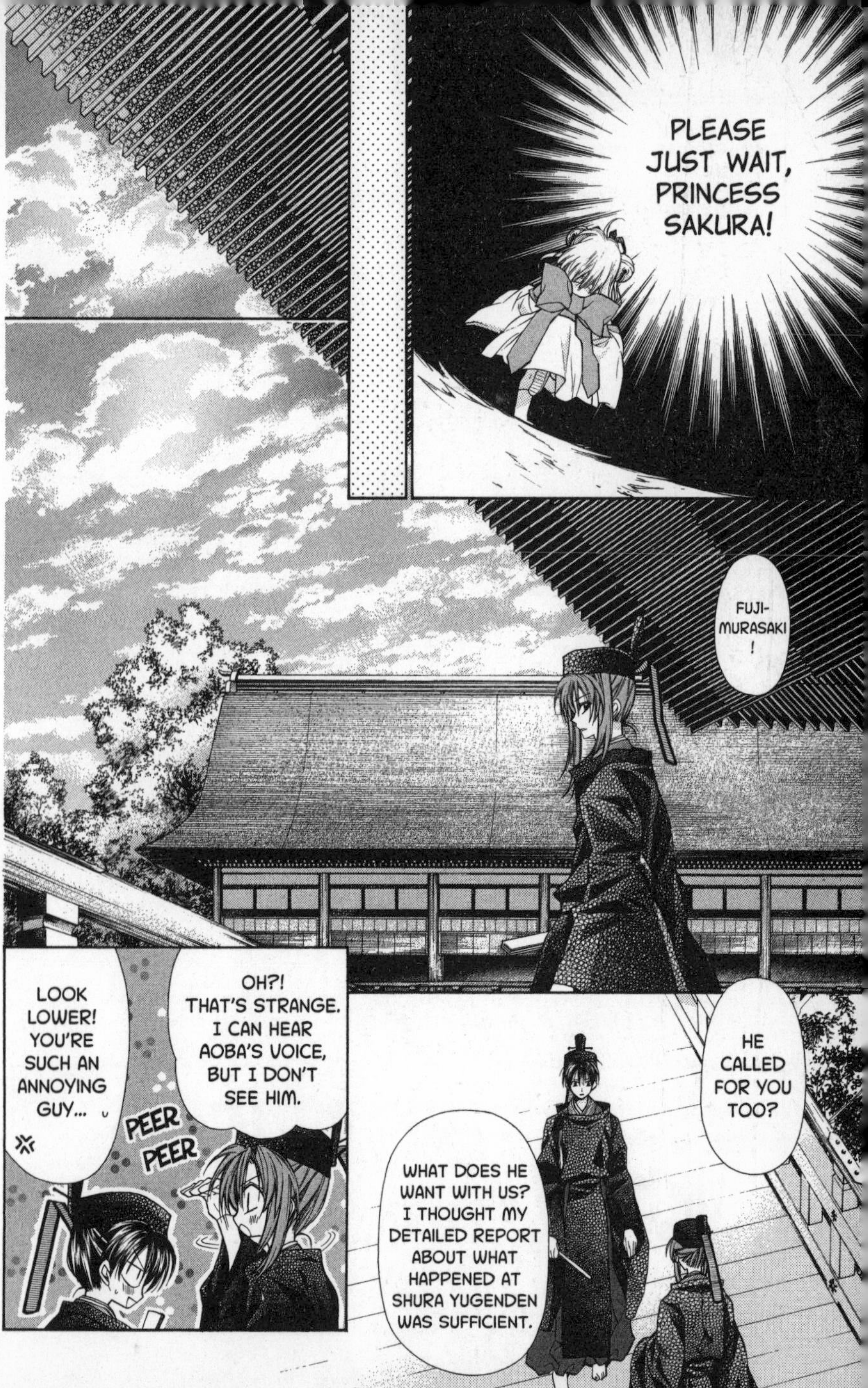
PLEASE JUST WAIT, PRINCESS SAKURA!
FUJI-MURASAKI!
HE CALLED FOR YOU TOO?
WHAT DOES HE WANT WITH US? I THOUGHT MY DETAILED REPORT ABOUT WHAT HAPPENED AT SHURA YUGENDEN WAS SUFFICIENT.
OH?! THAT'S STRANGE. I CAN HEAR AOBA'S VOICE, BUT I DON'T SEE HIM.
LOOK LOWER! YOU'RE SUCH AN ANNOYING GUY...
PEER PEER

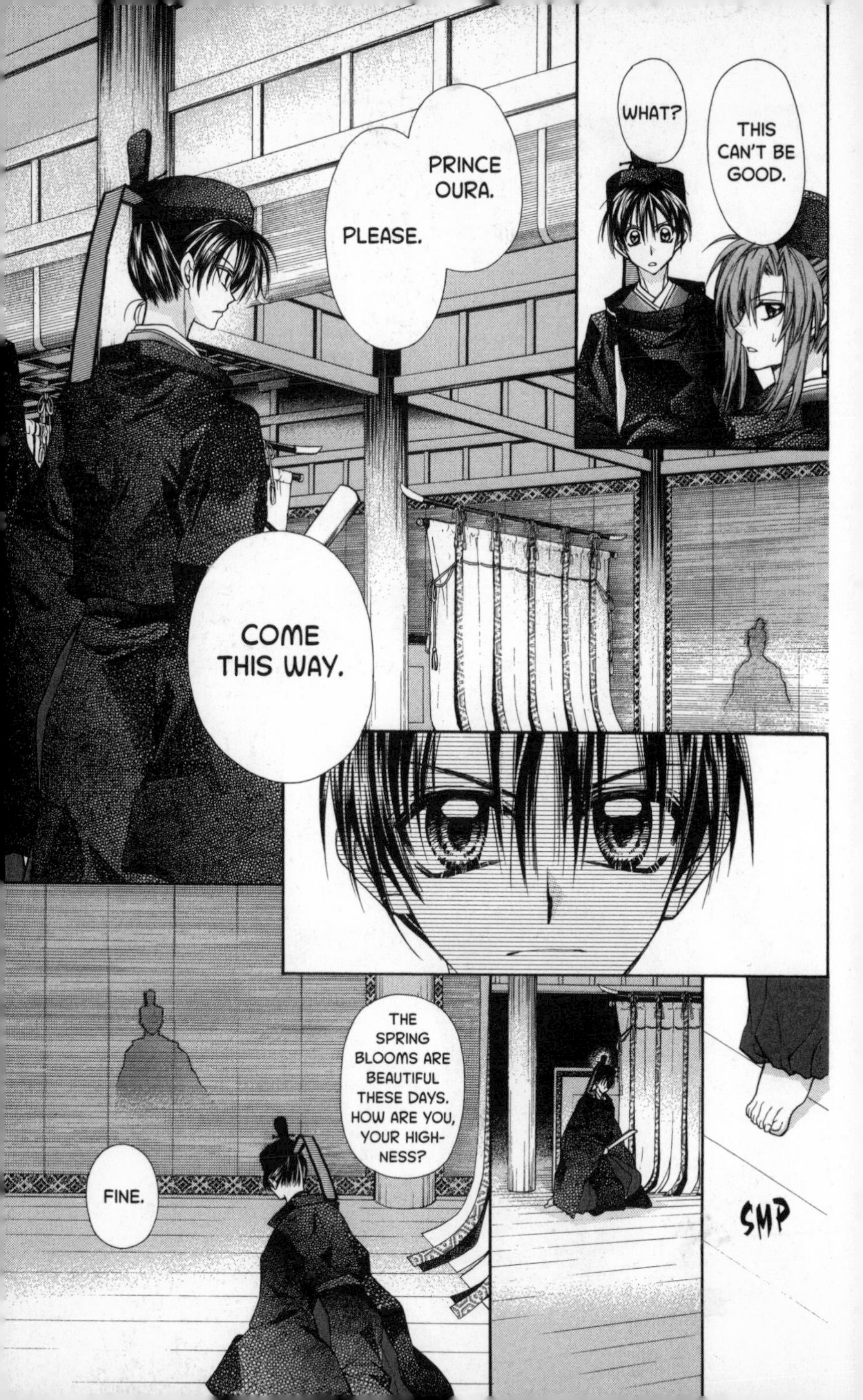
THIS CAN'T BE GOOD.
WHAT?
PRINCE OURA. PLEASE.
COME THIS WAY.
SMP
THE SPRING BLOOMS ARE BEAUTIFUL THESE DAYS. HOW ARE YOU, YOUR HIGH-NESS?
FINE.

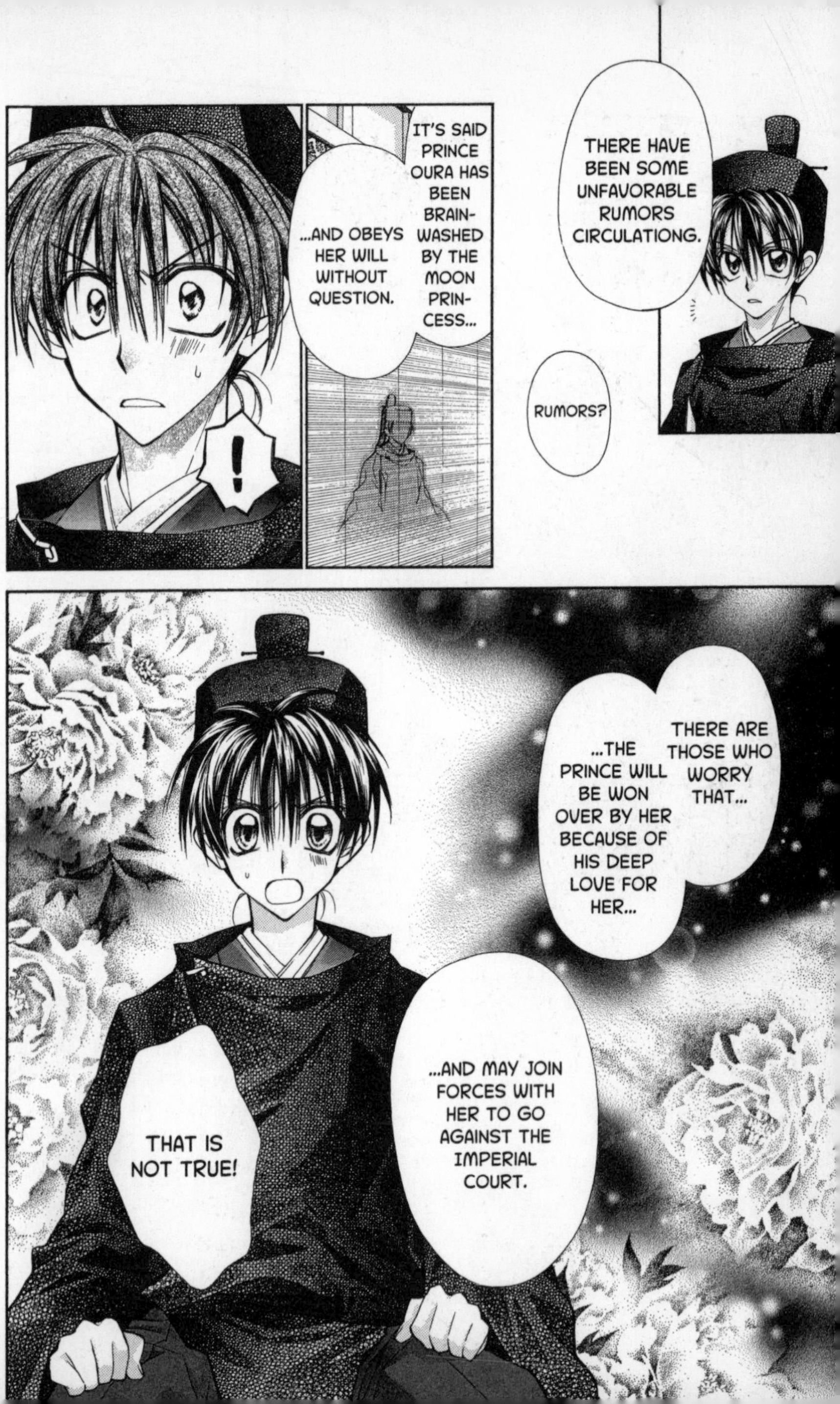
THERE HAVE BEEN SOME UNFAVORABLE RUMORS CIRCULATIONG.
RUMORS?
IT'S SAID PRINCE OURA HAS BEEN BRAIN-WASHED BY THE MOON PRIN-CESS...
...AND OBEYS HER WILL WITHOUT QUESTION.
!
THERE ARE THOSE WHO WORRY THAT...
...THE PRINCE WILL BE WON OVER BY HER BECAUSE OF HIS DEEP LOVE FOR HER...
...AND MAY JOIN FORCES WITH HER TO GO AGAINST THE IMPERIAL COURT.
THAT IS NOT TRUE!

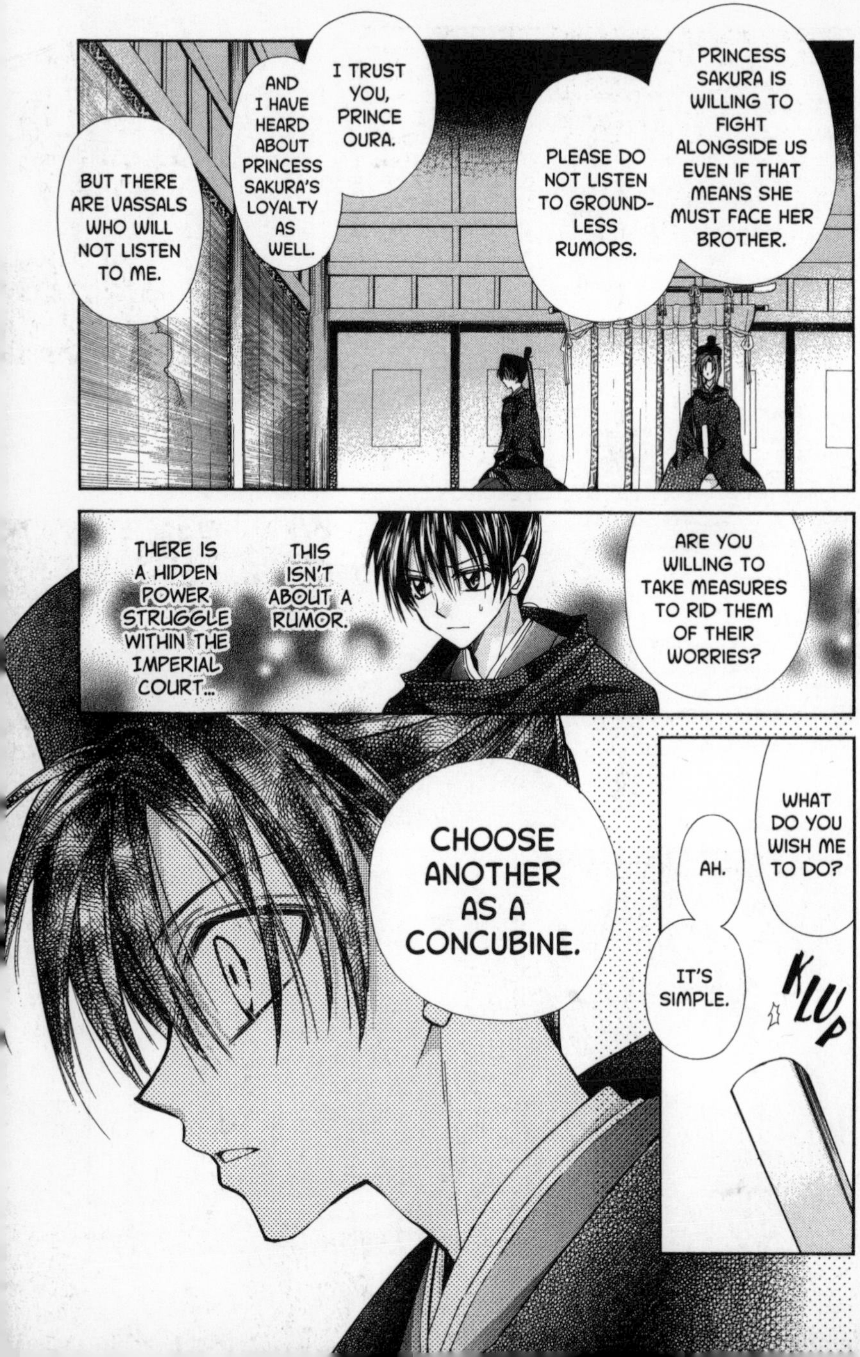
PRINCESS SAKURA IS WILLING TO FIGHT ALONGSIDE US EVEN IF THAT MEANS SHE MUST FACE HER BROTHER.
PLEASE DO NOT LISTEN TO GROUNDLESS RUMORS.
I TRUST YOU, PRINCE OURA.
AND I HAVE HEARD ABOUT PRINCESS SAKURA'S LOYALTY AS WELL.
BUT THERE ARE VASSALS WHO WILL NOT LISTEN TO ME.
ARE YOU WILLING TO TAKE MEASURES TO RID THEM OF THEIR WORRIES?
THIS ISN'T ABOUT A RUMOR.
THERE IS A HIDDEN POWER STRUGGLE WITHIN THE IMPERIAL COURT...
WHAT DO YOU WISH ME TO DO?
AH.
IT'S SIMPLE.
KLUP
CHOOSE ANOTHER AS A CONCUBINE.

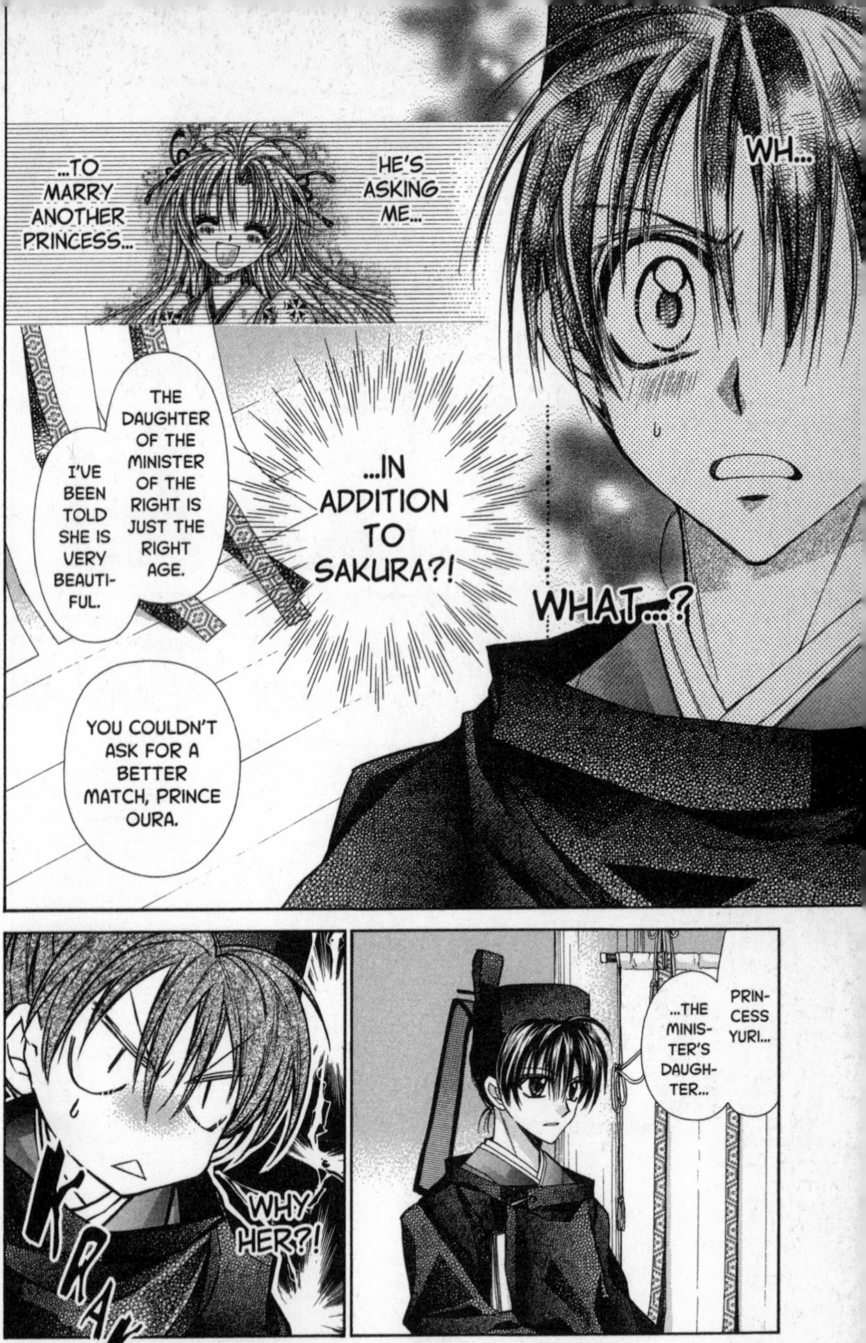
WH...
HE'S ASKING ME...
...TO MARRY ANOTHER PRINCESS...
...IN ADDITION TO SAKURA?!
WHAT...?
THE DAUGHTER OF THE MINISTER OF THE RIGHT IS JUST THE RIGHT AGE.
I'VE BEEN TOLD SHE IS VERY BEAUTIFUL.
YOU COULDN'T ASK FOR A BETTER MATCH, PRINCE OURA.
PRINCESS YURI...
...THE MINISTER'S DAUGHTER...
WHY HER?!
KRAKK

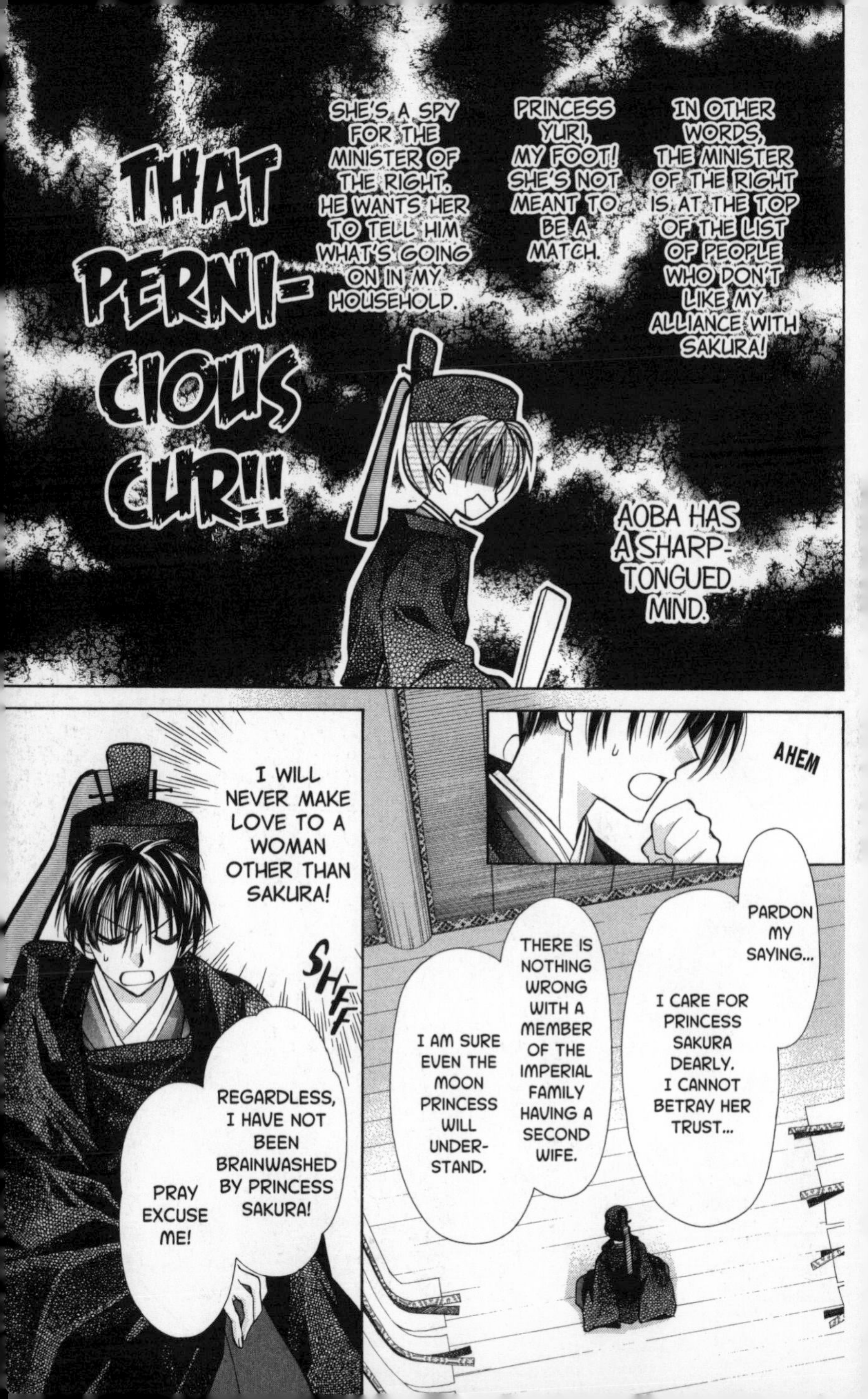
IN OTHER WORDS, THE MINISTER OF THE RIGHT IS AT THE TOP OF THE LIST OF PEOPLE WHO DON'T LIKE MY ALLIANCE WITH SAKURA!
PRINCESS YURI, MY FOOT! SHE'S NOT MEANT TO BE A MATCH.
SHE'S A SPY FOR THE MINISTER OF THE RIGHT. HE WANTS HER TO TELL HIM WHAT'S GOING ON IN MY HOUSEHOLD.
THAT PERNI-CIOUS CUR!!
AOBA HAS A SHARP-TONGUED MIND.
AHEM
PARDON MY SAYING...
I CARE FOR PRINCESS SAKURA DEARLY. I CANNOT BETRAY HER TRUST...
THERE IS NOTHING WRONG WITH A MEMBER OF THE IMPERIAL FAMILY HAVING A SECOND WIFE.
I AM SURE EVEN THE MOON PRINCESS WILL UNDER-STAND.
I WILL NEVER MAKE LOVE TO A WOMAN OTHER THAN SAKURA!
SHFF
REGARDLESS, I HAVE NOT BEEN BRAINWASHED BY PRINCESS SAKURA!
PRAY EXCUSE ME!

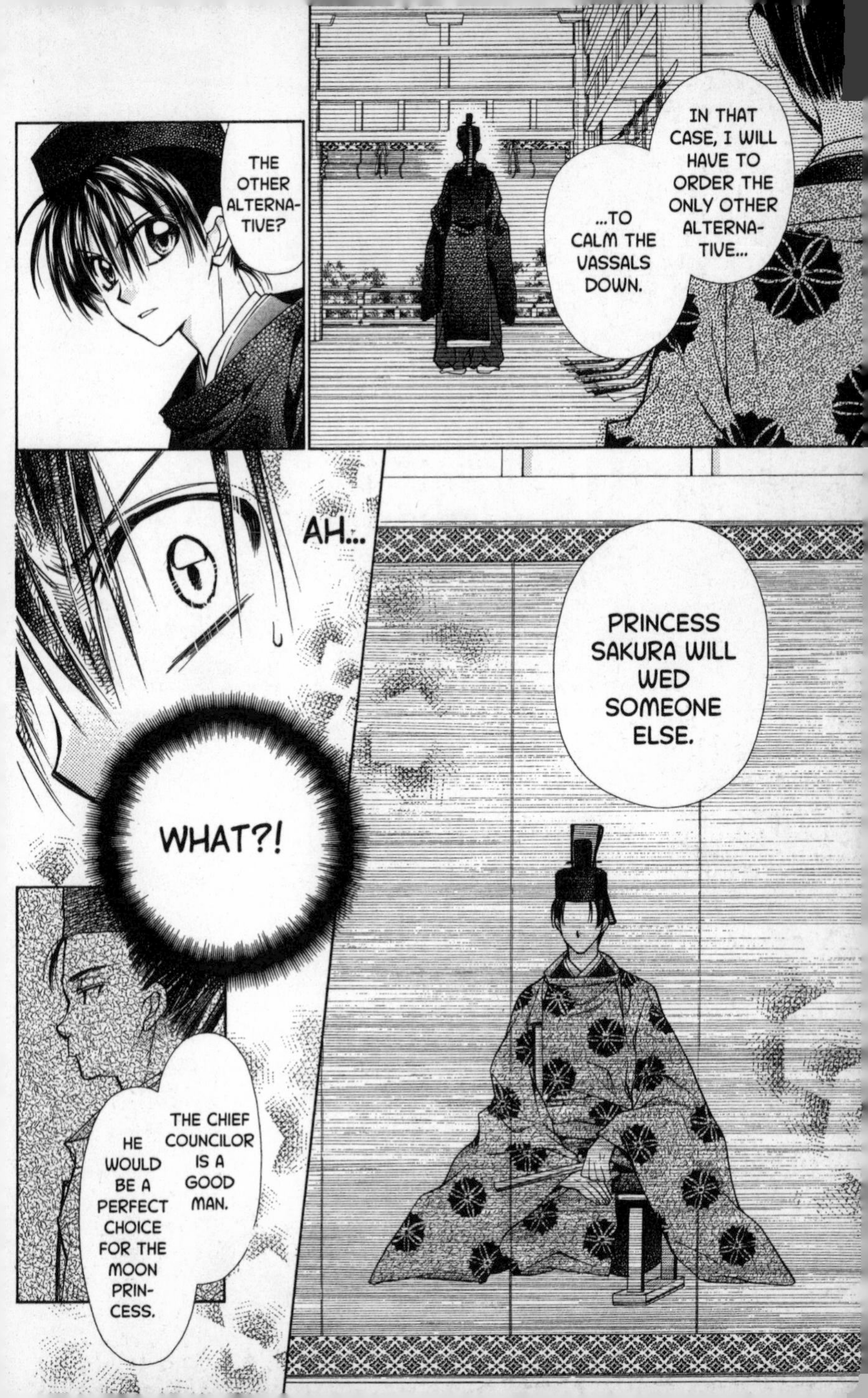
IN THAT CASE, I WILL HAVE TO ORDER THE ONLY OTHER ALTERNATIVE...
...TO CALM THE VASSALS DOWN.
THE OTHER ALTERNATIVE?
PRINCESS SAKURA WILL WED SOMEONE ELSE.
AH...
WHAT?!
THE CHIEF COUNCILOR IS A GOOD MAN.
HE WOULD BE A PERFECT CHOICE FOR THE MOON PRINCESS.

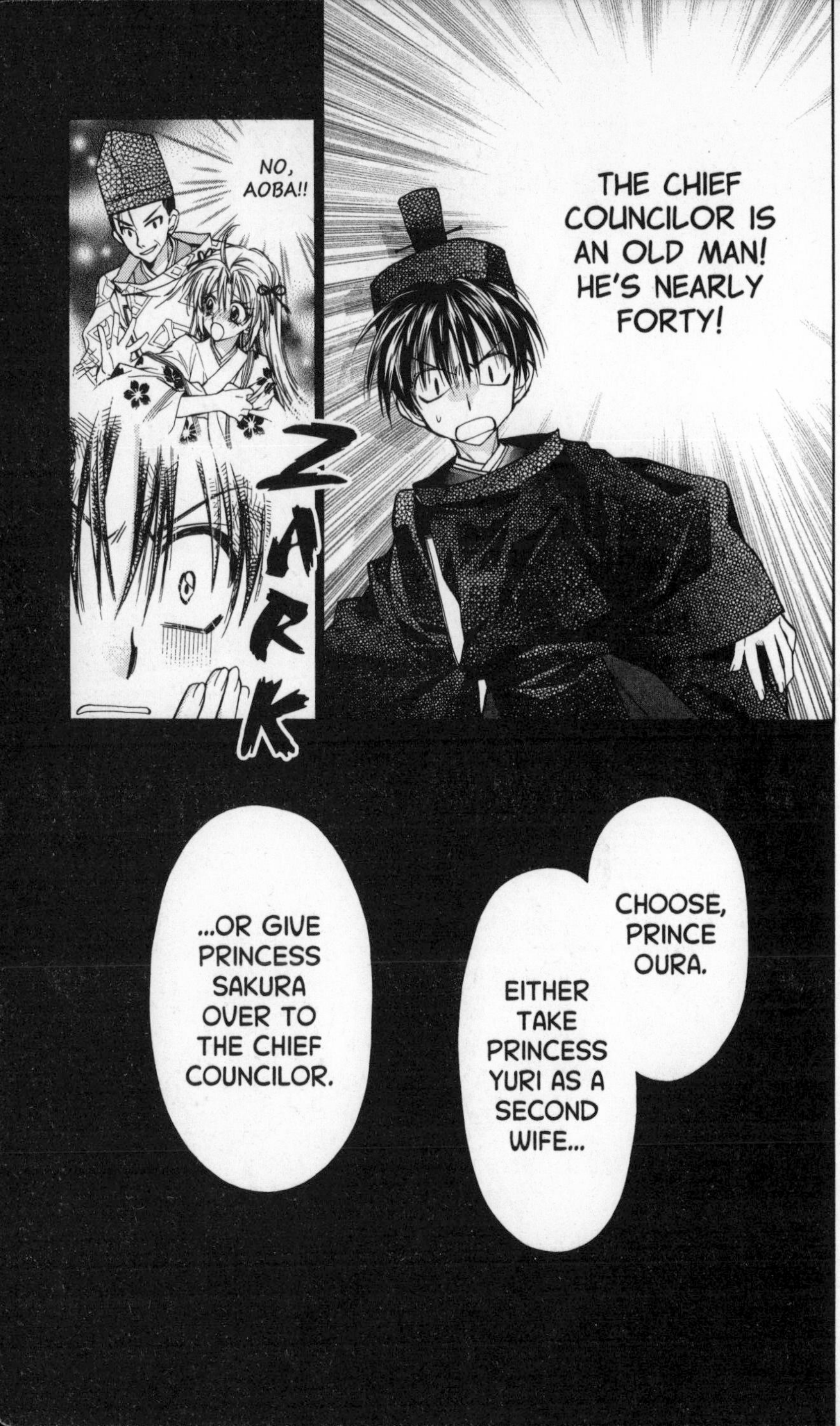
THE CHIEF COUNCILOR IS AN OLD MAN! HE'S NEARLY FORTY!
NO, AOBA!!
ZARK
CHOOSE, PRINCE OURA.
EITHER TAKE PRINCESS YURI AS A SECOND WIFE...
...OR GIVE PRINCESS SAKURA OVER TO THE CHIEF COUNCILOR.

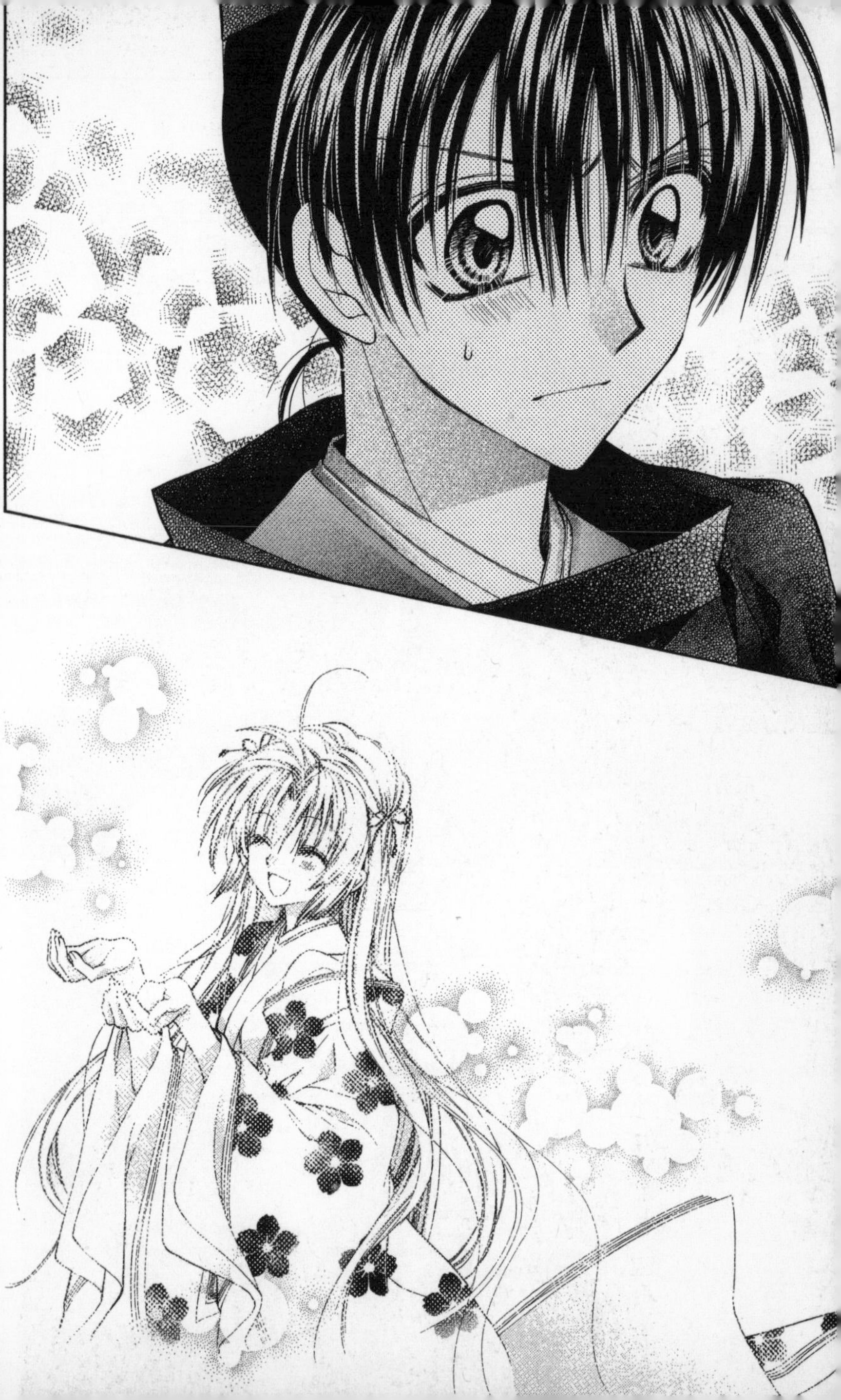

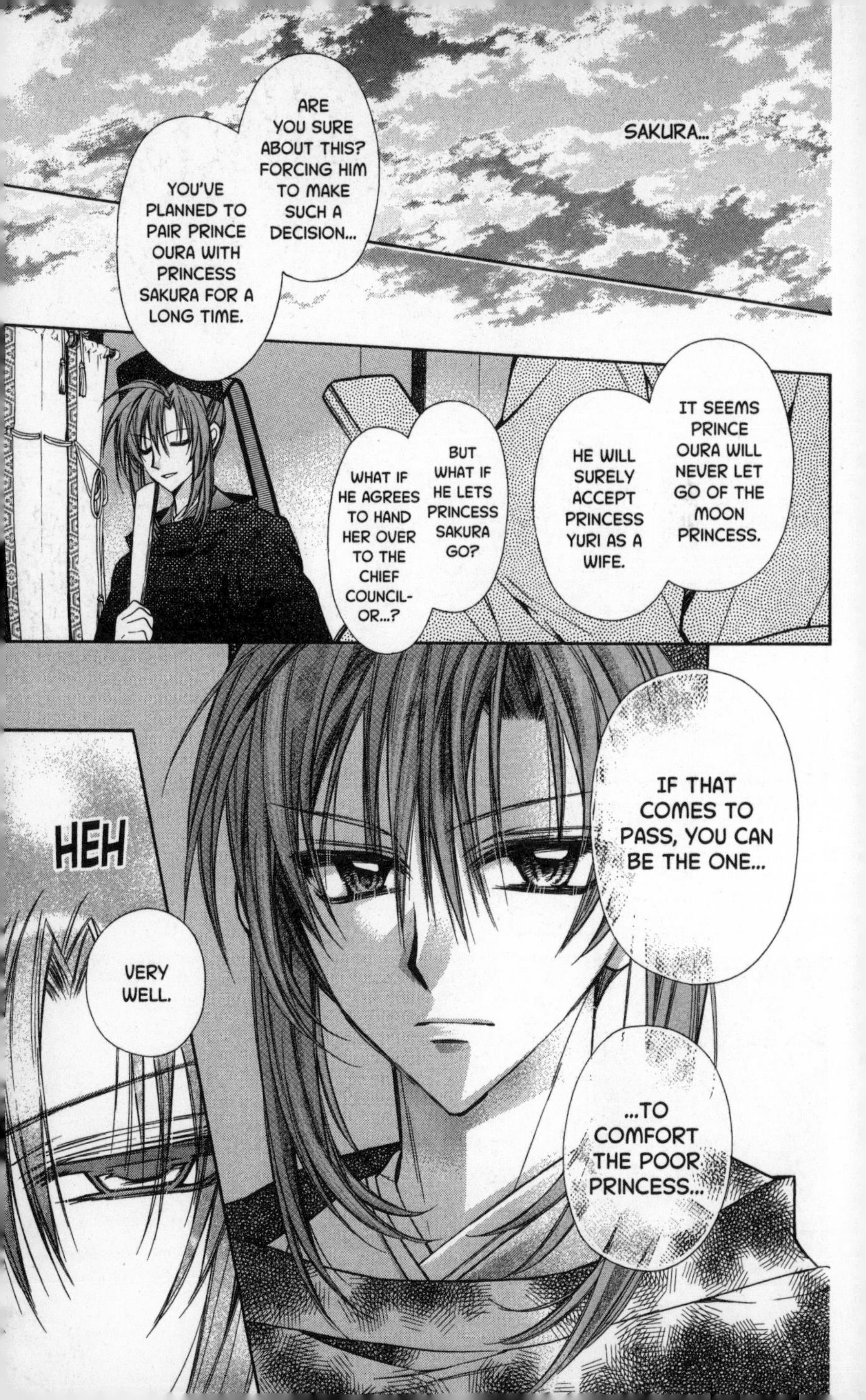
SAKURA...
ARE YOU SURE ABOUT THIS? FORCING HIM TO MAKE SUCH A DECISION...
YOU'VE PLANNED TO PAIR PRINCE OURA WITH PRINCESS SAKURA FOR A LONG TIME.
IT SEEMS PRINCE OURA WILL NEVER LET GO OF THE MOON PRINCESS.
HE WILL SURELY ACCEPT PRINCESS YURI AS A WIFE.
BUT WHAT IF HE LETS PRINCESS SAKURA GO?
WHAT IF HE AGREES TO HAND HER OVER TO THE CHIEF COUNCIL-OR...?
IF THAT COMES TO PASS, YOU CAN BE THE ONE...
...TO COMFORT THE POOR PRINCESS...
HEH
VERY WELL.

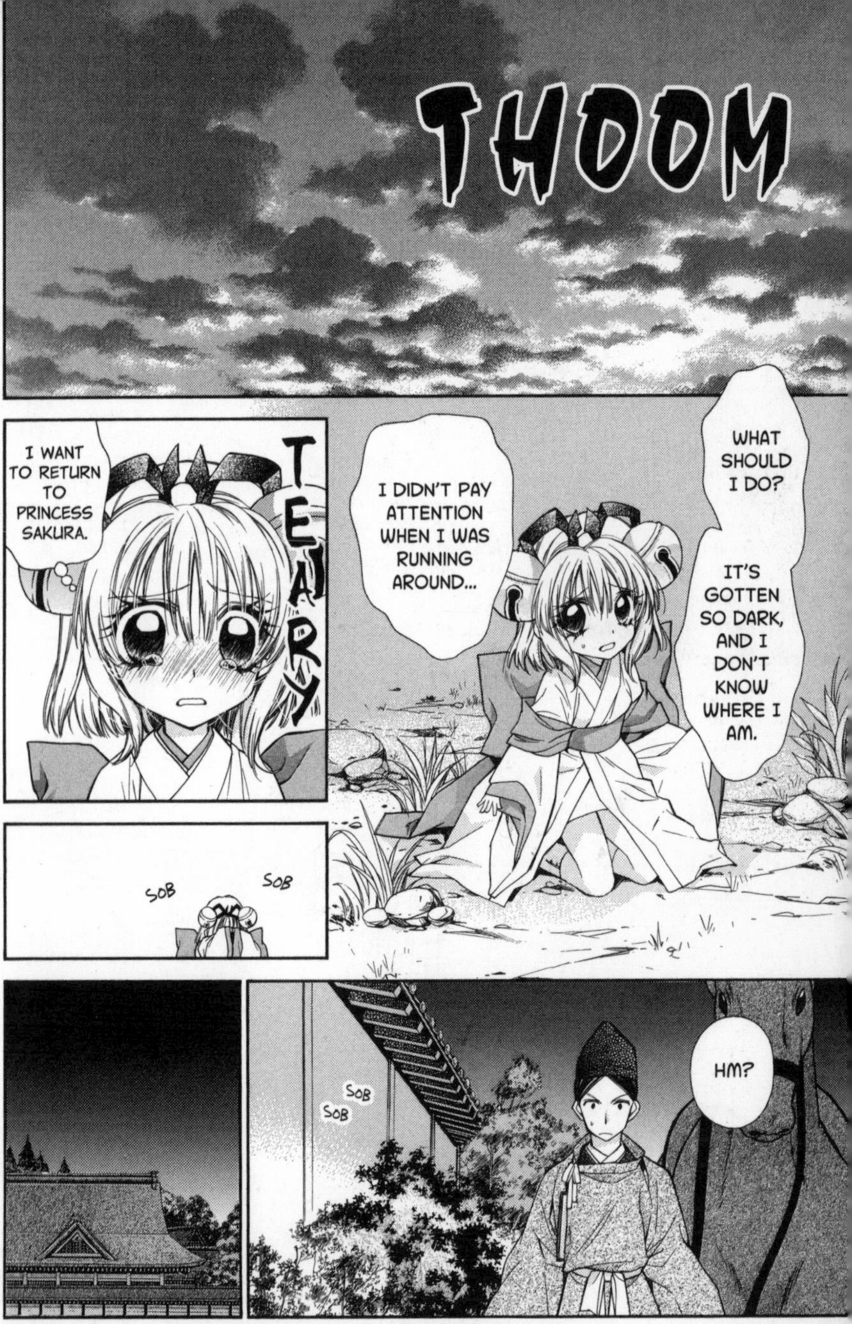
THOOM
WHAT SHOULD I DO?
IT'S GOTTEN SO DARK, AND I DON'T KNOW WHERE I AM.
I DIDN'T PAY ATTENTION WHEN I WAS RUNNING AROUND...
I WANT TO RETURN TO PRINCESS SAKURA.
TEARY
SOB
SOB
HM?
SOB
SOB

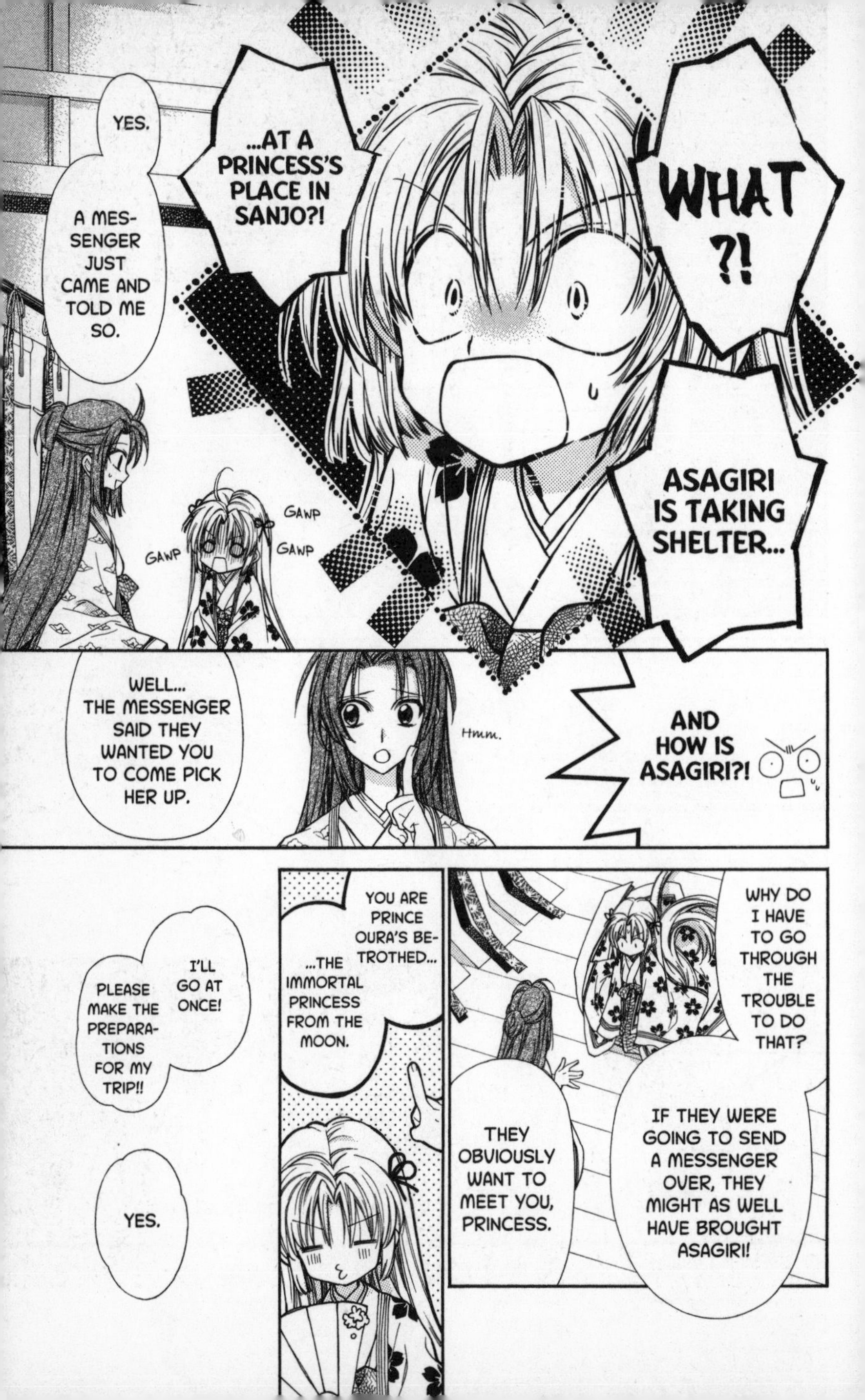
WHAT ?!
ASAGIRI IS TAKING SHELTER...
...AT A PRINCESS'S PLACE IN SANJO?!
YES.
A MES-SENGER JUST CAME AND TOLD ME SO.
GAWP
GAWP
GAWP
AND HOW IS ASAGIRI?!
Hmm.
WELL... THE MESSENGER SAID THEY WANTED YOU TO COME PICK HER UP.
WHY DO I HAVE TO GO THROUGH THE TROUBLE TO DO THAT?
IF THEY WERE GOING TO SEND A MESSENGER OVER, THEY MIGHT AS WELL HAVE BROUGHT ASAGIRI!
THEY OBVIOUSLY WANT TO MEET YOU, PRINCESS.
YOU ARE PRINCE OURA'S BE-TROTHED...
...THE IMMORTAL PRINCESS FROM THE MOON.
I'LL GO AT ONCE!
PLEASE MAKE THE PREPARA-TIONS FOR MY TRIP!!
YES.

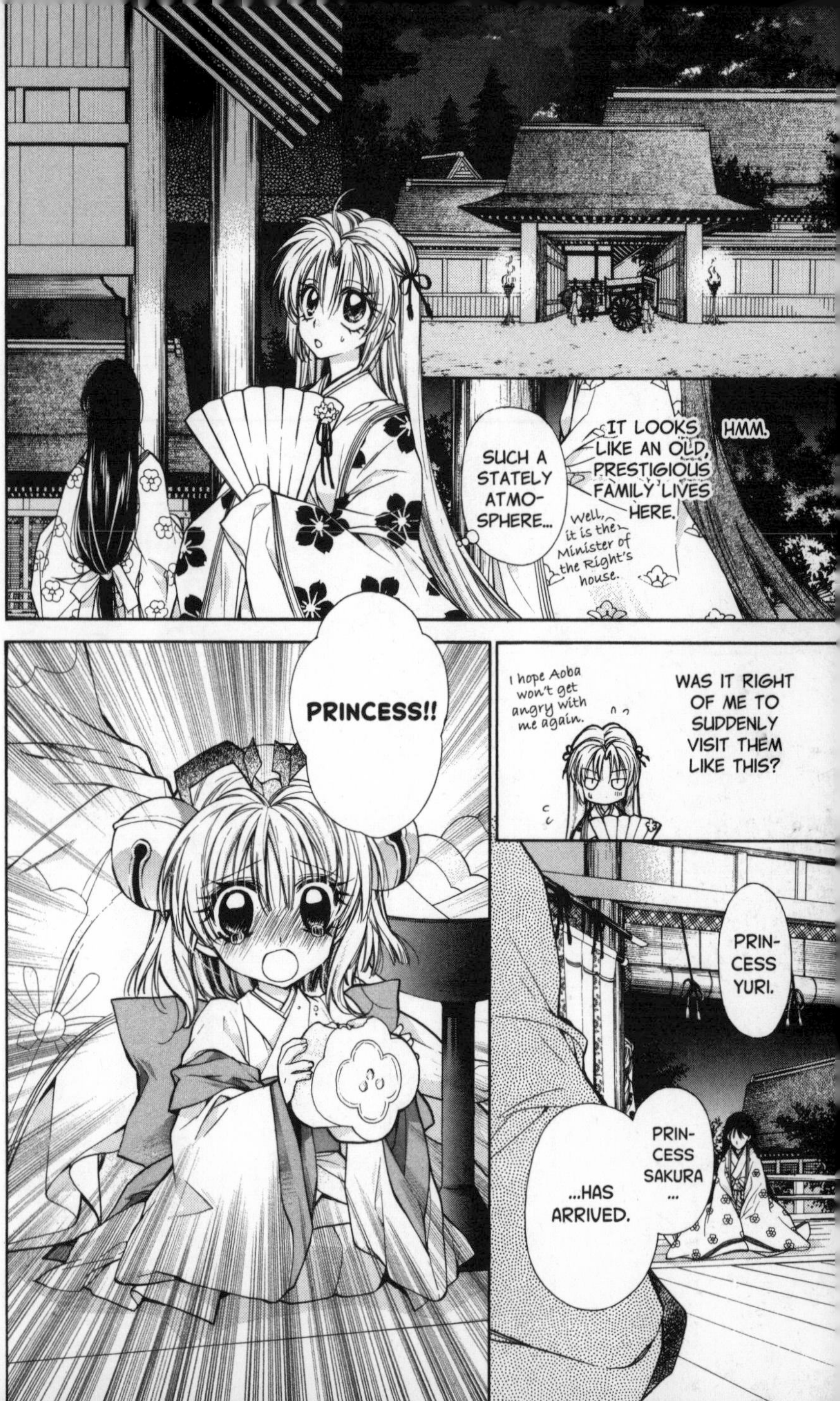
HMM.
IT LOOKS LIKE AN OLD, PRESTIGIOUS FAMILY LIVES HERE.
SUCH A STATELY ATMOSPHERE...
Well, it is the Minister of the Right's house.
WAS IT RIGHT OF ME TO SUDDENLY VISIT THEM LIKE THIS?
I hope Aoba won't get angry with me again.
PRINCESS YURI.
PRINCESS SAKURA ...
...HAS ARRIVED.
PRINCESS!!

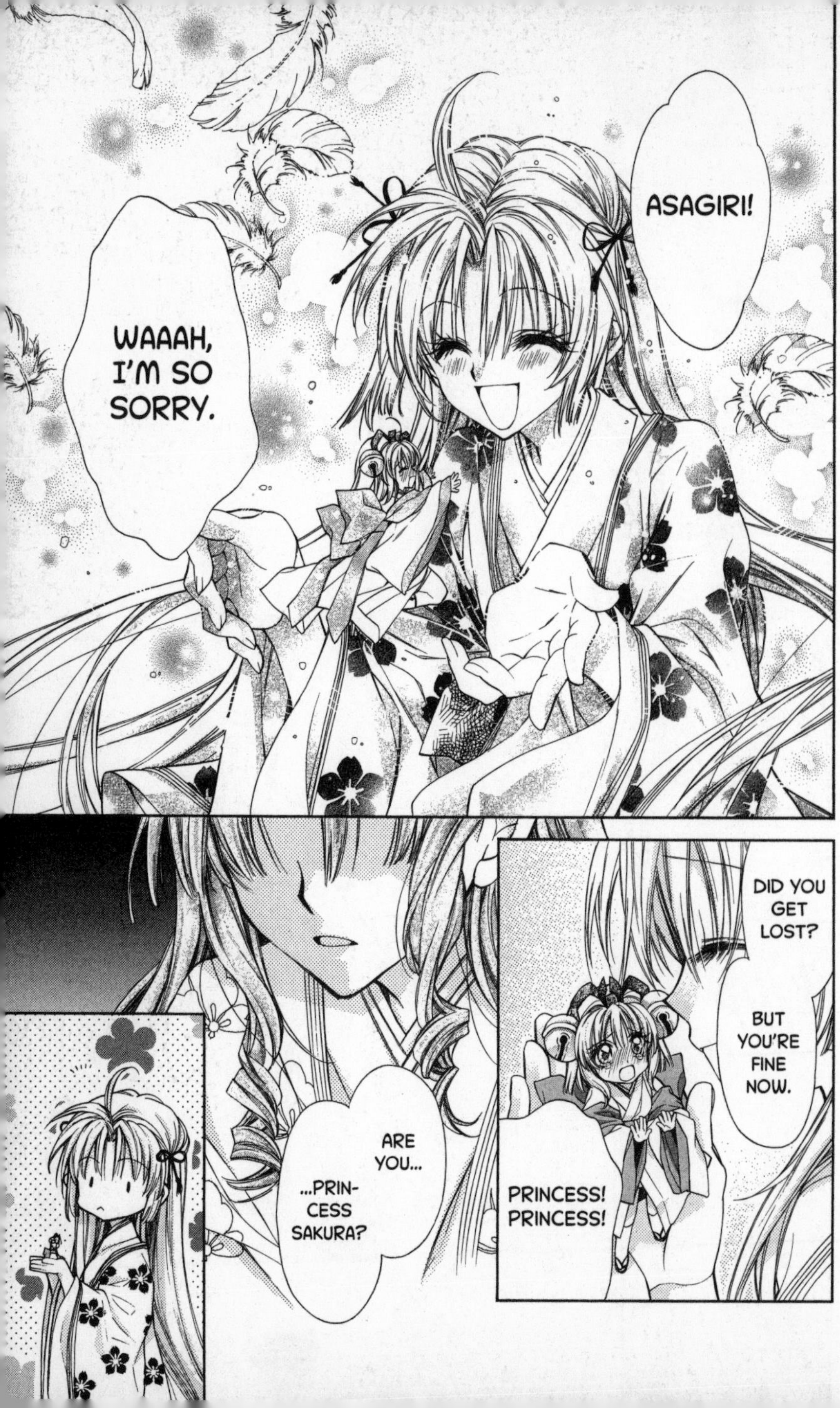
ASAGIRI!
WAAAH, I'M SO SORRY.
DID YOU GET LOST?
BUT YOU'RE FINE NOW.
PRINCESS! PRINCESS!
ARE YOU...
...PRIN-CESS SAKURA?

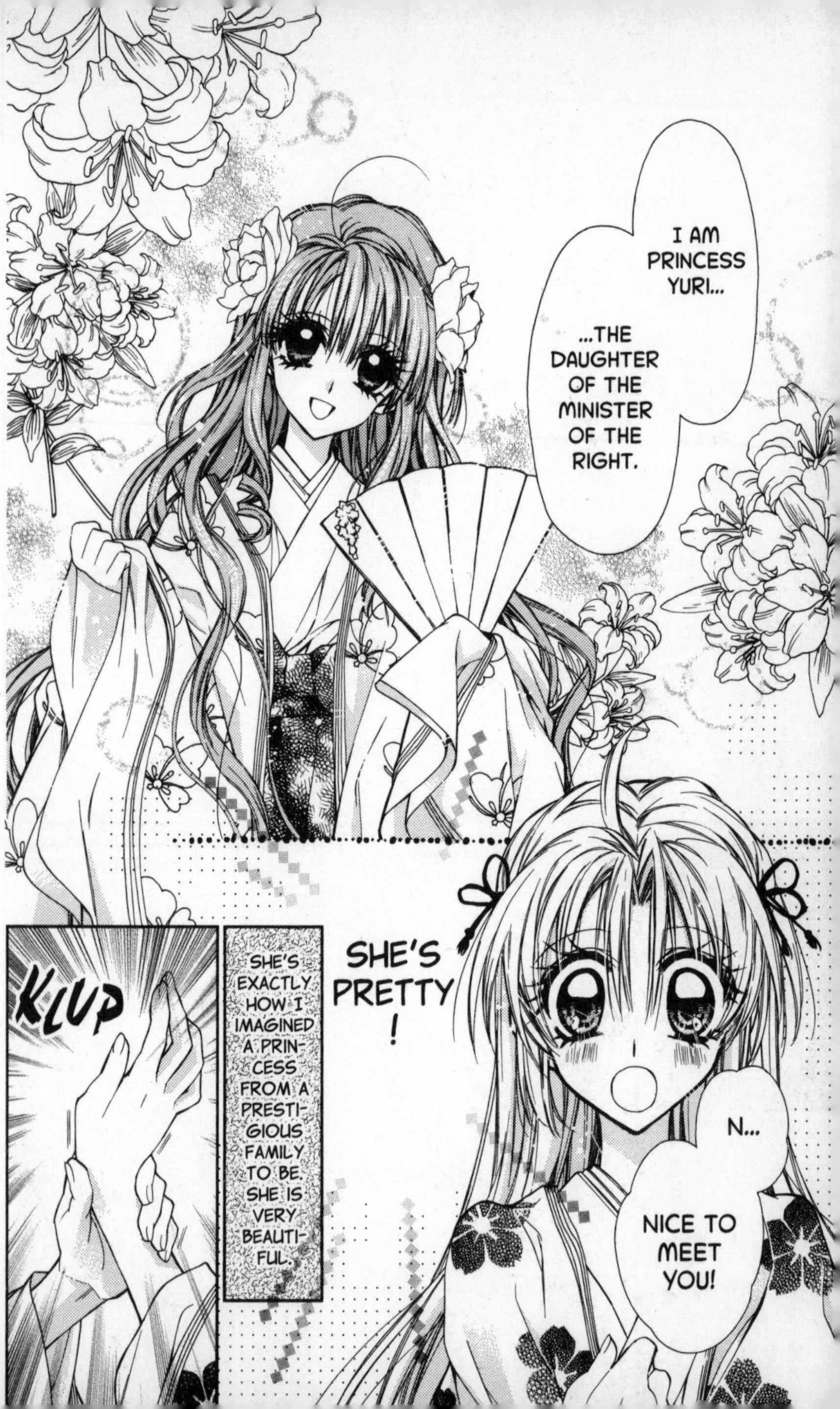
I AM PRINCESS YURI...
...THE DAUGHTER OF THE MINISTER OF THE RIGHT.
SHE'S PRETTY!
N...
NICE TO MEET YOU!
SHE'S EXACTLY HOW I IMAGINED A PRINCESS FROM A PRESTIGIOUS FAMILY TO BE. SHE IS VERY BEAUTIFUL.
KLUP

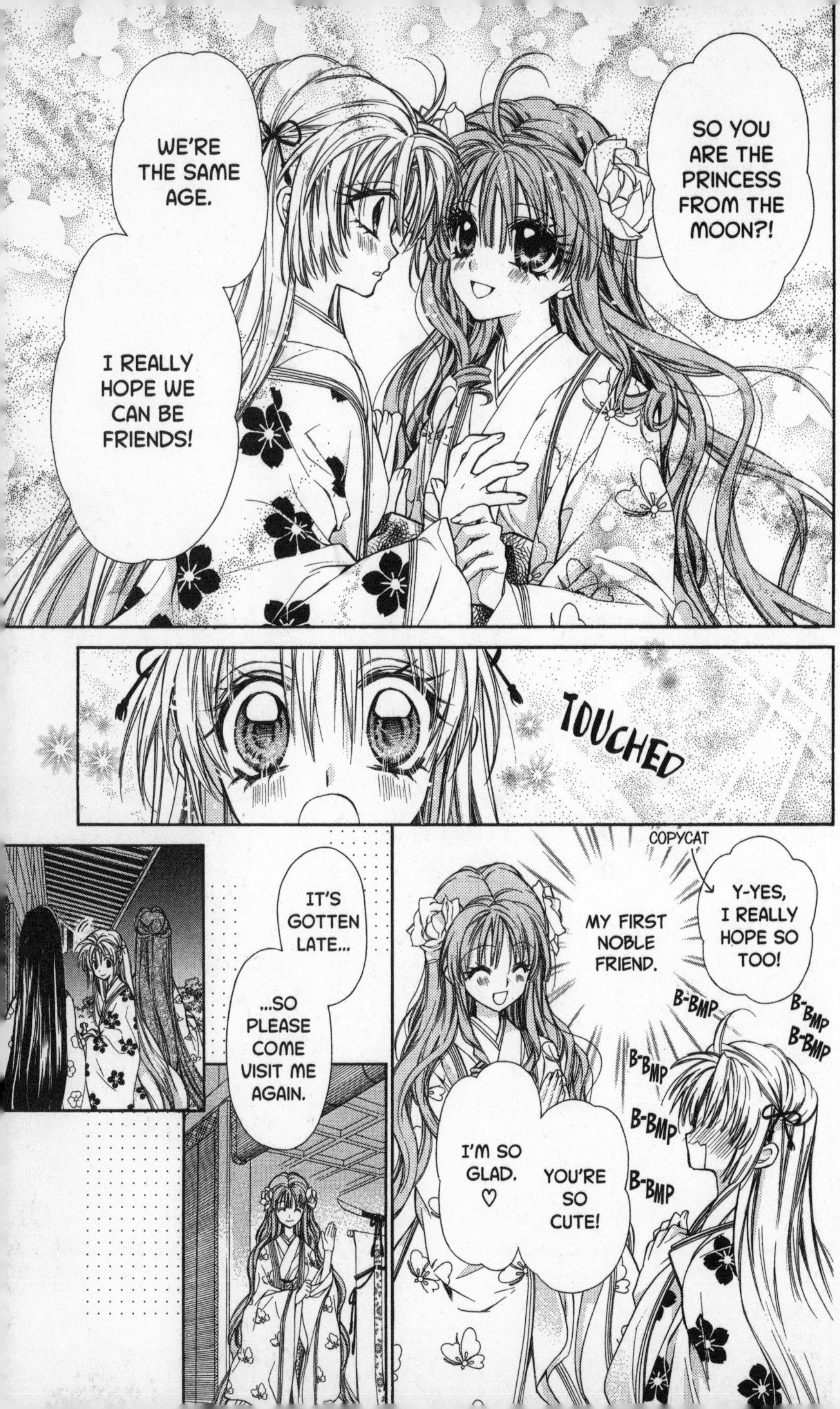
SO YOU ARE THE PRINCESS FROM THE MOON?!
WE'RE THE SAME AGE.
I REALLY HOPE WE CAN BE FRIENDS!
TOUCHED
COPYCAT
Y-YES, I REALLY HOPE SO TOO!
MY FIRST NOBLE FRIEND.
B-BMP
B-BMP B-BMP
B-BMP
B-BMP
B-BMP
YOU'RE SO CUTE!
I'M SO GLAD. ♡
IT'S GOTTEN LATE...
...SO PLEASE COME VISIT ME AGAIN.

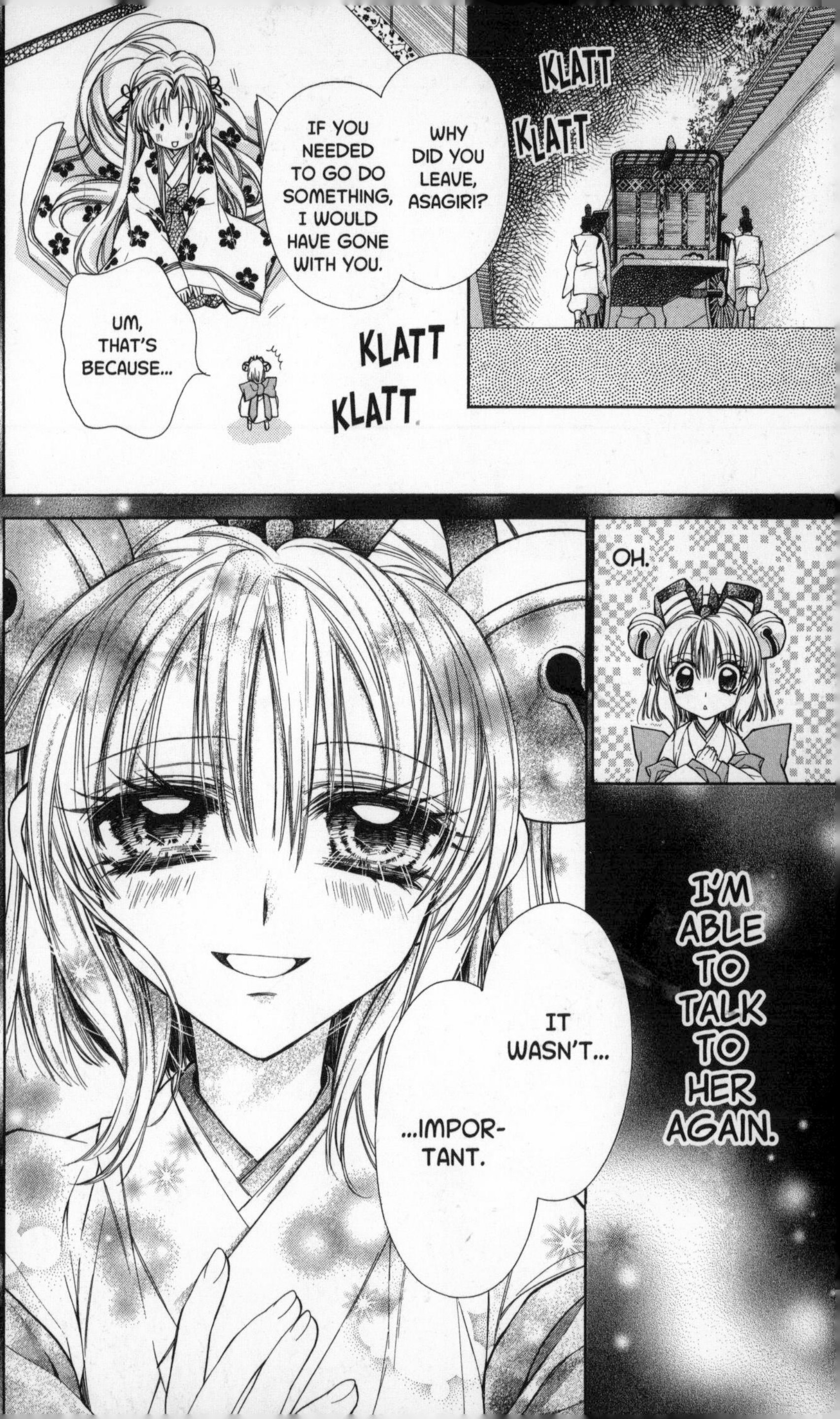
KLATT KLATT
WHY DID YOU LEAVE, ASAGIRI?
IF YOU NEEDED TO GO DO SOMETHING, I WOULD HAVE GONE WITH YOU.
KLATT KLATT
UM, THAT'S BECAUSE...
OH.
I'M ABLE TO TALK TO HER AGAIN.
IT WASN'T...
...IMPOR-TANT.

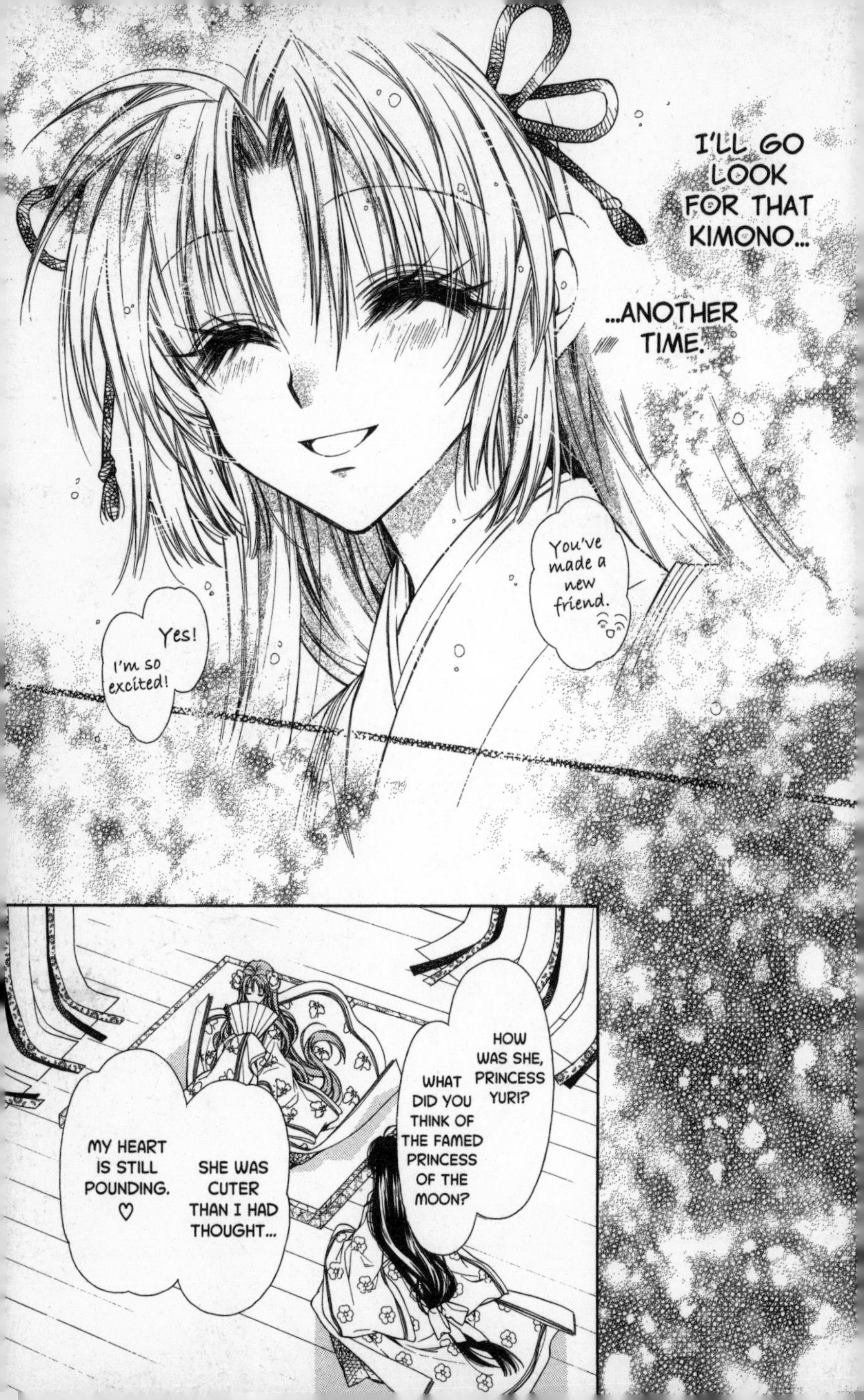
I'LL GO LOOK FOR THAT KIMONO...
...ANOTHER TIME.
You've made a new friend.
Yes! I'm so excited!
HOW WAS SHE, PRINCESS YURI?
WHAT DID YOU THINK OF THE FAMED PRINCESS OF THE MOON?
SHE WAS CUTER THAN I HAD THOUGHT...
MY HEART IS STILL POUNDING. ♡

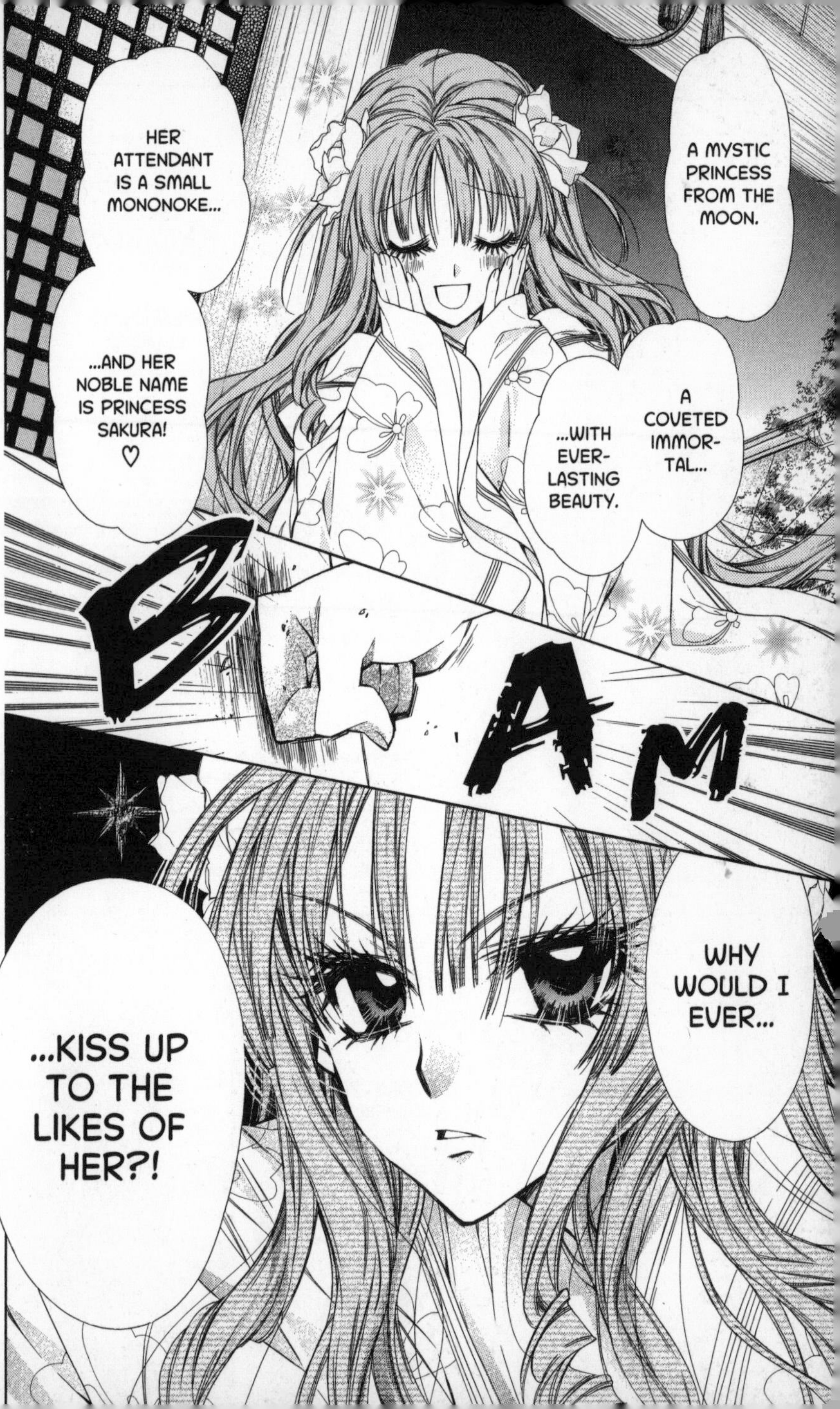
A MYSTIC PRINCESS FROM THE MOON.
A COVETED IMMOR-TAL...
...WITH EVER-LASTING BEAUTY.
HER ATTENDANT IS A SMALL MONONOKE...
...AND HER NOBLE NAME IS PRINCESS SAKURA! ♡
BAM
WHY WOULD I EVER...
...KISS UP TO THE LIKES OF HER?!

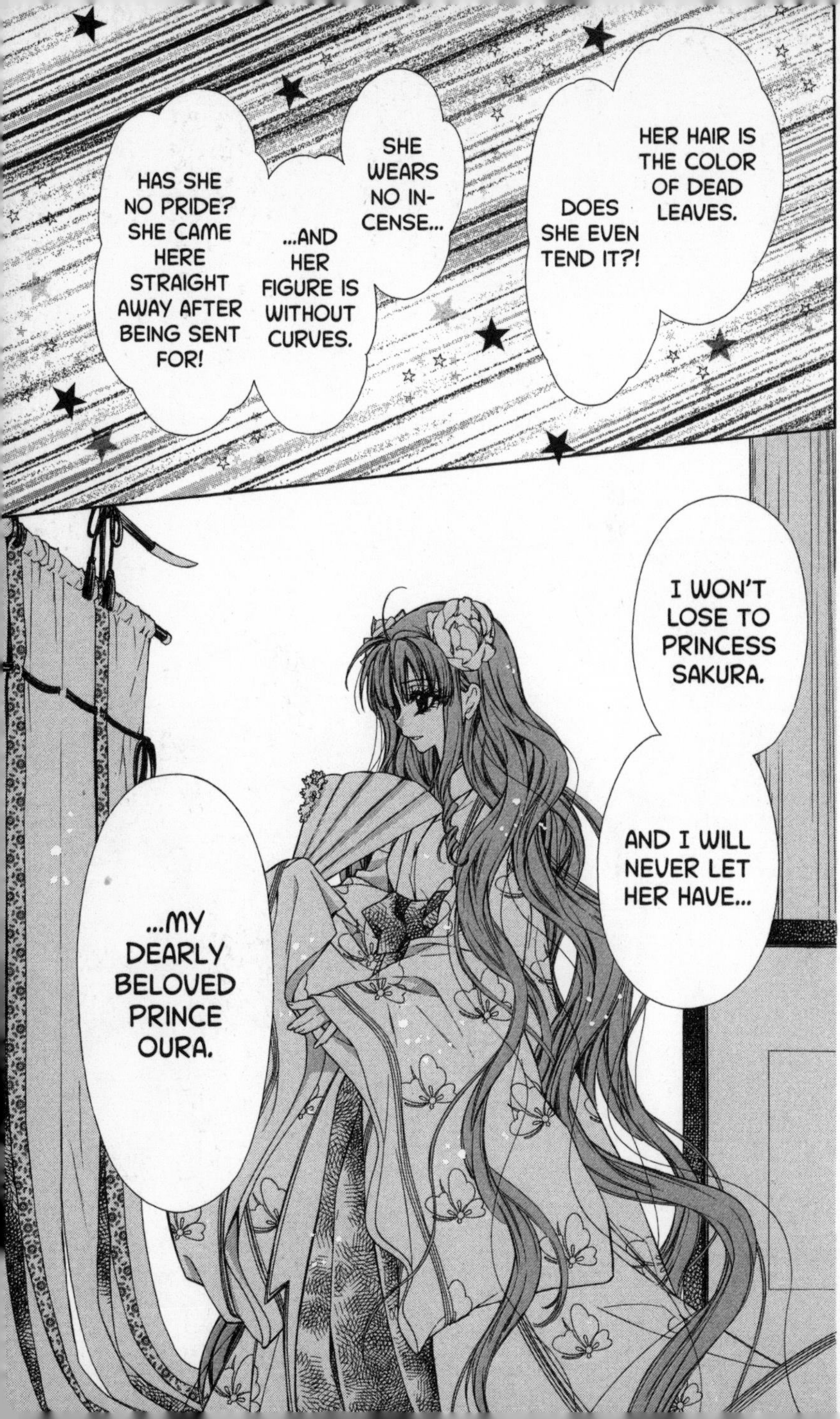
HER HAIR IS THE COLOR OF DEAD LEAVES.
DOES SHE EVEN TEND IT?!
SHE WEARS NO IN-CENSE...
...AND HER FIGURE IS WITHOUT CURVES.
HAS SHE NO PRIDE? SHE CAME HERE STRAIGHT AWAY AFTER BEING SENT FOR!
I WON'T LOSE TO PRINCESS SAKURA.
AND I WILL NEVER LET HER HAVE...
...MY DEARLY BELOVED PRINCE OURA.

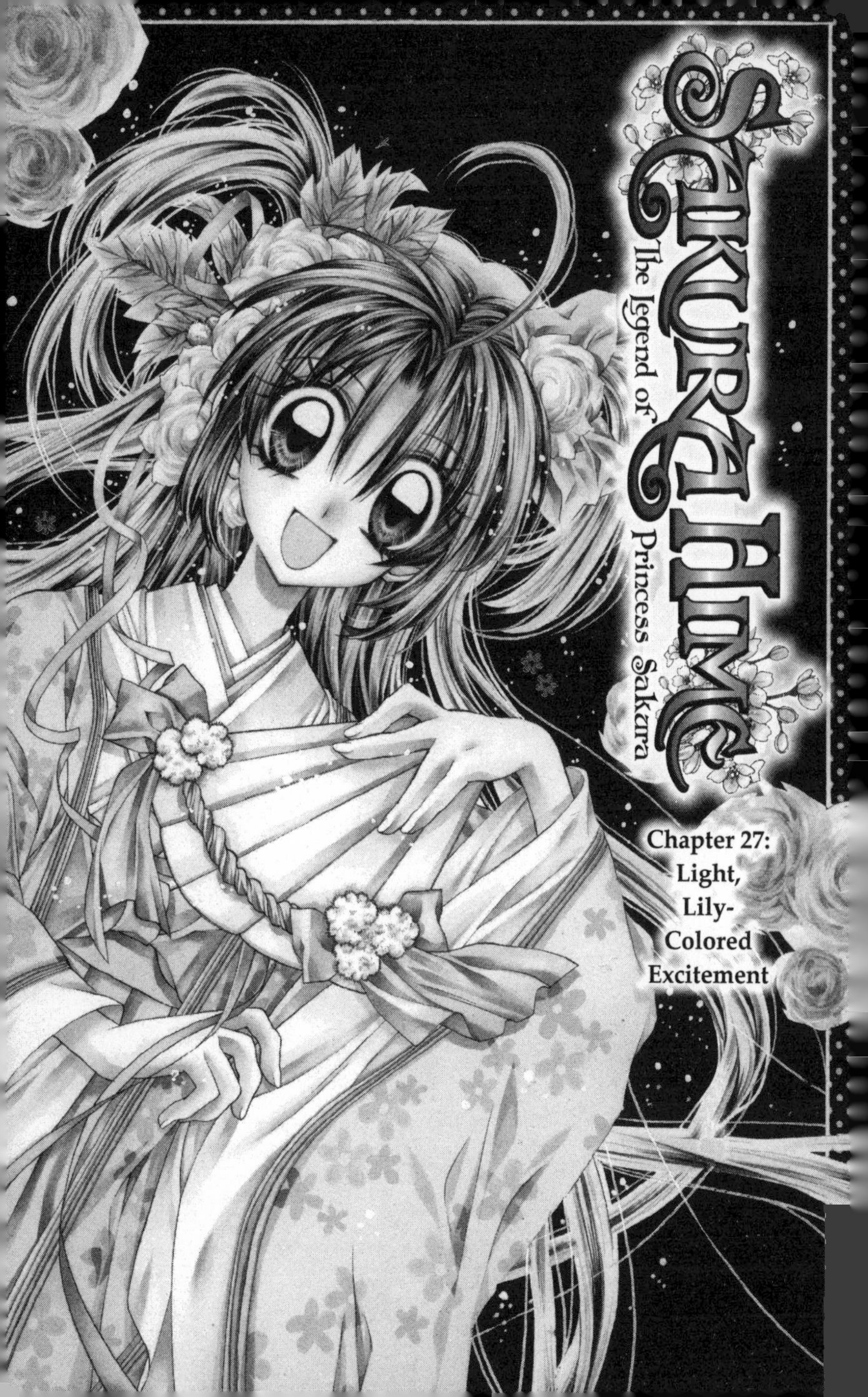
Sakura Hime
The Legend of Princess Sakura
Chapter 27:
Light,
Lily-
Colored
Excitement

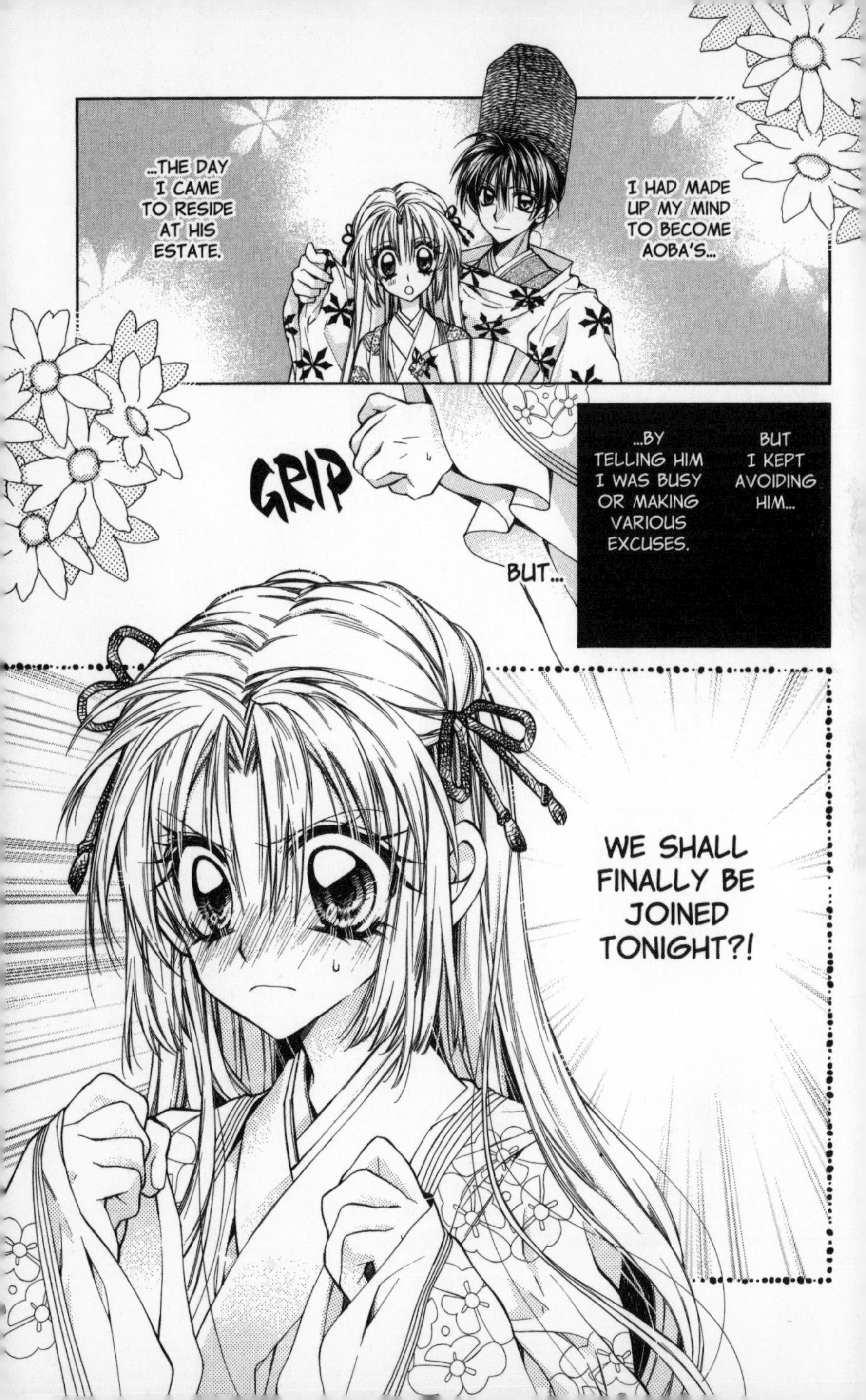
I HAD MADE UP MY MIND TO BECOME AOBA'S...
...THE DAY I CAME TO RESIDE AT HIS ESTATE.
BUT I KEPT AVOIDING HIM...
...BY TELLING HIM I WAS BUSY OR MAKING VARIOUS EXCUSES.
GRIP
BUT...
WE SHALL FINALLY BE JOINED TONIGHT?!

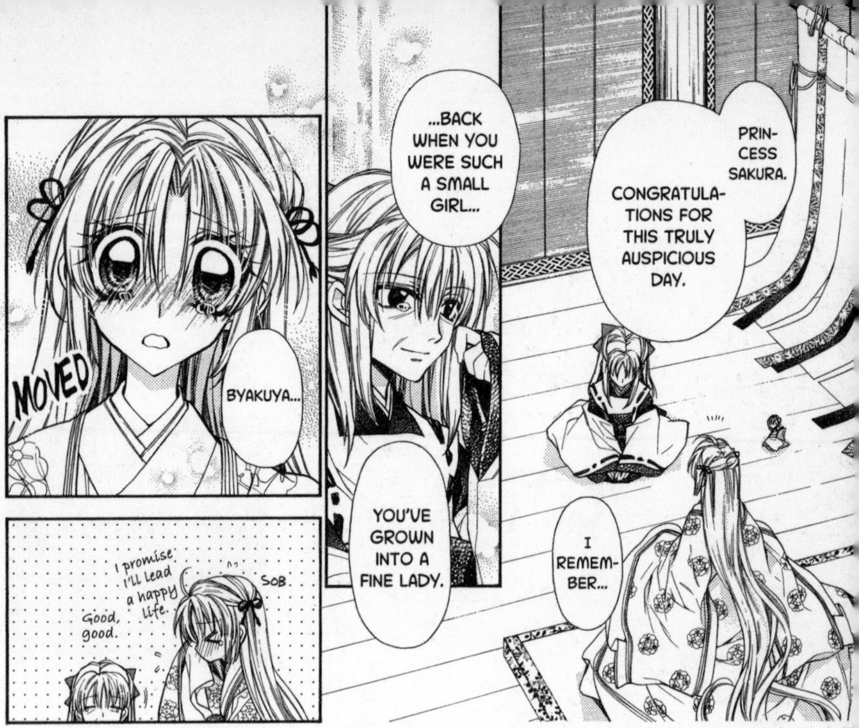
PRINCESS SAKURA.
CONGRATULATIONS FOR THIS TRULY AUSPICIOUS DAY.
I REMEMBER...
...BACK WHEN YOU WERE SUCH A SMALL GIRL...
YOU'VE GROWN INTO A FINE LADY.
MOVED
BYAKUYA...
SOB
I promise I'll lead a happy life.
Good, good.

Chapter 27: Light, Lily-Colored Excitement

※ I'm giving away the story.

In chapter 27 you get to see Aoba's popularity plummet. (laugh) Princess Sakura is an honest girl who cannot lie, and all Princess Yuri can do is the opposite... I think Princess Yuri has the lead right now. Aoba is in a tight spot too. But it looks like a lot of things are going on inside Aoba's head as well. I don't usually do this, but I couldn't help smiling when my assistants and friends asked me, "Why is Aoba's room so messy?" and "What is Princess Yuri after?" (Because they're all worried about him.) I had a lot of fun drawing a Sakura who wants Aoba to look at her but keeps failing to succeed. I am a Sakura-type person who cannot lie, so I was impressed by Yuri. I thought, "Wow, Princess Yuri is something, huh..." Lying to people is really tiring, isn't it? (But I think manga artists have to be good at lying to be able to draw manga. ← To hold off from revealing what happens in the future.) So I feel slightly uncomfortable having to develop the story a little bit at a time. I want everything revealed right away.

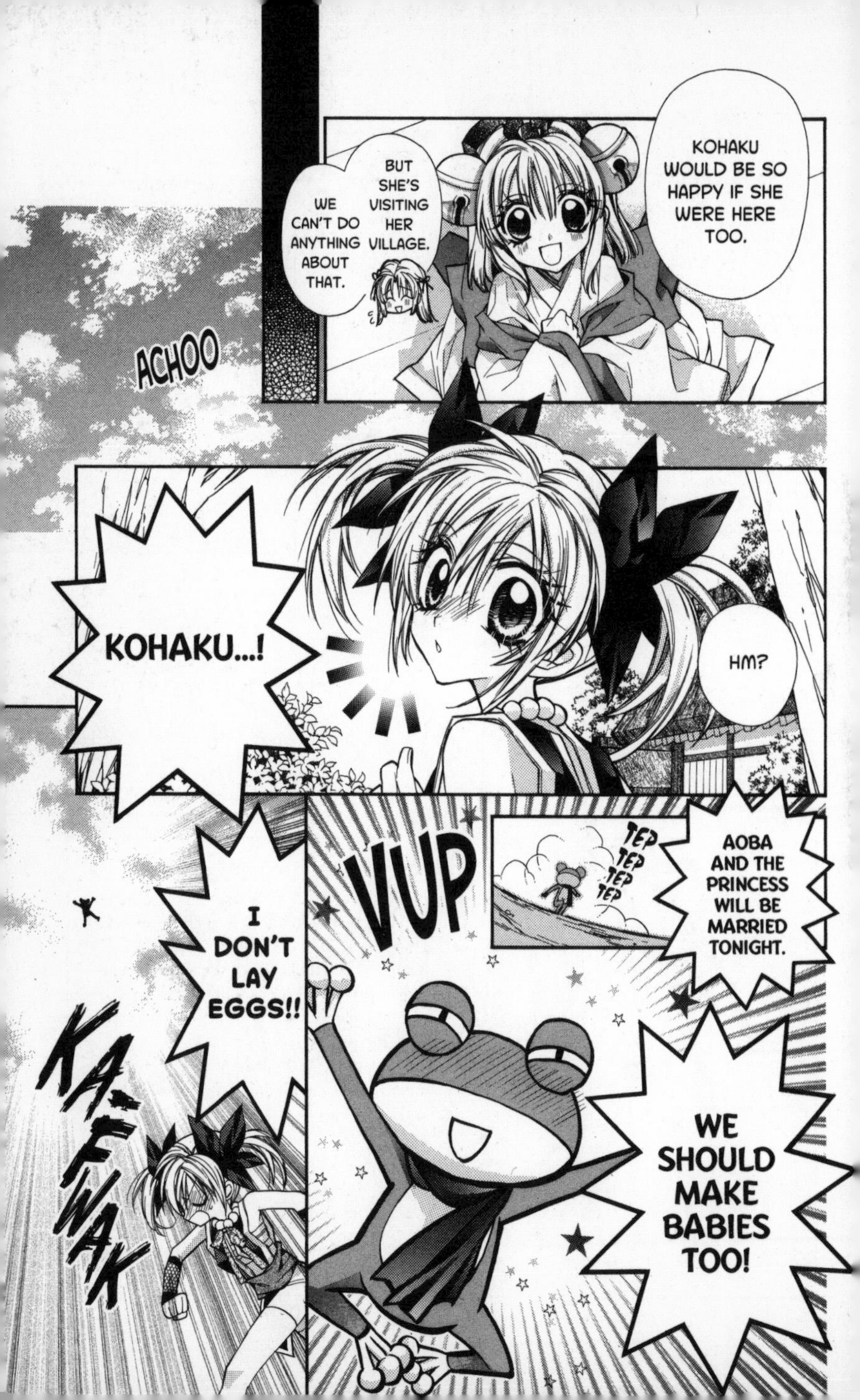
KOHAKU WOULD BE SO HAPPY IF SHE WERE HERE TOO.
BUT SHE'S VISITING HER VILLAGE.
WE CAN'T DO ANYTHING ABOUT THAT.
ACHOO
HM?
KOHAKU...!
AOBA AND THE PRINCESS WILL BE MARRIED TONIGHT.
TEP TEP TEP TEP
VUP
WE SHOULD MAKE BABIES TOO!
I DON'T LAY EGGS!!
KA-FWAK

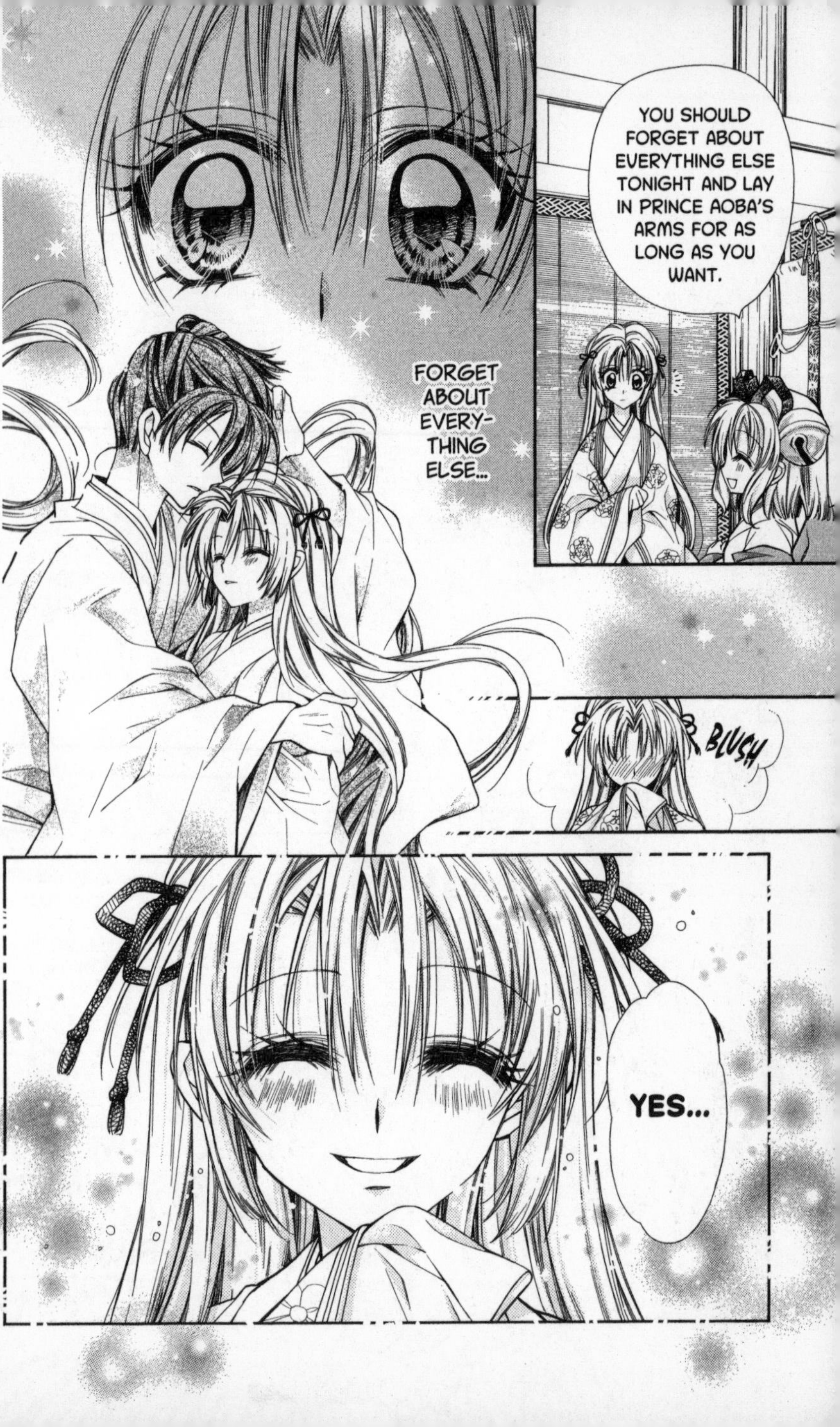
YOU SHOULD FORGET ABOUT EVERYTHING ELSE TONIGHT AND LAY IN PRINCE AOBA'S ARMS FOR AS LONG AS YOU WANT.
BLUSH
FORGET ABOUT EVERY-THING ELSE...
YES...

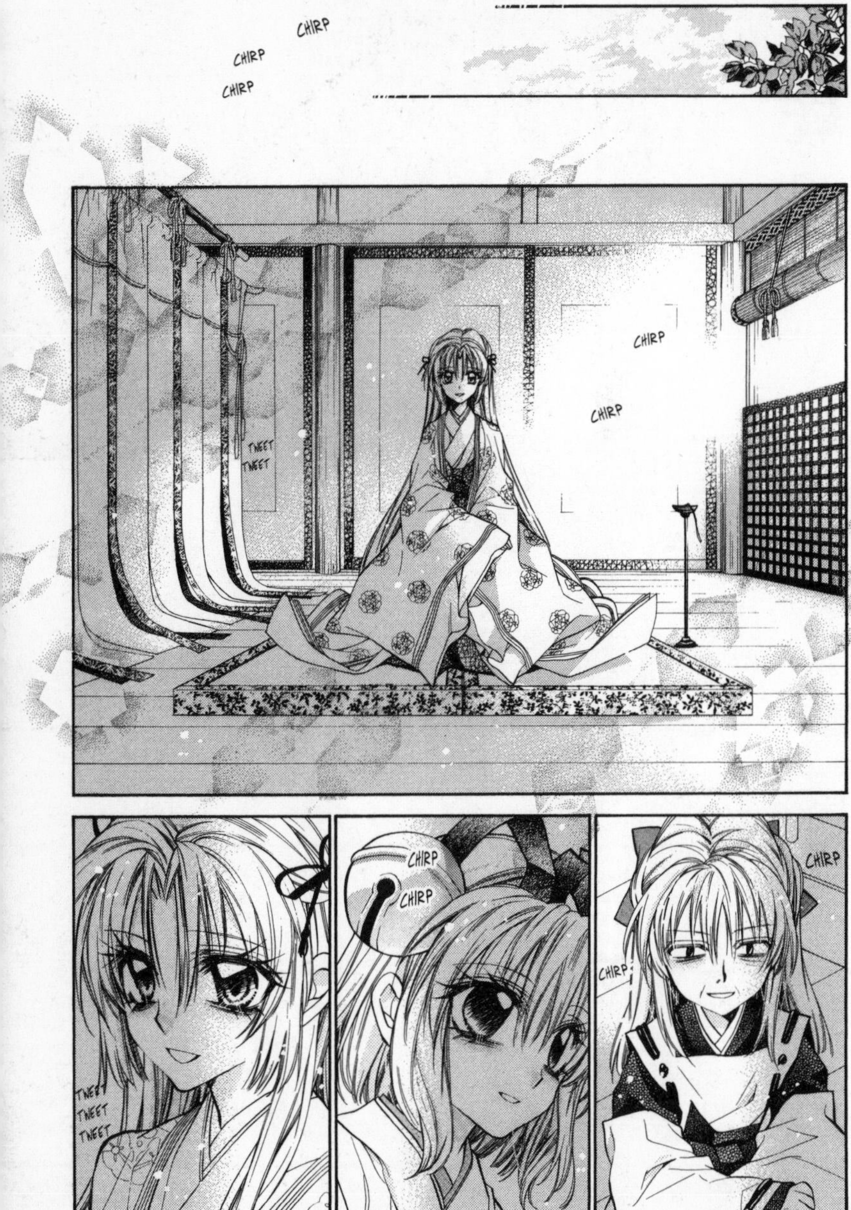
CHIRP
CHIRP
CHIRP
CHIRP
CHIRP
TWEET
TWEET
CHIRP
CHIRP
CHIRP
CHIRP
TWEET
TWEET
TWEET

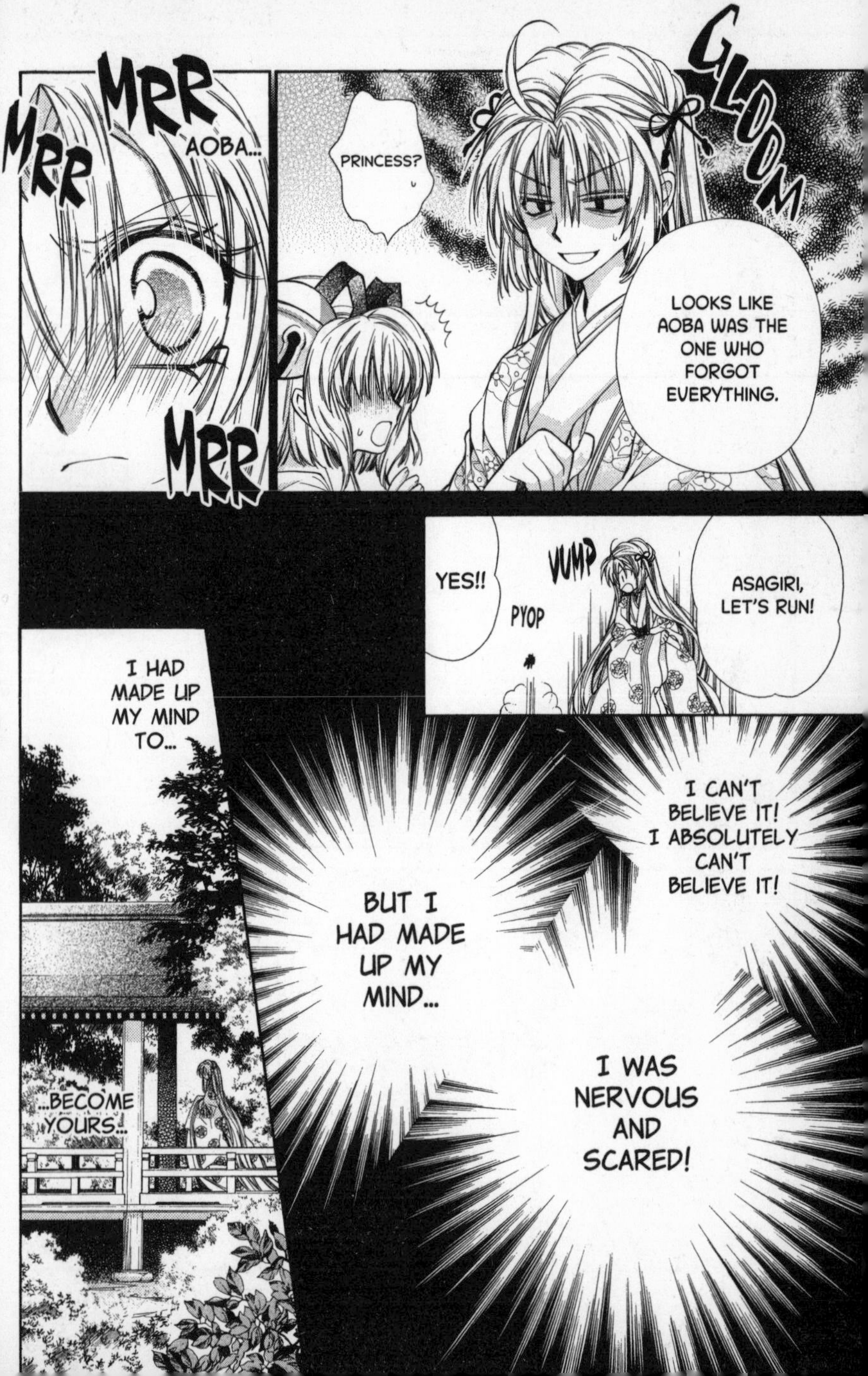
GLOOM
PRINCESS?
LOOKS LIKE AOBA WAS THE ONE WHO FORGOT EVERYTHING.
MRR
MRR
AOBA...
MRR
ASAGIRI, LET'S RUN!
VUMP
YES!!
PYOP
I CAN'T BELIEVE IT! I ABSOLUTELY CAN'T BELIEVE IT!
BUT I HAD MADE UP MY MIND...
I WAS NERVOUS AND SCARED!
I HAD MADE UP MY MIND TO...
...BECOME YOURS...

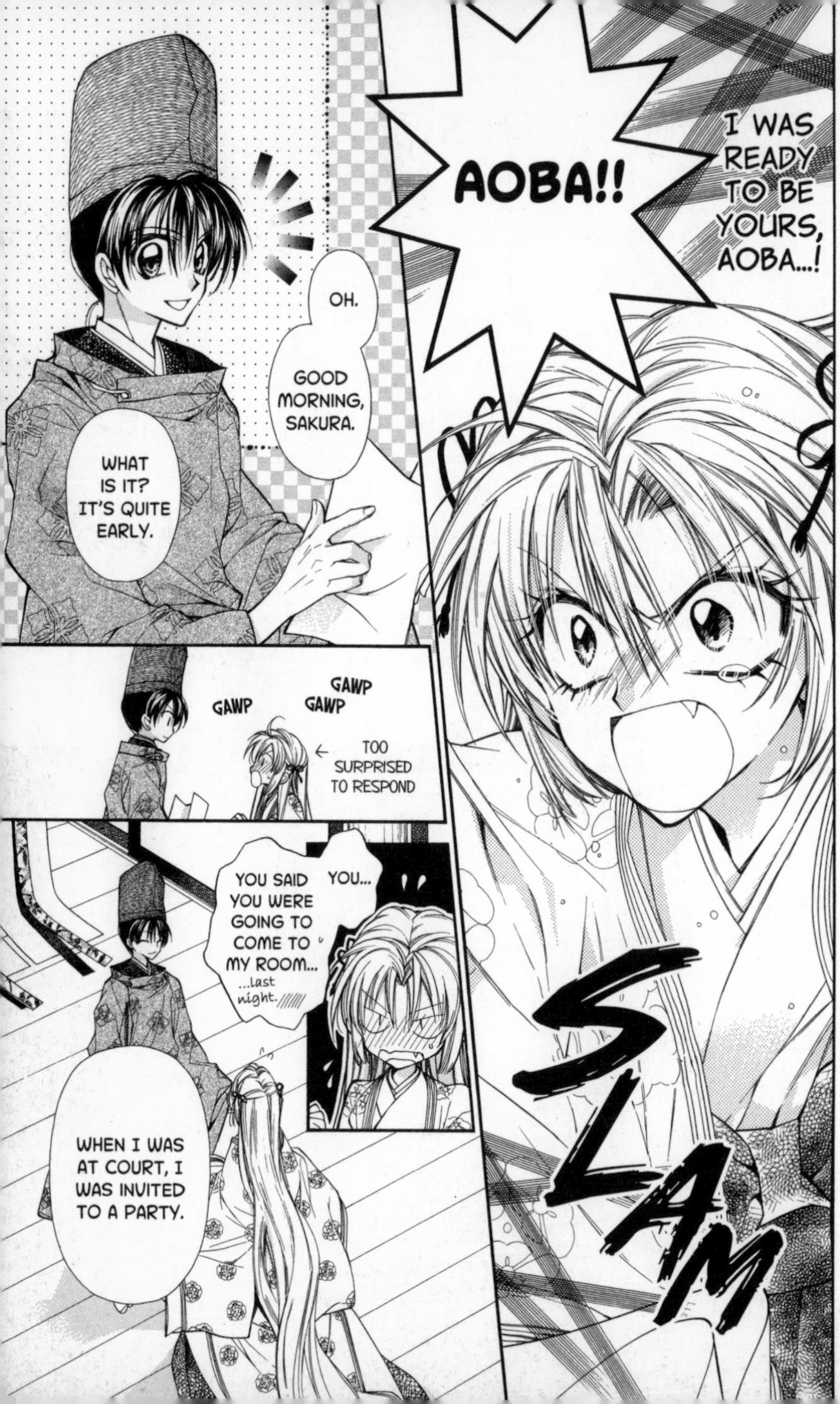
I WAS READY TO BE YOURS, AOBA...!
AOBA!!
SLAM
OH.
GOOD MORNING, SAKURA.
WHAT IS IT? IT'S QUITE EARLY.
GAWP
GAWP
GAWP
TOO SURPRISED TO RESPOND
YOU...
YOU SAID YOU WERE GOING TO COME TO MY ROOM...
...last night.
WHEN I WAS AT COURT, I WAS INVITED TO A PARTY.

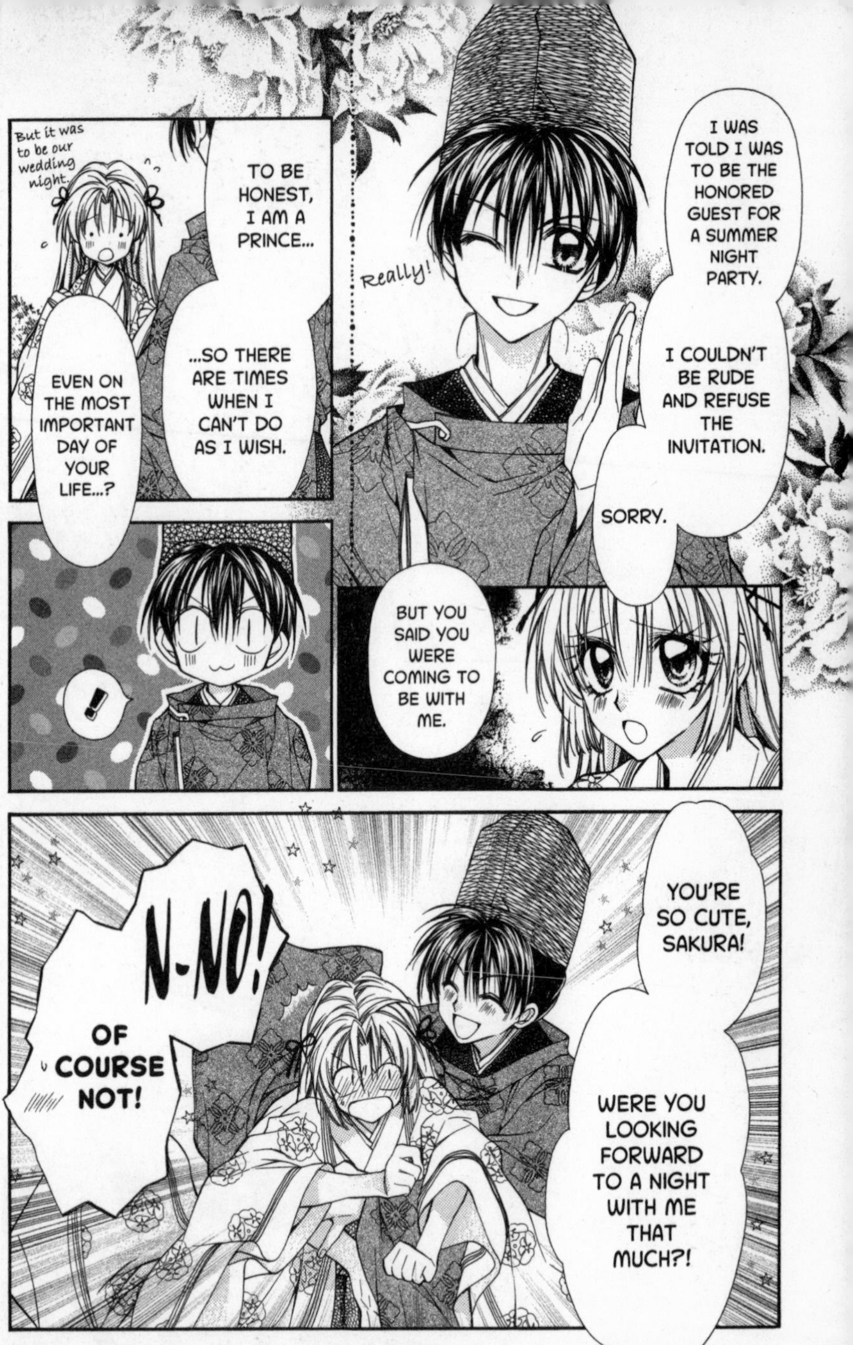
I WAS TOLD I WAS TO BE THE HONORED GUEST FOR A SUMMER NIGHT PARTY.
I COULDN'T BE RUDE AND REFUSE THE INVITATION.
SORRY.
Really!
TO BE HONEST, I AM A PRINCE...
...SO THERE ARE TIMES WHEN I CAN'T DO AS I WISH.
But it was to be our wedding night.
EVEN ON THE MOST IMPORTANT DAY OF YOUR LIFE...?
BUT YOU SAID YOU WERE COMING TO BE WITH ME.
!
YOU'RE SO CUTE, SAKURA!
WERE YOU LOOKING FORWARD TO A NIGHT WITH ME THAT MUCH?!
N-NO!
OF COURSE NOT!

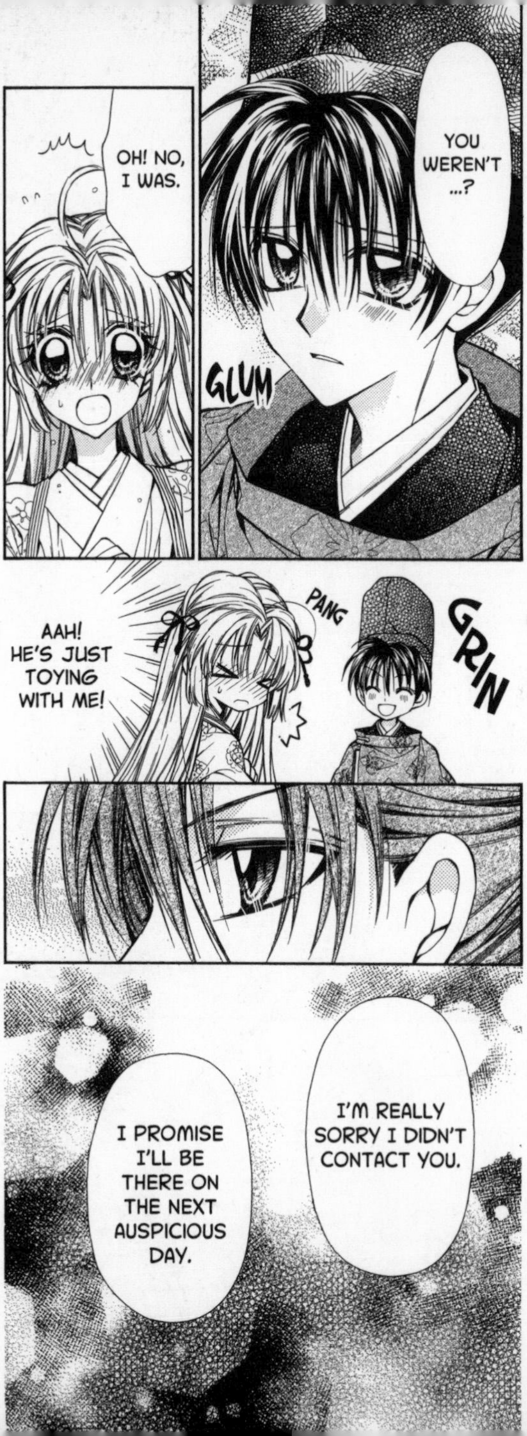
YOU WEREN'T ...?
GLUM
OH! NO, I WAS.
GRIN
PANG
AAH! HE'S JUST TOYING WITH ME!
I'M REALLY SORRY I DIDN'T CONTACT YOU.
I PROMISE I'LL BE THERE ON THE NEXT AUSPICIOUS DAY.

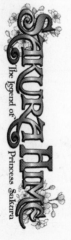

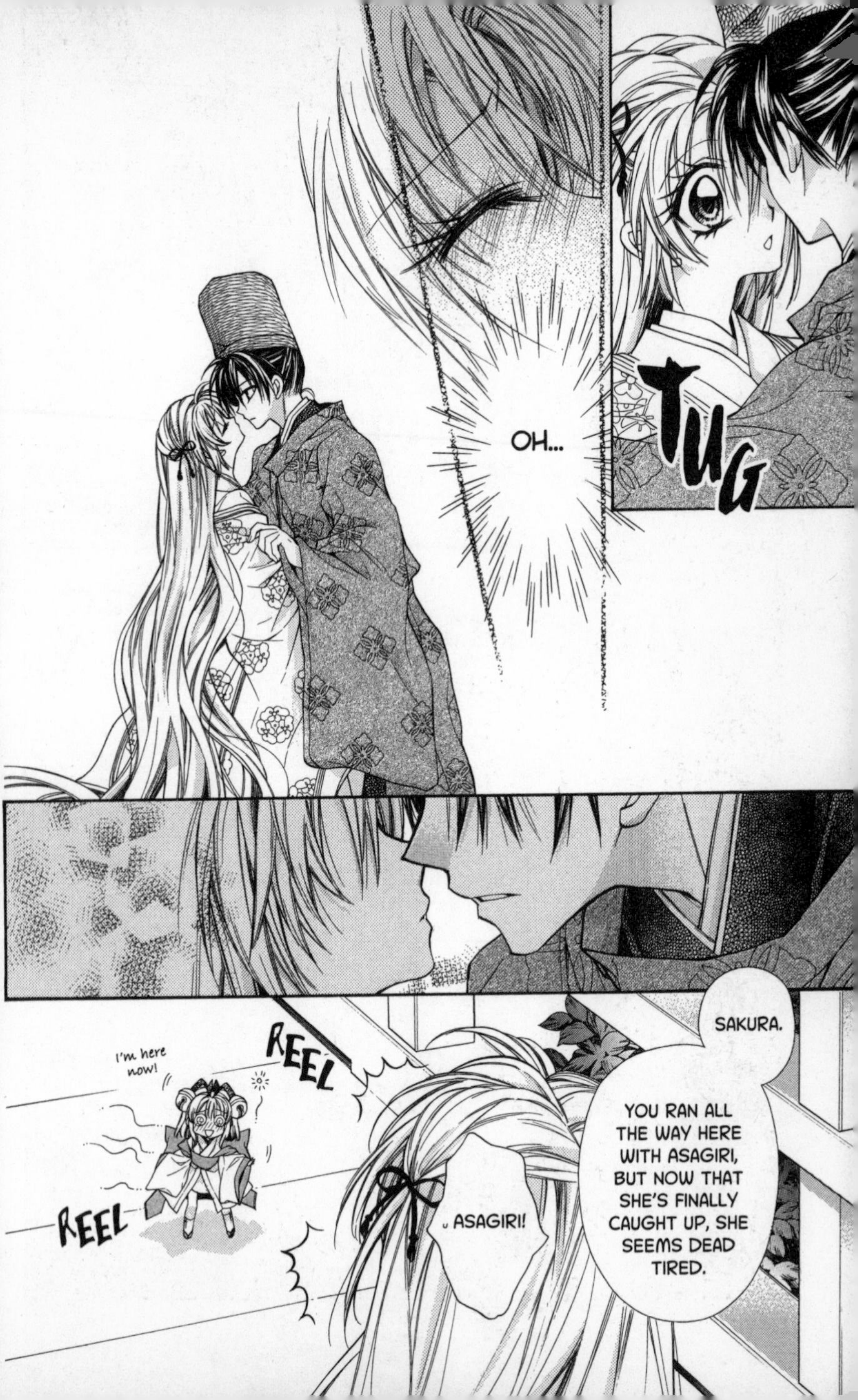
TUG
OH...
SAKURA.
YOU RAN ALL THE WAY HERE WITH ASAGIRI, BUT NOW THAT SHE'S FINALLY CAUGHT UP, SHE SEEMS DEAD TIRED.
ASAGIRI!
REEL
I'm here now!
REEL

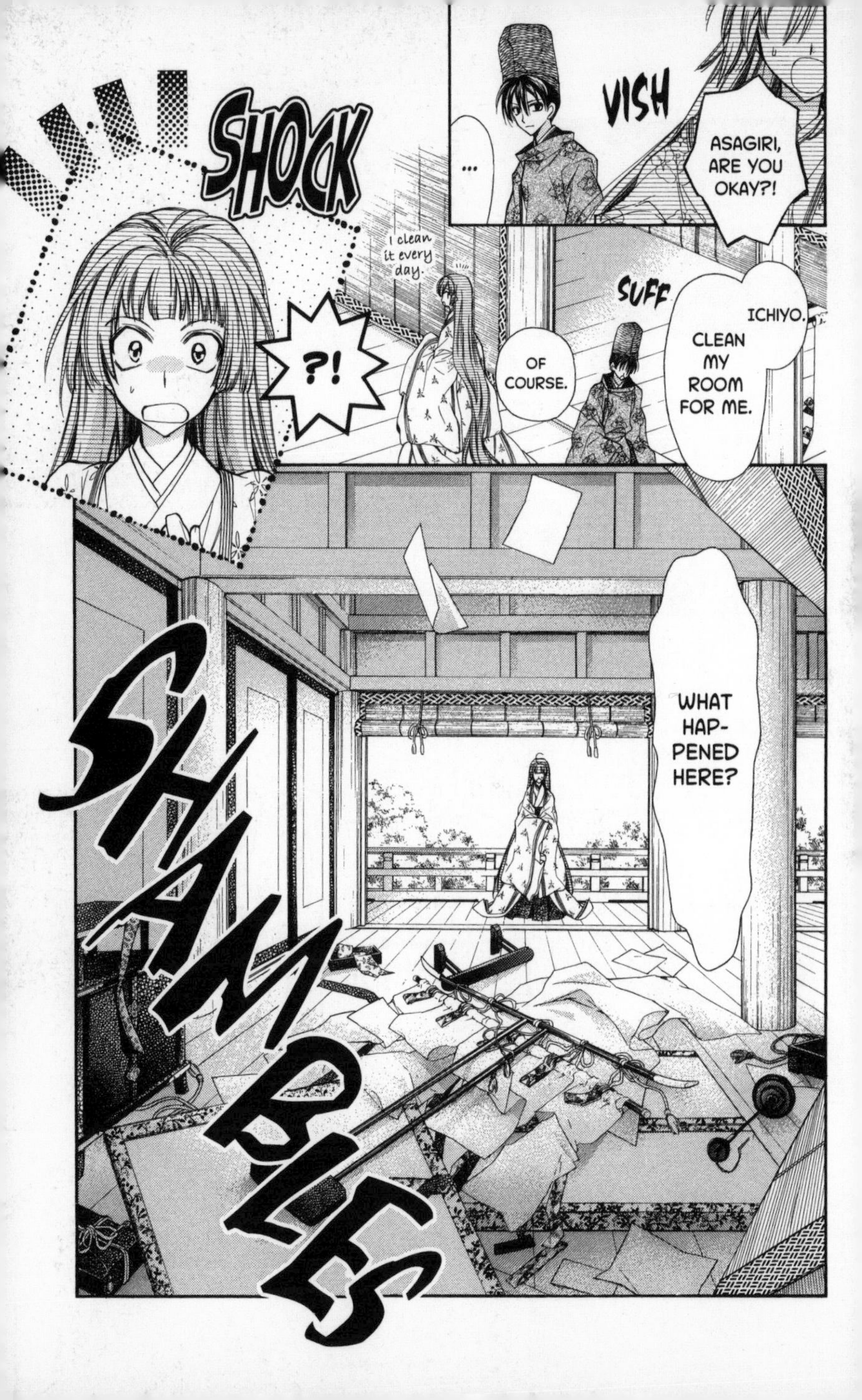
VISH
ASAGIRI, ARE YOU OKAY?!
...
SUFF
ICHIYO. CLEAN MY ROOM FOR ME.
OF COURSE.
I clean it every day.
SHOCK
?!
WHAT HAP-PENED HERE?
SHAMBLES

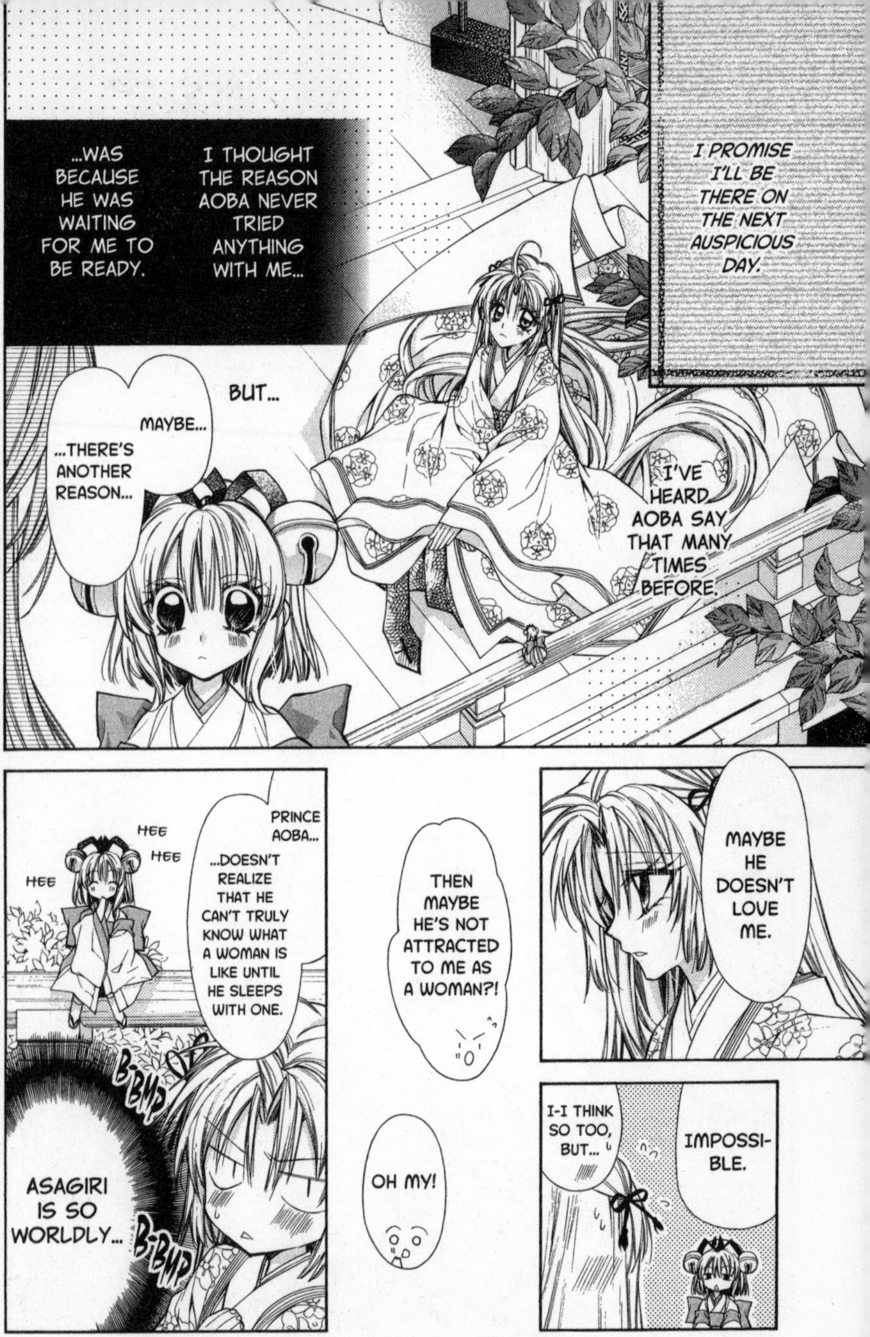
I PROMISE I'LL BE THERE ON THE NEXT AUSPICIOUS DAY.
I THOUGHT THE REASON AOBA NEVER TRIED ANYTHING WITH ME...
...WAS BECAUSE HE WAS WAITING FOR ME TO BE READY.
I'VE HEARD AOBA SAY THAT MANY TIMES BEFORE.
BUT...
MAYBE...
...THERE'S ANOTHER REASON...
MAYBE HE DOESN'T LOVE ME.
THEN MAYBE HE'S NOT ATTRACTED TO ME AS A WOMAN?!
IMPOSSIBLE.
I-I THINK SO TOO, BUT...
OH MY!
PRINCE AOBA...
...DOESN'T REALIZE THAT HE CAN'T TRULY KNOW WHAT A WOMAN IS LIKE UNTIL HE SLEEPS WITH ONE.
HEE
HEE
HEE
B-BMP
ASAGIRI IS SO WORLDLY...
B-BMP

Mon-Hun 3

Yes, it's the famous *Monster Hunter Portable 3rd* (A PSP game).

I'm totally hooked! ♪

I've been playing it when I have spare time in between my work. I'm currently at Hunter Rank 6, and I've completed all the village quests except the "The End" quest. (I can defeat Deviljho, but I get beaten to a pulp by the slapstick pair after it [Tigrex and Nargacuga]. I currently feel like giving up. (|||| ᵕ)

I had the Long Sword (used about 250 times) that I started using in *Monster Hunter Freedom 2*, but after that I changed to a Gunlance (used about 300 times). Now I'm hooked on the Light Bowgun (used about 200 times).

Phew, things are so much easier when I use the Light Bowgun. I just can't stop using it...

HUFF HUFF

By the way, I really like Jinouga and Hapurubokka. ♪
(I'll fish and catch him!!)

I'm wearing Alatreon armor now. (But I'm kind of attracted to the gunner's Ingot armor as well.)

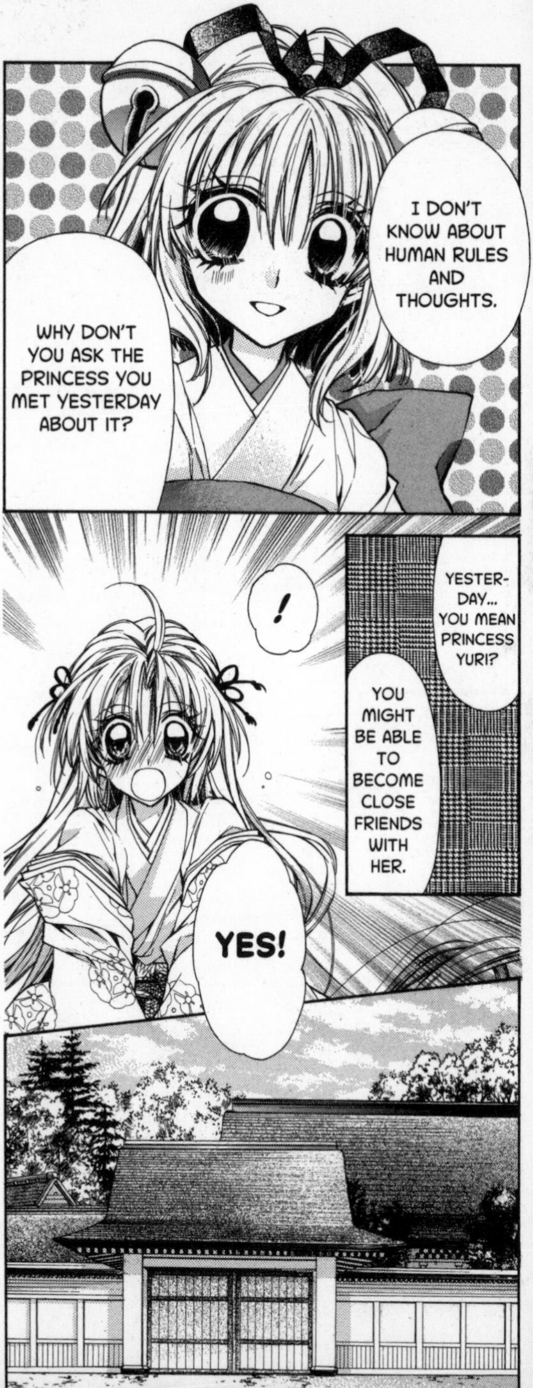

I DON'T KNOW ABOUT HUMAN RULES AND THOUGHTS.
WHY DON'T YOU ASK THE PRINCESS YOU MET YESTERDAY ABOUT IT?
YESTER-DAY... YOU MEAN PRINCESS YURI?
!
YOU MIGHT BE ABLE TO BECOME CLOSE FRIENDS WITH HER.
YES!

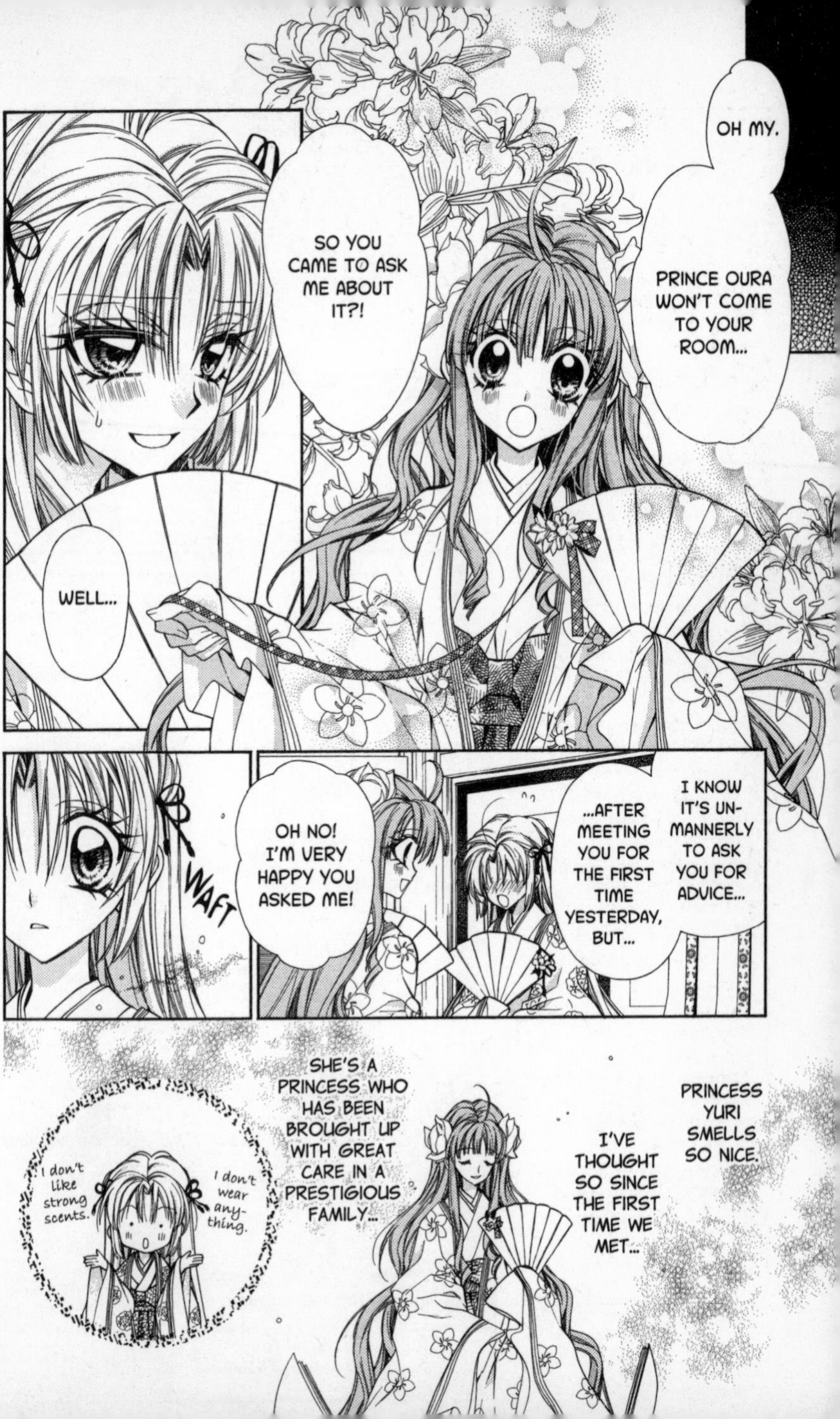
OH MY.
PRINCE OURA WON'T COME TO YOUR ROOM...
SO YOU CAME TO ASK ME ABOUT IT?!
WELL...
I KNOW IT'S UN-MANNERLY TO ASK YOU FOR ADVICE...
...AFTER MEETING YOU FOR THE FIRST TIME YESTERDAY, BUT...
OH NO! I'M VERY HAPPY YOU ASKED ME!
WAFT
PRINCESS YURI SMELLS SO NICE.
I'VE THOUGHT SO SINCE THE FIRST TIME WE MET...
SHE'S A PRINCESS WHO HAS BEEN BROUGHT UP WITH GREAT CARE IN A PRESTIGIOUS FAMILY...
I don't wear anything.
I don't like strong scents.

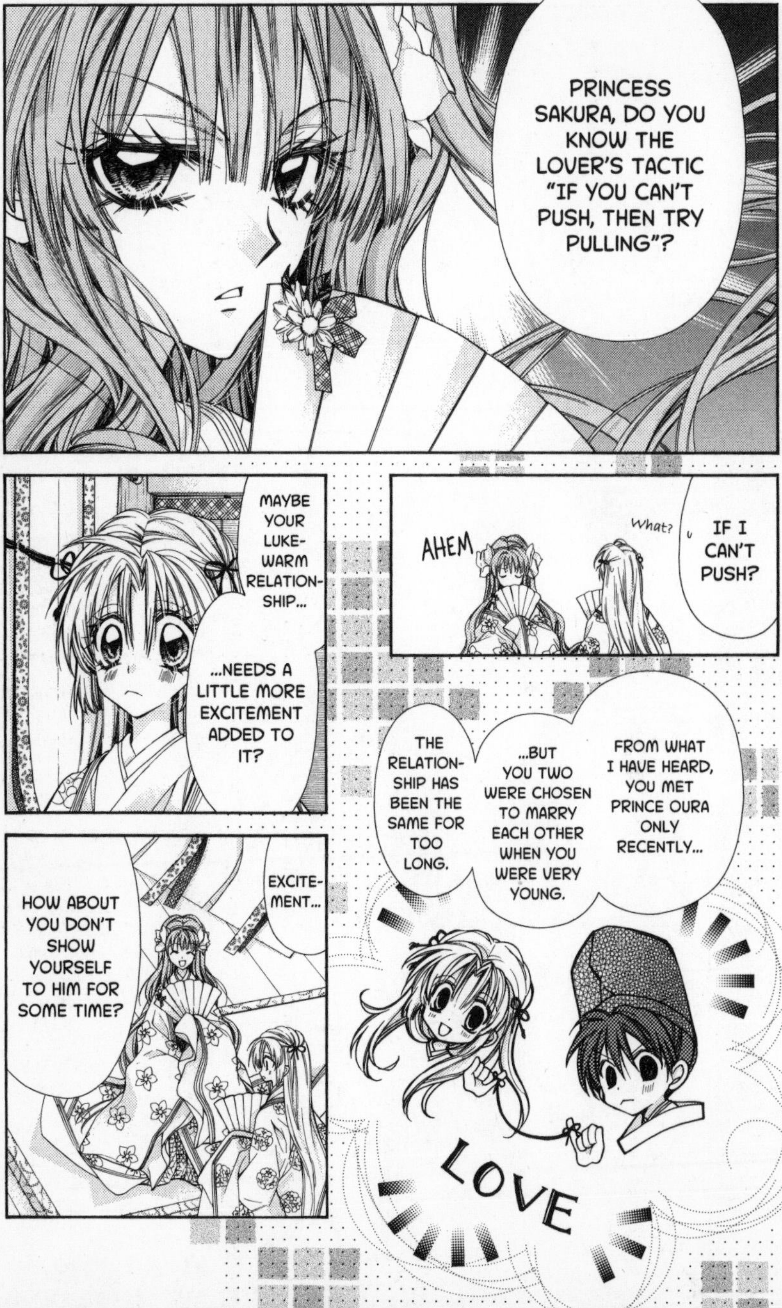
PRINCESS SAKURA, DO YOU KNOW THE LOVER'S TACTIC "IF YOU CAN'T PUSH, THEN TRY PULLING"?
IF I CAN'T PUSH?
What?
AHEM
FROM WHAT I HAVE HEARD, YOU MET PRINCE OURA ONLY RECENTLY...
...BUT YOU TWO WERE CHOSEN TO MARRY EACH OTHER WHEN YOU WERE VERY YOUNG.
THE RELATIONSHIP HAS BEEN THE SAME FOR TOO LONG.
LOVE
MAYBE YOUR LUKEWARM RELATIONSHIP...
...NEEDS A LITTLE MORE EXCITEMENT ADDED TO IT?
EXCITEMENT...
HOW ABOUT YOU DON'T SHOW YOURSELF TO HIM FOR SOME TIME?

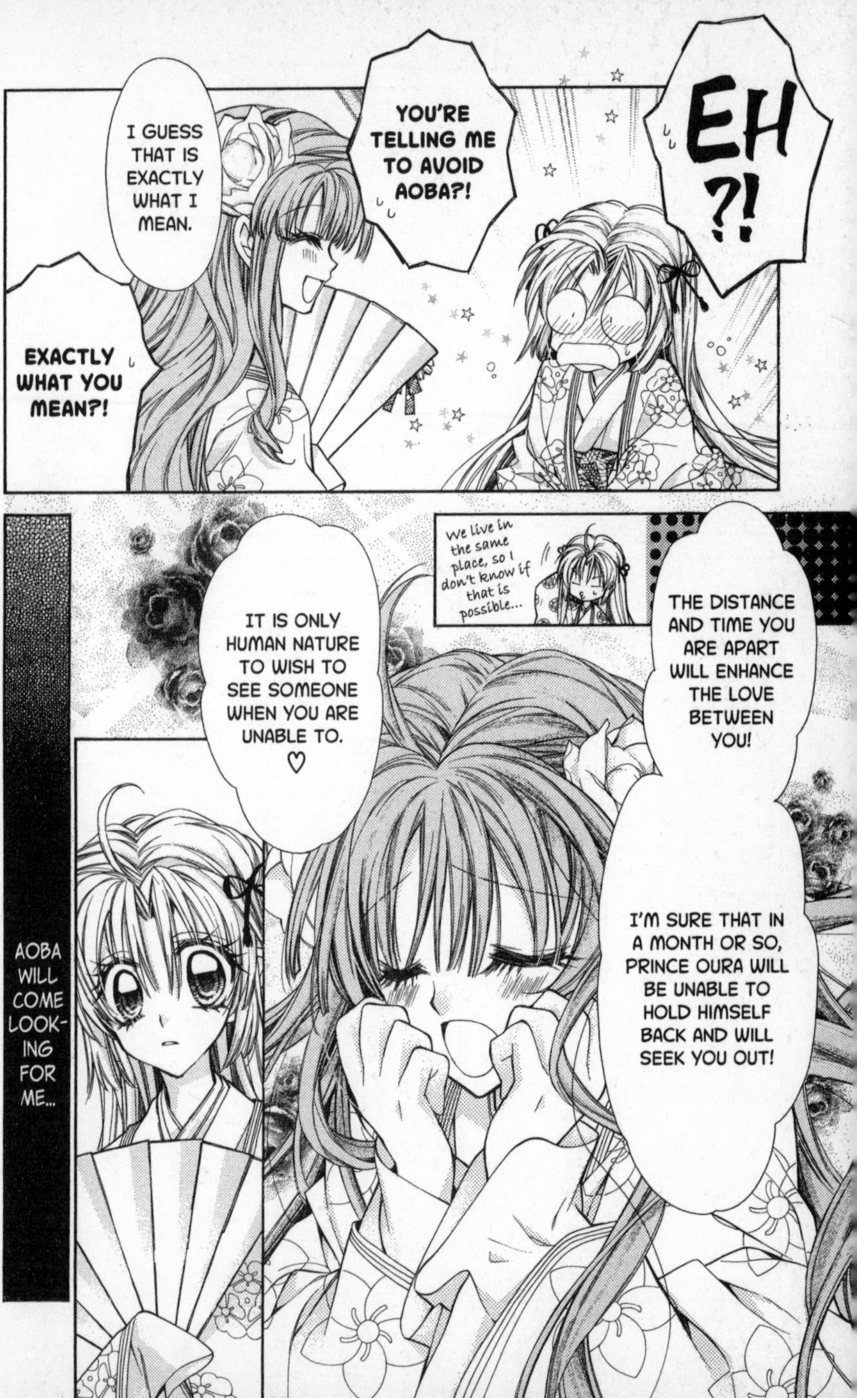
EH ?!
YOU'RE TELLING ME TO AVOID AOBA?!
I GUESS THAT IS EXACTLY WHAT I MEAN.
EXACTLY WHAT YOU MEAN?!
THE DISTANCE AND TIME YOU ARE APART WILL ENHANCE THE LOVE BETWEEN YOU!
We live in the same place, so I don't know if that is possible...
IT IS ONLY HUMAN NATURE TO WISH TO SEE SOMEONE WHEN YOU ARE UNABLE TO. ♡
I'M SURE THAT IN A MONTH OR SO, PRINCE OURA WILL BE UNABLE TO HOLD HIMSELF BACK AND WILL SEEK YOU OUT!
AOBA WILL COME LOOKING FOR ME...

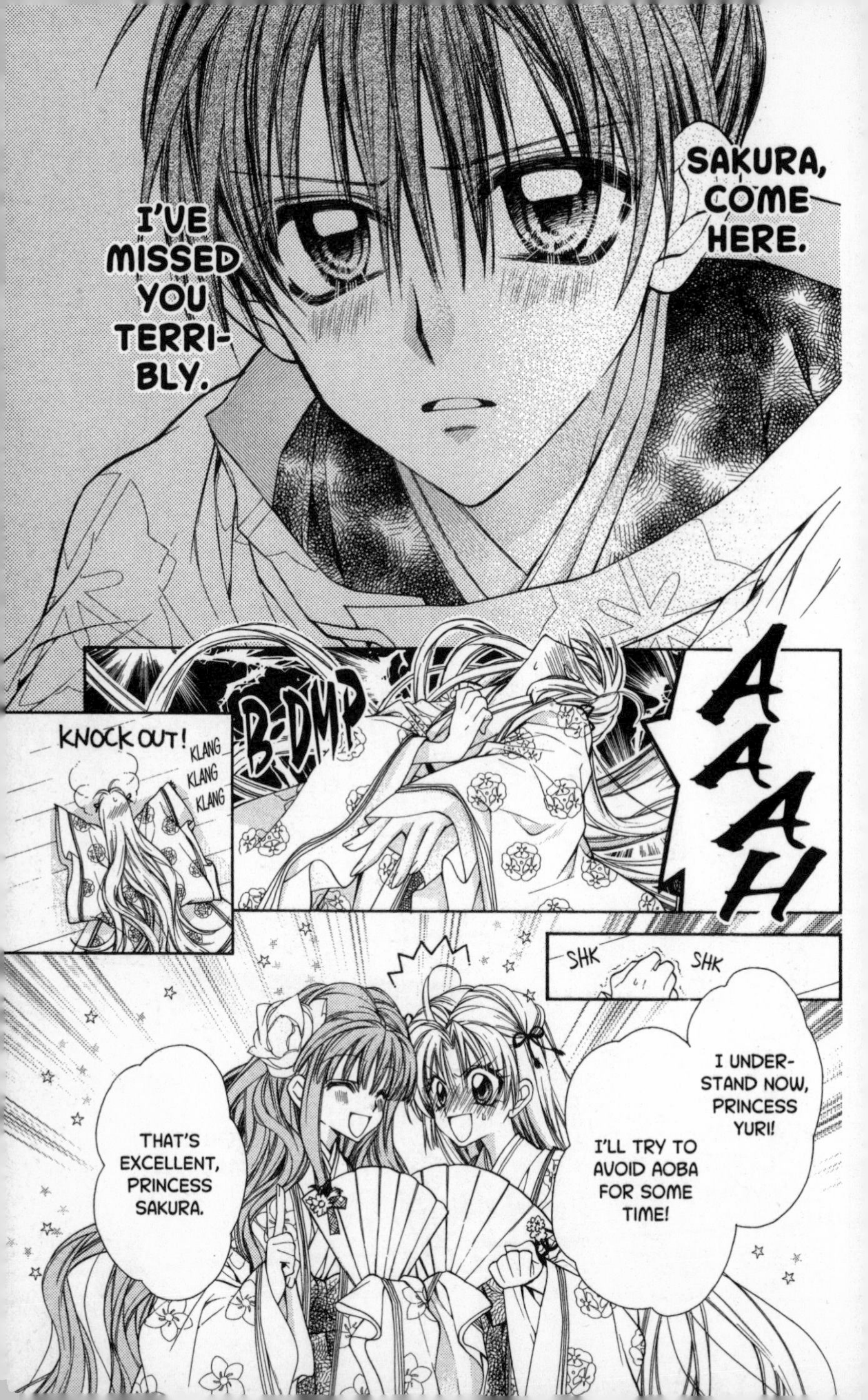
SAKURA, COME HERE.
I'VE MISSED YOU TERRI-BLY.
AAAH
B-DMP
KNOCK OUT!
KLANG KLANG KLANG
SHK SHK
I UNDER-STAND NOW, PRINCESS YURI!
I'LL TRY TO AVOID AOBA FOR SOME TIME!
THAT'S EXCELLENT, PRINCESS SAKURA.

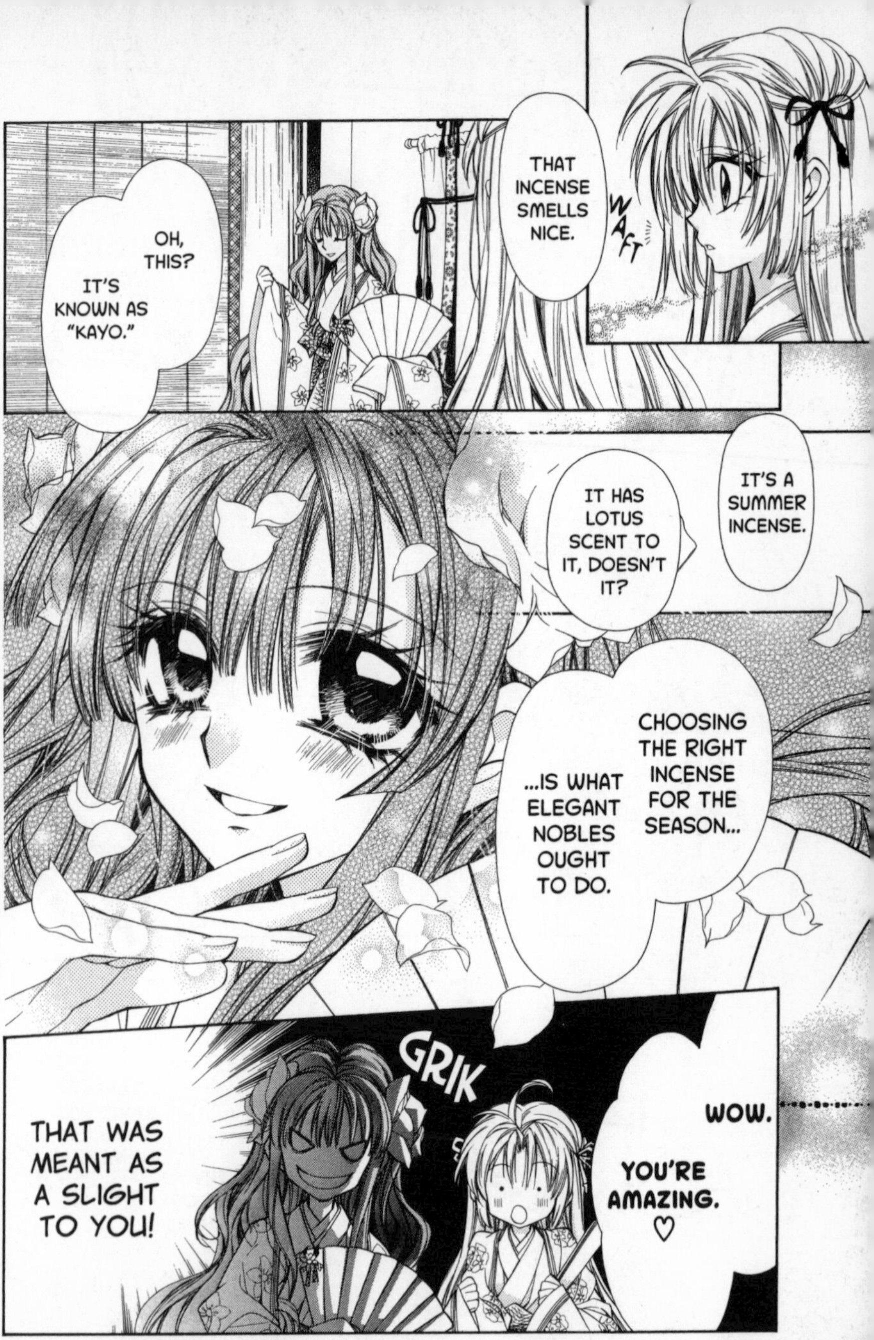
THAT INCENSE SMELLS NICE.
WAFT
OH, THIS?
IT'S KNOWN AS "KAYO."
IT'S A SUMMER INCENSE.
IT HAS LOTUS SCENT TO IT, DOESN'T IT?
CHOOSING THE RIGHT INCENSE FOR THE SEASON...
...IS WHAT ELEGANT NOBLES OUGHT TO DO.
WOW.
YOU'RE AMAZING. ♡
GRIK
THAT WAS MEANT AS A SLIGHT TO YOU!

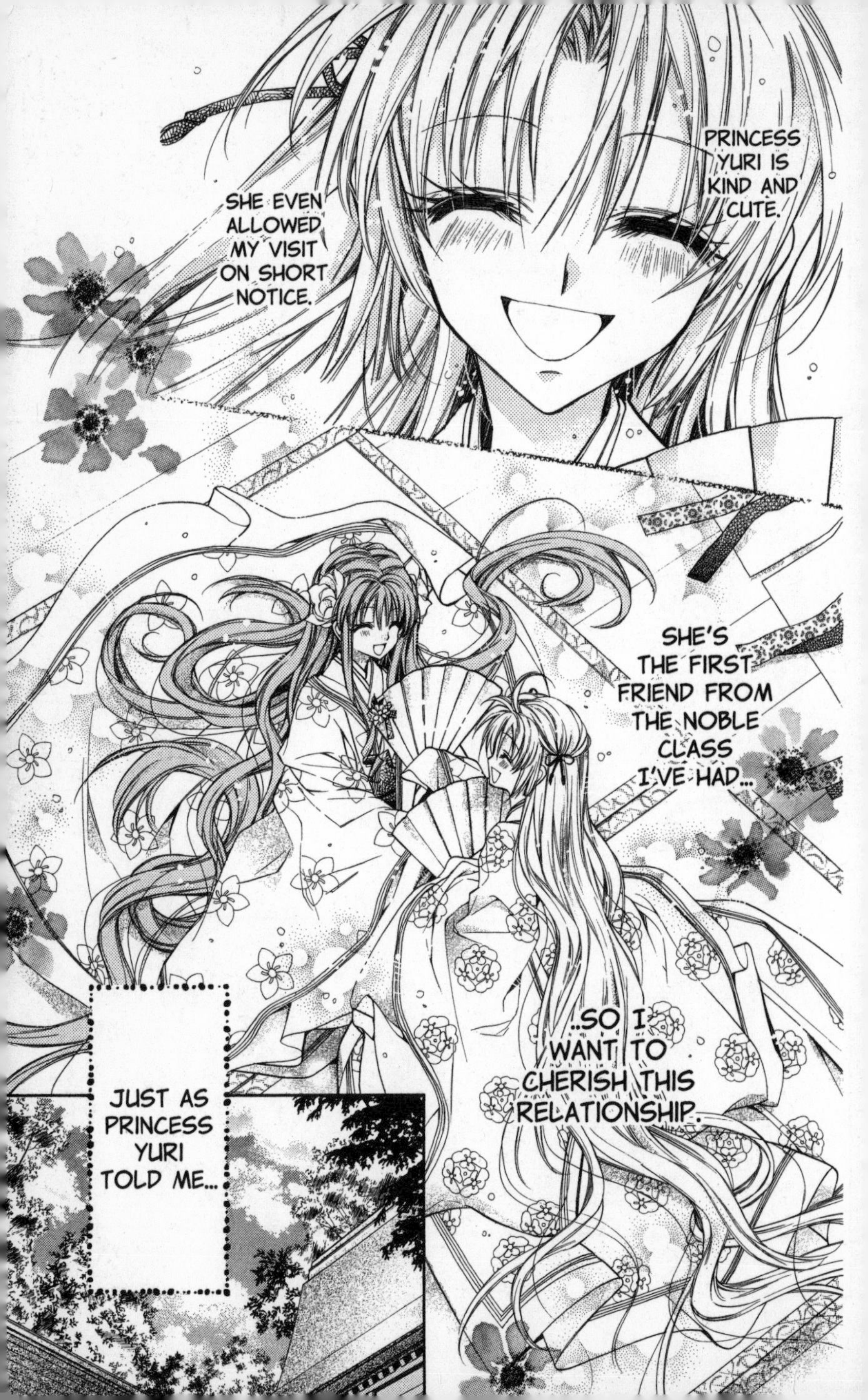
PRINCESS YURI IS KIND AND CUTE.
SHE EVEN ALLOWED MY VISIT ON SHORT NOTICE.
SHE'S THE FIRST FRIEND FROM THE NOBLE CLASS I'VE HAD...
...SO I WANT TO CHERISH THIS RELATIONSHIP.
JUST AS PRINCESS YURI TOLD ME...

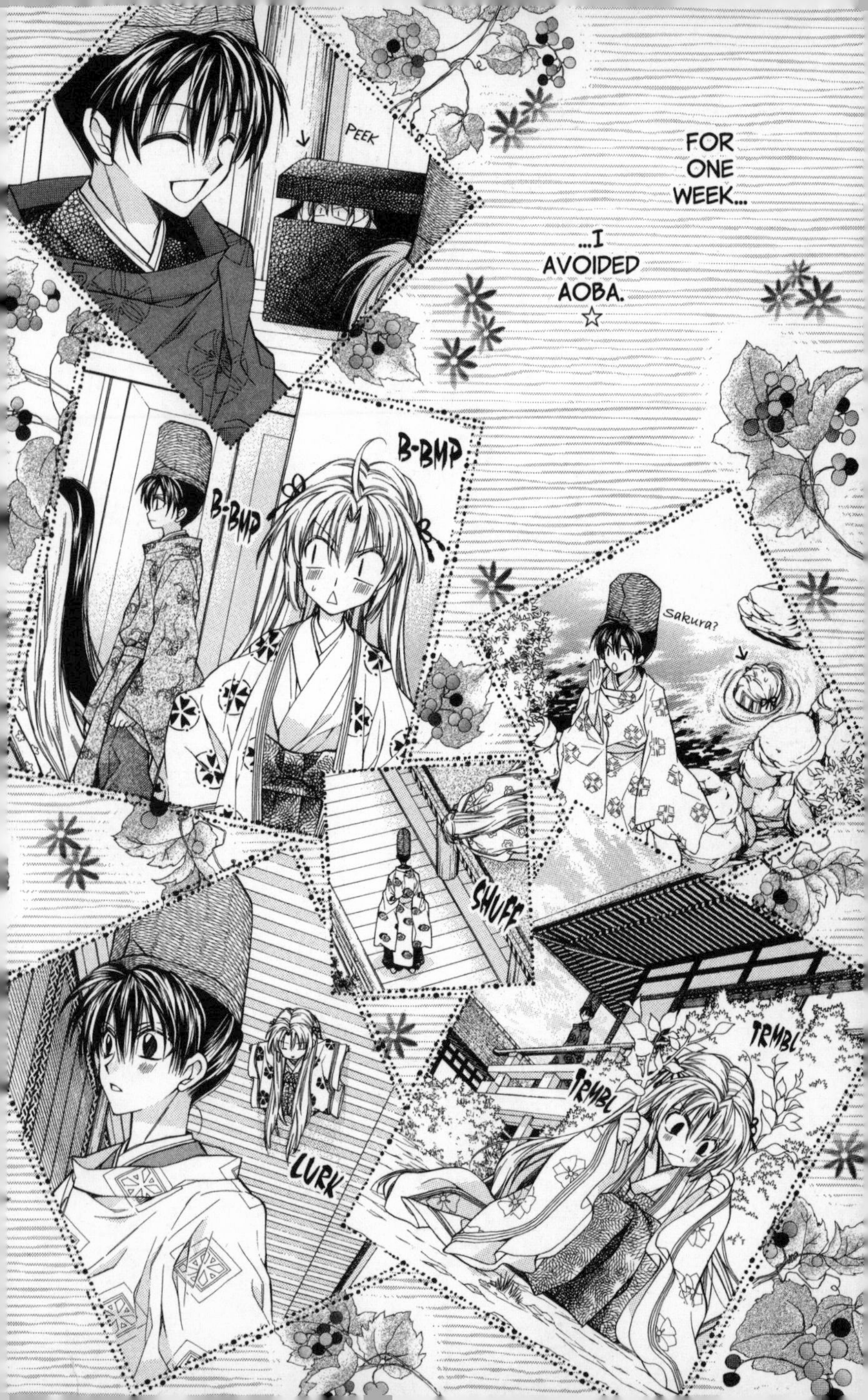
FOR ONE WEEK...
...I AVOIDED AOBA. ☆
PEEK
Sakura?
B-BMP
B-BMP
SHUFF
TRMBL
TRMBL
LURK

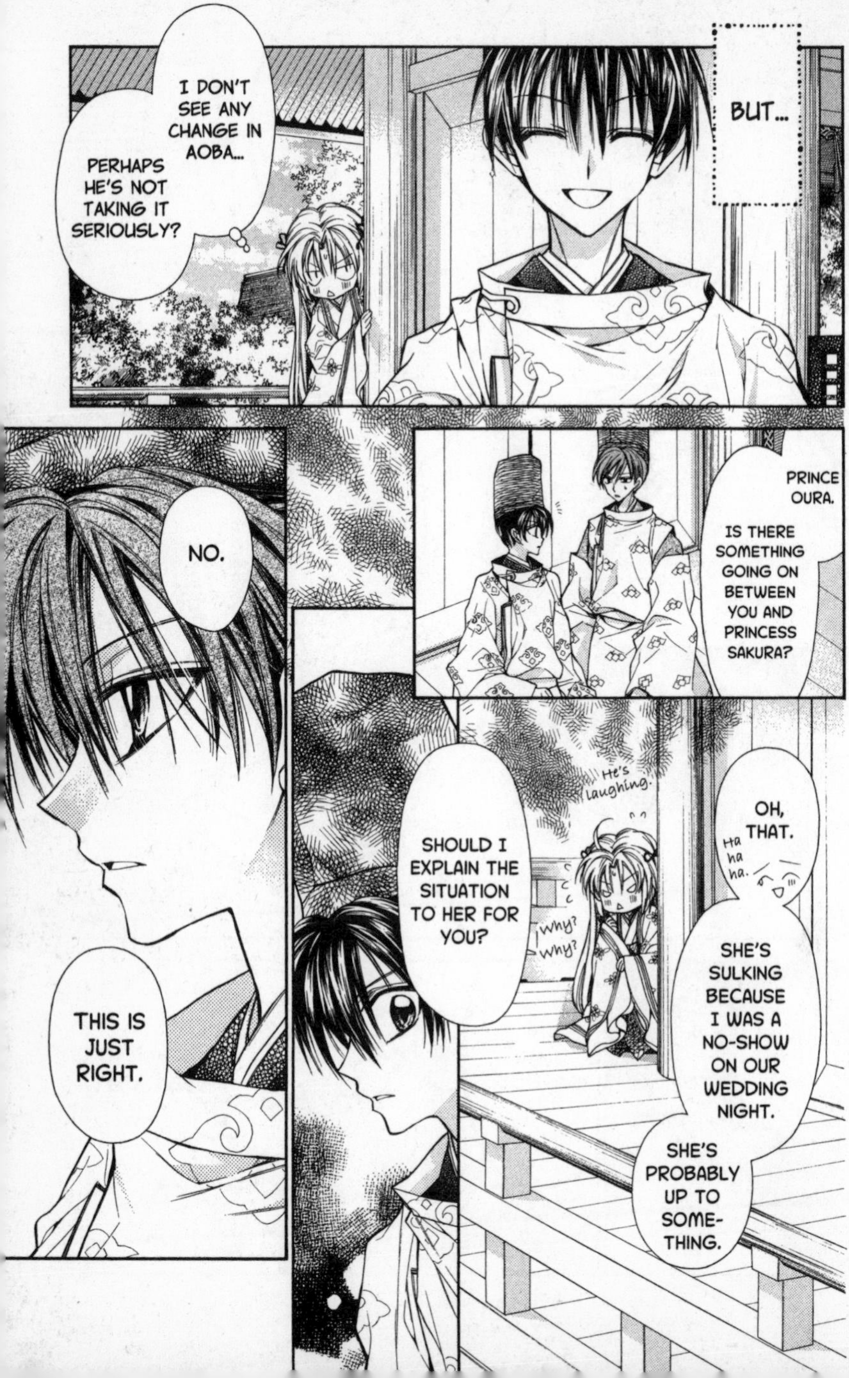
BUT...
I DON'T SEE ANY CHANGE IN AOBA... PERHAPS HE'S NOT TAKING IT SERIOUSLY?
PRINCE OURA.
IS THERE SOMETHING GOING ON BETWEEN YOU AND PRINCESS SAKURA?
OH, THAT.
Ha ha ha.
He's laughing.
SHE'S SULKING BECAUSE I WAS A NO-SHOW ON OUR WEDDING NIGHT.
SHE'S PROBABLY UP TO SOME-THING.
why? why?
SHOULD I EXPLAIN THE SITUATION TO HER FOR YOU?
NO.
THIS IS JUST RIGHT.

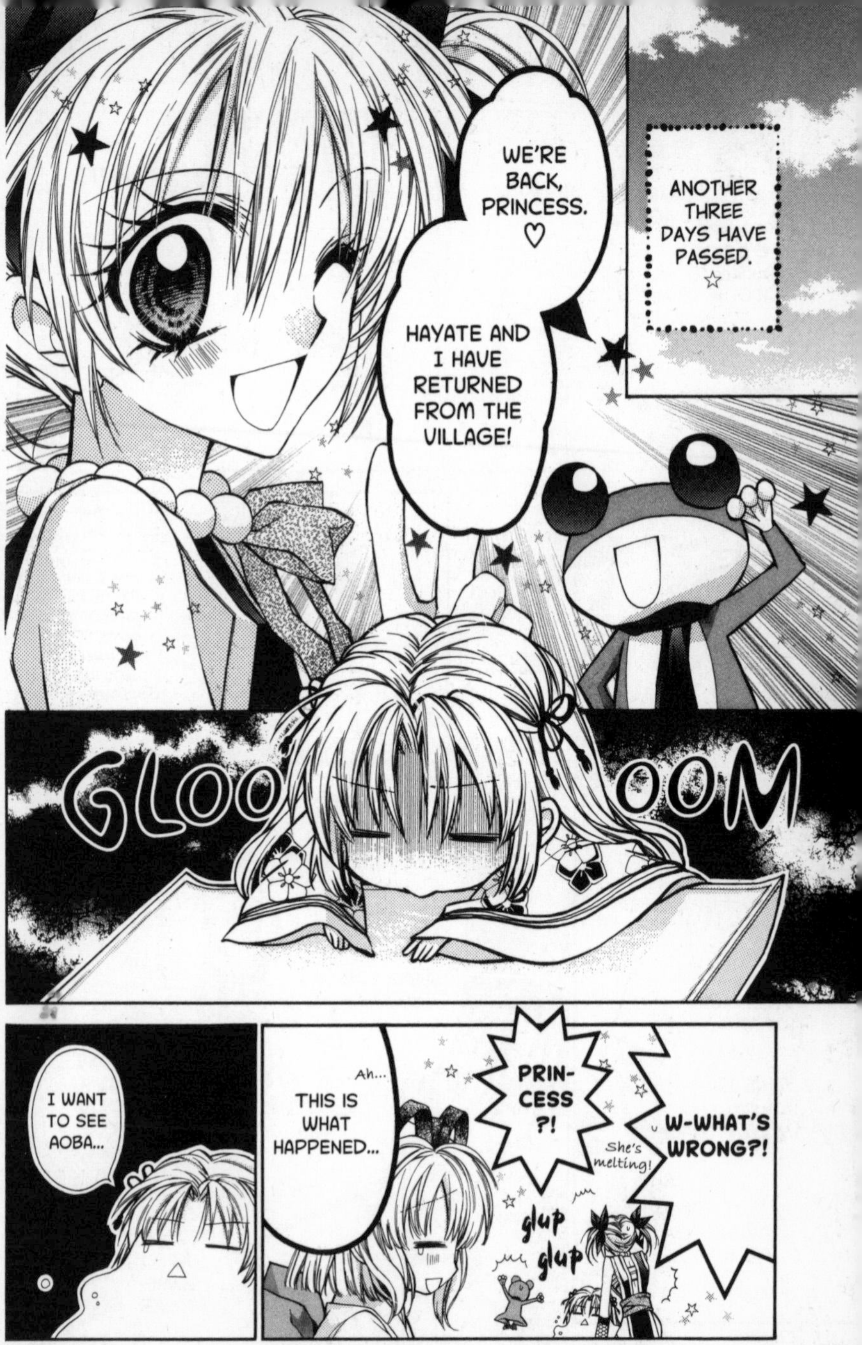
ANOTHER THREE DAYS HAVE PASSED. ☆
WE'RE BACK, PRINCESS. ♡
HAYATE AND I HAVE RETURNED FROM THE VILLAGE!
GLOOOOM
PRIN-CESS?!
W-WHAT'S WRONG?!
She's melting!
glup glup
Ah...
THIS IS WHAT HAPPENED...
I WANT TO SEE AOBA...

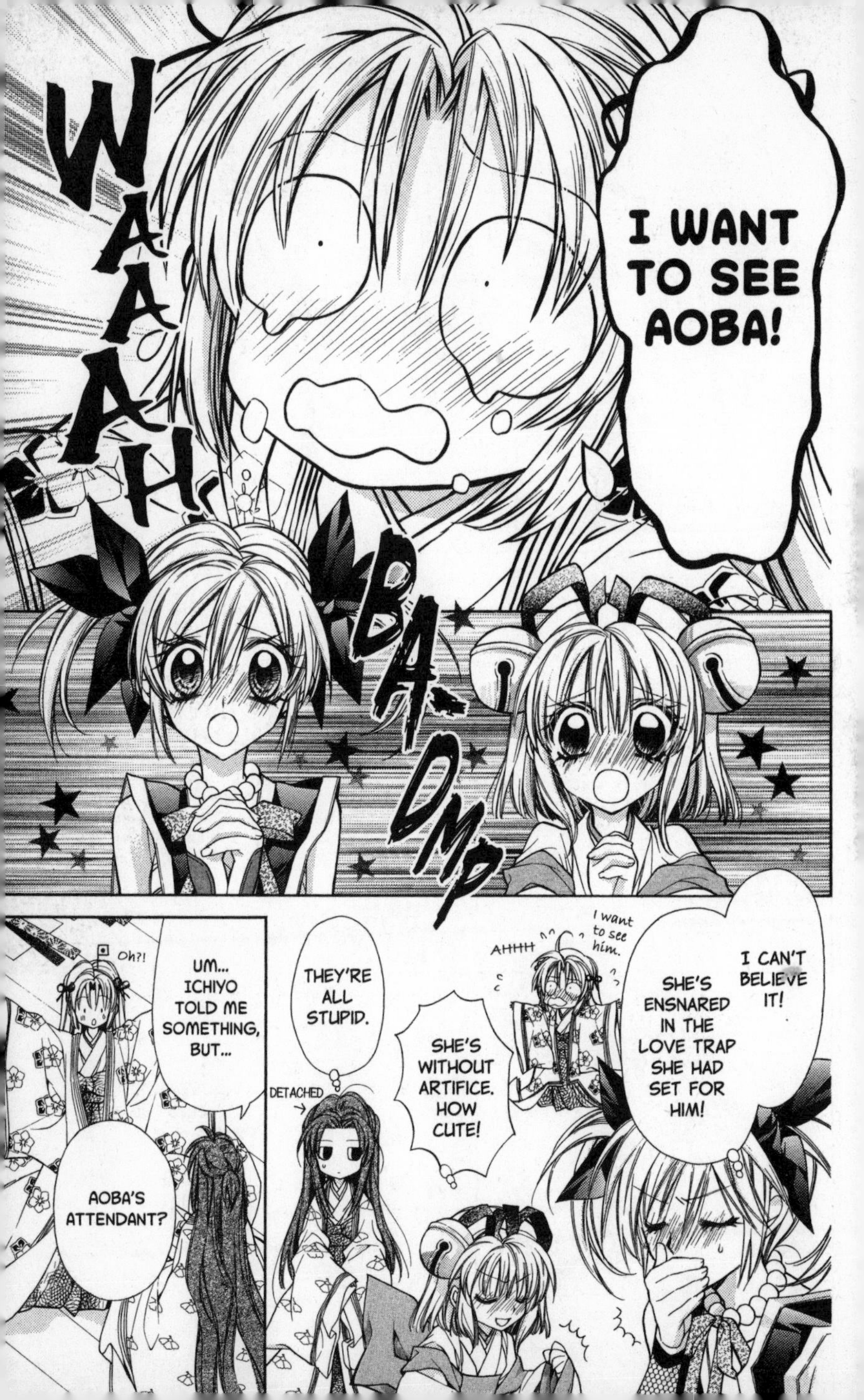
I WANT TO SEE AOBA!
WAAAH
BA-DMP
I CAN'T BELIEVE IT!
SHE'S ENSNARED IN THE LOVE TRAP SHE HAD SET FOR HIM!
I want to see him.
AHHHH
SHE'S WITHOUT ARTIFICE. HOW CUTE!
THEY'RE ALL STUPID.
DETACHED
UM... ICHIYO TOLD ME SOMETHING, BUT...
Oh?!
AOBA'S ATTENDANT?

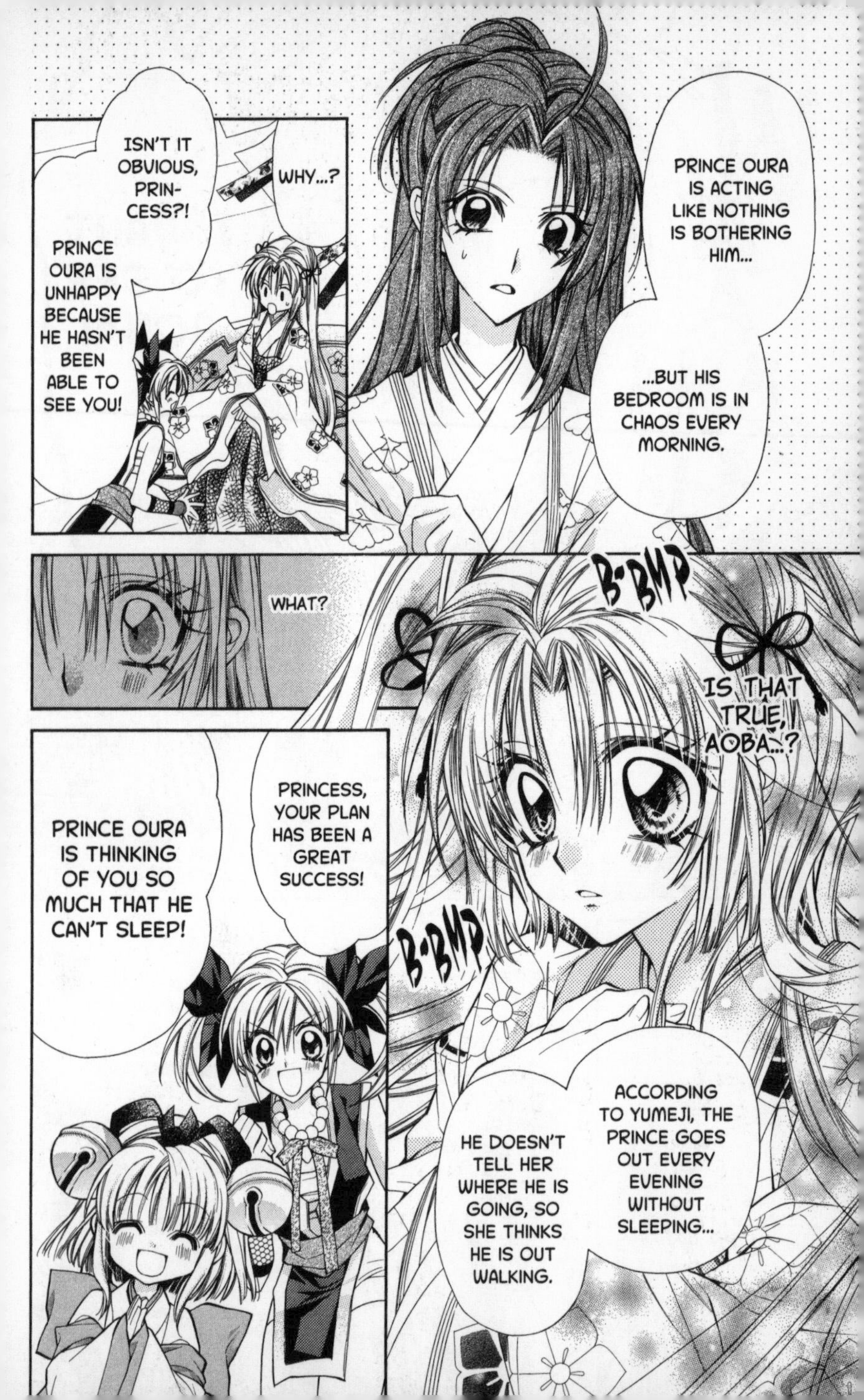
PRINCE OURA IS ACTING LIKE NOTHING IS BOTHERING HIM...
...BUT HIS BEDROOM IS IN CHAOS EVERY MORNING.
WHY...?
ISN'T IT OBVIOUS, PRIN-CESS?!
PRINCE OURA IS UNHAPPY BECAUSE HE HASN'T BEEN ABLE TO SEE YOU!
B-BMP
IS THAT TRUE, AOBA...?
B-BMP
ACCORDING TO YUMEJI, THE PRINCE GOES OUT EVERY EVENING WITHOUT SLEEPING...
HE DOESN'T TELL HER WHERE HE IS GOING, SO SHE THINKS HE IS OUT WALKING.
WHAT?
PRINCESS, YOUR PLAN HAS BEEN A GREAT SUCCESS!
PRINCE OURA IS THINKING OF YOU SO MUCH THAT HE CAN'T SLEEP!

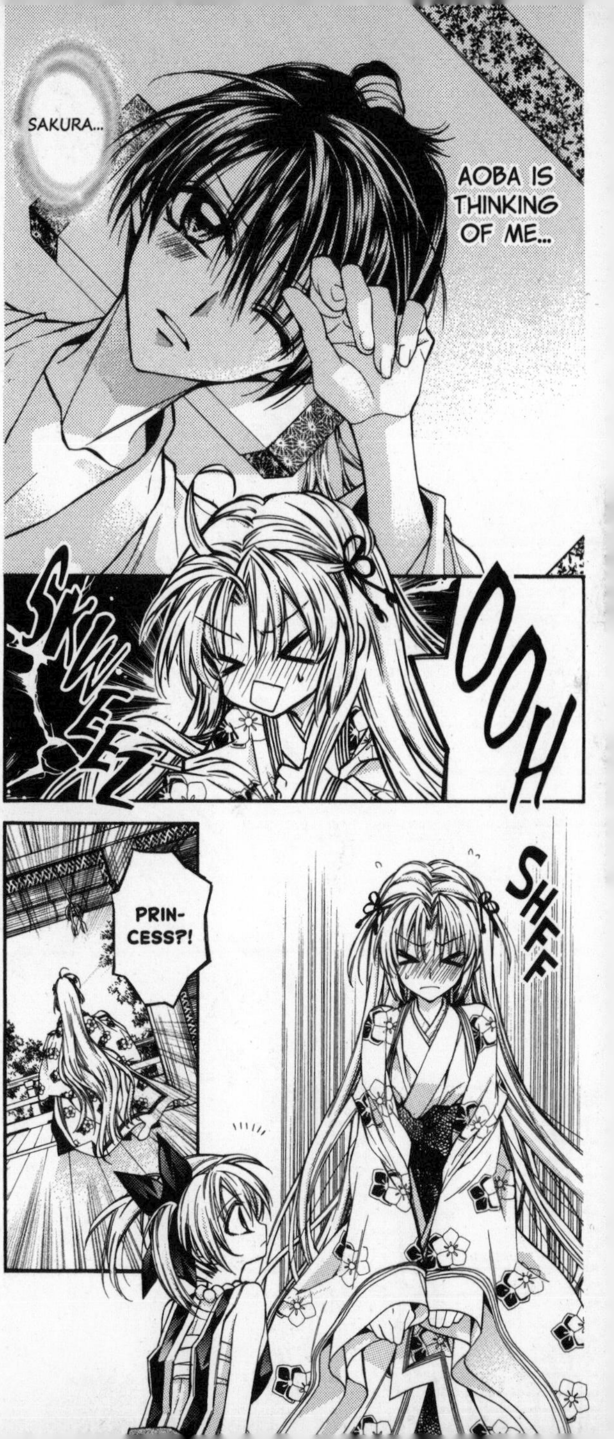
SAKURA...
AOBA IS THINKING OF ME...
OOOH
SKWEEZ
SHFF
PRIN-CESS?!

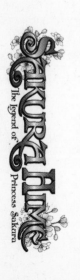

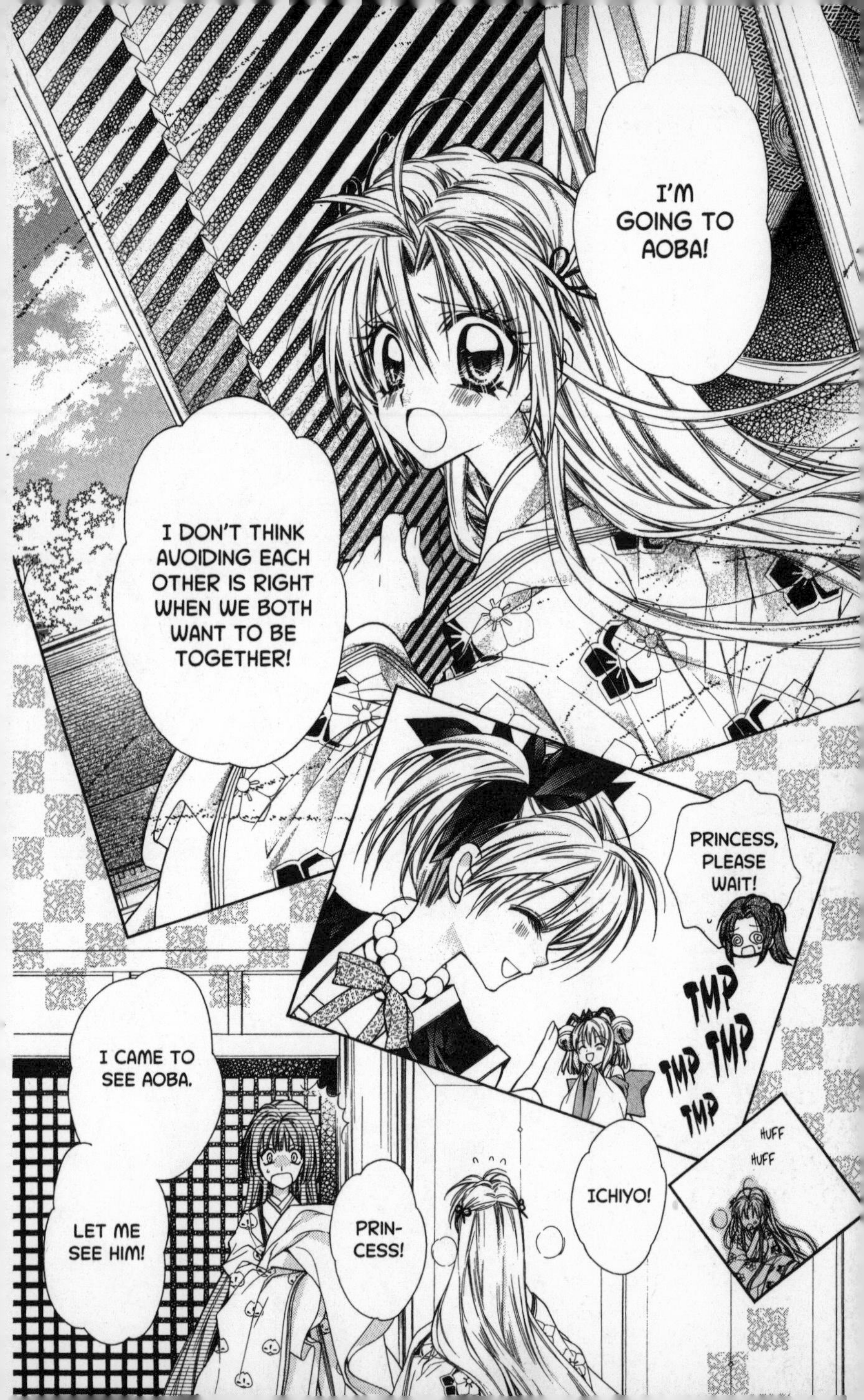
I'M GOING TO AOBA!
I DON'T THINK AVOIDING EACH OTHER IS RIGHT WHEN WE BOTH WANT TO BE TOGETHER!
PRINCESS, PLEASE WAIT!
TMP TMP TMP TMP TMP
HUFF HUFF
ICHIYO!
PRIN-CESS!
I CAME TO SEE AOBA.
LET ME SEE HIM!

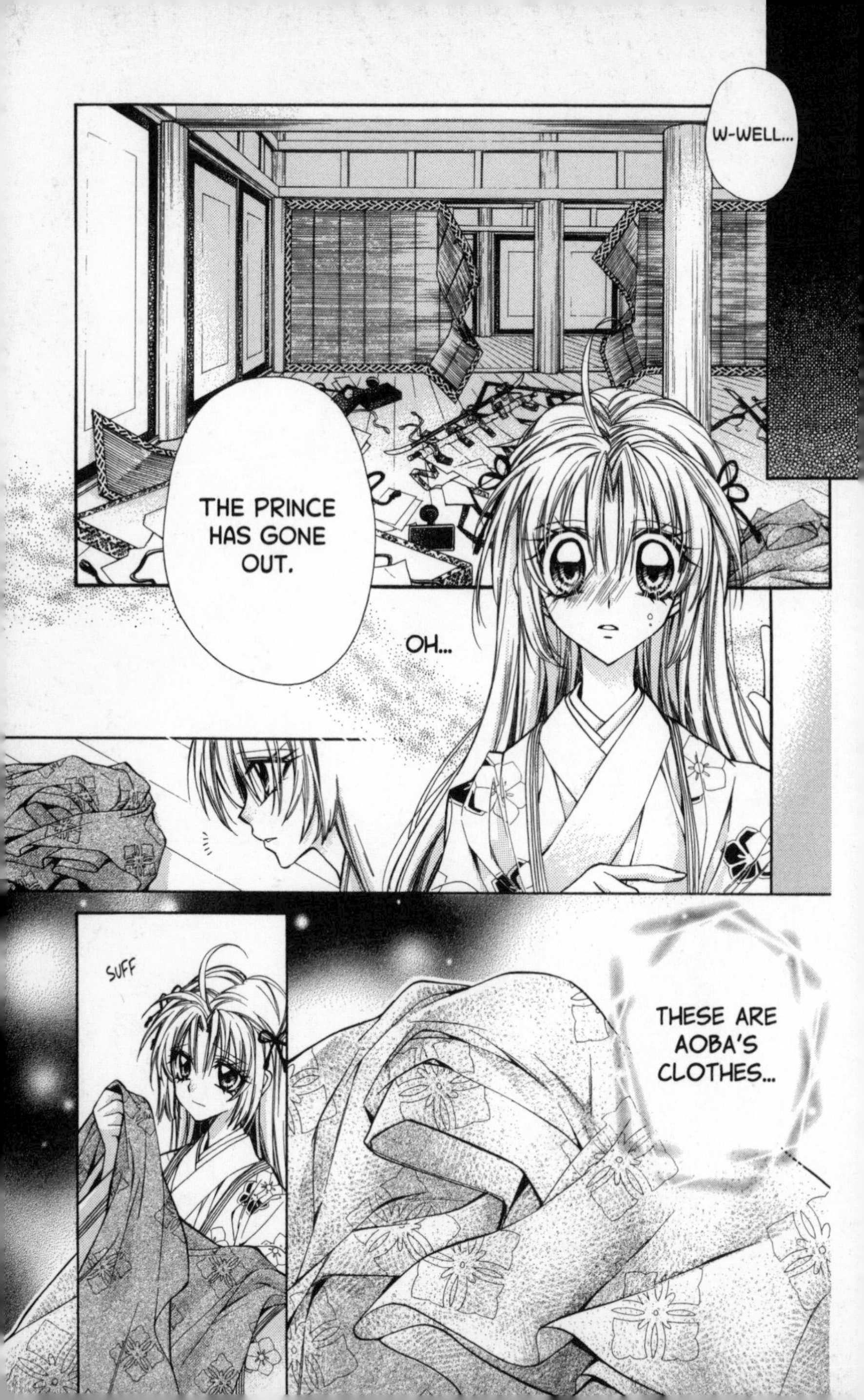
W-WELL...
THE PRINCE HAS GONE OUT.
OH...
THESE ARE AOBA'S CLOTHES...
SUFF

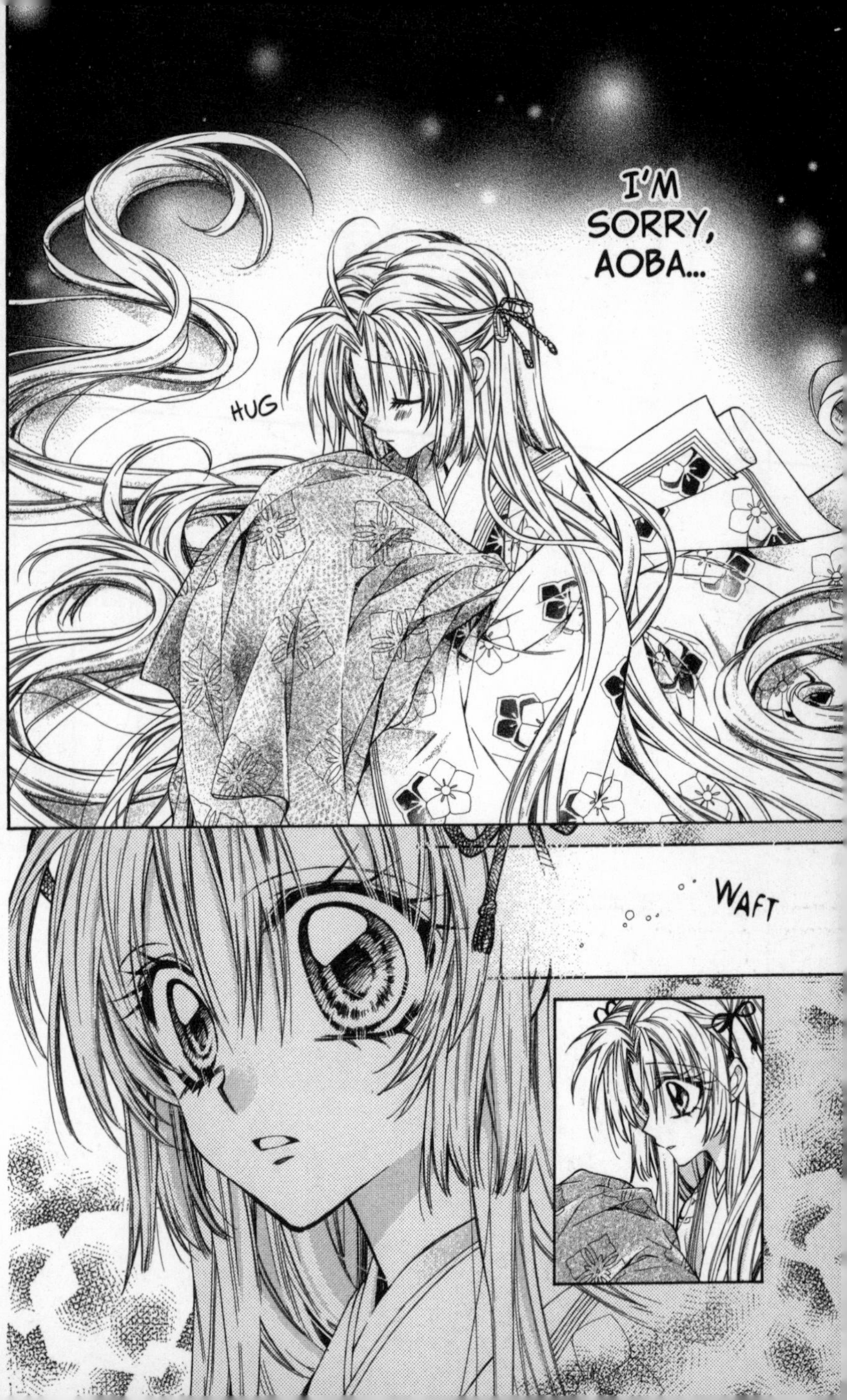
I'M SORRY, AOBA...
HUG
WAFT

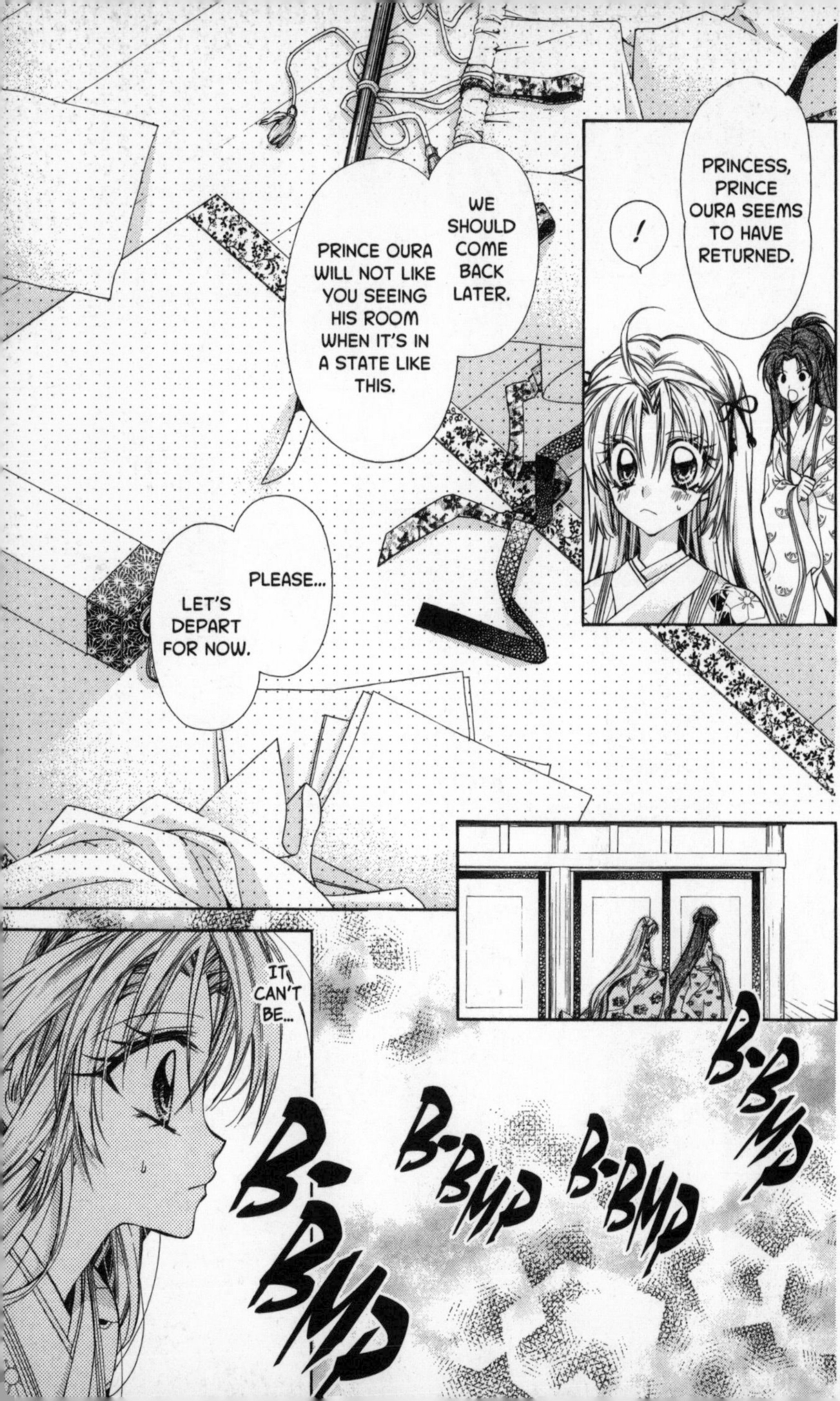
PRINCESS, PRINCE OURA SEEMS TO HAVE RETURNED.
!
WE SHOULD COME BACK LATER.
PRINCE OURA WILL NOT LIKE YOU SEEING HIS ROOM WHEN IT'S IN A STATE LIKE THIS.
PLEASE... LET'S DEPART FOR NOW.
IT CAN'T BE...
B-BMP
B-BMP
B-BMP
B-BMP

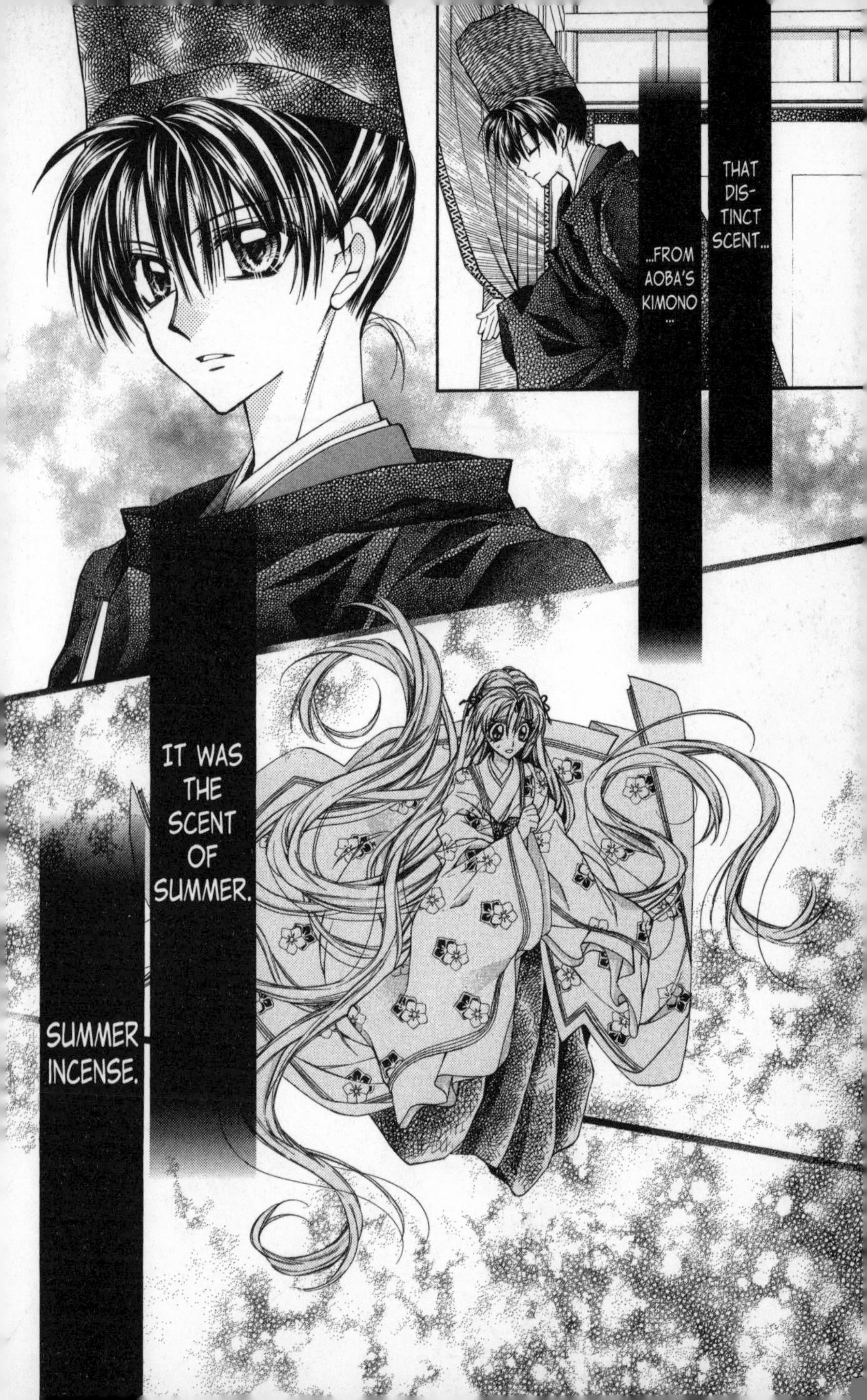
THAT DIS-TINCT SCENT...
...FROM AOBA'S KIMONO...
IT WAS THE SCENT OF SUMMER.
SUMMER INCENSE.

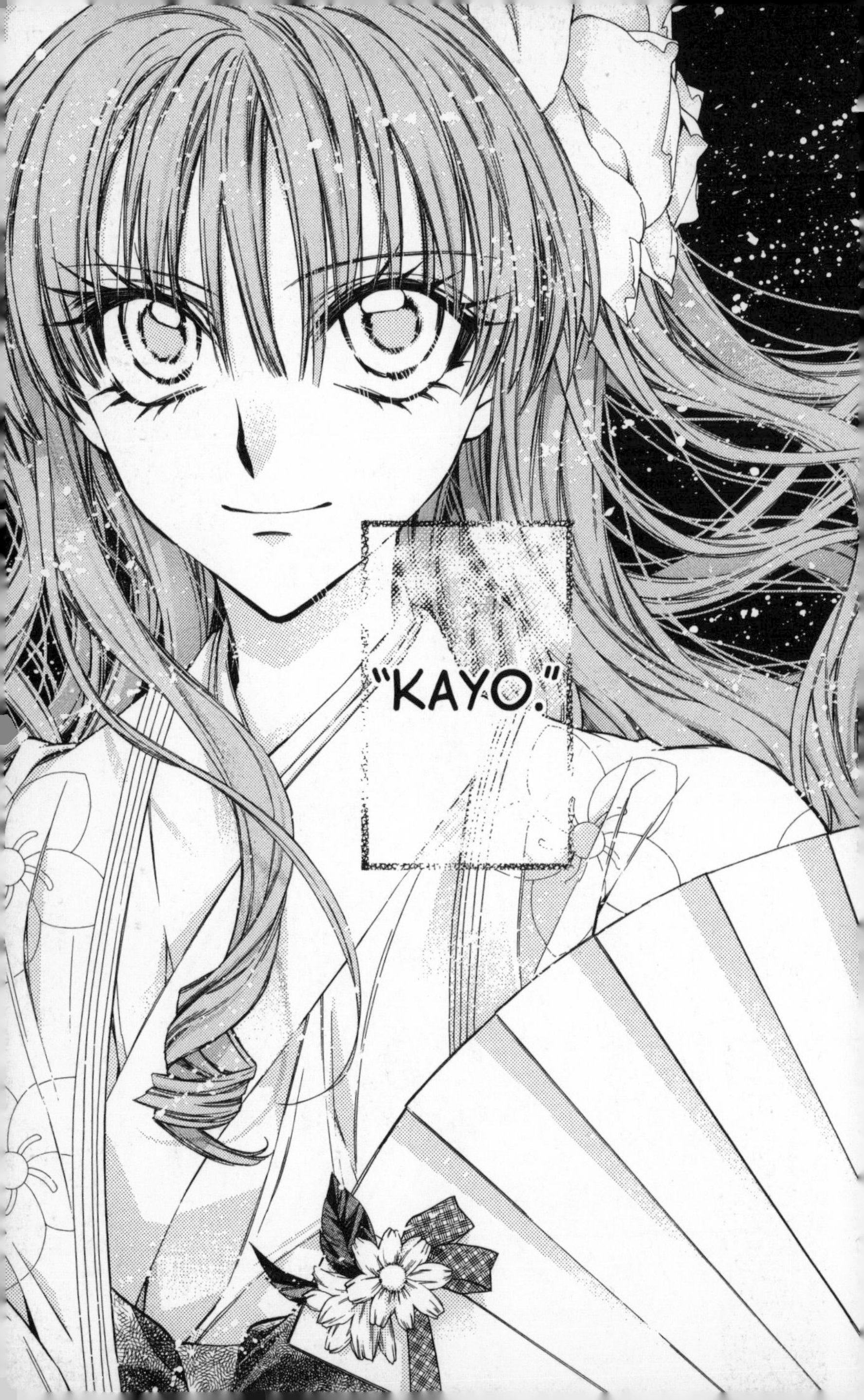
"KAYO."

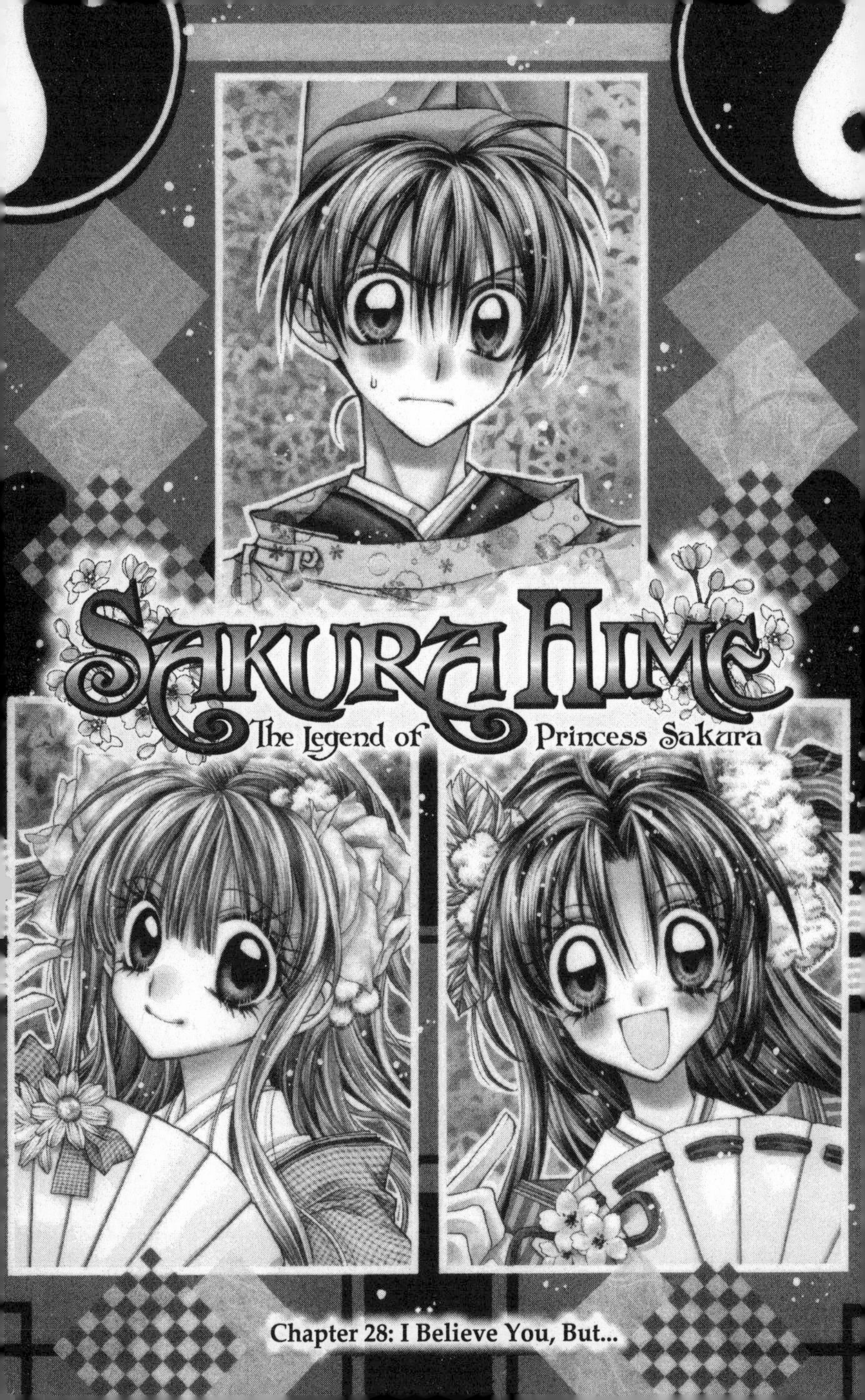
SAKURA HIME
The Legend of Princess Sakura
Chapter 28: I Believe You, But...

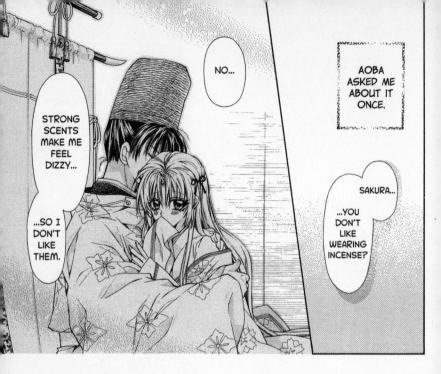

AOBA ASKED ME ABOUT IT ONCE.
SAKURA...
...YOU DON'T LIKE WEARING INCENSE?
NO...
STRONG SCENTS MAKE ME FEEL DIZZY...
...SO I DON'T LIKE THEM.

Chapter 28: I Believe You, But...

※ I'm giving away the story.

In this chapter you get to see Princess Yuri explode. ☆ I wrote in the last chapter that Princess Yuri can only lie, but she doesn't seem to be very good at it. So maybe we can say Aoba is caught in a dilemma...? It's tough, but being the good boy he is, he has to at least go and meet Princess Yuri. Just the mere existence of Princess Yuri...seems to add a strong comedic tone to this chapter. The last volume was very serious, so while I was working on it, I was surprised that this was the same manga series. Starting with chapter 27, each chapter is now 32 pages (chapters used to be 40 pages), so I couldn't squeeze in the entire story here. That is why there are so many small panels. The scene with Princess Yuri's father winking was tough... (But the inking was very easy.)

↑ It was emotionally tough. (laugh)

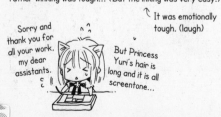

Sorry and thank you for all your work, my dear assistants.

But Princess Yuri's hair is long and it is all screentone...

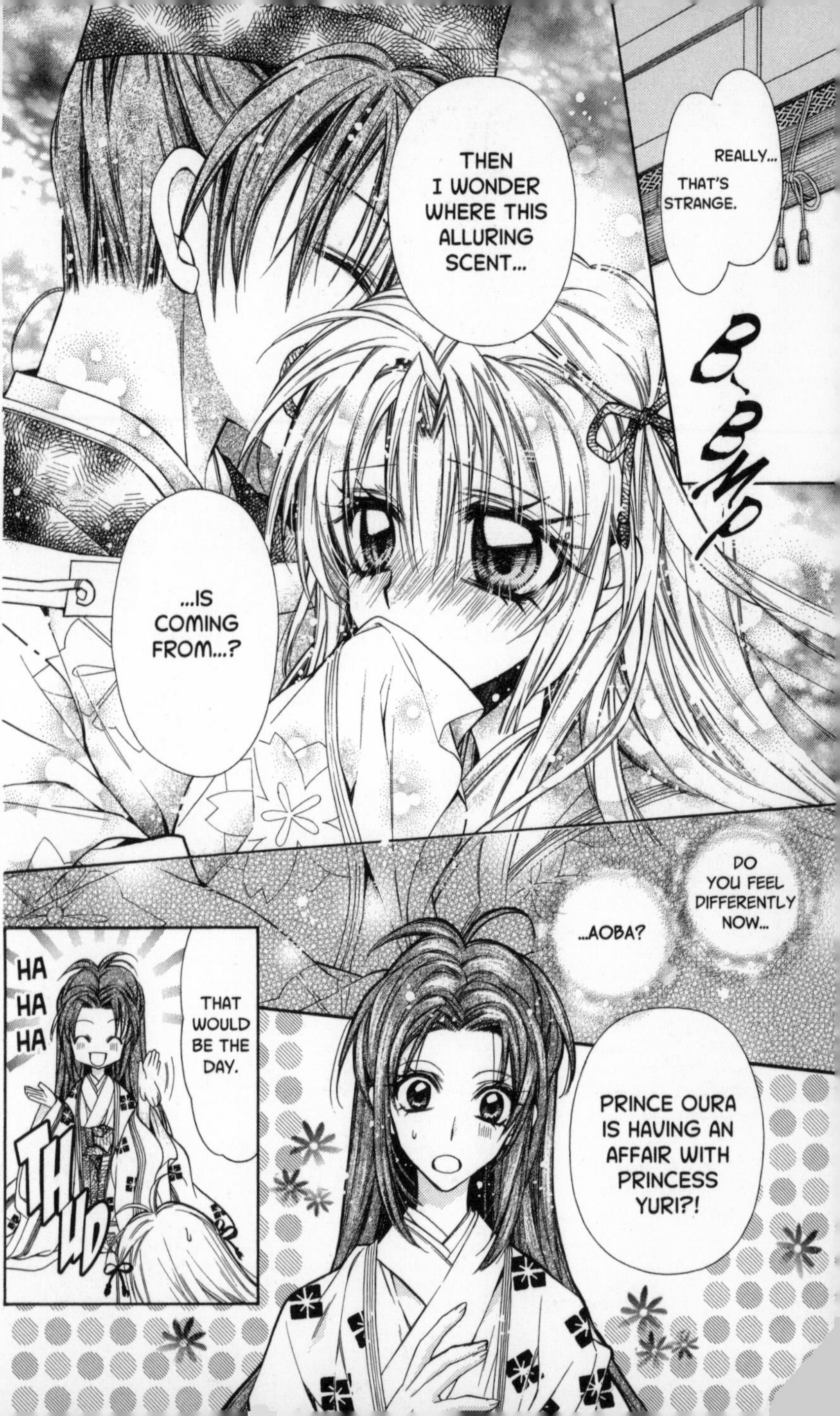
REALLY...
THAT'S STRANGE.
B-BMP
THEN I WONDER WHERE THIS ALLURING SCENT...
...IS COMING FROM...?
DO YOU FEEL DIFFERENTLY NOW...
...AOBA?
PRINCE OURA IS HAVING AN AFFAIR WITH PRINCESS YURI?!
THAT WOULD BE THE DAY.
HA HA HA
THUD

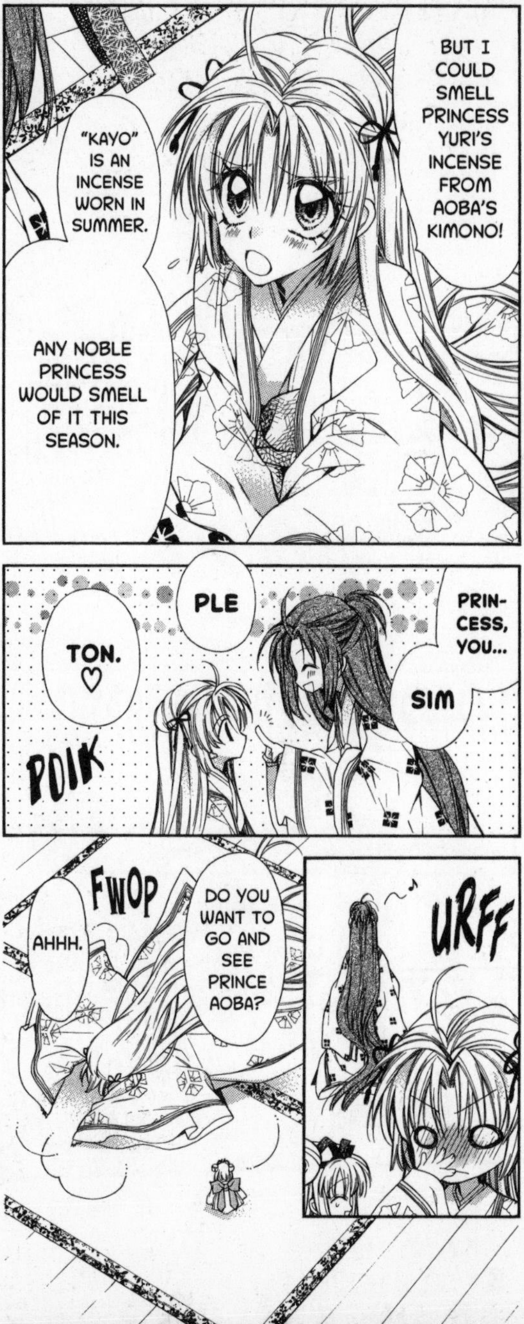
BUT I COULD SMELL PRINCESS YURI'S INCENSE FROM AOBA'S KIMONO!
"KAYO" IS AN INCENSE WORN IN SUMMER.
ANY NOBLE PRINCESS WOULD SMELL OF IT THIS SEASON.
PRIN-CESS, YOU...
SIM
PLE
TON. ♡
POIK
URFF
DO YOU WANT TO GO AND SEE PRINCE AOBA?
FWOP
AHHH.

Hay Fever

I've had hay fever for over ten years now. I love spring, but it's a tough season for me.

I get a runny nose, which drips on my work when drawing.

↓

I blow my nose too much and it starts to get irritated.

↓

I drink medicine to stop my runny nose.

↓

I get thirsty and dozy.

↓

The top and bottom of my eyelids start to stick together.

↓

I sleep (faint).

↓

The effect of the medicine wears off and my nose starts running again. (Endless...)

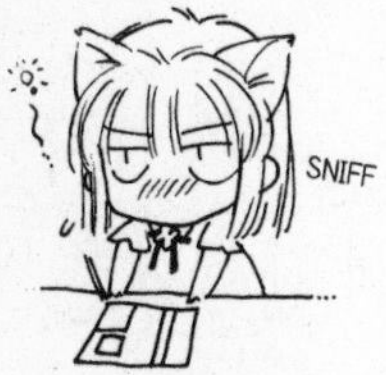
SNIFF

There are years I get hay fever, and there are years I don't.

How odd.

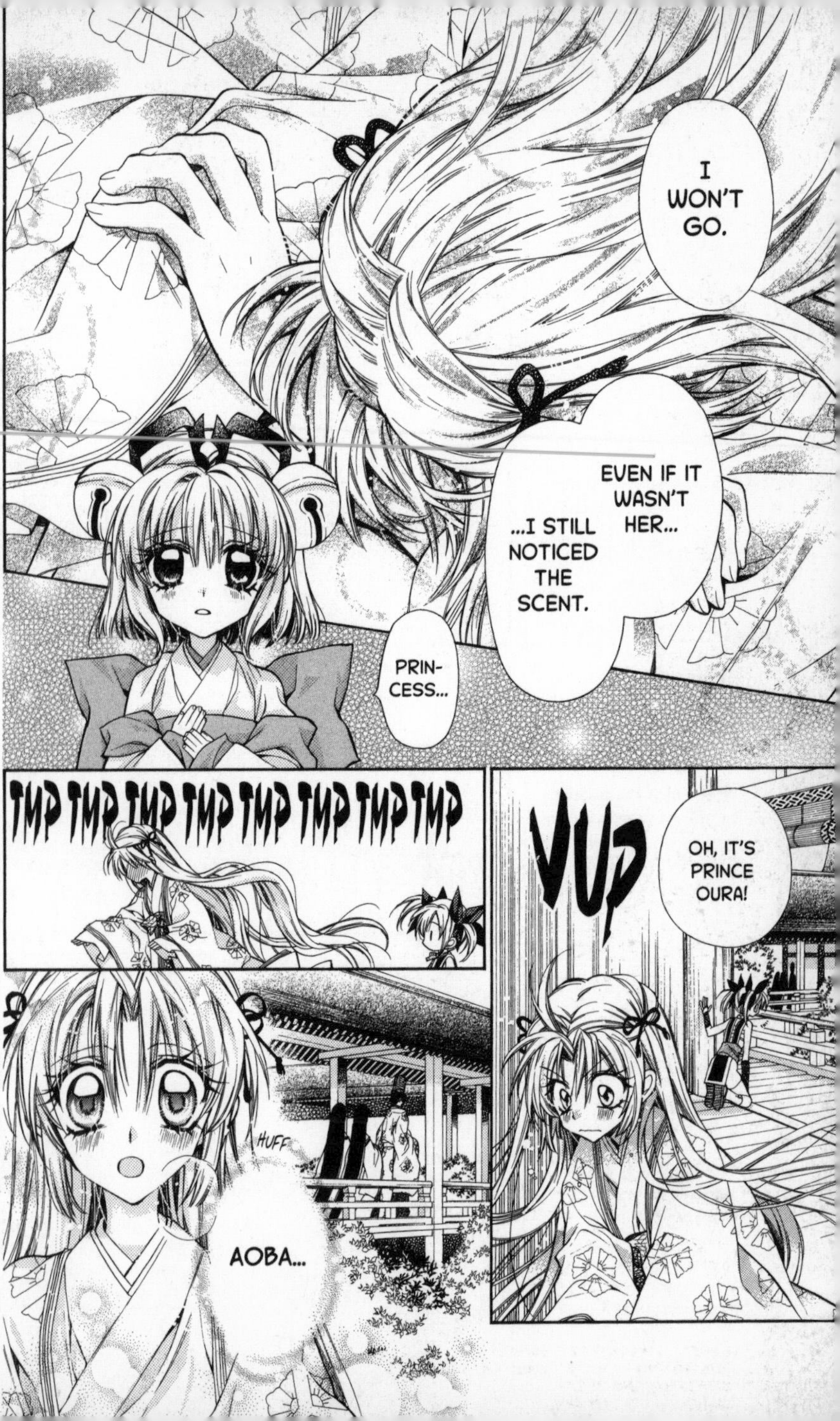
I WON'T GO.
EVEN IF IT WASN'T HER...
...I STILL NOTICED THE SCENT.
PRIN-CESS...
VUP
OH, IT'S PRINCE OURA!
TMP TMP TMP TMP TMP TMP TMP TMP
HUFF
AOBA...

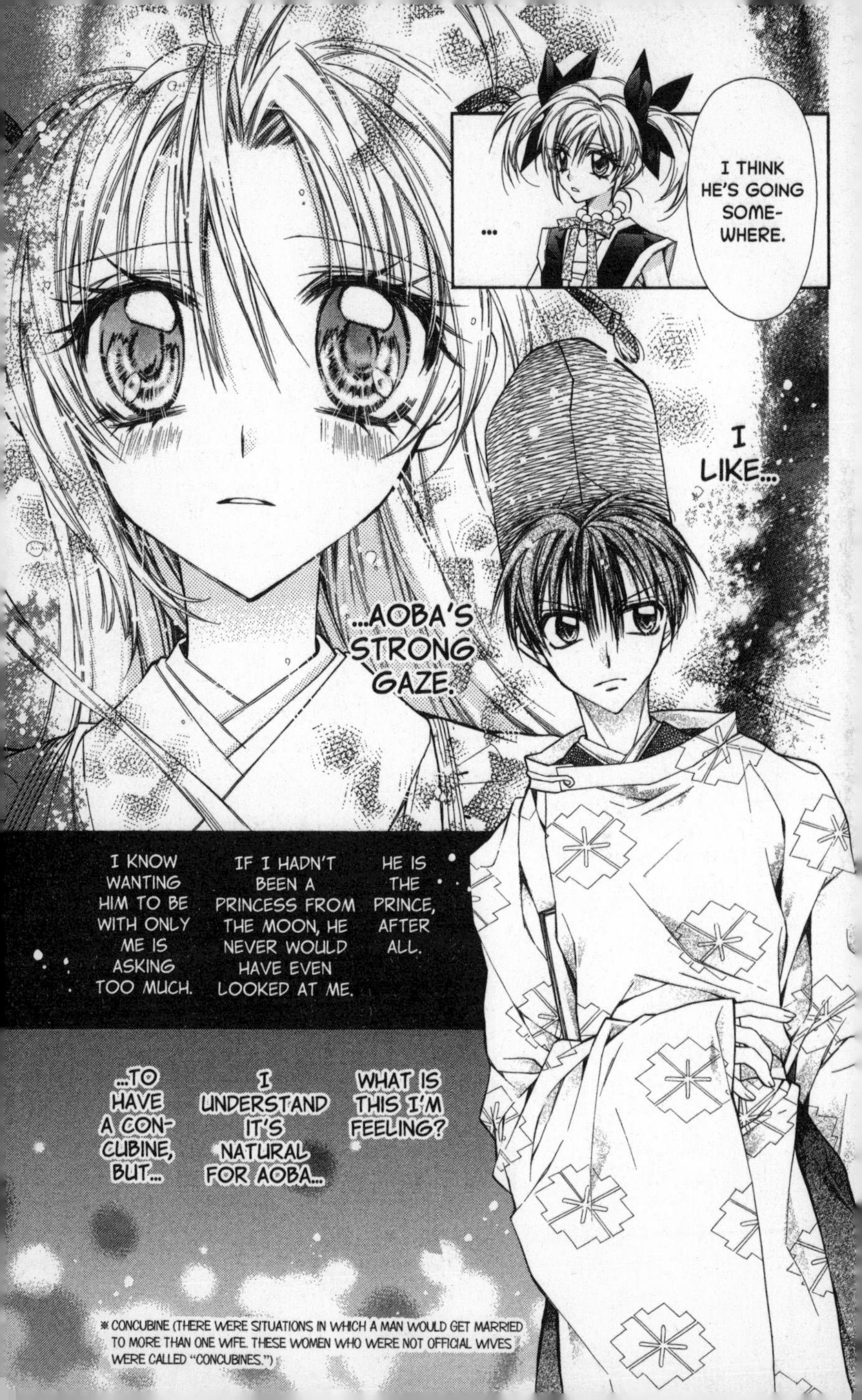
I THINK HE'S GOING SOME-WHERE.
...
I LIKE...
...AOBA'S STRONG GAZE.
HE IS THE PRINCE, AFTER ALL.
IF I HADN'T BEEN A PRINCESS FROM THE MOON, HE NEVER WOULD HAVE EVEN LOOKED AT ME.
I KNOW WANTING HIM TO BE WITH ONLY ME IS ASKING TOO MUCH.
WHAT IS THIS I'M FEELING?
I UNDERSTAND IT'S NATURAL FOR AOBA...
...TO HAVE A CON-CUBINE, BUT...
※ CONCUBINE (THERE WERE SITUATIONS IN WHICH A MAN WOULD GET MARRIED TO MORE THAN ONE WIFE. THESE WOMEN WHO WERE NOT OFFICIAL WIVES WERE CALLED "CONCUBINES.")

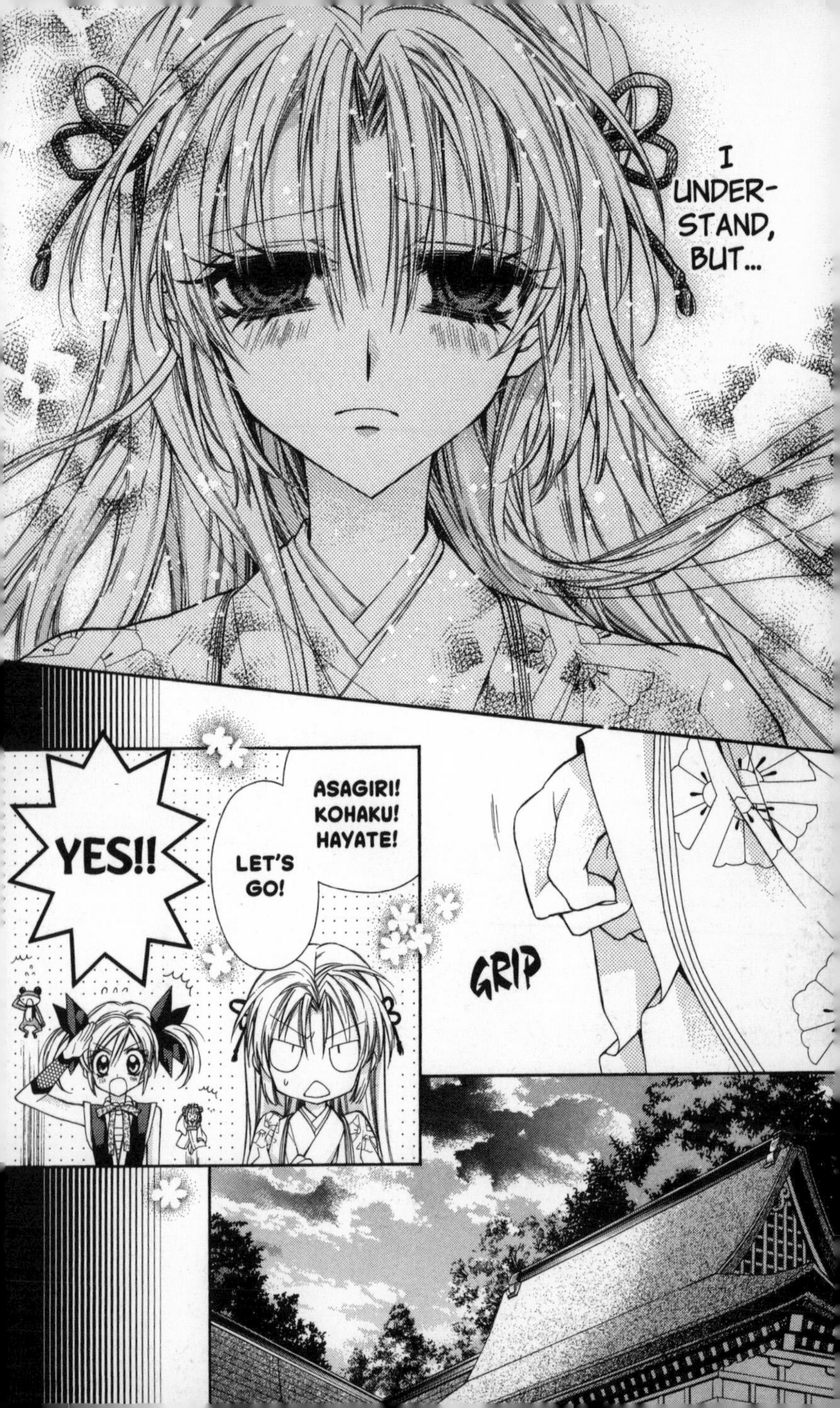
I UNDER-STAND, BUT...
GRIP
ASAGIRI! KOHAKU! HAYATE!
LET'S GO!
YES!!

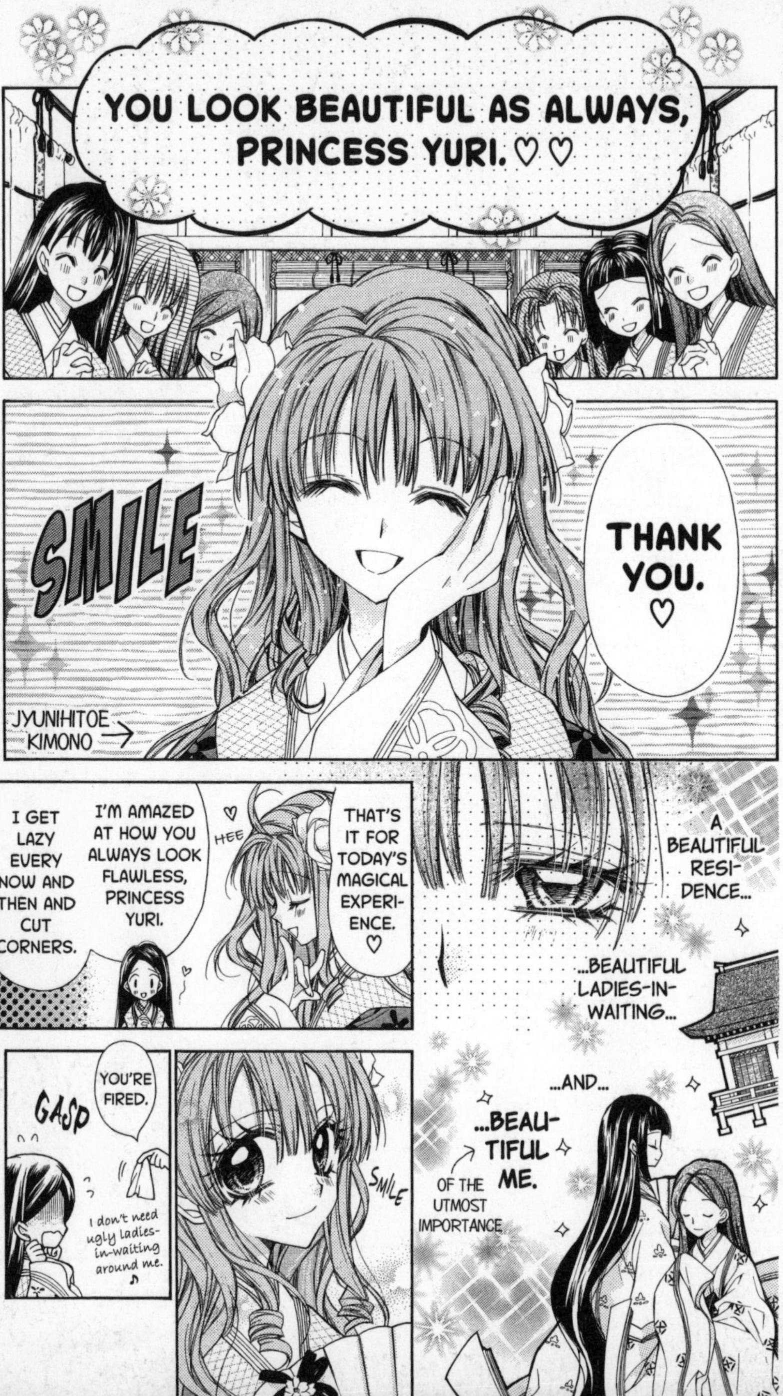
YOU LOOK BEAUTIFUL AS ALWAYS, PRINCESS YURI. ♡ ♡
THANK YOU. ♡
SMILE
JYUNIHITOE KIMONO
A BEAUTIFUL RESIDENCE...
...BEAUTIFUL LADIES-IN-WAITING...
...AND...
...BEAUTIFUL ME.
OF THE UTMOST IMPORTANCE
THAT'S IT FOR TODAY'S MAGICAL EXPERIENCE. ♡
HEE
I'M AMAZED AT HOW YOU ALWAYS LOOK FLAWLESS, PRINCESS YURI.
I GET LAZY EVERY NOW AND THEN AND CUT CORNERS.
SMILE
YOU'RE FIRED.
GASP
I don't need ugly ladies-in-waiting around me. ♪

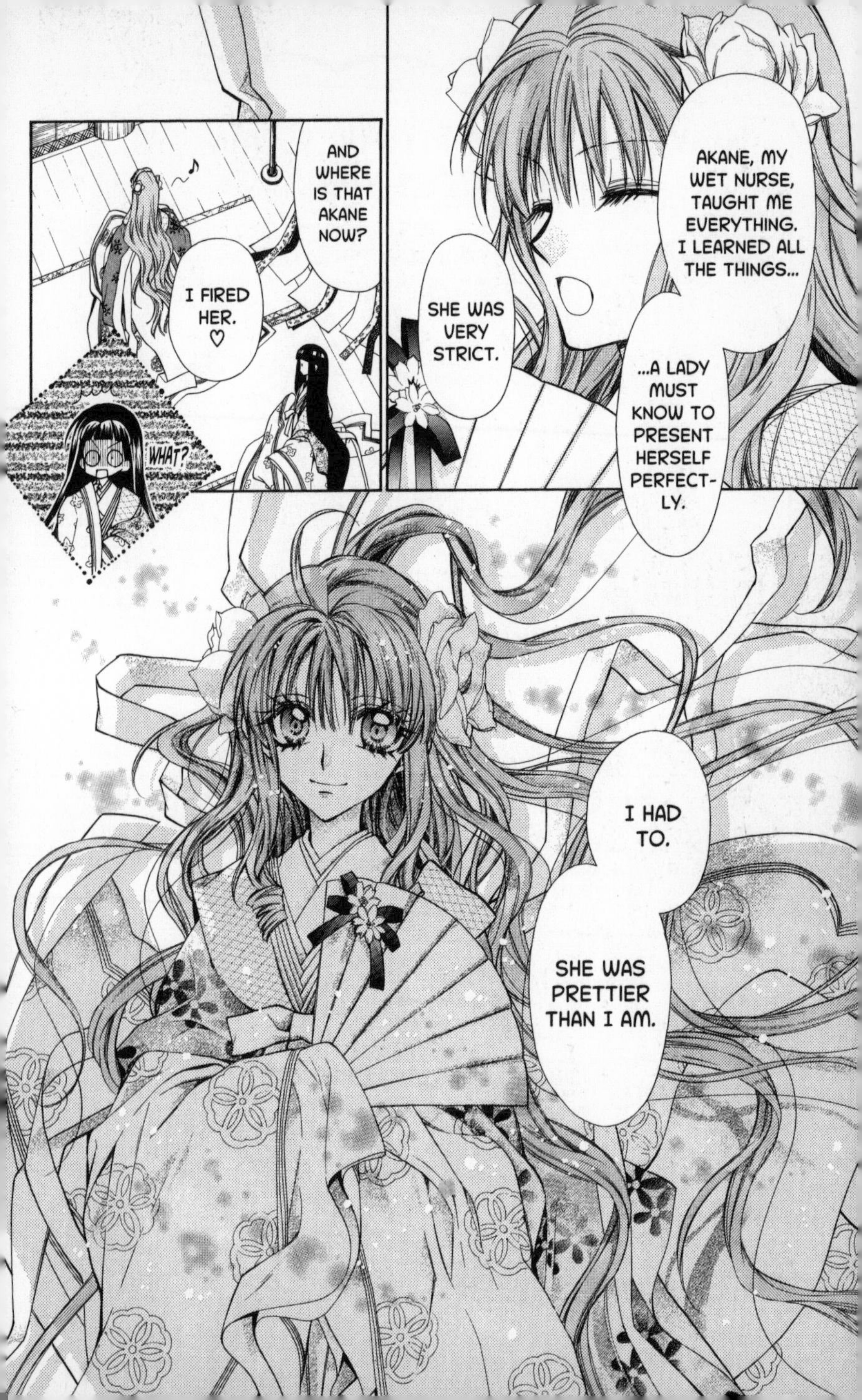
AKANE, MY WET NURSE, TAUGHT ME EVERYTHING. I LEARNED ALL THE THINGS...
...A LADY MUST KNOW TO PRESENT HERSELF PERFECT-LY.
SHE WAS VERY STRICT.
AND WHERE IS THAT AKANE NOW?
I FIRED HER. ♡
WHAT?
I HAD TO.
SHE WAS PRETTIER THAN I AM.

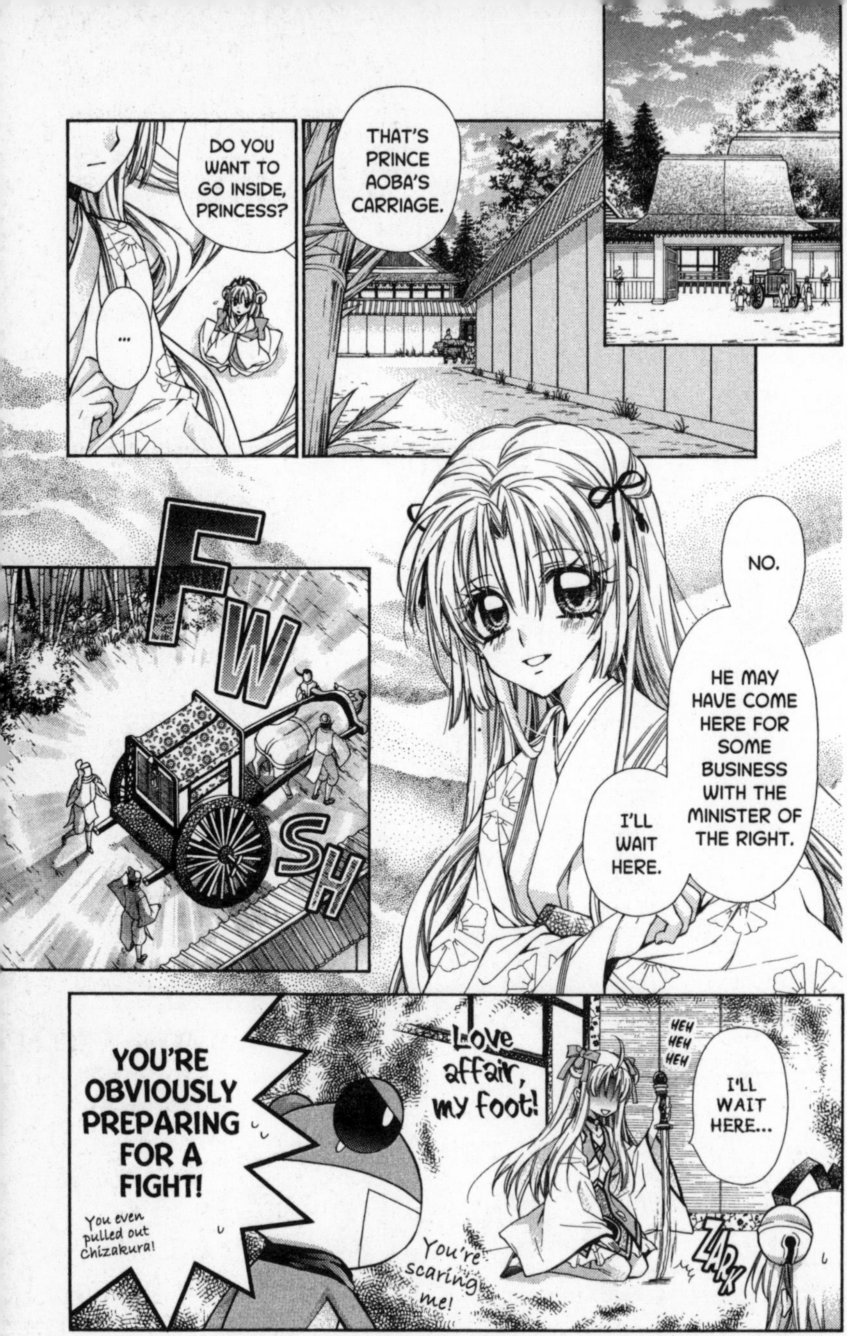
THAT'S PRINCE AOBA'S CARRIAGE.
DO YOU WANT TO GO INSIDE, PRINCESS?
...
NO.
HE MAY HAVE COME HERE FOR SOME BUSINESS WITH THE MINISTER OF THE RIGHT.
I'LL WAIT HERE.
FWSH
HEH HEH HEH
I'LL WAIT HERE...
ZARK
Love affair, my foot!
You're scaring me!
YOU'RE OBVIOUSLY PREPARING FOR A FIGHT!
You even pulled out Chizakura!

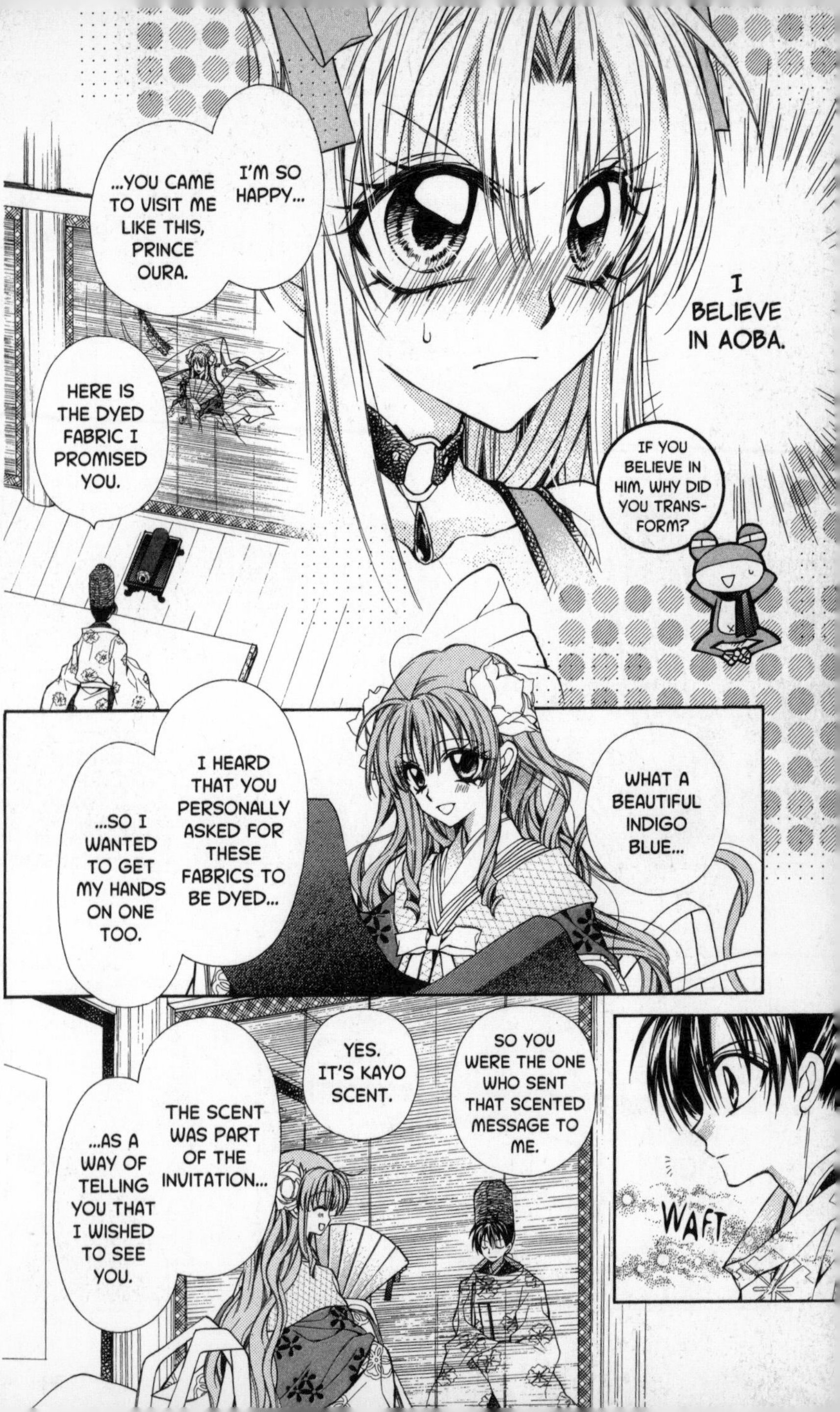
I BELIEVE IN AOBA.
IF YOU BELIEVE IN HIM, WHY DID YOU TRANS-FORM?
I'M SO HAPPY...
...YOU CAME TO VISIT ME LIKE THIS, PRINCE OURA.
HERE IS THE DYED FABRIC I PROMISED YOU.
WHAT A BEAUTIFUL INDIGO BLUE...
I HEARD THAT YOU PERSONALLY ASKED FOR THESE FABRICS TO BE DYED...
...SO I WANTED TO GET MY HANDS ON ONE TOO.
WAFT
SO YOU WERE THE ONE WHO SENT THAT SCENTED MESSAGE TO ME.
YES. IT'S KAYO SCENT.
THE SCENT WAS PART OF THE INVITATION...
...AS A WAY OF TELLING YOU THAT I WISHED TO SEE YOU.

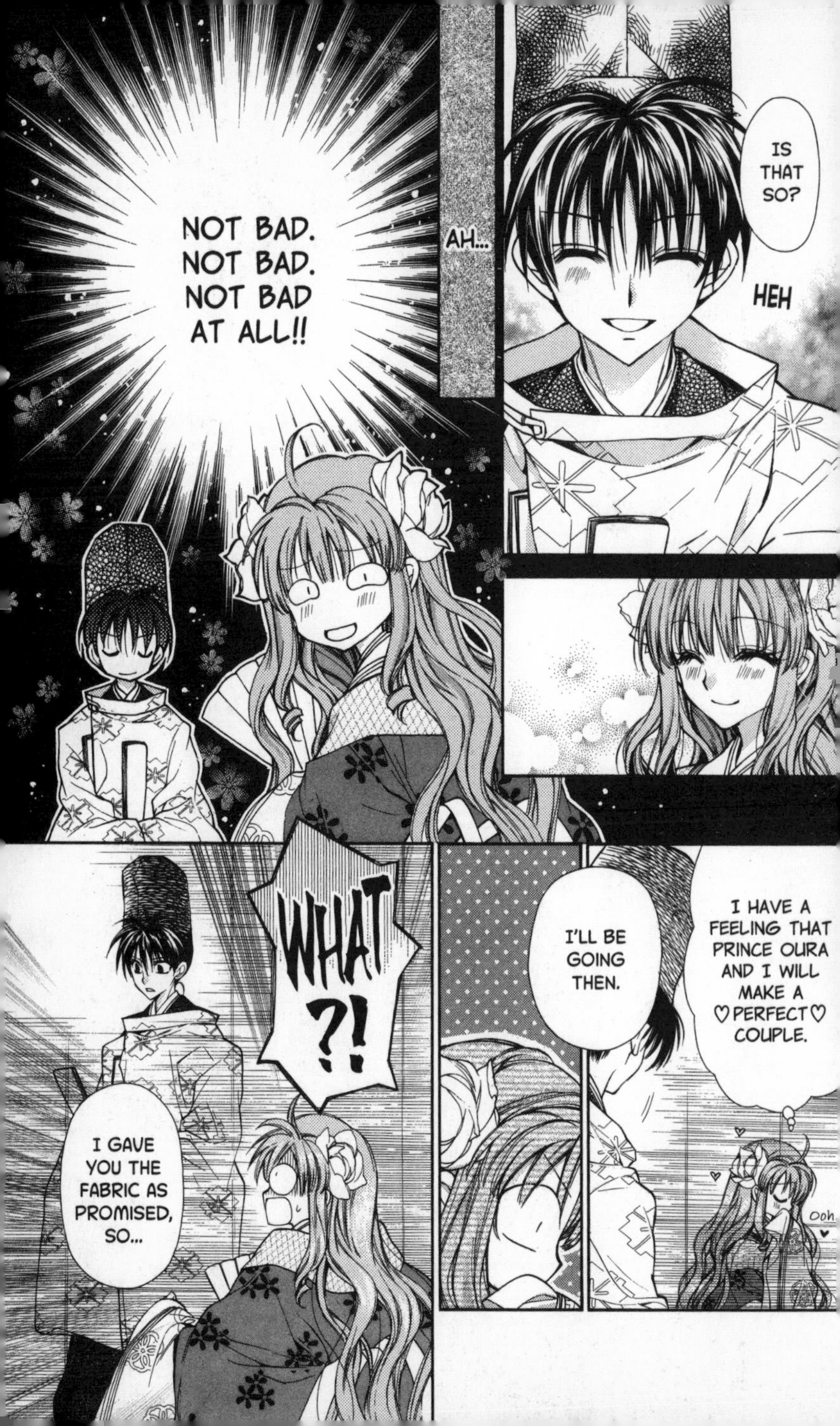

IS THAT SO?
HEH
AH...
NOT BAD. NOT BAD. NOT BAD AT ALL!!
I HAVE A FEELING THAT PRINCE OURA AND I WILL MAKE A ♡PERFECT♡ COUPLE.
Ooh.
I'LL BE GOING THEN.
WHAT?!
I GAVE YOU THE FABRIC AS PROMISED, SO...

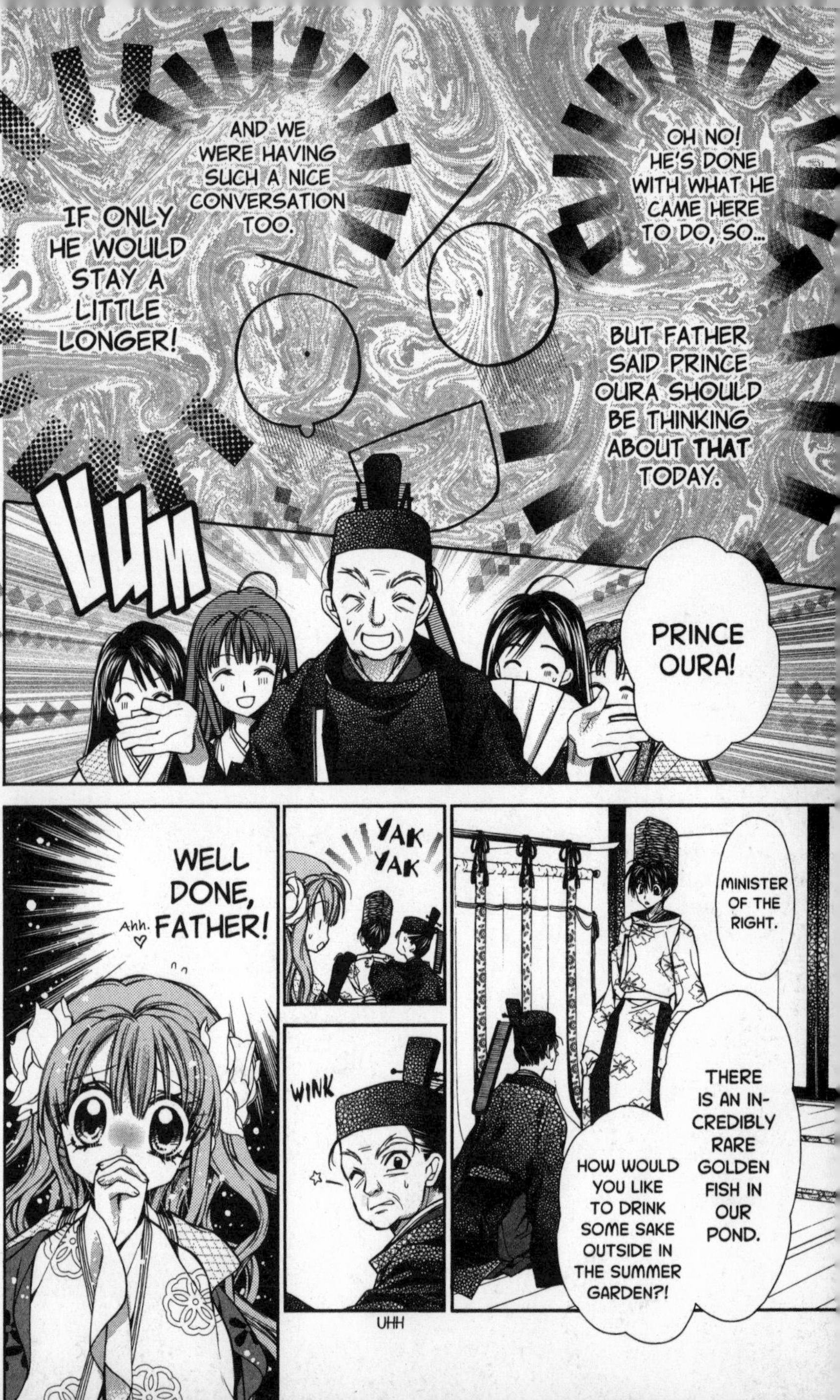
OH NO! HE'S DONE WITH WHAT HE CAME HERE TO DO, SO...
BUT FATHER SAID PRINCE OURA SHOULD BE THINKING ABOUT **THAT** TODAY.
AND WE WERE HAVING SUCH A NICE CONVERSATION TOO.
IF ONLY HE WOULD STAY A LITTLE LONGER!
PRINCE OURA!
VUUM
MINISTER OF THE RIGHT.
THERE IS AN INCREDIBLY RARE GOLDEN FISH IN OUR POND.
HOW WOULD YOU LIKE TO DRINK SOME SAKE OUTSIDE IN THE SUMMER GARDEN?!
YAK YAK
WINK
UHH
WELL DONE, FATHER!
Ahh. ♡

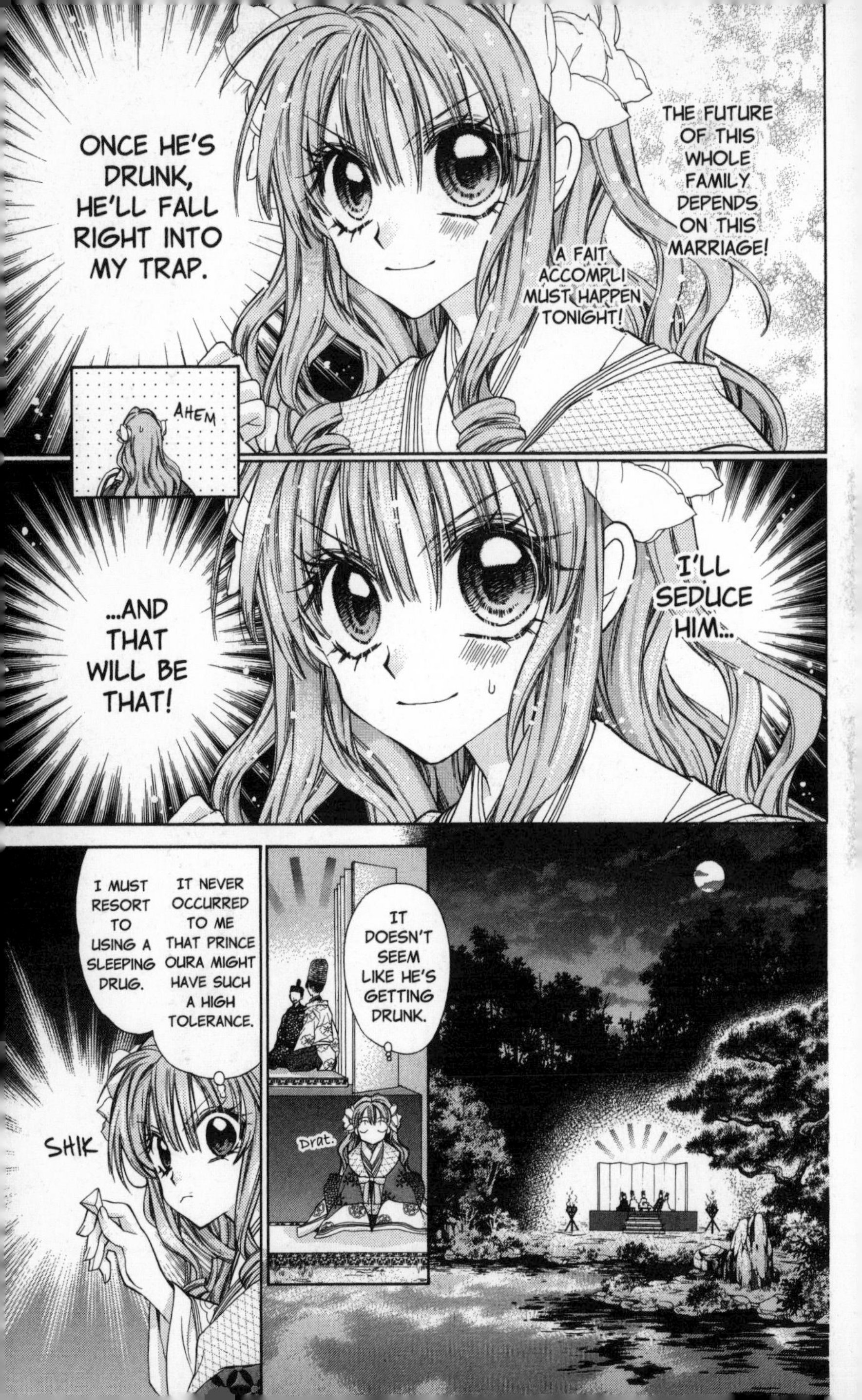
THE FUTURE OF THIS WHOLE FAMILY DEPENDS ON THIS MARRIAGE!
A FAIT ACCOMPLI MUST HAPPEN TONIGHT!
ONCE HE'S DRUNK, HE'LL FALL RIGHT INTO MY TRAP.
AHEM
I'LL SEDUCE HIM...
...AND THAT WILL BE THAT!
IT DOESN'T SEEM LIKE HE'S GETTING DRUNK.
Drat.
IT NEVER OCCURRED TO ME THAT PRINCE OURA MIGHT HAVE SUCH A HIGH TOLERANCE.
I MUST RESORT TO USING A SLEEPING DRUG.
SHIK

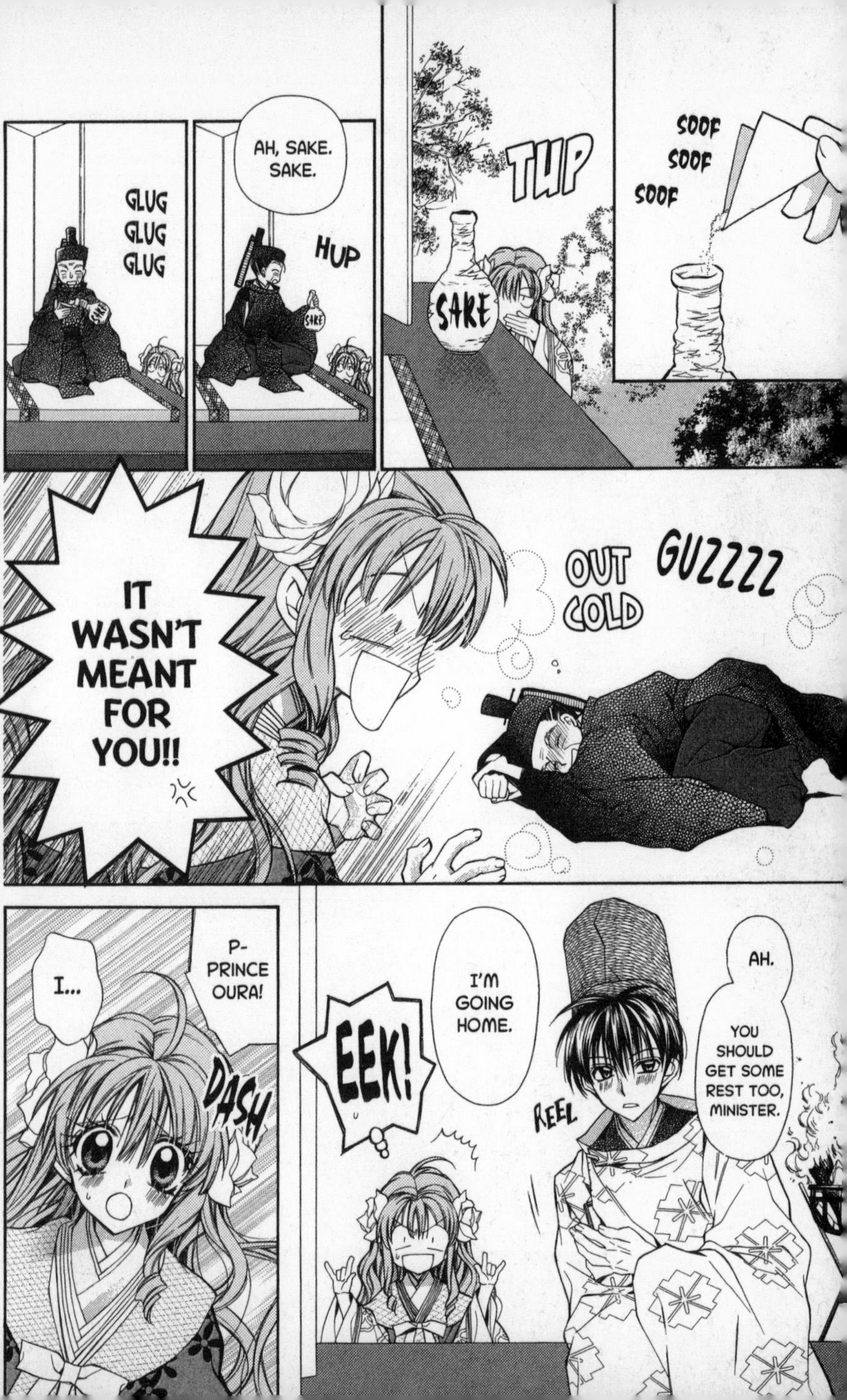
SOOF
SOOF
SOOF
TUP
SAKE
AH, SAKE. SAKE.
HUP
SAKE
GLUG
GLUG
GLUG
GUZZZZ
OUT COLD
IT WASN'T MEANT FOR YOU!!
AH.
YOU SHOULD GET SOME REST TOO, MINISTER.
I'M GOING HOME.
REEL
EEK!
P-PRINCE OURA!
I...
DASH

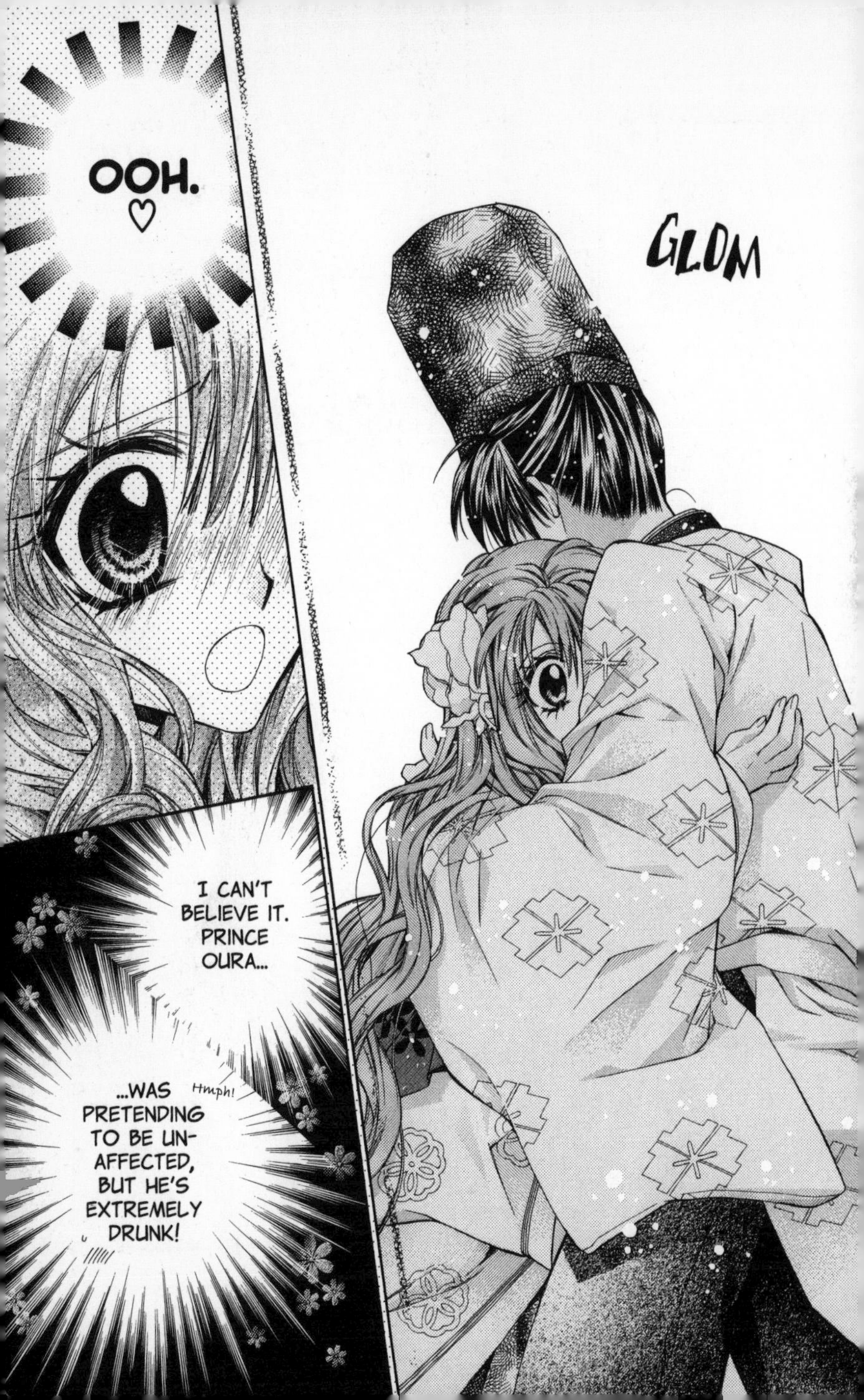
GLOM
OOH. ♡
I CAN'T BELIEVE IT. PRINCE OURA...
...WAS PRETENDING TO BE UN-AFFECTED, BUT HE'S EXTREMELY DRUNK!
Hmph!

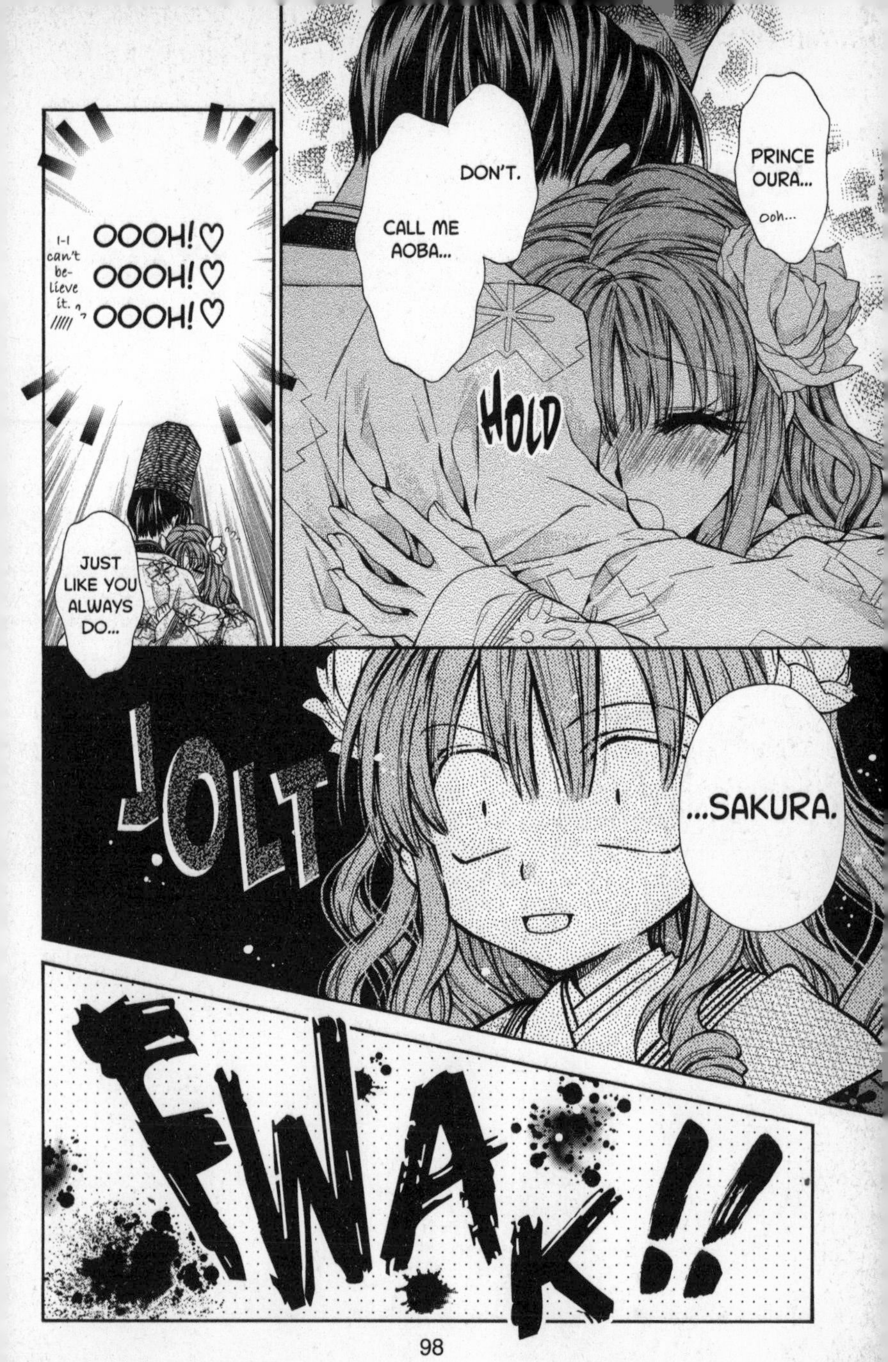
PRINCE OURA...
Ooh...
DON'T.
CALL ME AOBA...
HOLD
OOOH! ♡ OOOH! ♡ OOOH! ♡
I-I can't be-lieve it.
JUST LIKE YOU ALWAYS DO...
...SAKURA.
JOLT
FWAK!!

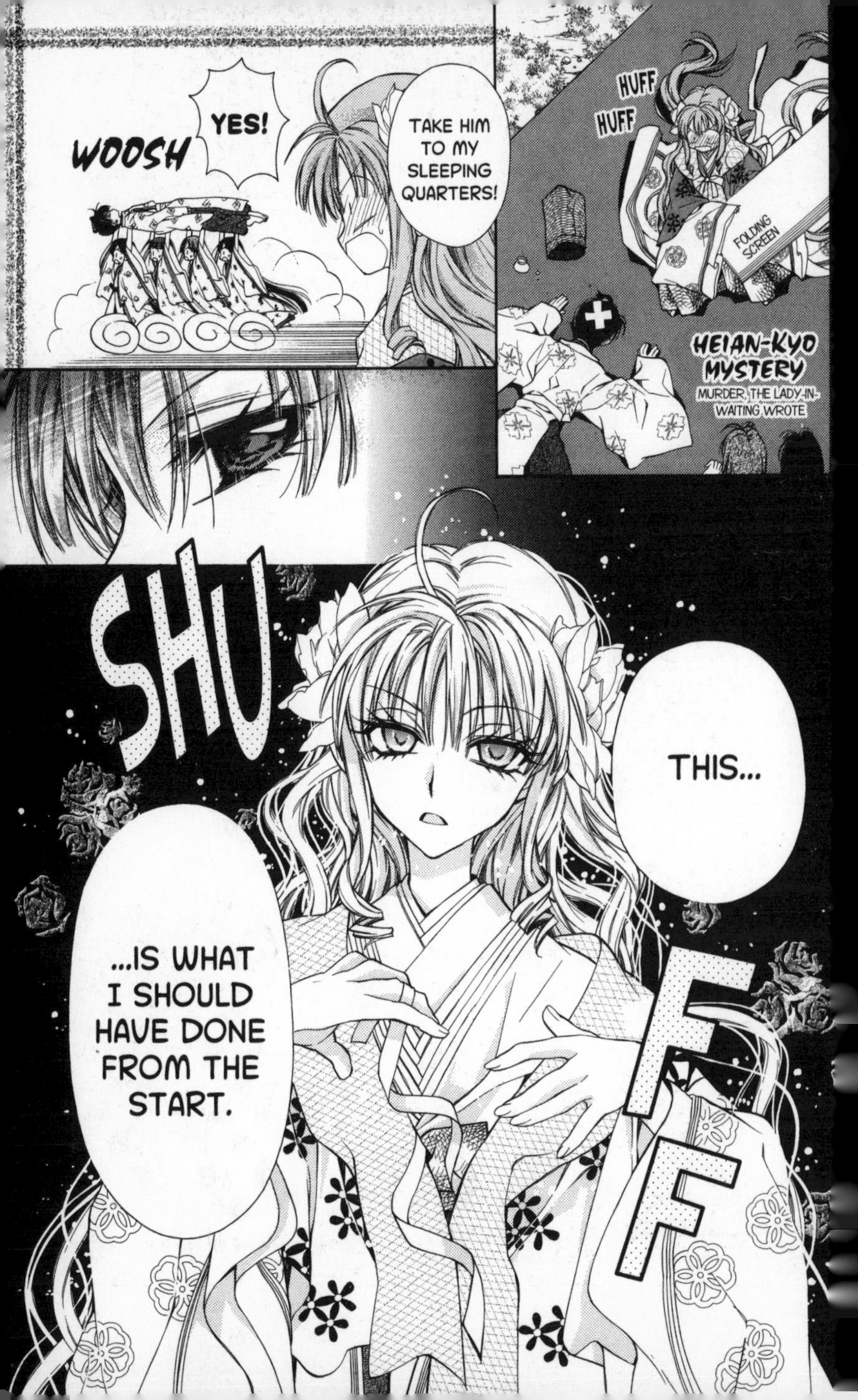
HUFF
HUFF
FOLDING SCREEN
HEIAN-KYO MYSTERY
MURDER, THE LADY-IN-WAITING WROTE
TAKE HIM TO MY SLEEPING QUARTERS!
YES!
WOOSH
THIS...
...IS WHAT I SHOULD HAVE DONE FROM THE START.
SHUFF

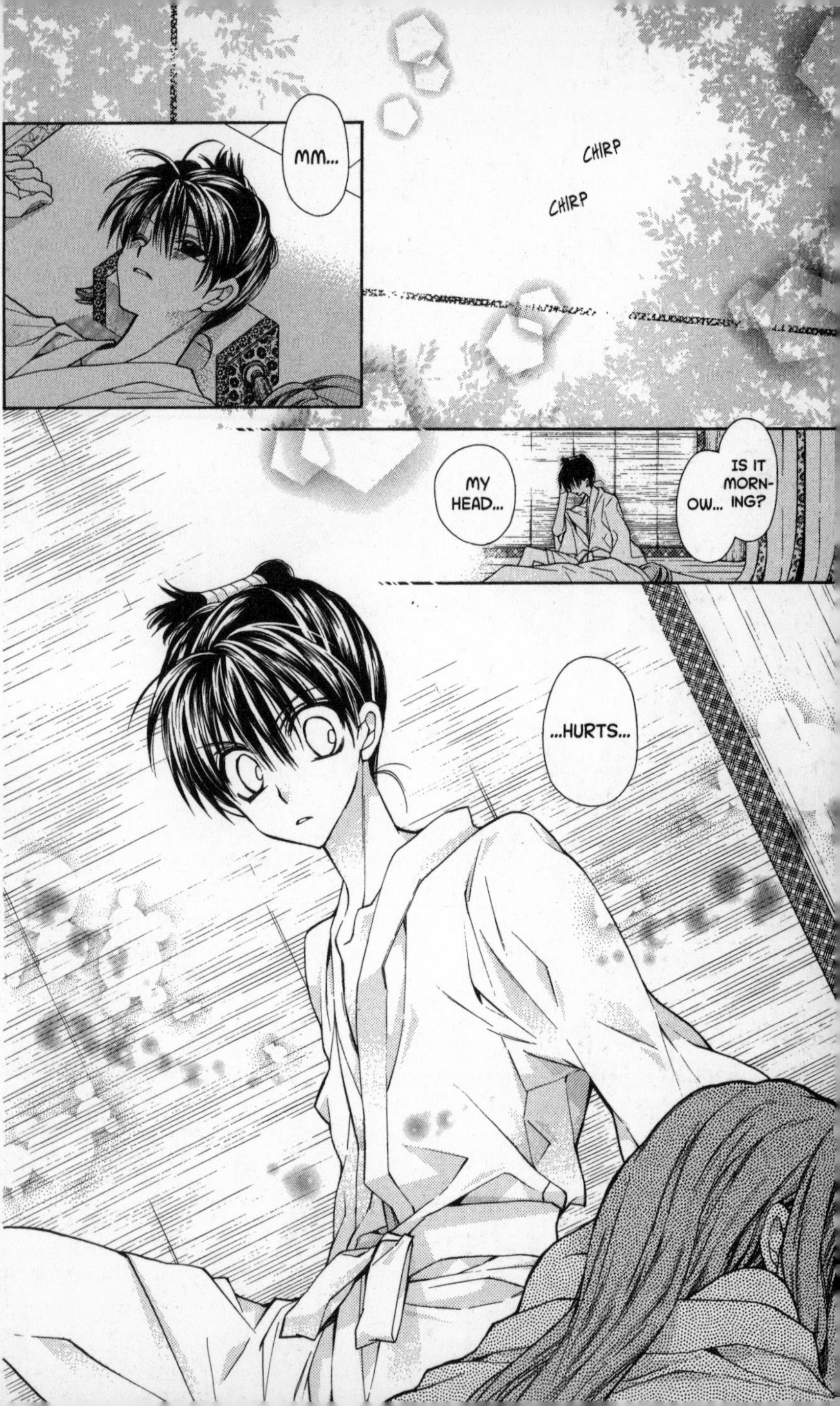

CHIRP
CHIRP
MM...
IS IT MORN-ING? OW...
MY HEAD...
...HURTS...

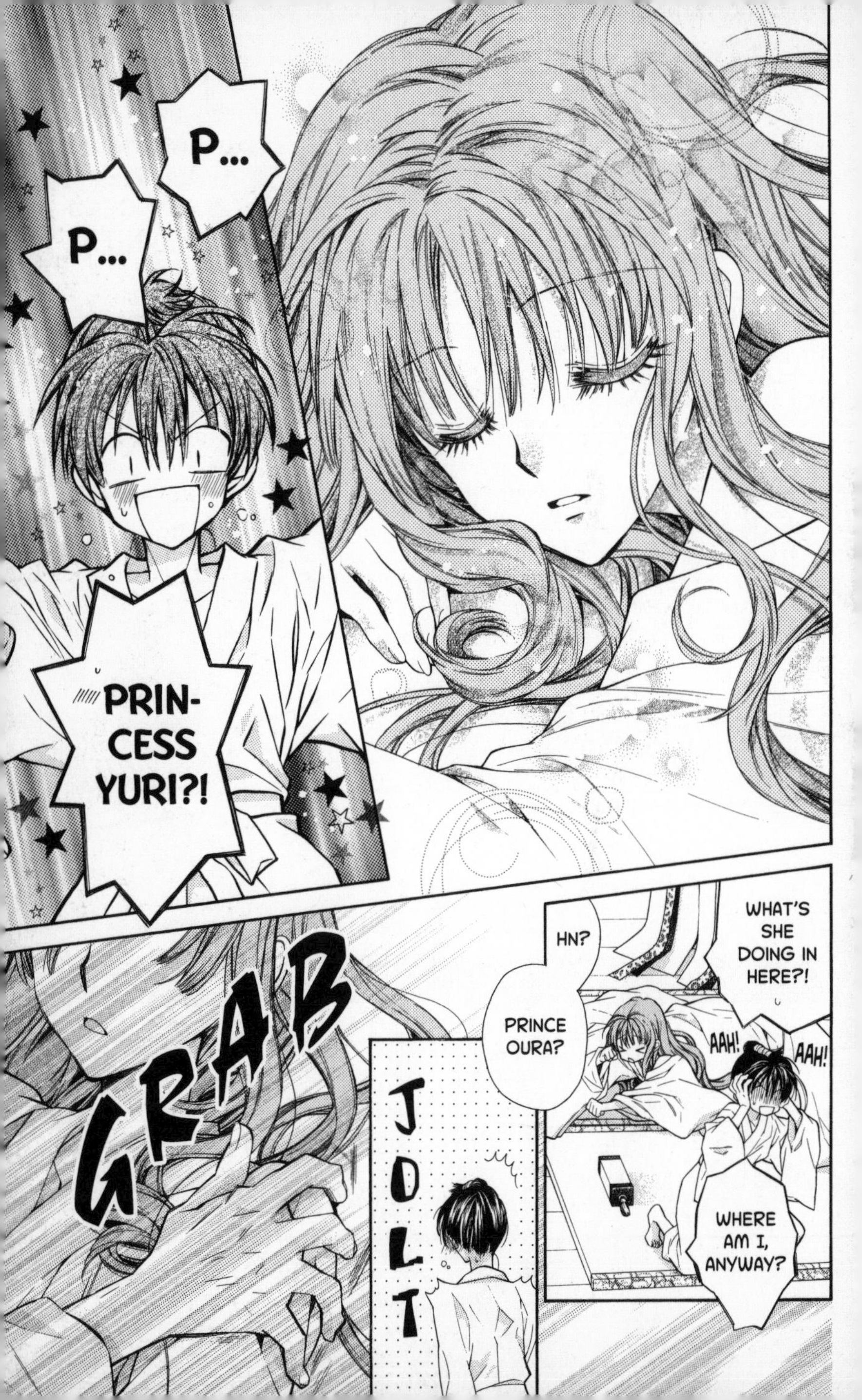
P...
P...
PRIN-
CESS
YURI?!
WHAT'S
SHE
DOING IN
HERE?!
AAH!
AAH!
HN?
PRINCE
OURA?
WHERE
AM I,
ANYWAY?
JOLT
GRAB

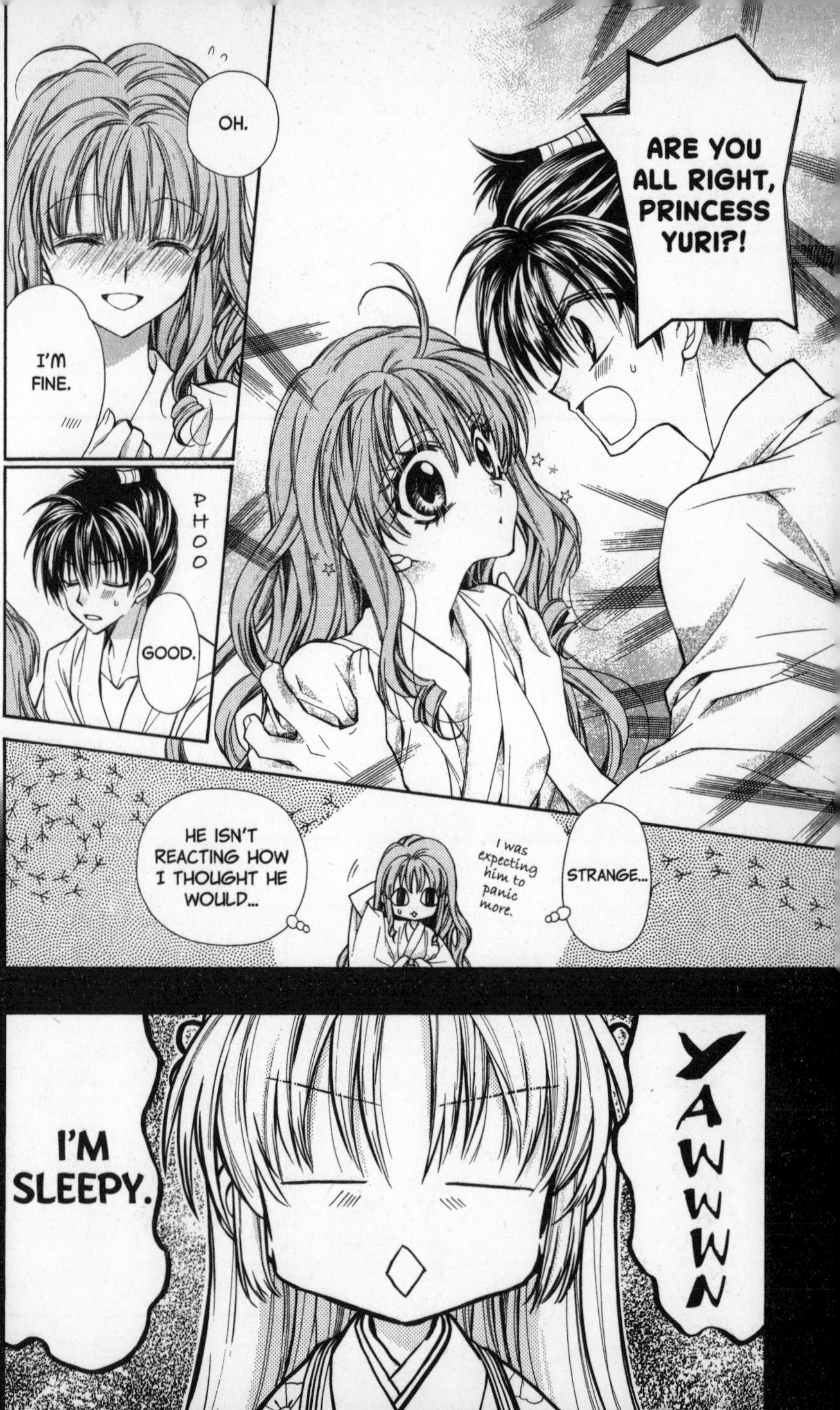

ARE YOU ALL RIGHT, PRINCESS YURI?!
OH.
I'M FINE.
PHOO
GOOD.
STRANGE...
I was expecting him to panic more.
HE ISN'T REACTING HOW I THOUGHT HE WOULD...
YAWWWN
I'M SLEEPY.

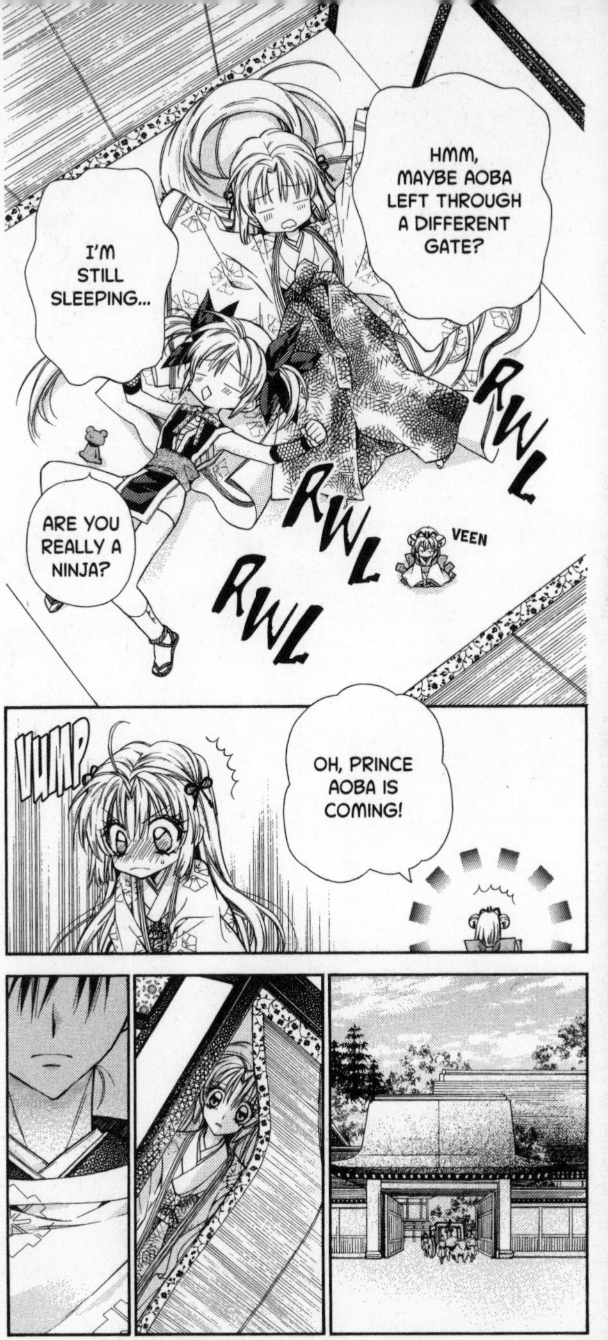
HMM, MAYBE AOBA LEFT THROUGH A DIFFERENT GATE?
I'M STILL SLEEPING...
RWL
RWL
RWL
RWL
VEEN
ARE YOU REALLY A NINJA?
OH, PRINCE AOBA IS COMING!
VUMP

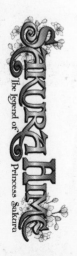

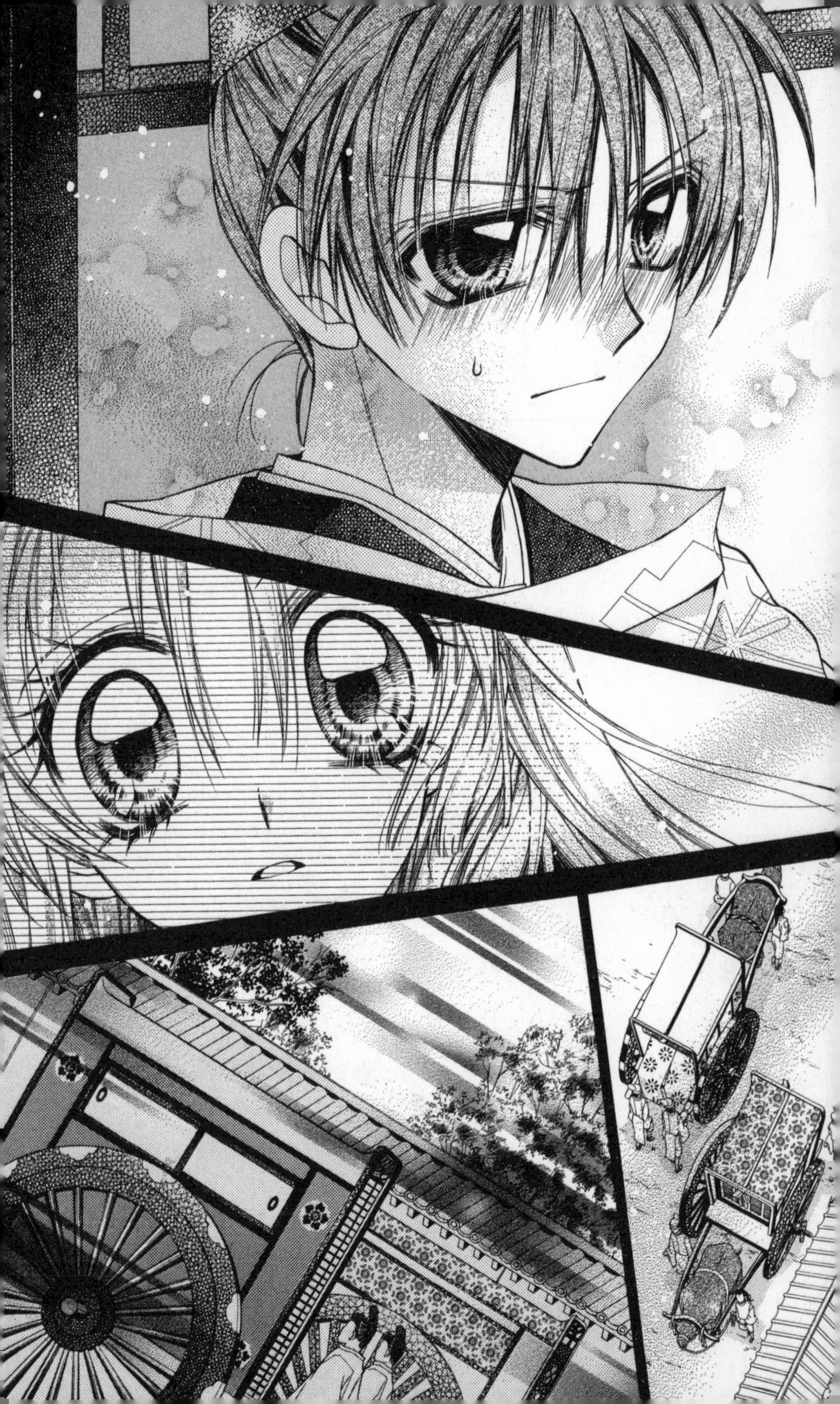

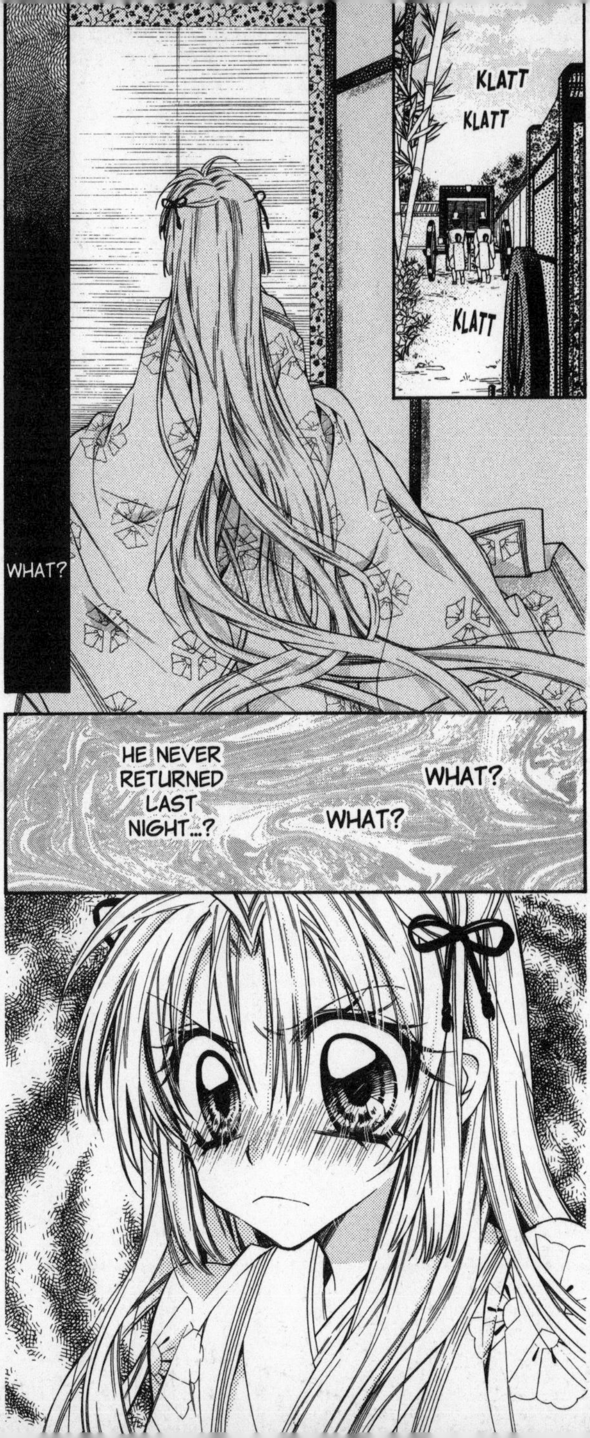
KLATT
KLATT
KLATT
WHAT?
WHAT?
WHAT?
HE NEVER RETURNED LAST NIGHT...?

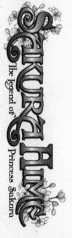

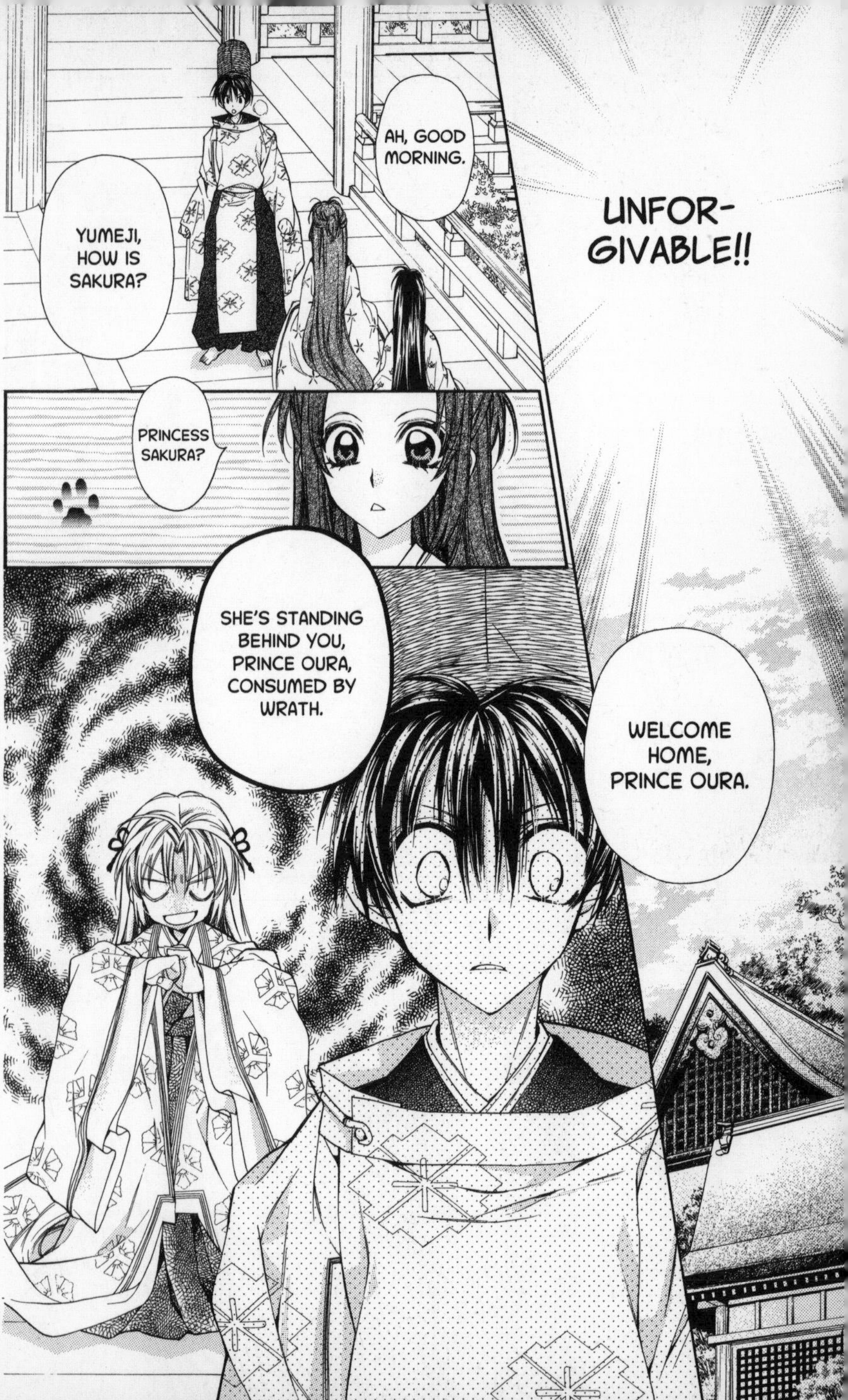
UNFOR-GIVABLE!!
WELCOME HOME, PRINCE OURA.
AH, GOOD MORNING.
YUMEJI, HOW IS SAKURA?
PRINCESS SAKURA?
SHE'S STANDING BEHIND YOU, PRINCE OURA, CONSUMED BY WRATH.

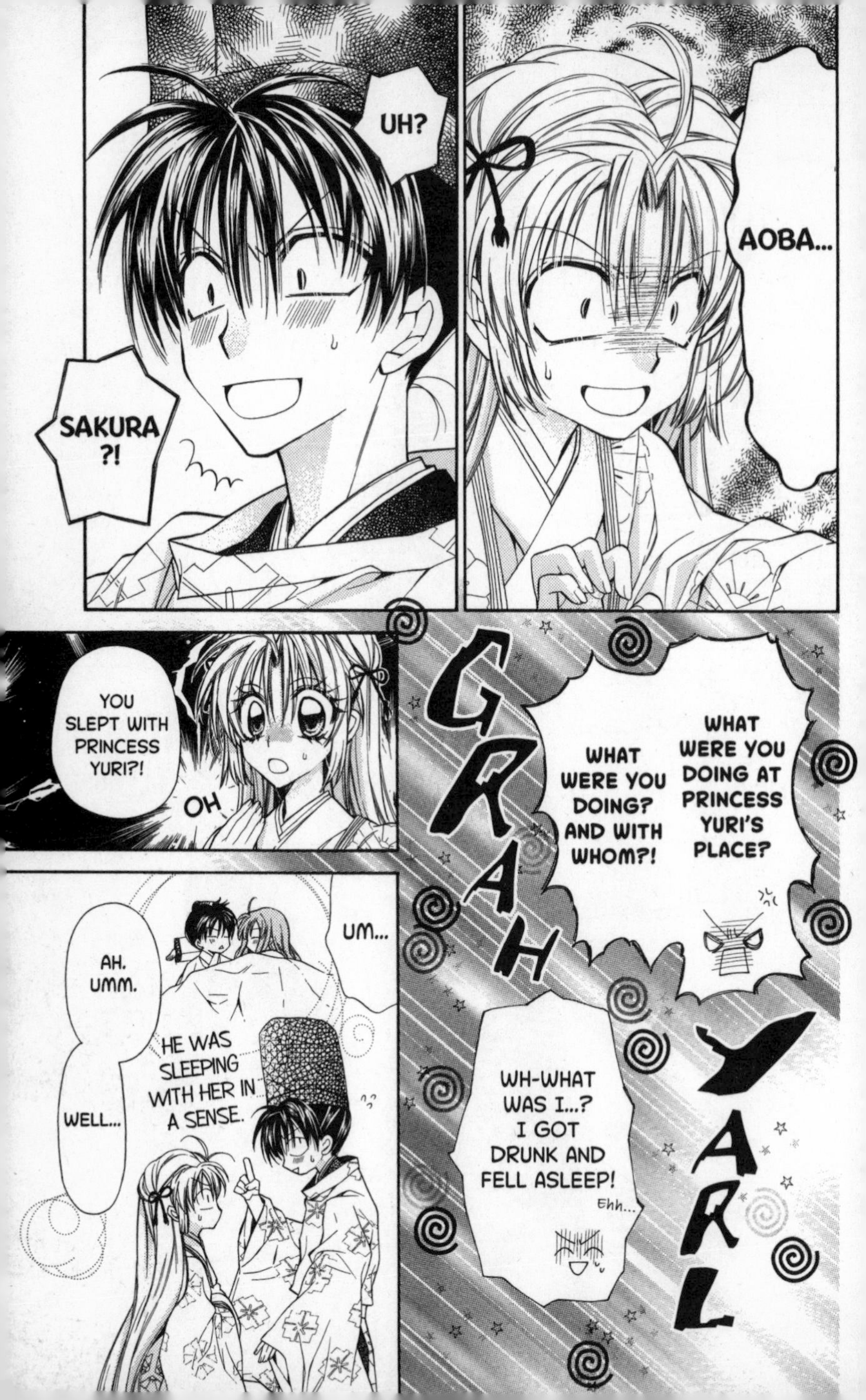
AOBA...
UH?
SAKURA ?!
GRAH
WHAT WERE YOU DOING AT PRINCESS YURI'S PLACE?
WHAT WERE YOU DOING? AND WITH WHOM?!
WH-WHAT WAS I...? I GOT DRUNK AND FELL ASLEEP!
Ehh...
YARL
YOU SLEPT WITH PRINCESS YURI?!
OH
UM...
AH. UMM.
HE WAS SLEEPING WITH HER IN A SENSE.
WELL...

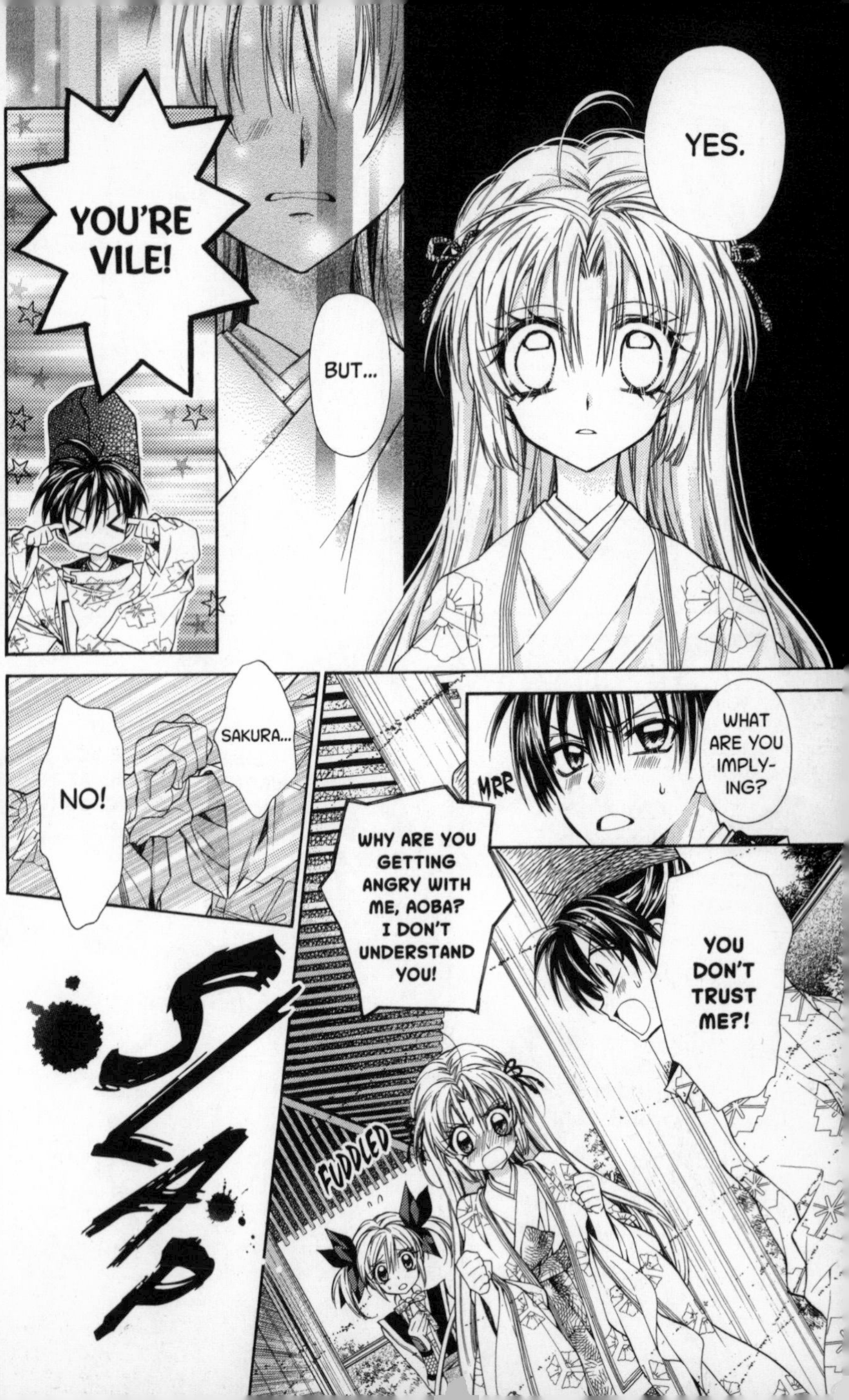
YES.
BUT...
YOU'RE VILE!
MRR
WHAT ARE YOU IMPLYING?
YOU DON'T TRUST ME?!
WHY ARE YOU GETTING ANGRY WITH ME, AOBA? I DON'T UNDERSTAND YOU!
FUDDLED
SAKURA...
NO!
SLAP

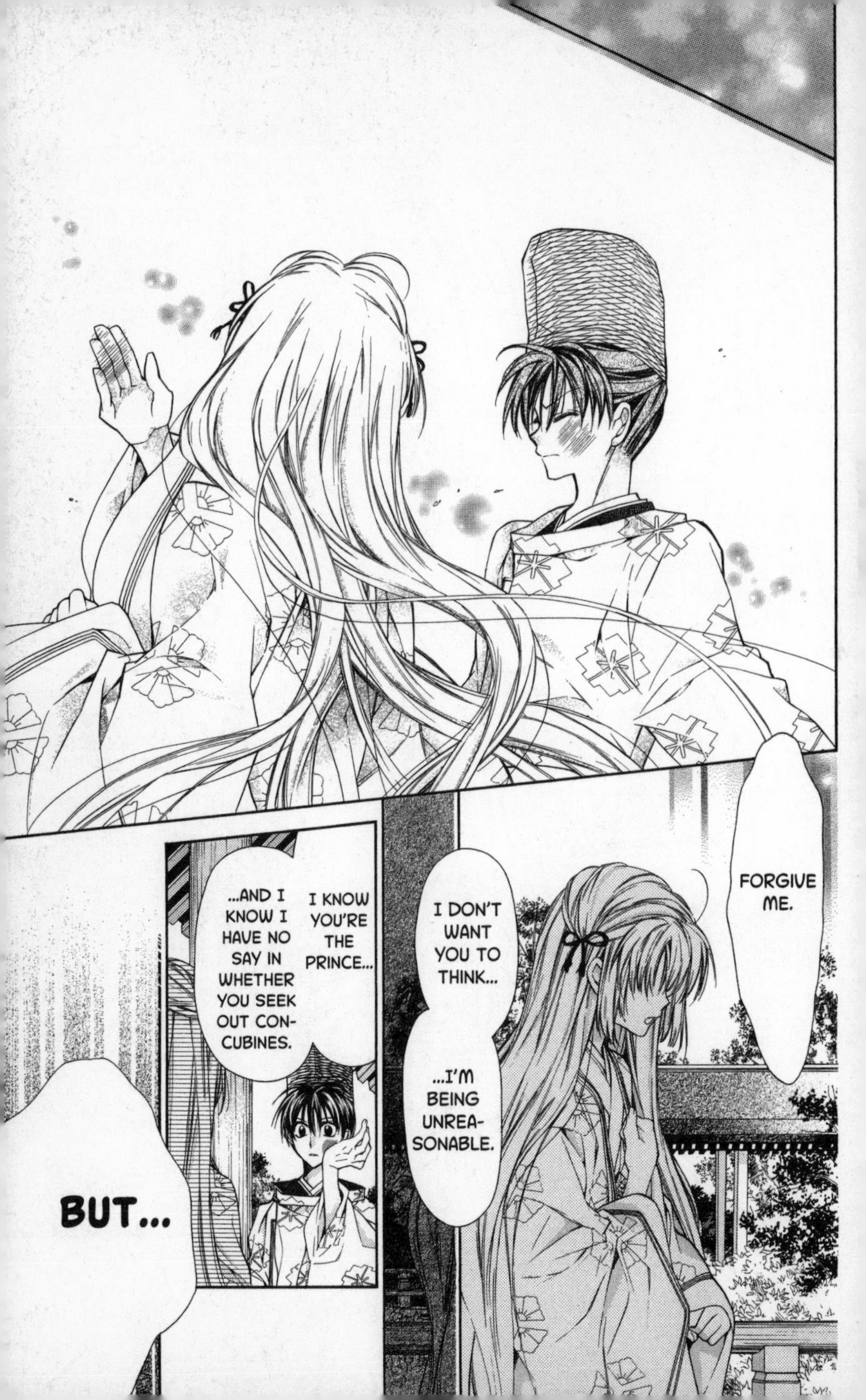
FORGIVE ME.
I DON'T WANT YOU TO THINK...
...I'M BEING UNREASONABLE.
I KNOW YOU'RE THE PRINCE...
...AND I KNOW I HAVE NO SAY IN WHETHER YOU SEEK OUT CONCUBINES.
BUT...

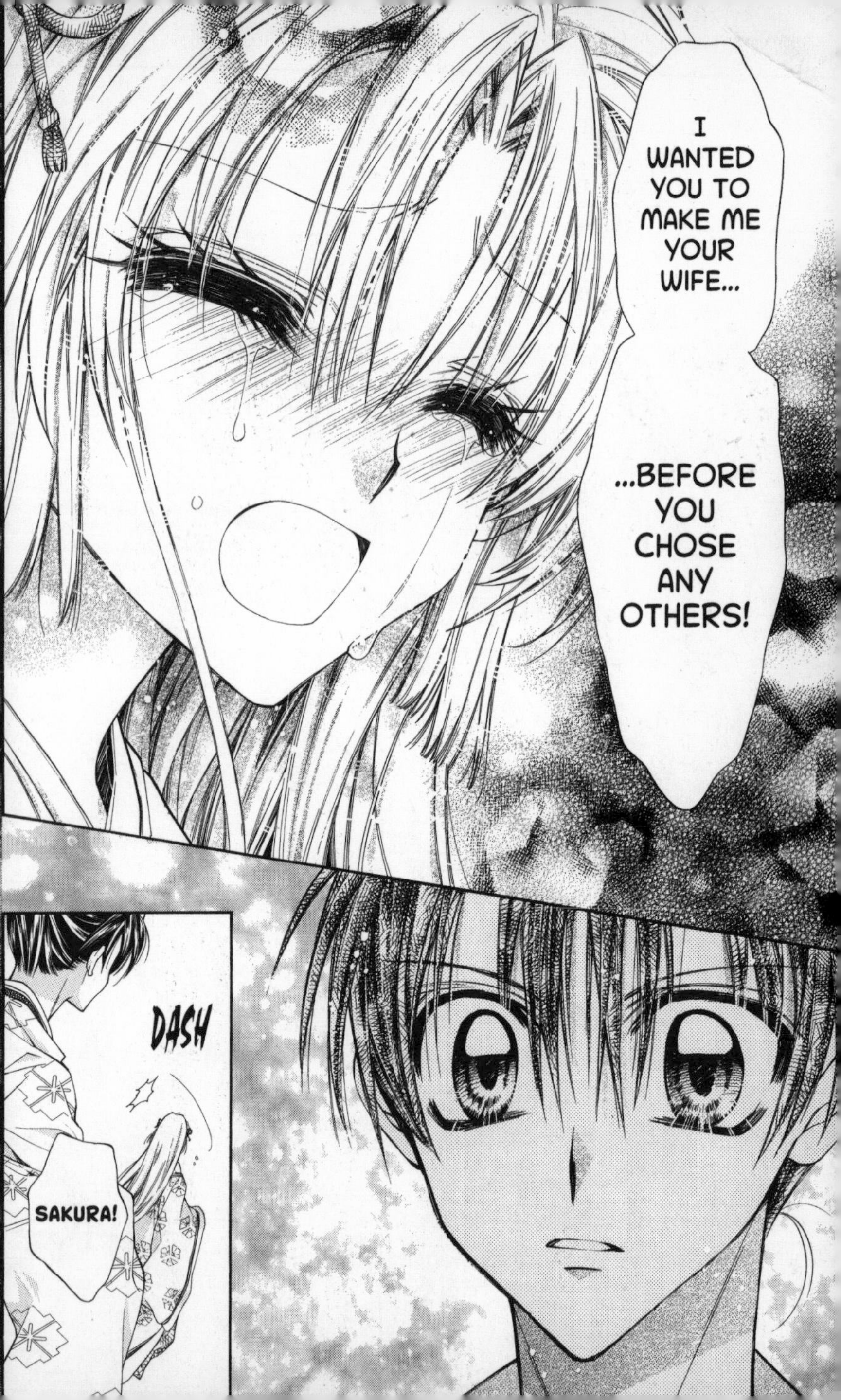
I WANTED YOU TO MAKE ME YOUR WIFE...
...BEFORE YOU CHOSE ANY OTHERS!
DASH
SAKURA!

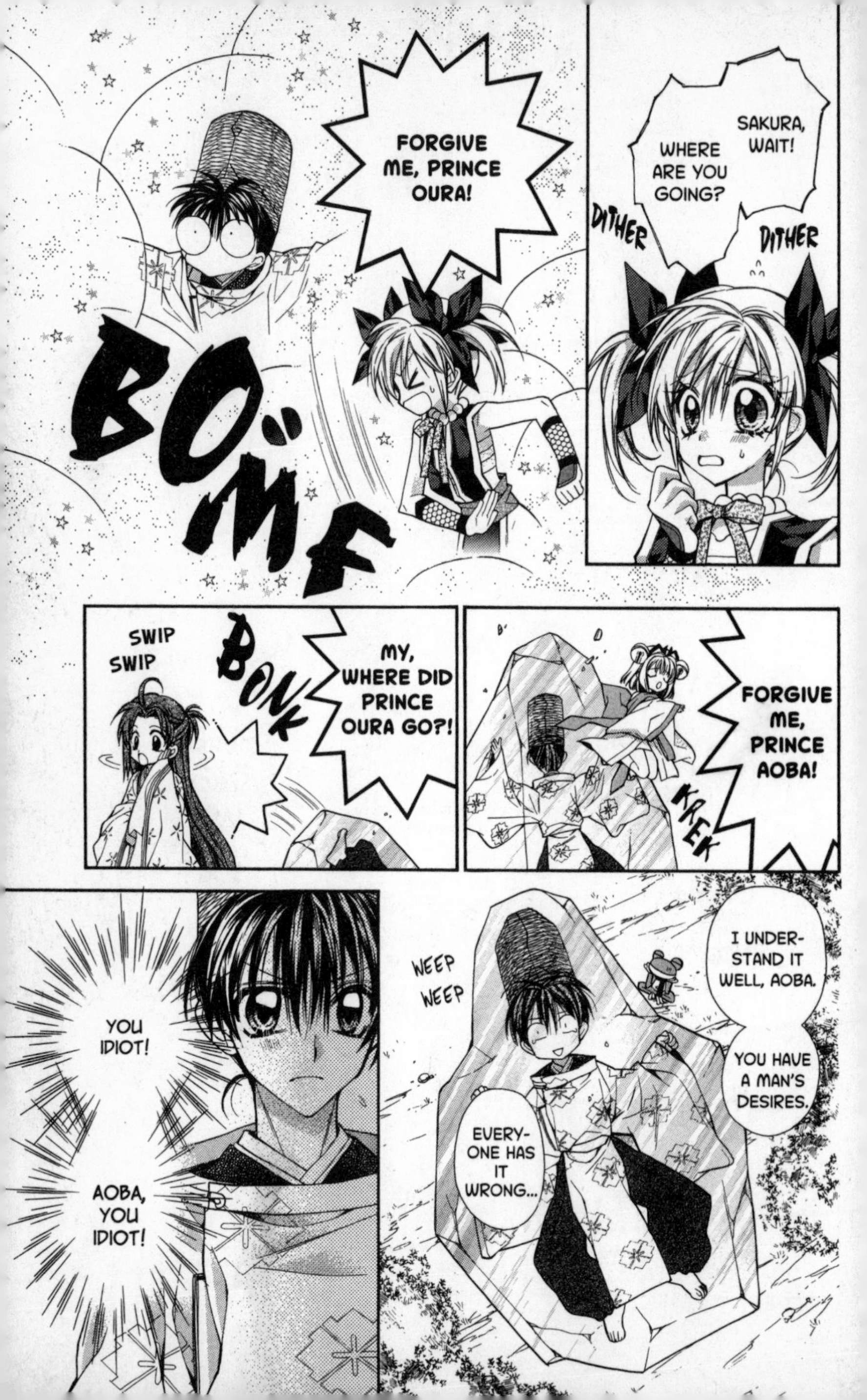
SAKURA, WAIT!
WHERE ARE YOU GOING?
DITHER
DITHER
FORGIVE ME, PRINCE OURA!
BOMF
FORGIVE ME, PRINCE AOBA!
KREK
SWIP SWIP
BONK
MY, WHERE DID PRINCE OURA GO?!
WEEP WEEP
I UNDERSTAND IT WELL, AOBA.
YOU HAVE A MAN'S DESIRES.
EVERYONE HAS IT WRONG...
YOU IDIOT!
AOBA, YOU IDIOT!

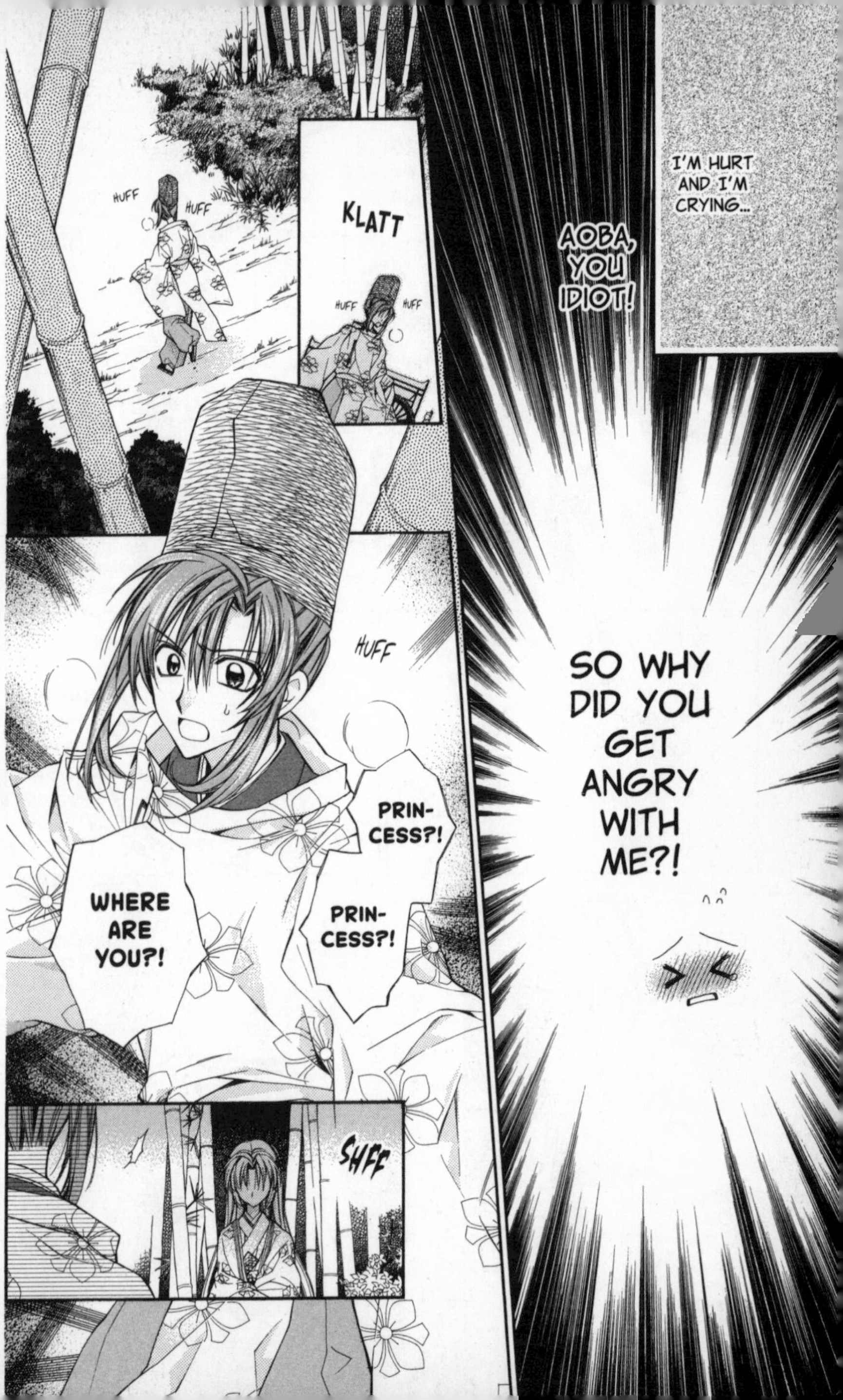
I'M HURT AND I'M CRYING...
AOBA, YOU IDIOT!
SO WHY DID YOU GET ANGRY WITH ME?!
KLATT
HUFF HUFF
HUFF HUFF
HUFF
PRIN-CESS?!
PRIN-CESS?!
WHERE ARE YOU?!
SHFF

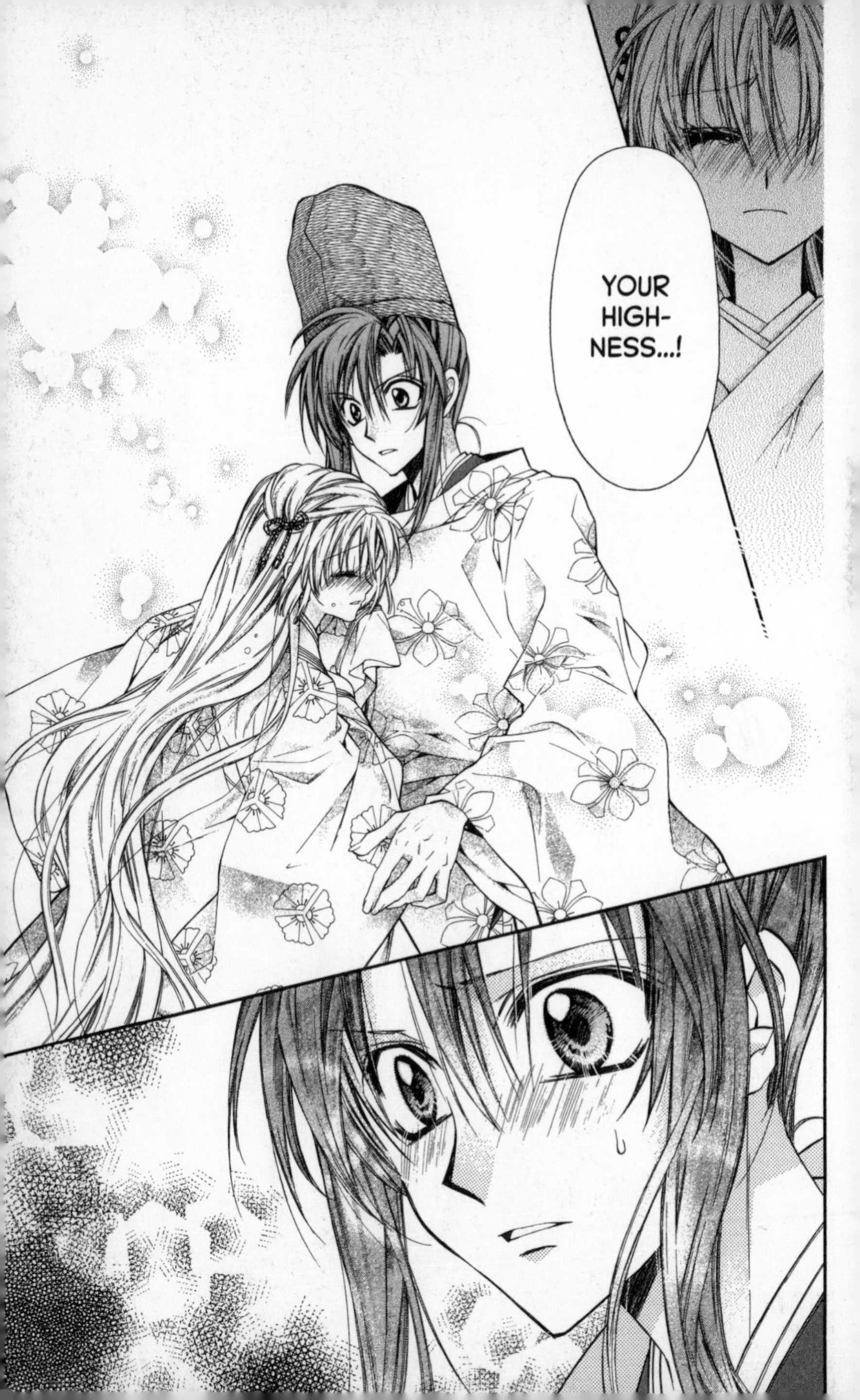
YOUR HIGH- NESS...!

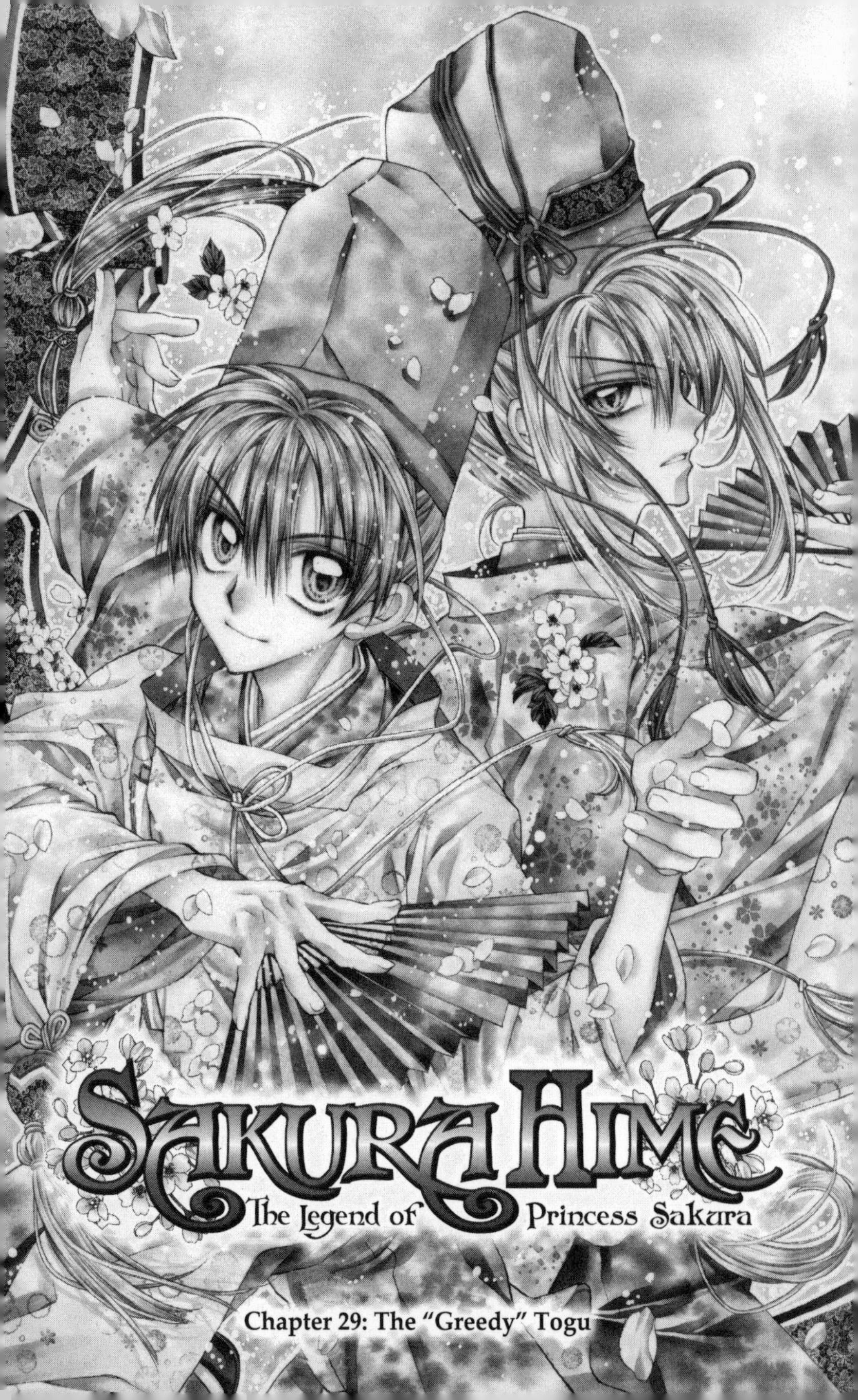
SAKURA HIME
The Legend of Princess Sakura
Chapter 29: The "Greedy" Togu

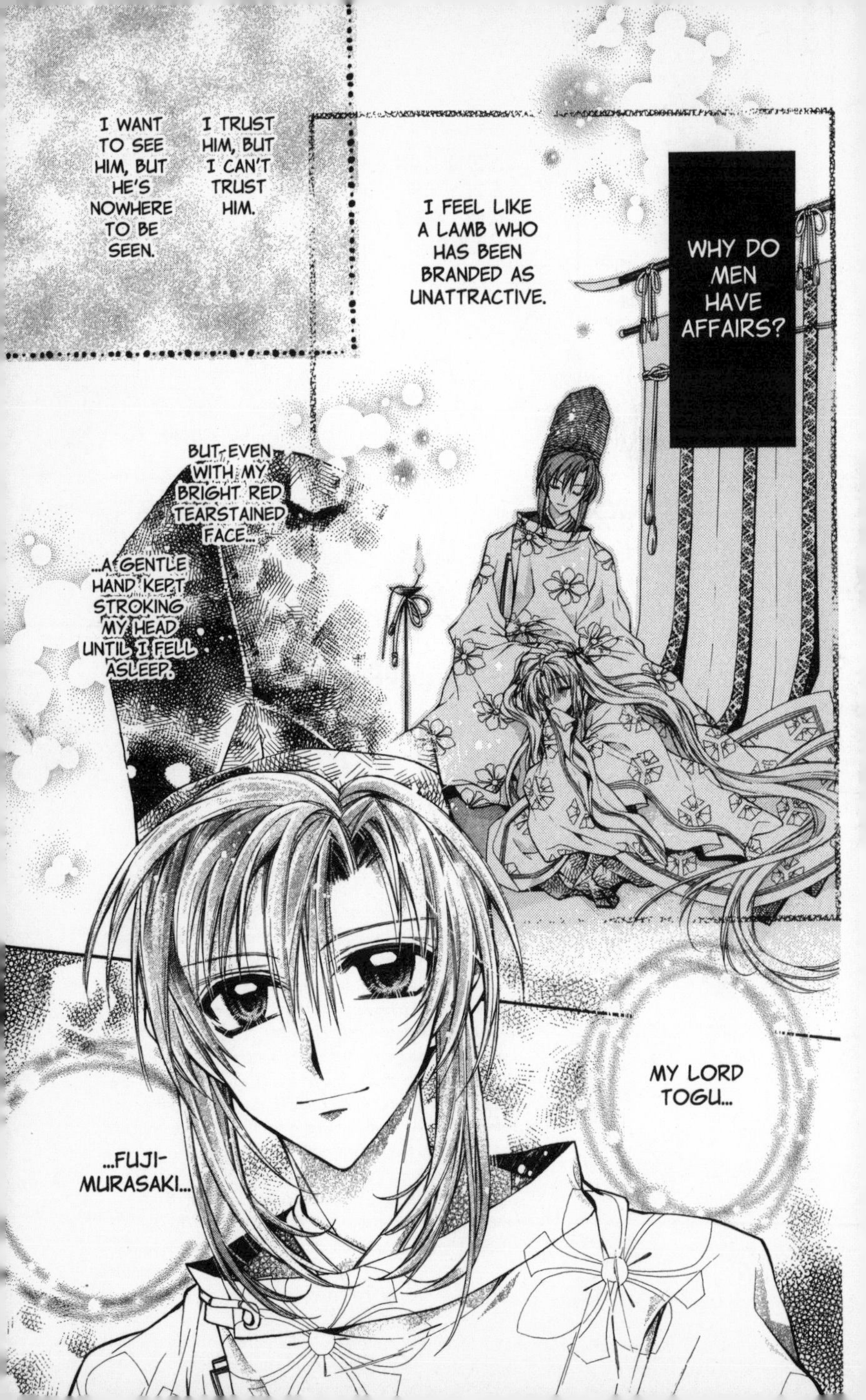
WHY DO MEN HAVE AFFAIRS?
I FEEL LIKE A LAMB WHO HAS BEEN BRANDED AS UNATTRACTIVE.
I TRUST HIM, BUT I CAN'T TRUST HIM.
I WANT TO SEE HIM, BUT HE'S NOWHERE TO BE SEEN.
BUT EVEN WITH MY BRIGHT RED TEARSTAINED FACE...
...A GENTLE HAND KEPT STROKING MY HEAD UNTIL I FELL ASLEEP.
MY LORD TOGU...
...FUJI-MURASAKI...

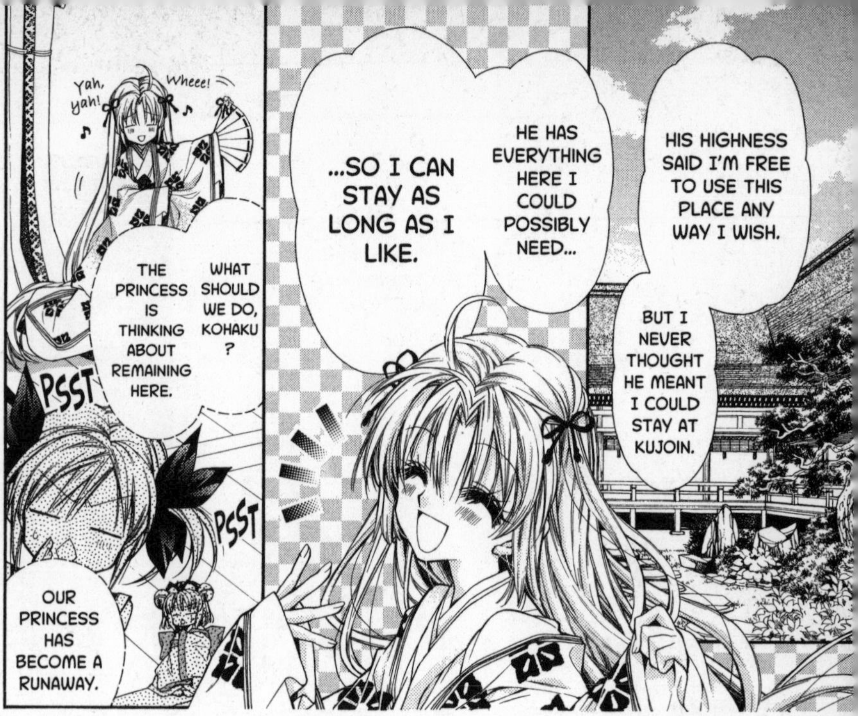
HIS HIGHNESS SAID I'M FREE TO USE THIS PLACE ANY WAY I WISH.
BUT I NEVER THOUGHT HE MEANT I COULD STAY AT KUJOIN.
HE HAS EVERYTHING HERE I COULD POSSIBLY NEED...
...SO I CAN STAY AS LONG AS I LIKE.
Wheee!
Yah, yah!
WHAT SHOULD WE DO, KOHAKU?
THE PRINCESS IS THINKING ABOUT REMAINING HERE.
PSST
PSST
OUR PRINCESS HAS BECOME A RUNAWAY.

Chapter 29: The "Greedy" Togu

※ I'm giving away the story.

This chapter... Well, basically I wanted to write about Lord Fujimurasaki's soul symbol in a side story, but as the story is developing in this way, I thought this was the perfect opportunity to share it. In here are Lord Fujimurasaki's thoughts that I have kept hidden all this time.
Some of his feelings I can relate to... That is, he reflects some of my thoughts. There are times when I empathize with someone too much, but on the other hand, there are times when I am extremely cool about things, and that makes me worry that I may be a coldhearted person. Lord Fujimurasaki's thoughts are a little different, but he too is unable to open up to other people about his worries. It's especially true in his case because he has been avoiding people after being misunderstood in regards to his soul symbol. I hope you will watch over him with a warm heart.

Thank you.

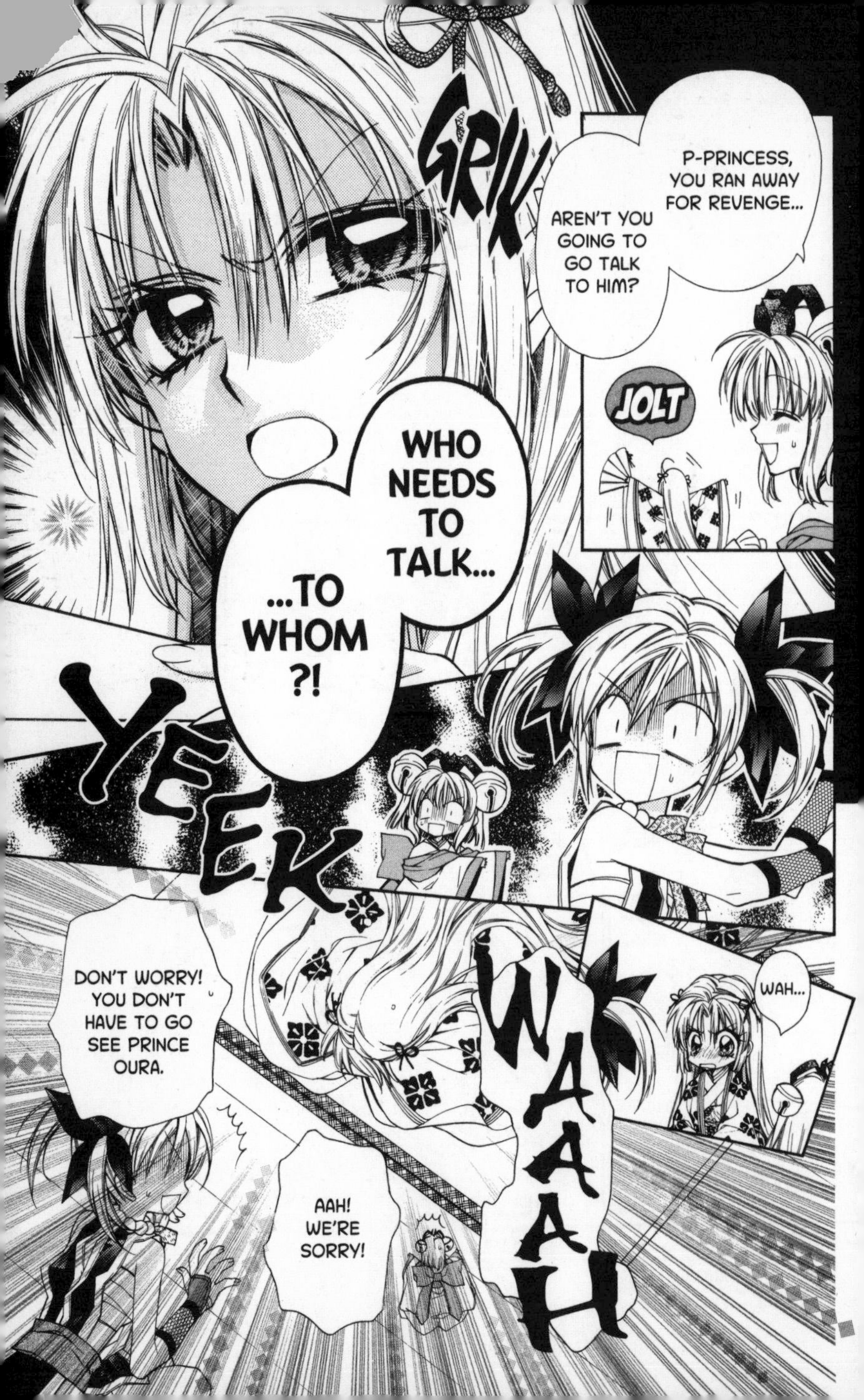
P-PRINCESS, YOU RAN AWAY FOR REVENGE...
AREN'T YOU GOING TO GO TALK TO HIM?
JOLT
GRIIK
WHO NEEDS TO TALK...
...TO WHOM?!
YEEK
WAH...
WAAAH
DON'T WORRY! YOU DON'T HAVE TO GO SEE PRINCE OURA.
AAH! WE'RE SORRY!

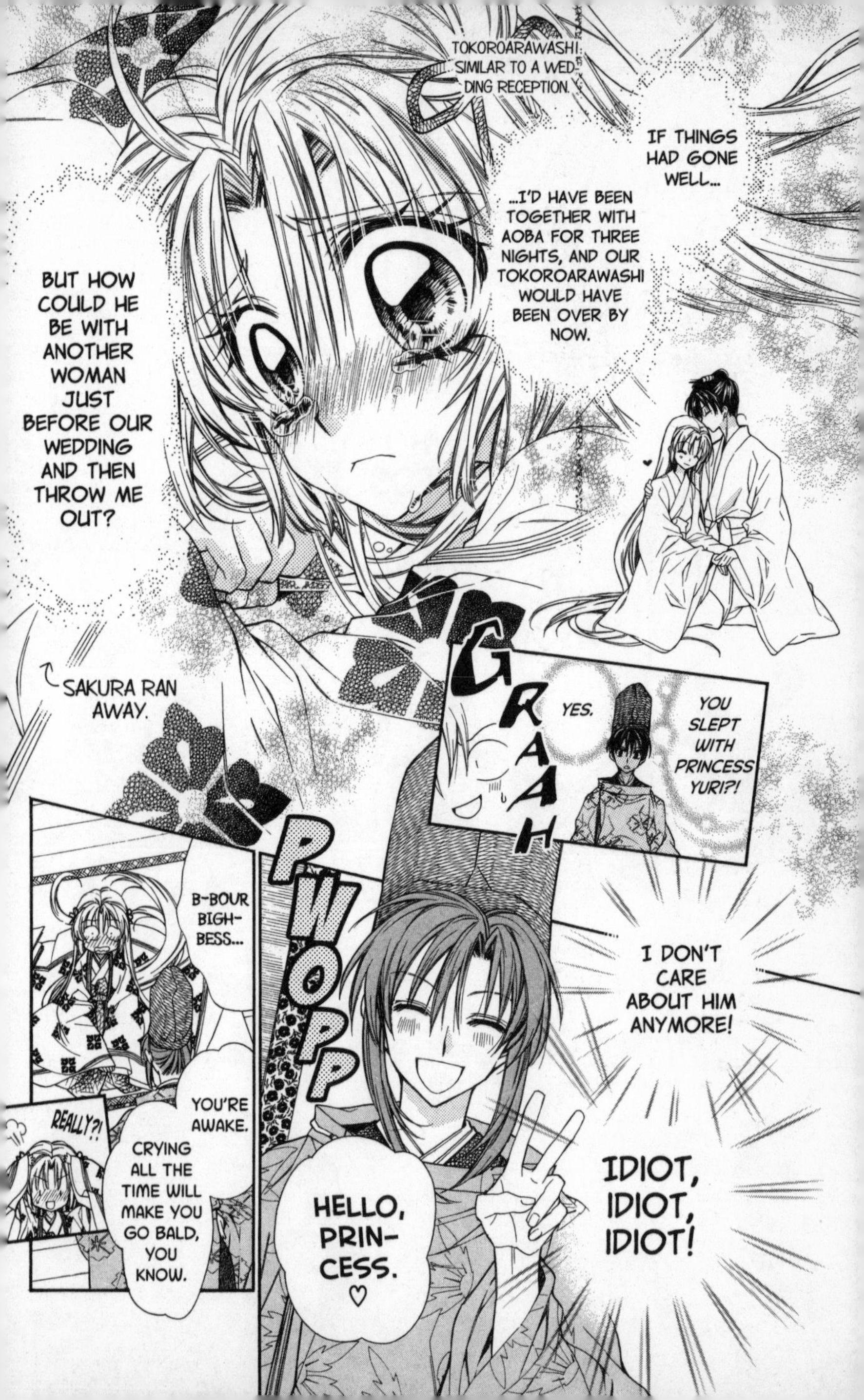
TOKOROARAWASHI: SIMILAR TO A WEDDING RECEPTION.
IF THINGS HAD GONE WELL...
...I'D HAVE BEEN TOGETHER WITH AOBA FOR THREE NIGHTS, AND OUR TOKOROARAWASHI WOULD HAVE BEEN OVER BY NOW.
BUT HOW COULD HE BE WITH ANOTHER WOMAN JUST BEFORE OUR WEDDING AND THEN THROW ME OUT?
SAKURA RAN AWAY.
YOU SLEPT WITH PRINCESS YURI?!
YES.
GRAAH
I DON'T CARE ABOUT HIM ANYMORE!
IDIOT, IDIOT, IDIOT!
PWOPP
HELLO, PRINCESS. ♡
YOU'RE AWAKE.
CRYING ALL THE TIME WILL MAKE YOU GO BALD, YOU KNOW.
B-BOUR BIGH-BESS...
REALLY?!

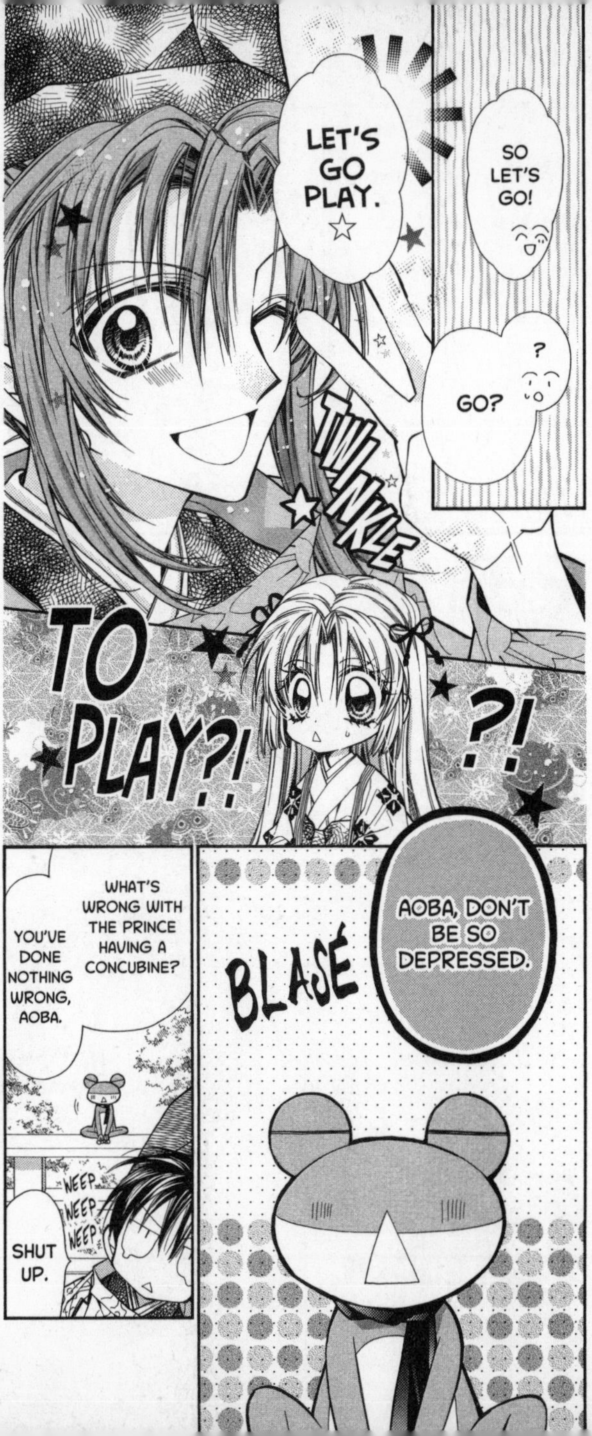
SO LET'S GO!
GO?
?
LET'S GO PLAY. ☆
TWINKLE
TO PLAY?!
?!
AOBA, DON'T BE SO DEPRESSED.
BLASÉ
WHAT'S WRONG WITH THE PRINCE HAVING A CONCUBINE?
YOU'VE DONE NOTHING WRONG, AOBA.
WEEP WEEP WEEP
SHUT UP.

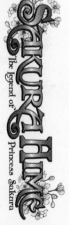

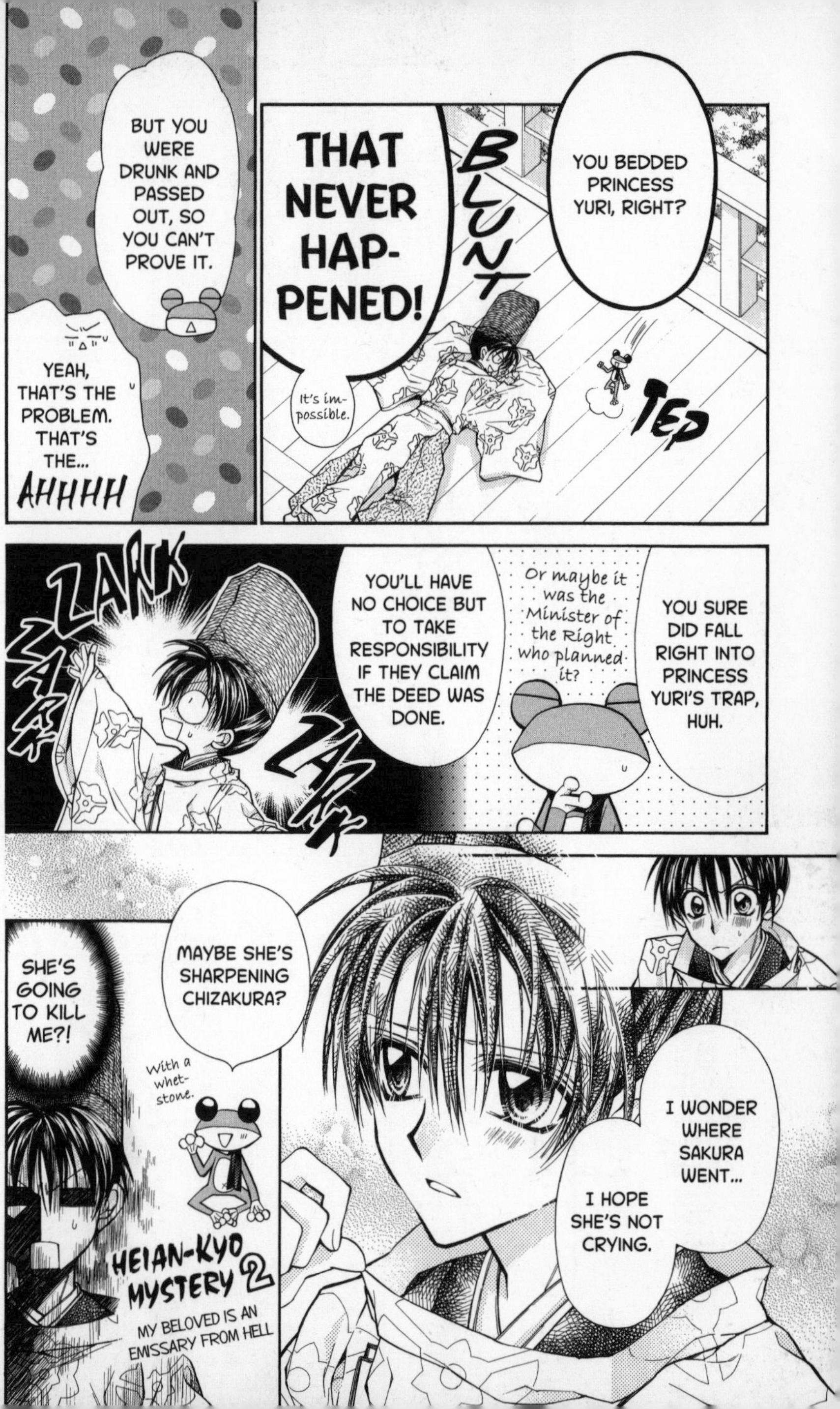
YOU BEDDED PRINCESS YURI, RIGHT?
TEP
BLUNT
THAT NEVER HAP-PENED!
It's impossible.
BUT YOU WERE DRUNK AND PASSED OUT, SO YOU CAN'T PROVE IT.
YEAH, THAT'S THE PROBLEM. THAT'S THE...
AHHHH
YOU SURE DID FALL RIGHT INTO PRINCESS YURI'S TRAP, HUH.
Or maybe it was the Minister of the Right who planned it?
YOU'LL HAVE NO CHOICE BUT TO TAKE RESPONSIBILITY IF THEY CLAIM THE DEED WAS DONE.
ZAKK
ZAKK
ZAKK
I WONDER WHERE SAKURA WENT...
I HOPE SHE'S NOT CRYING.
MAYBE SHE'S SHARPENING CHIZAKURA?
With a whet-stone.
SHE'S GOING TO KILL ME?!
HEIAN-KYO MYSTERY 2
MY BELOVED IS AN EMISSARY FROM HELL

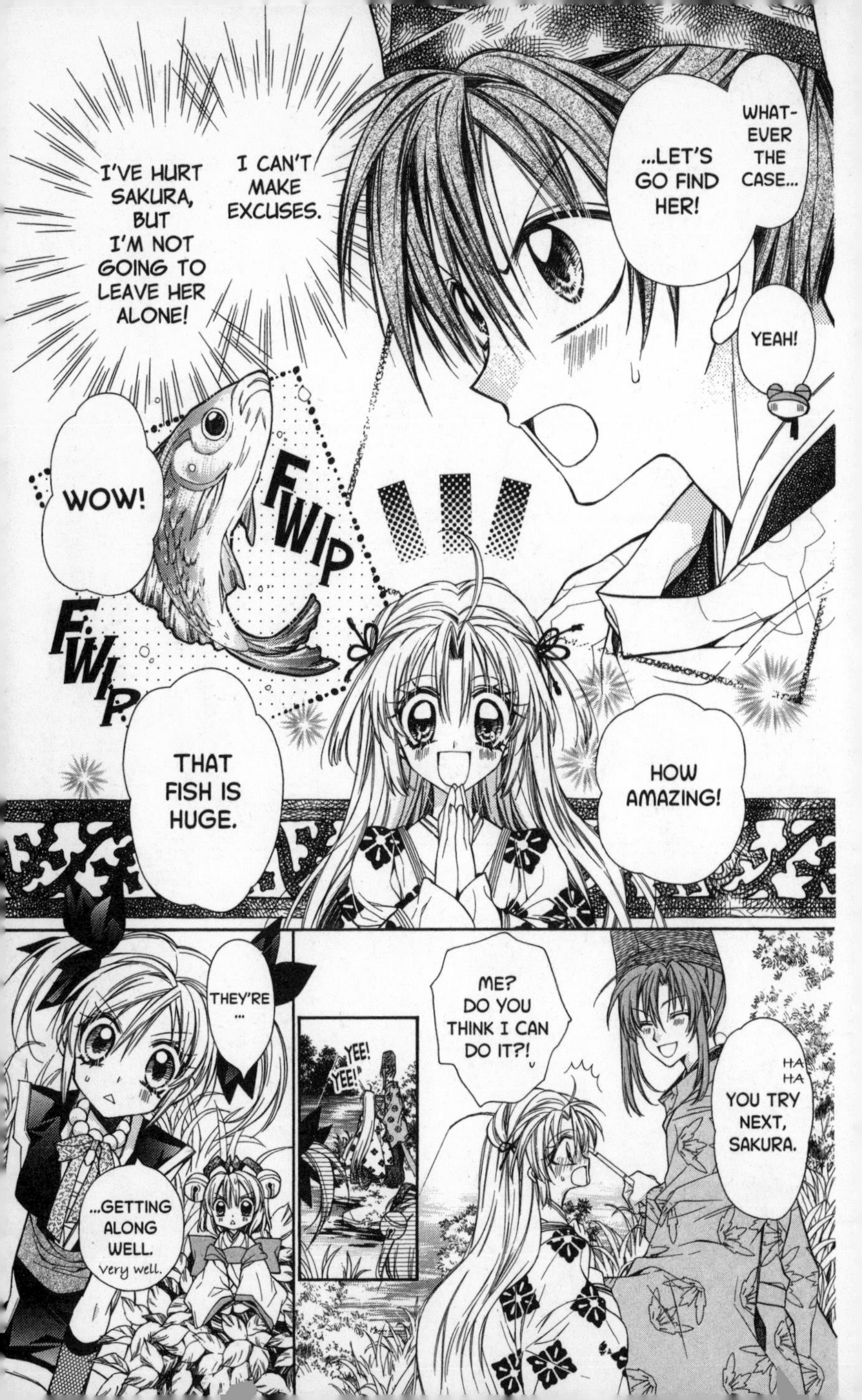
WHAT-EVER THE CASE...
...LET'S GO FIND HER!
YEAH!
I CAN'T MAKE EXCUSES.
I'VE HURT SAKURA, BUT I'M NOT GOING TO LEAVE HER ALONE!
WOW!
FWIP
FWIP
HOW AMAZING!
THAT FISH IS HUGE.
HA HA
YOU TRY NEXT, SAKURA.
ME? DO YOU THINK I CAN DO IT?!
YEE! YEE!
THEY'RE...
...GETTING ALONG WELL.
Very well.

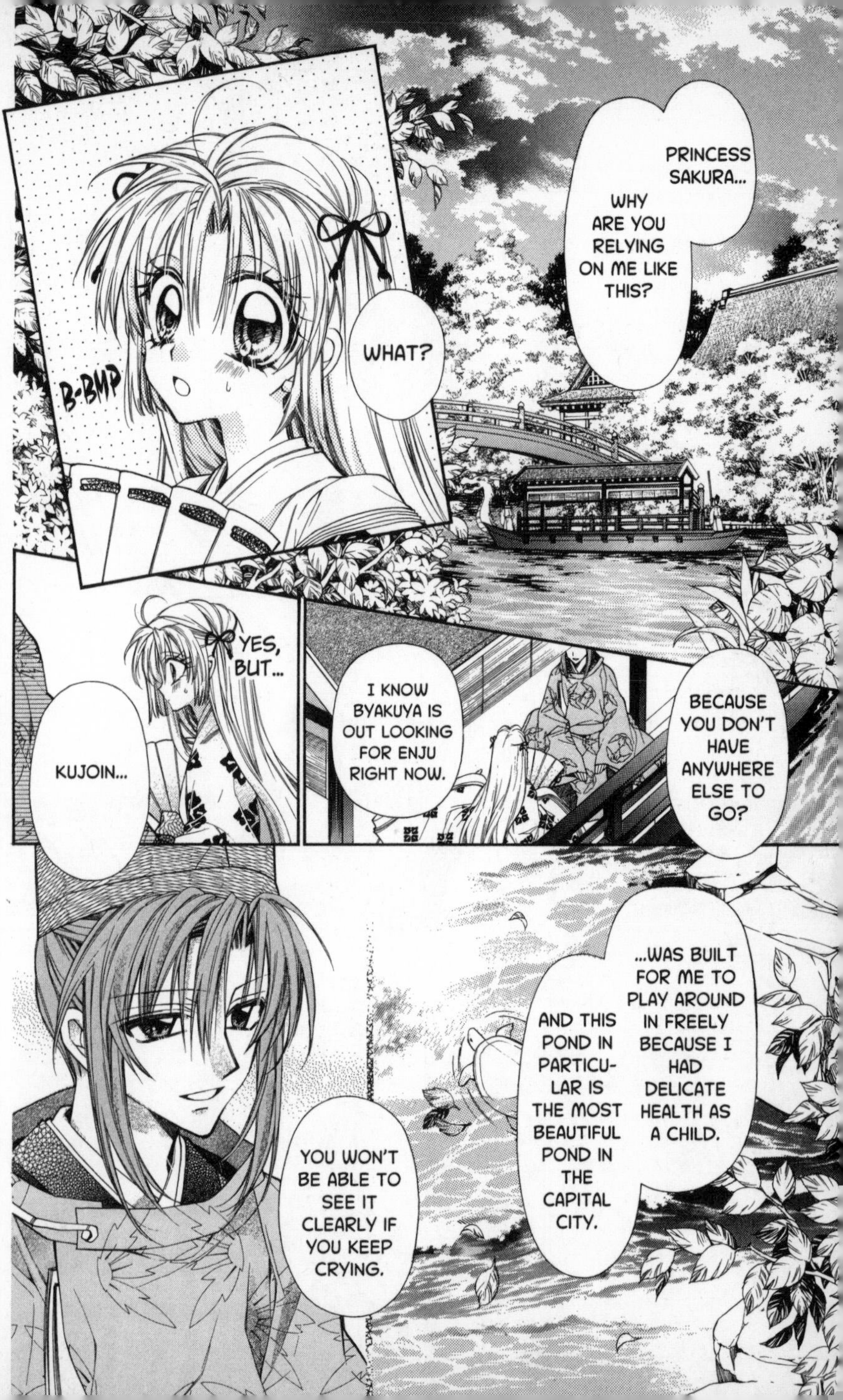
PRINCESS SAKURA...
WHY ARE YOU RELYING ON ME LIKE THIS?
WHAT?
B-BMP
BECAUSE YOU DON'T HAVE ANYWHERE ELSE TO GO?
I KNOW BYAKUYA IS OUT LOOKING FOR ENJU RIGHT NOW.
YES, BUT...
KUJOIN...
...WAS BUILT FOR ME TO PLAY AROUND IN FREELY BECAUSE I HAD DELICATE HEALTH AS A CHILD.
AND THIS POND IN PARTICULAR IS THE MOST BEAUTIFUL POND IN THE CAPITAL CITY.
YOU WON'T BE ABLE TO SEE IT CLEARLY IF YOU KEEP CRYING.

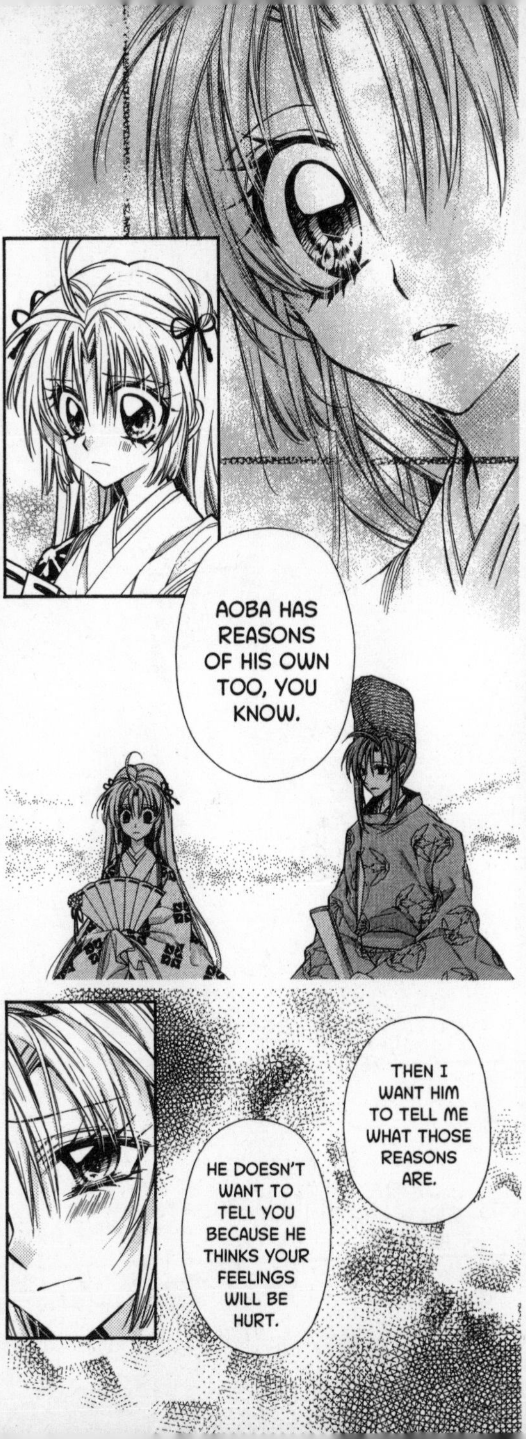
AOBA HAS REASONS OF HIS OWN TOO, YOU KNOW.
THEN I WANT HIM TO TELL ME WHAT THOSE REASONS ARE.
HE DOESN'T WANT TO TELL YOU BECAUSE HE THINKS YOUR FEELINGS WILL BE HURT.

Embarrassed

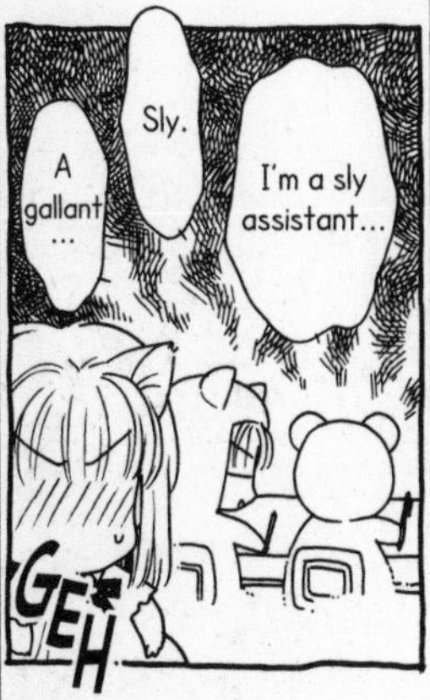
I'm a sly assistant...
Sly.
A gallant...
GEH

As you can see above, my assistants try to embarrass me by using phrases from the manga while working on it. (laugh)

Sooner or later, they'll start saying, "The sly sensei. The sly and...gallant..."

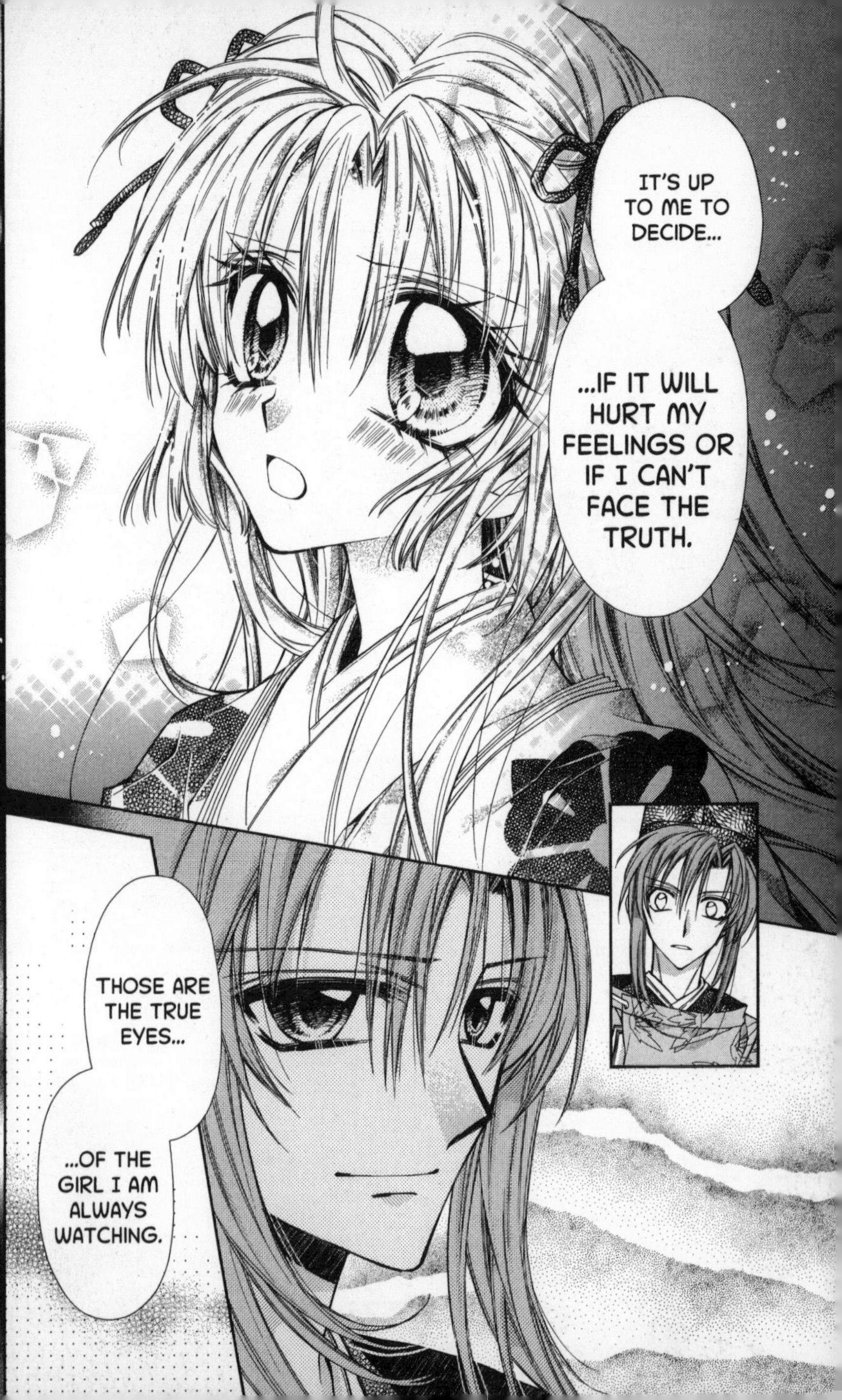
IT'S UP TO ME TO DECIDE...
...IF IT WILL HURT MY FEELINGS OR IF I CAN'T FACE THE TRUTH.
THOSE ARE THE TRUE EYES...
...OF THE GIRL I AM ALWAYS WATCHING.

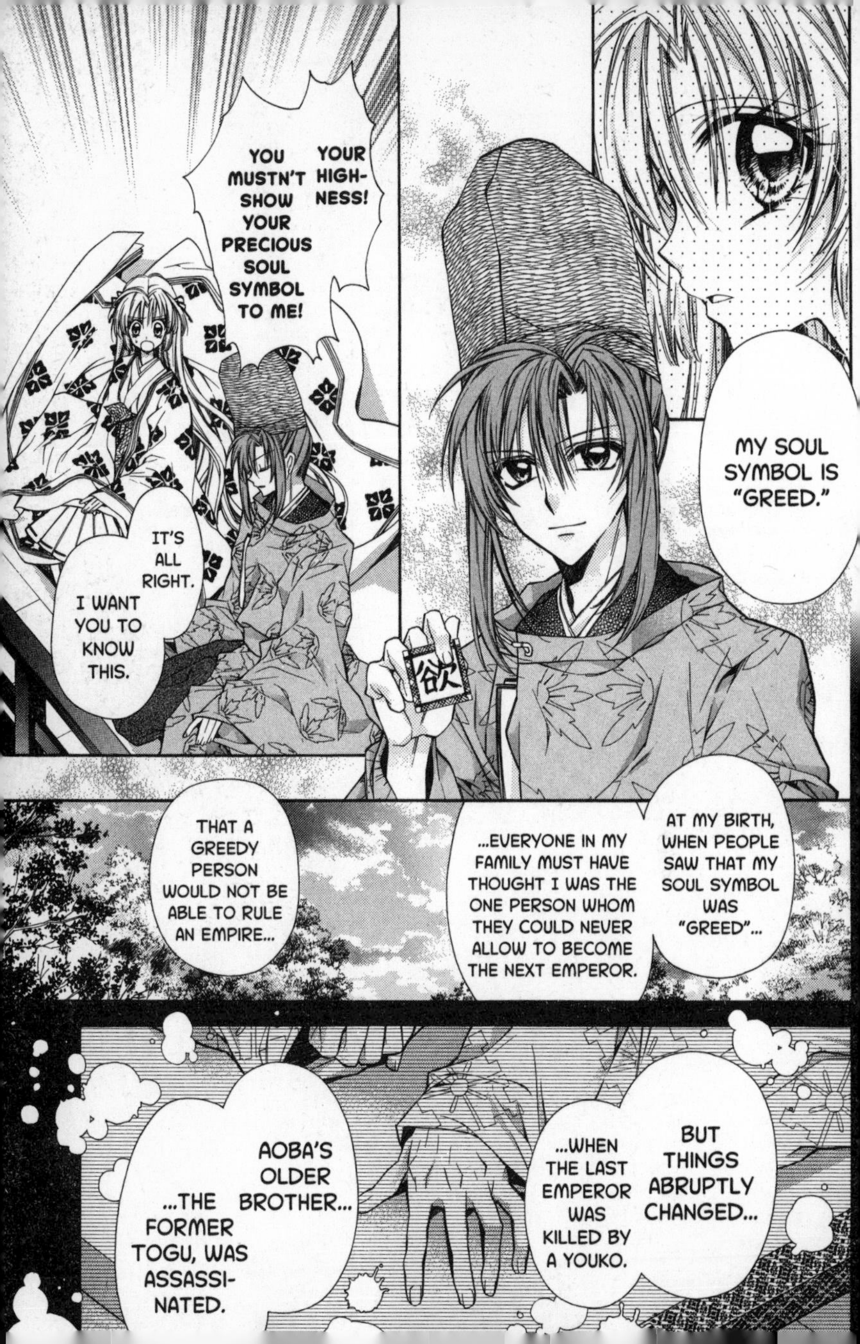
MY SOUL SYMBOL IS "GREED."
欲
YOUR HIGHNESS!
YOU MUSTN'T SHOW YOUR PRECIOUS SOUL SYMBOL TO ME!
IT'S ALL RIGHT. I WANT YOU TO KNOW THIS.
AT MY BIRTH, WHEN PEOPLE SAW THAT MY SOUL SYMBOL WAS "GREED"...
...EVERYONE IN MY FAMILY MUST HAVE THOUGHT I WAS THE ONE PERSON WHOM THEY COULD NEVER ALLOW TO BECOME THE NEXT EMPEROR.
THAT A GREEDY PERSON WOULD NOT BE ABLE TO RULE AN EMPIRE...
BUT THINGS ABRUPTLY CHANGED...
...WHEN THE LAST EMPEROR WAS KILLED BY A YOUKO.
AOBA'S OLDER BROTHER...
...THE FORMER TOGU, WAS ASSASSINATED.

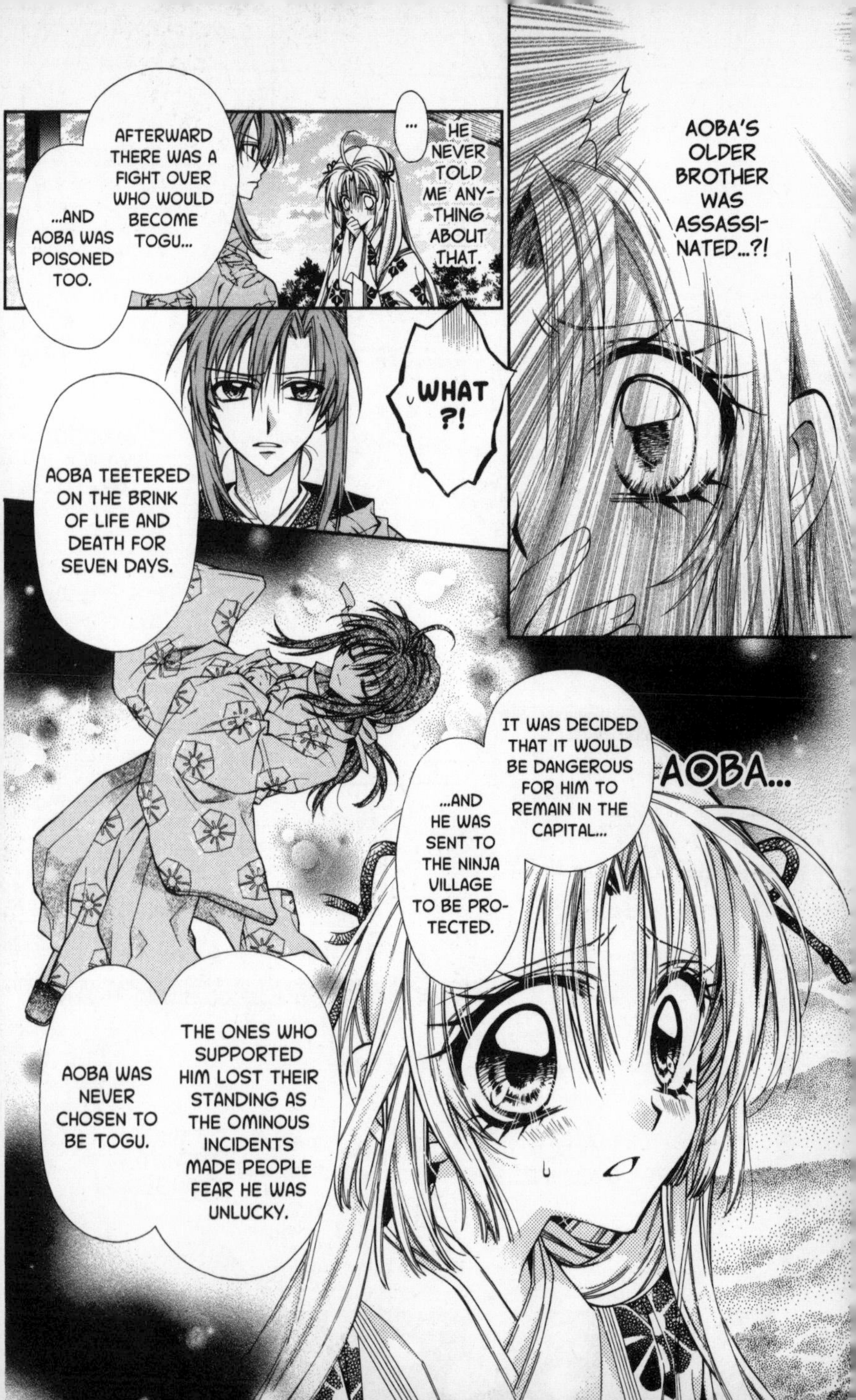
AOBA'S OLDER BROTHER WAS ASSASSI-NATED...?!
...
HE NEVER TOLD ME ANY-THING ABOUT THAT.
AFTERWARD THERE WAS A FIGHT OVER WHO WOULD BECOME TOGU...
...AND AOBA WAS POISONED TOO.
WHAT ?!
AOBA TEETERED ON THE BRINK OF LIFE AND DEATH FOR SEVEN DAYS.
AOBA...
IT WAS DECIDED THAT IT WOULD BE DANGEROUS FOR HIM TO REMAIN IN THE CAPITAL...
...AND HE WAS SENT TO THE NINJA VILLAGE TO BE PRO-TECTED.
THE ONES WHO SUPPORTED HIM LOST THEIR STANDING AS THE OMINOUS INCIDENTS MADE PEOPLE FEAR HE WAS UNLUCKY.
AOBA WAS NEVER CHOSEN TO BE TOGU.

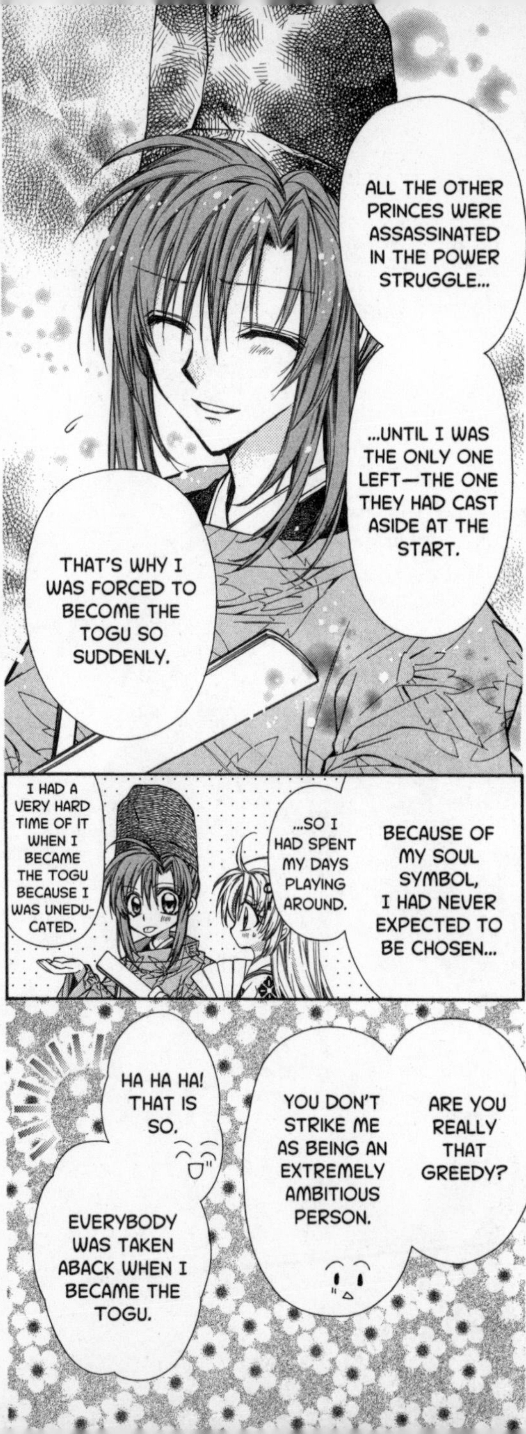
ALL THE OTHER PRINCES WERE ASSASSINATED IN THE POWER STRUGGLE...
...UNTIL I WAS THE ONLY ONE LEFT—THE ONE THEY HAD CAST ASIDE AT THE START.
THAT'S WHY I WAS FORCED TO BECOME THE TOGU SO SUDDENLY.
BECAUSE OF MY SOUL SYMBOL, I HAD NEVER EXPECTED TO BE CHOSEN...
...SO I HAD SPENT MY DAYS PLAYING AROUND.
I HAD A VERY HARD TIME OF IT WHEN I BECAME THE TOGU BECAUSE I WAS UNEDUCATED.
ARE YOU REALLY THAT GREEDY?
YOU DON'T STRIKE ME AS BEING AN EXTREMELY AMBITIOUS PERSON.
HA HA HA! THAT IS SO.
EVERYBODY WAS TAKEN ABACK WHEN I BECAME THE TOGU.

Afterword

You'll find a side story for *I.O.N* at the end of this volume. When I counted, it had been thirteen years since I had created anything new for this series. I reread the manga and tried to make my artwork look similar to it again. I put a lot of work into that because I didn't want to destroy the "mood" of the original series. I hope you enjoy it.

✿ Special Thanks ✿

Nakame

Kawanishi-san Mari
Momoko-chan Kawamura-san
Itakura-san Ikurun
Minami-san Konako
Yuki-chan Momo-san

Shueisha, Ribon

Fujikawa-san
Kunta-san

Kawatani-san

Sobisha

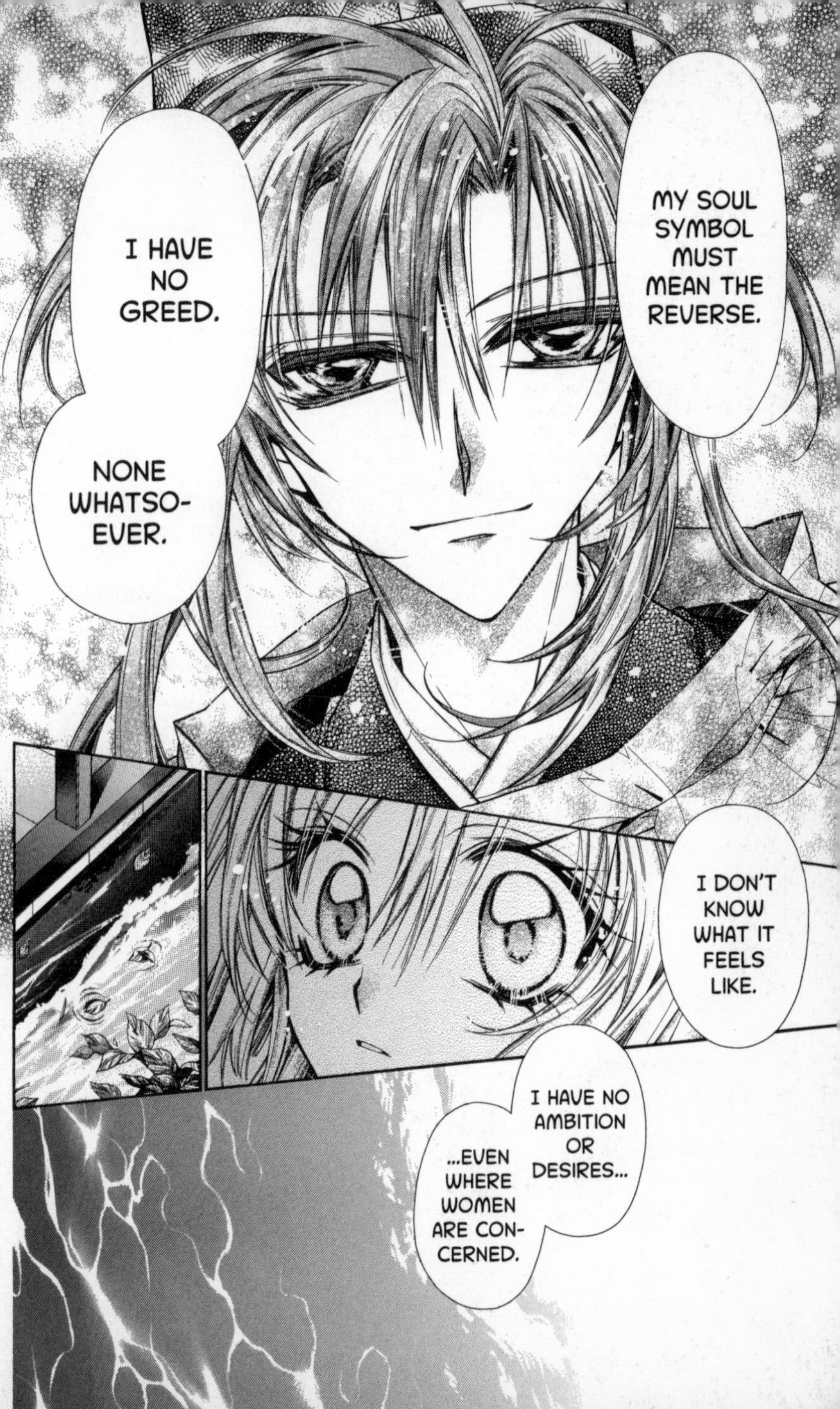
MY SOUL SYMBOL MUST MEAN THE REVERSE.
I HAVE NO GREED.
NONE WHATSO-EVER.
I DON'T KNOW WHAT IT FEELS LIKE.
I HAVE NO AMBITION OR DESIRES...
...EVEN WHERE WOMEN ARE CON-CERNED.

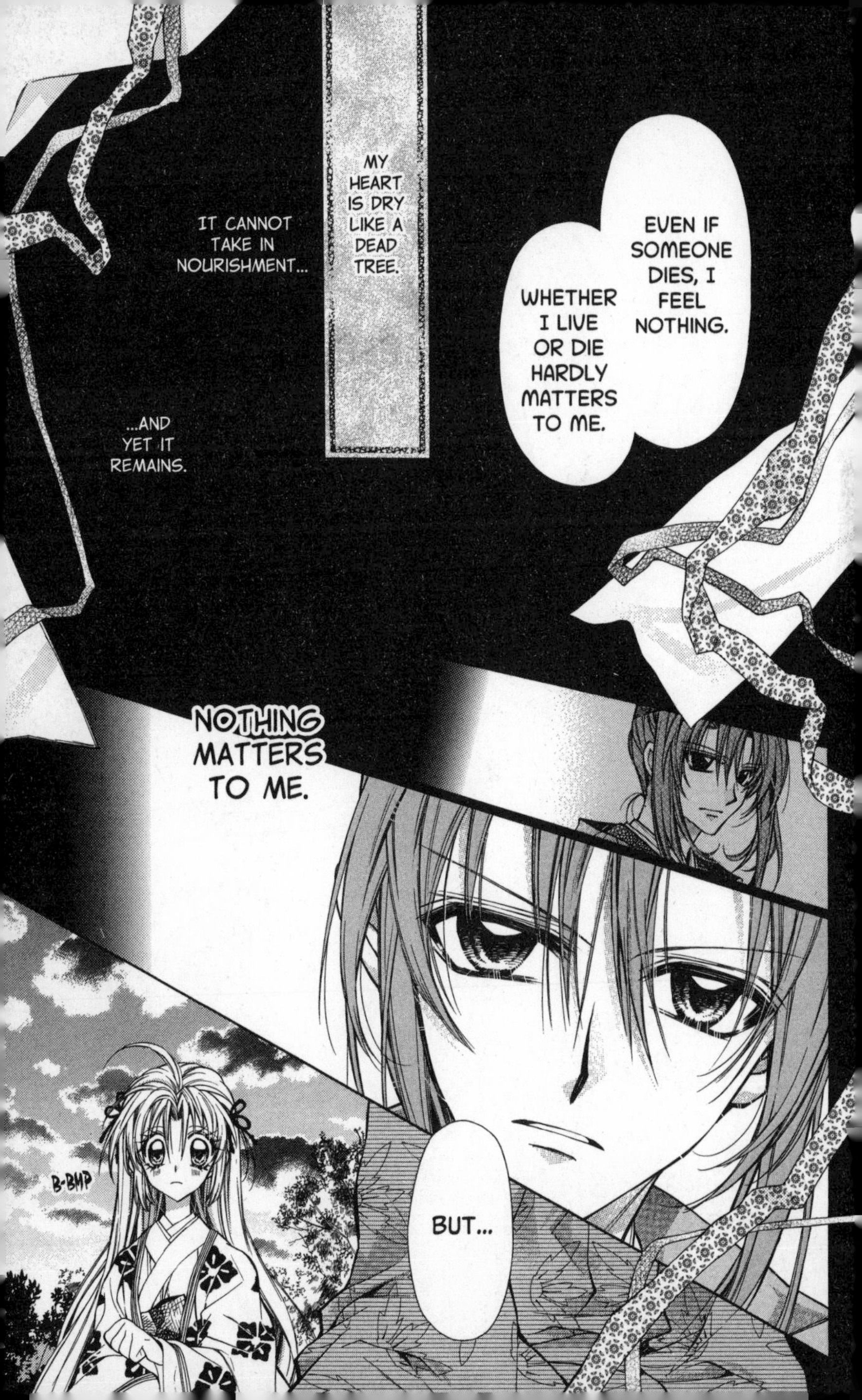
EVEN IF SOMEONE DIES, I FEEL NOTHING.
WHETHER I LIVE OR DIE HARDLY MATTERS TO ME.
MY HEART IS DRY LIKE A DEAD TREE.
IT CANNOT TAKE IN NOURISHMENT...
...AND YET IT REMAINS.
NOTHING MATTERS TO ME.
BUT...
B-BMP

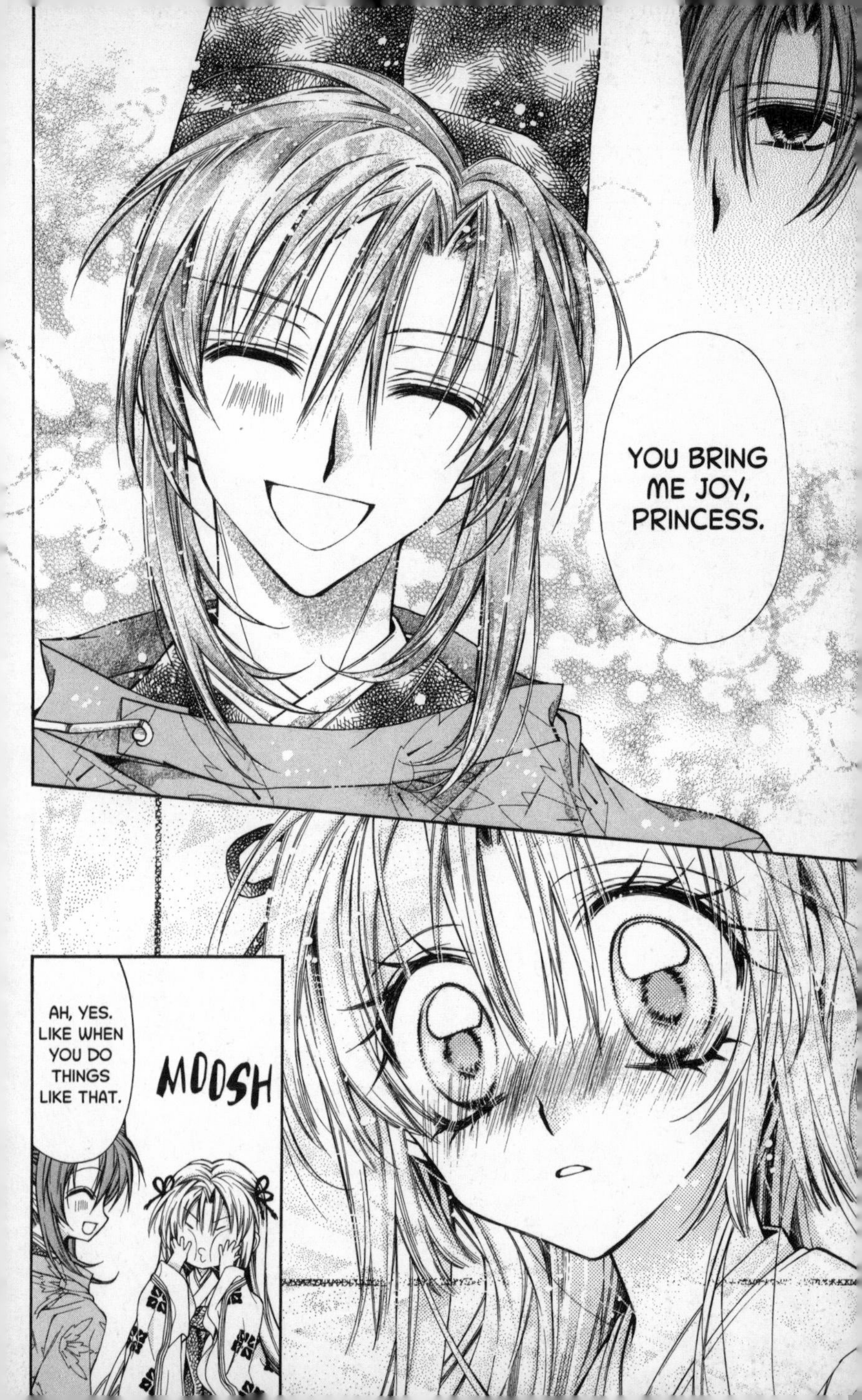
YOU BRING ME JOY, PRINCESS.
AH, YES. LIKE WHEN YOU DO THINGS LIKE THAT.
MOOSH

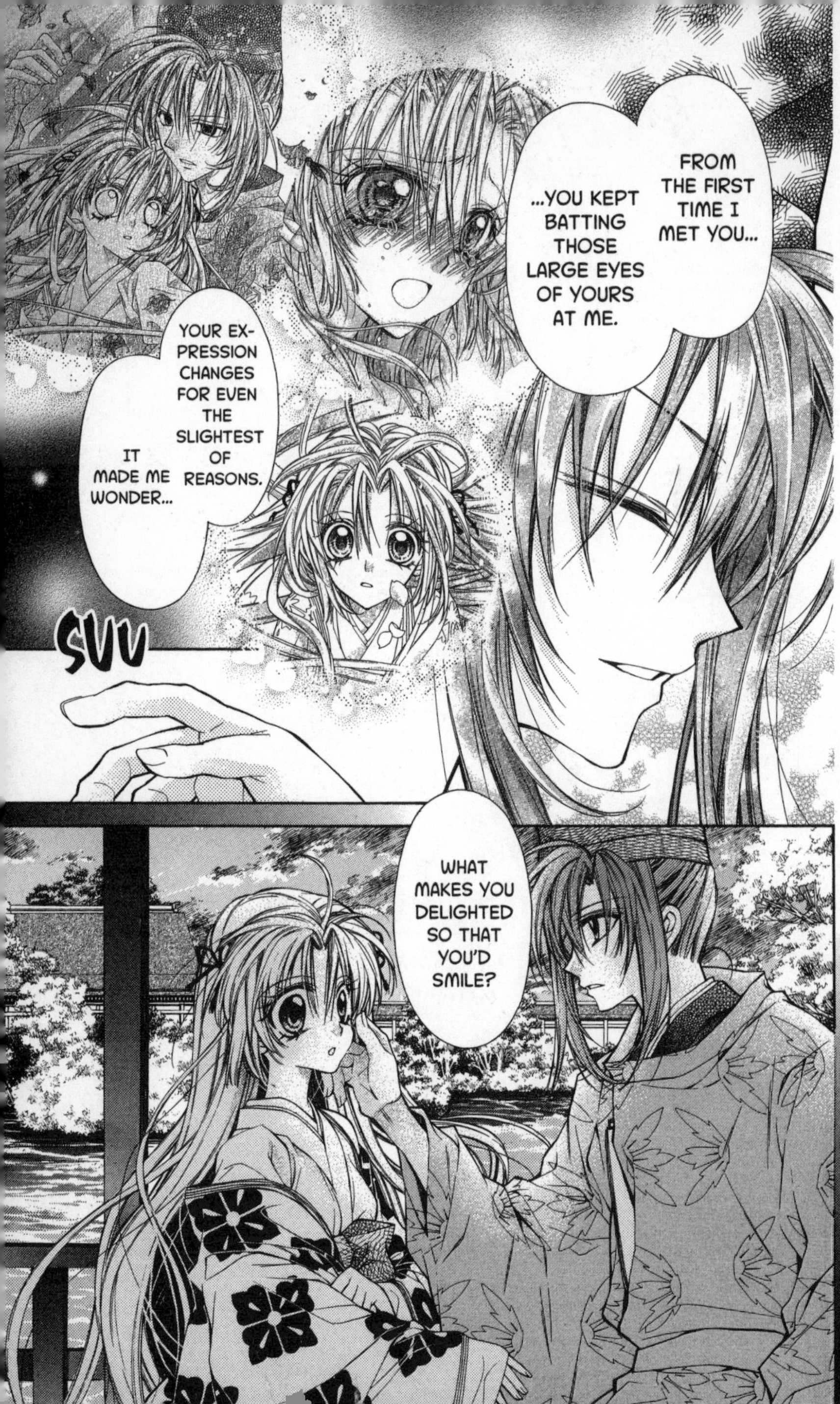
FROM THE FIRST TIME I MET YOU...
...YOU KEPT BATTING THOSE LARGE EYES OF YOURS AT ME.
YOUR EX-PRESSION CHANGES FOR EVEN THE SLIGHTEST OF REASONS.
IT MADE ME WONDER...
SVU
WHAT MAKES YOU DELIGHTED SO THAT YOU'D SMILE?

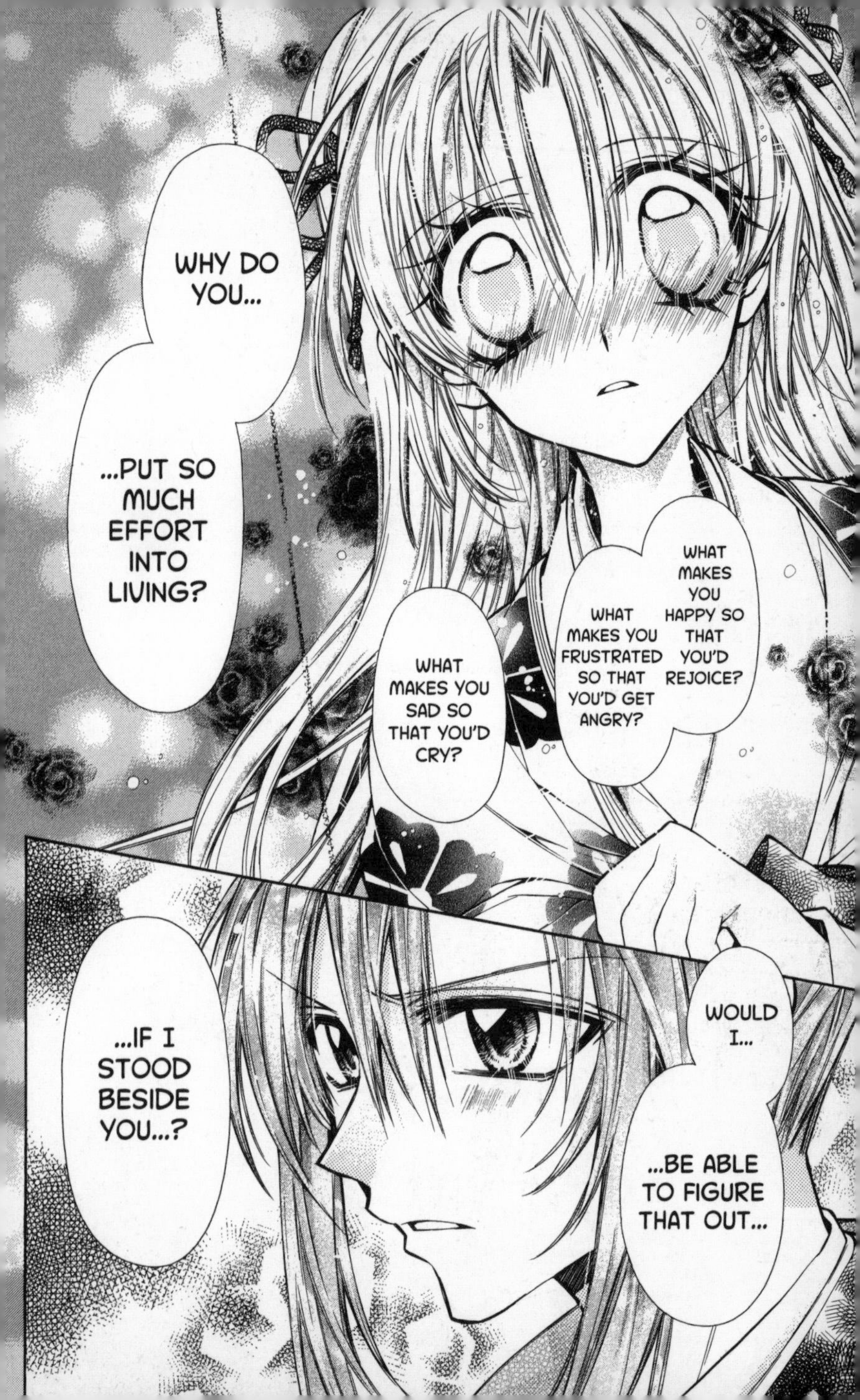
WHY DO YOU...
...PUT SO MUCH EFFORT INTO LIVING?
WHAT MAKES YOU HAPPY SO THAT YOU'D REJOICE?
WHAT MAKES YOU FRUSTRATED SO THAT YOU'D GET ANGRY?
WHAT MAKES YOU SAD SO THAT YOU'D CRY?
WOULD I...
...BE ABLE TO FIGURE THAT OUT...
...IF I STOOD BESIDE YOU...?

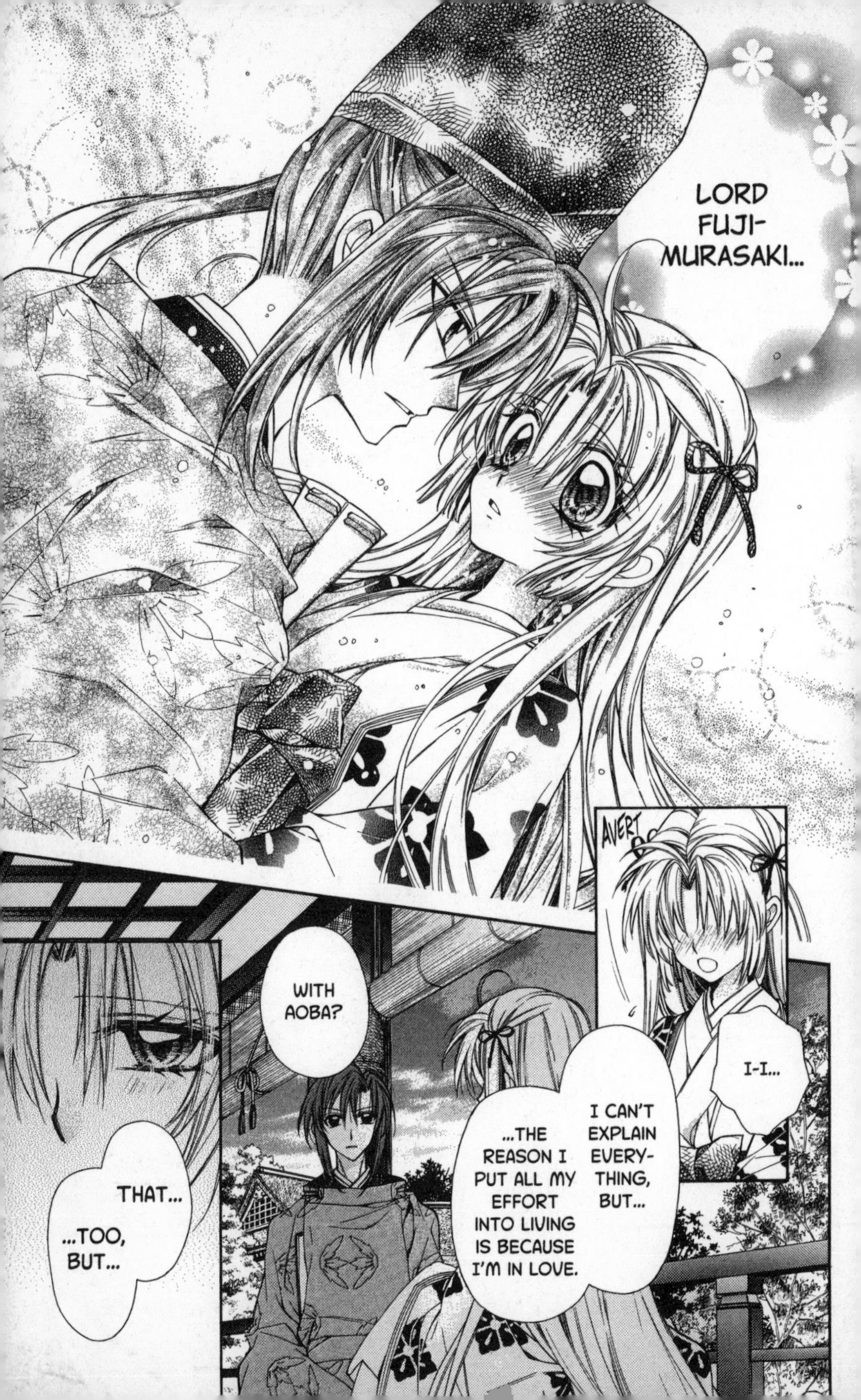
LORD FUJI-MURASAKI...
AVERT
I-I...
I CAN'T EXPLAIN EVERY-THING, BUT...
...THE REASON I PUT ALL MY EFFORT INTO LIVING IS BECAUSE I'M IN LOVE.
WITH AOBA?
THAT...
...TOO, BUT...

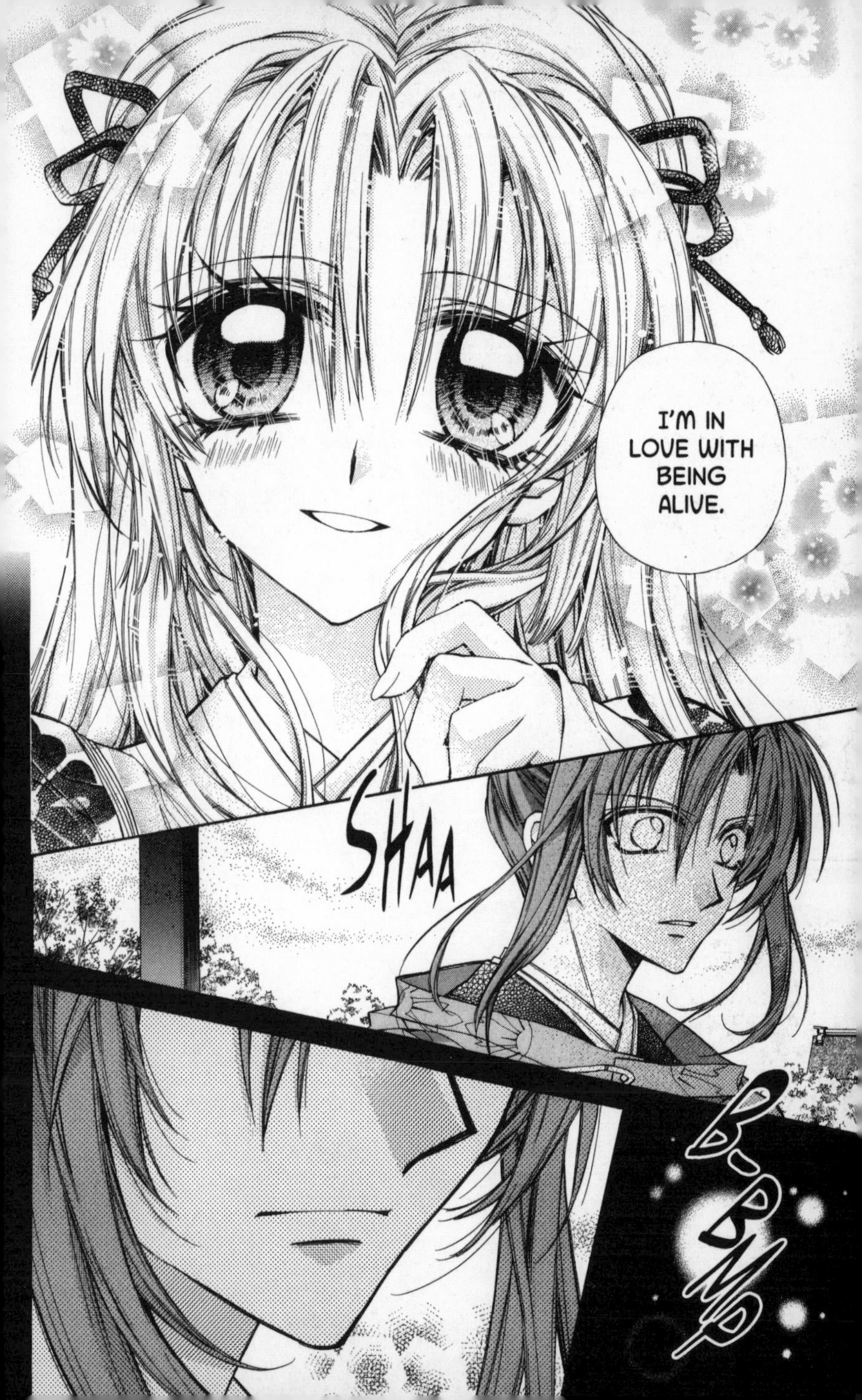
I'M IN LOVE WITH BEING ALIVE.
SHAA
B-BMP

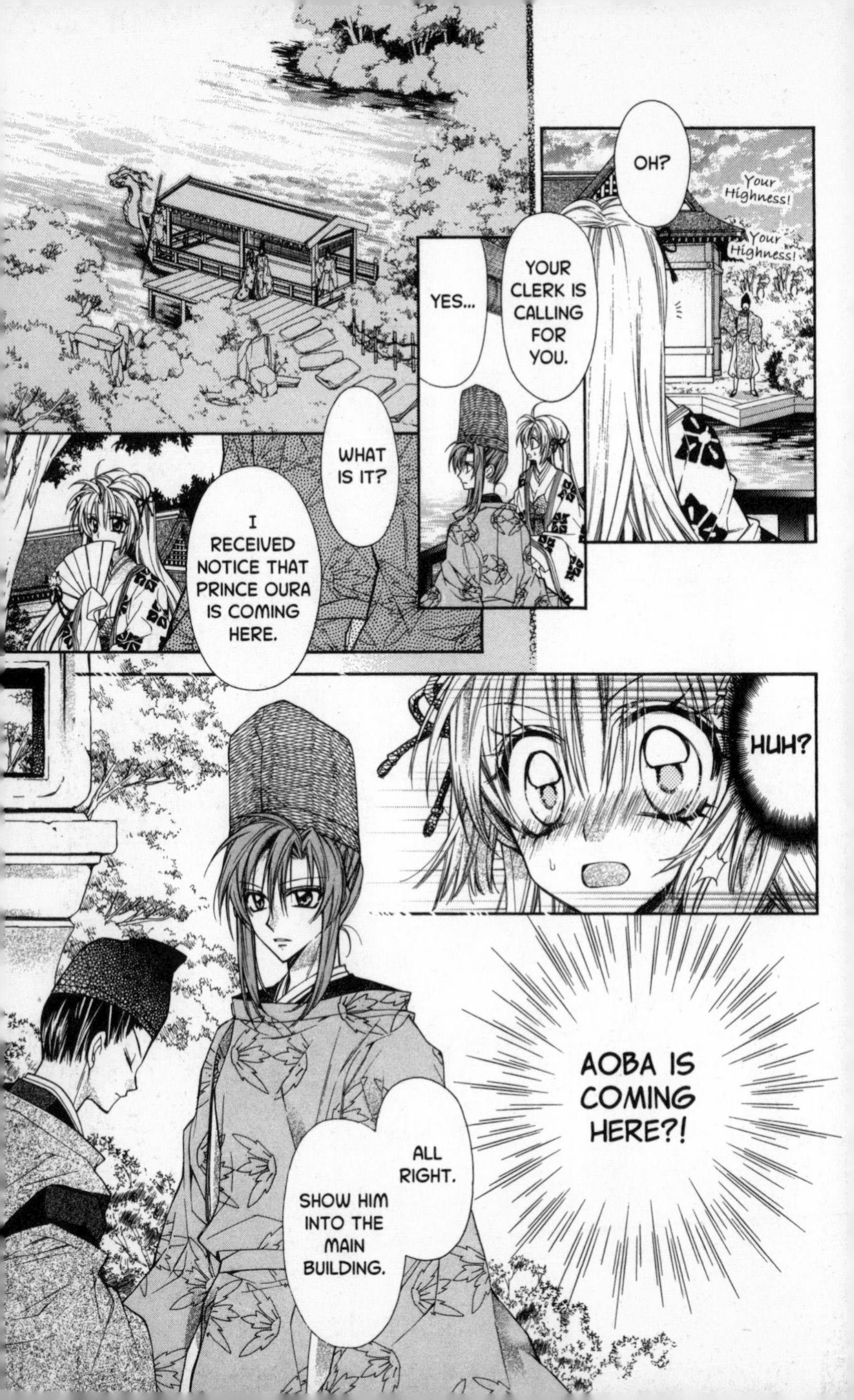
OH?
Your Highness!
Your Highness!
YOUR CLERK IS CALLING FOR YOU.
YES...
WHAT IS IT?
I RECEIVED NOTICE THAT PRINCE OURA IS COMING HERE.
HUH?
AOBA IS COMING HERE?!
ALL RIGHT.
SHOW HIM INTO THE MAIN BUILDING.

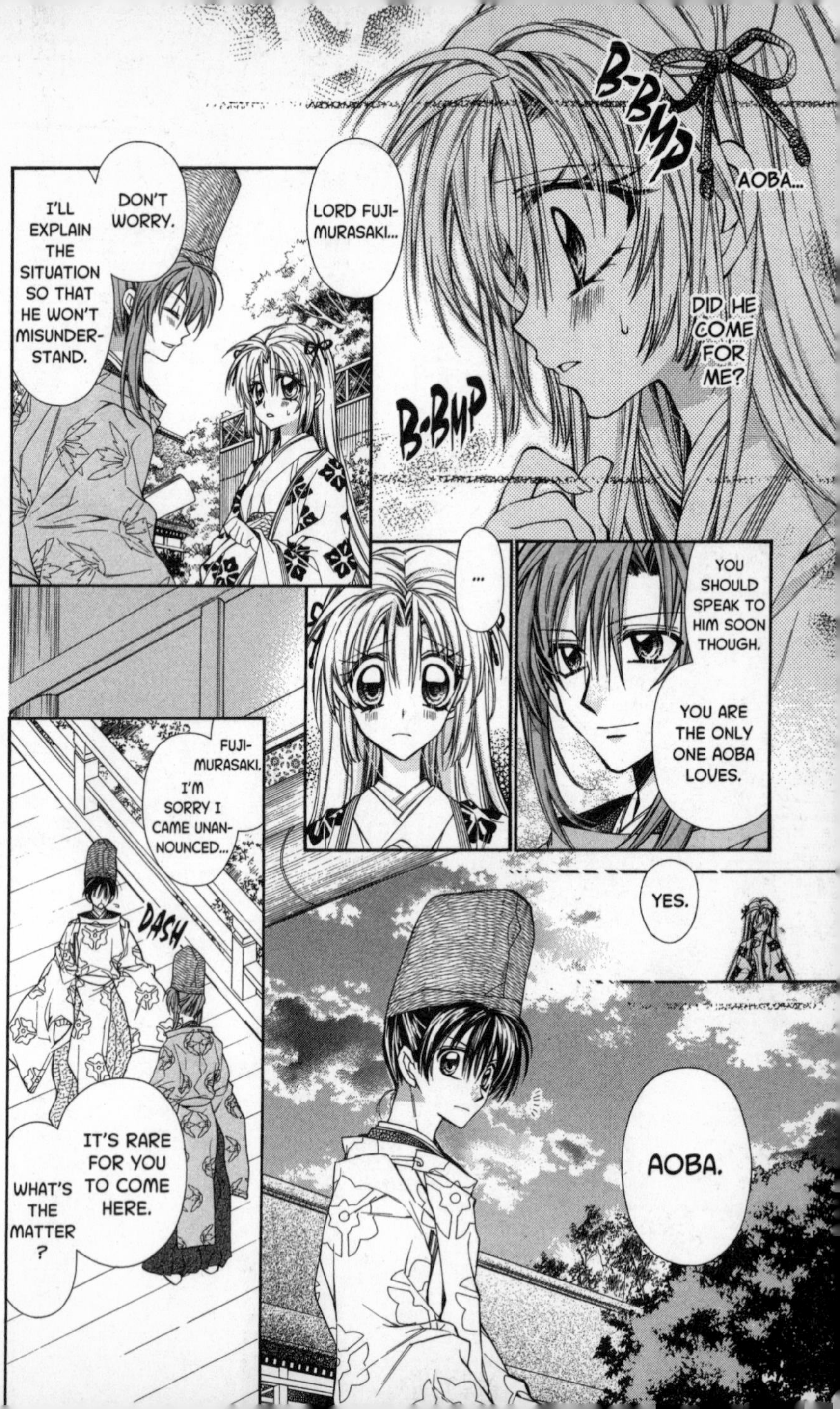
B-BMP
AOBA...
DID HE COME FOR ME?
B-BMP
LORD FUJI-MURASAKI...
DON'T WORRY.
I'LL EXPLAIN THE SITUATION SO THAT HE WON'T MISUNDERSTAND.
YOU SHOULD SPEAK TO HIM SOON THOUGH.
YOU ARE THE ONLY ONE AOBA LOVES.
...
YES.
AOBA.
FUJI-MURASAKI. I'M SORRY I CAME UNANNOUNCED...
DASH
IT'S RARE FOR YOU TO COME HERE.
WHAT'S THE MATTER?

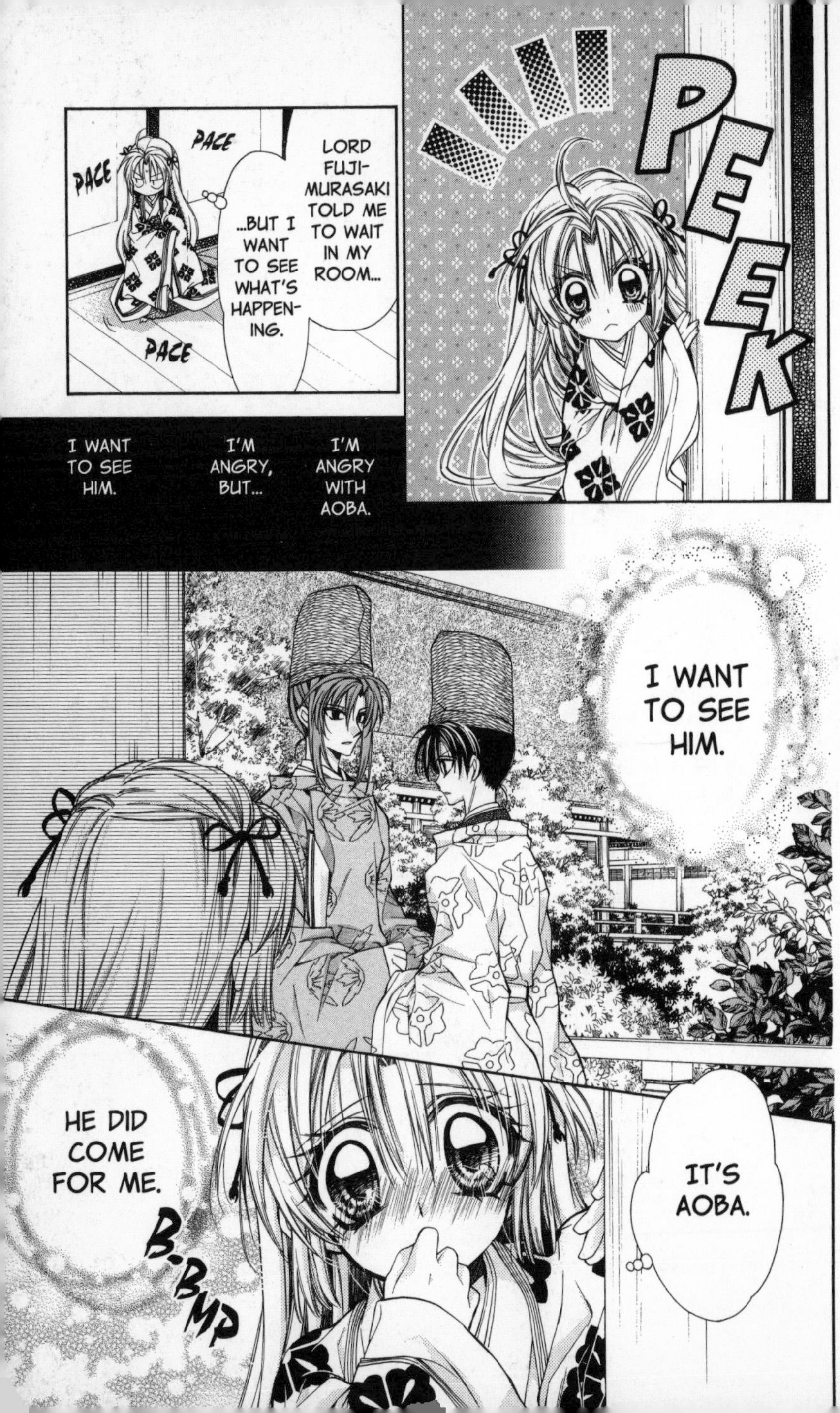
PEEK
PACE PACE PACE
LORD FUJI-MURASAKI TOLD ME TO WAIT IN MY ROOM...
...BUT I WANT TO SEE WHAT'S HAPPENING.
I'M ANGRY WITH AOBA.
I'M ANGRY, BUT...
I WANT TO SEE HIM.
I WANT TO SEE HIM.
IT'S AOBA.
HE DID COME FOR ME.
B-BMP

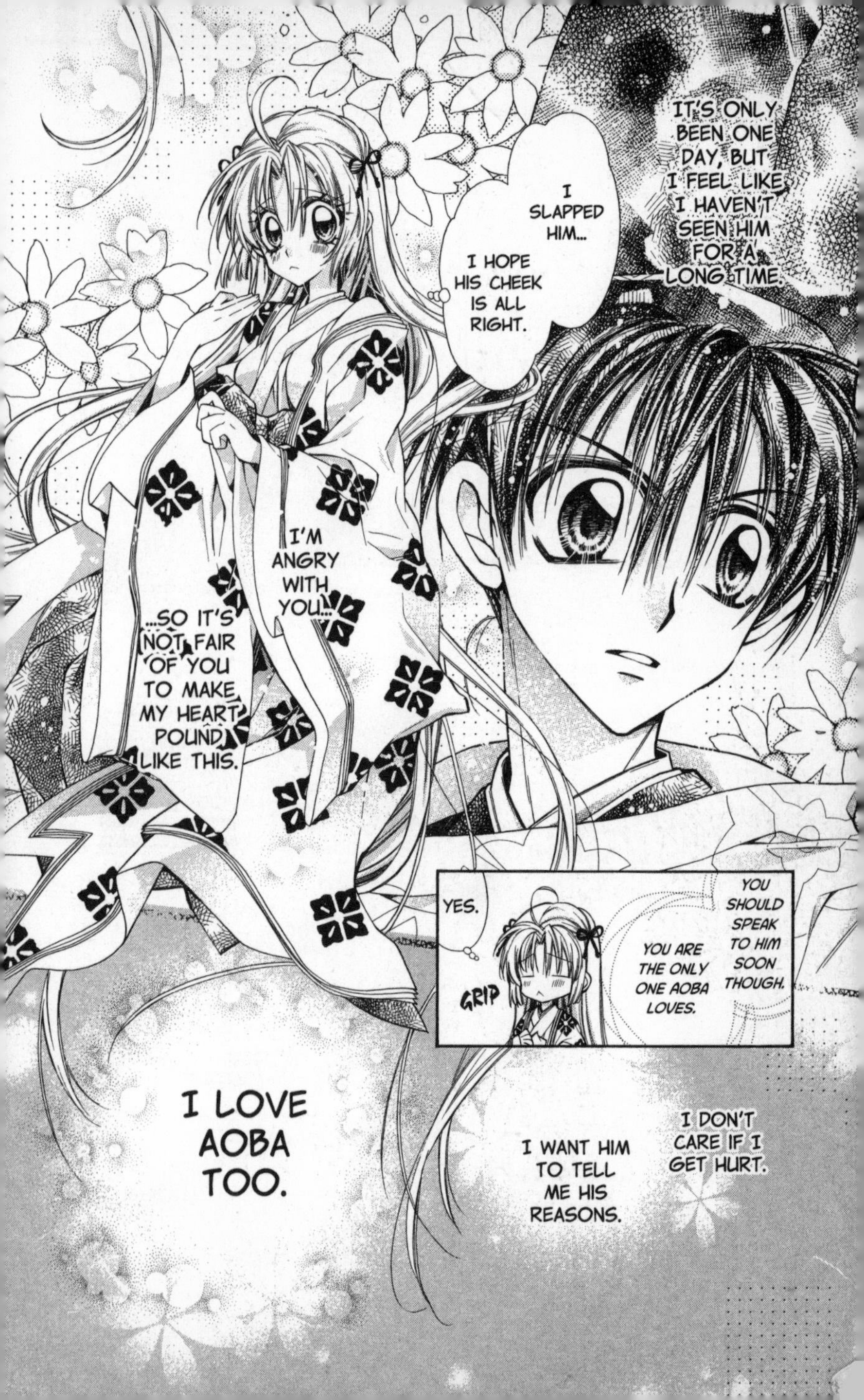
IT'S ONLY BEEN ONE DAY, BUT I FEEL LIKE I HAVEN'T SEEN HIM FOR A LONG TIME.
I SLAPPED HIM...
I HOPE HIS CHEEK IS ALL RIGHT.
I'M ANGRY WITH YOU...
...SO IT'S NOT FAIR OF YOU TO MAKE MY HEART POUND LIKE THIS.
YOU SHOULD SPEAK TO HIM SOON THOUGH.
YOU ARE THE ONLY ONE AOBA LOVES.
YES.
GRIP
I DON'T CARE IF I GET HURT.
I WANT HIM TO TELL ME HIS REASONS.
I LOVE AOBA TOO.

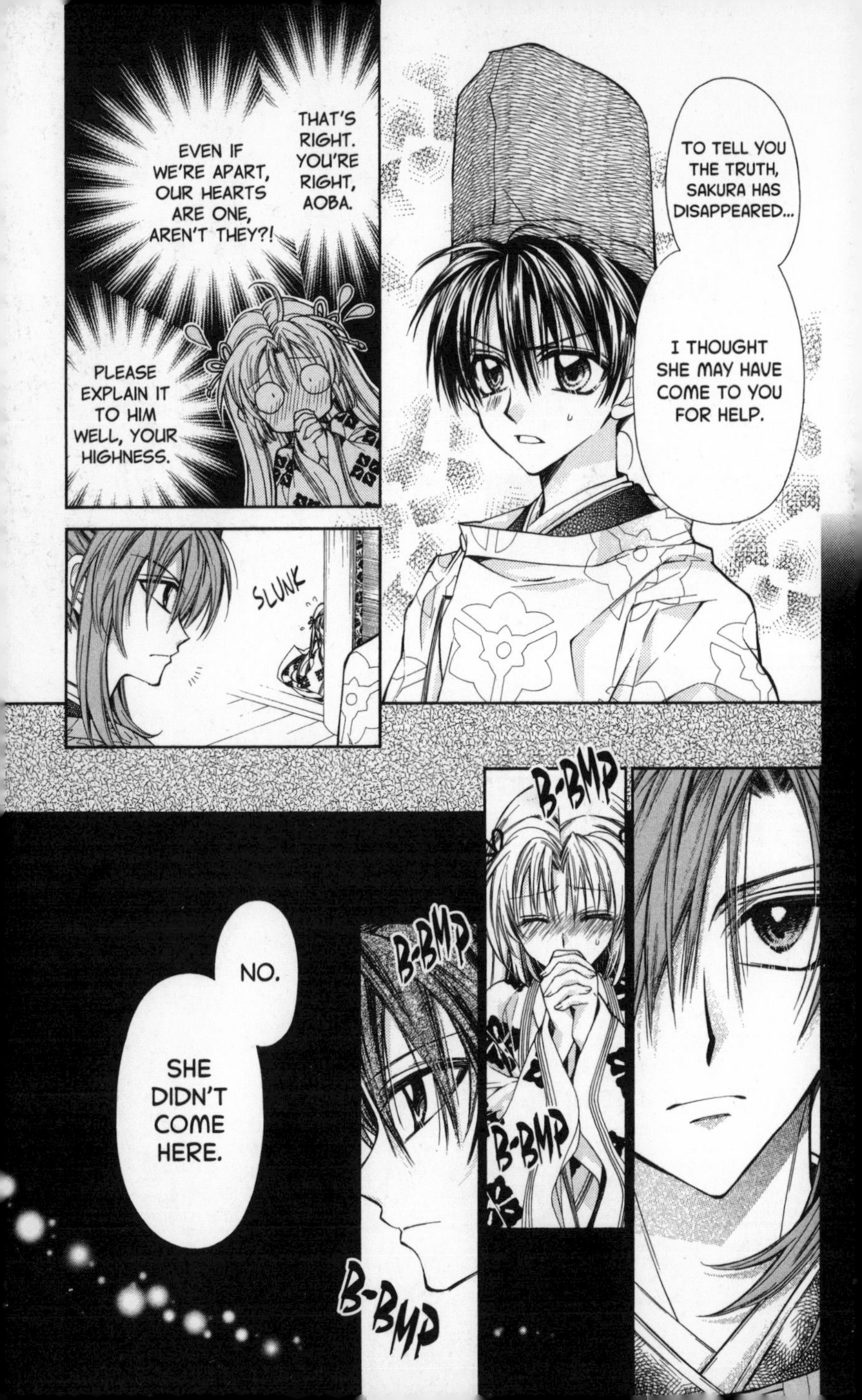
TO TELL YOU THE TRUTH, SAKURA HAS DISAPPEARED...
I THOUGHT SHE MAY HAVE COME TO YOU FOR HELP.
THAT'S RIGHT. YOU'RE RIGHT, AOBA.
EVEN IF WE'RE APART, OUR HEARTS ARE ONE, AREN'T THEY?!
PLEASE EXPLAIN IT TO HIM WELL, YOUR HIGHNESS.
SLUNK
B-BMP
B-BMP
B-BMP
B-BMP
NO.
SHE DIDN'T COME HERE.

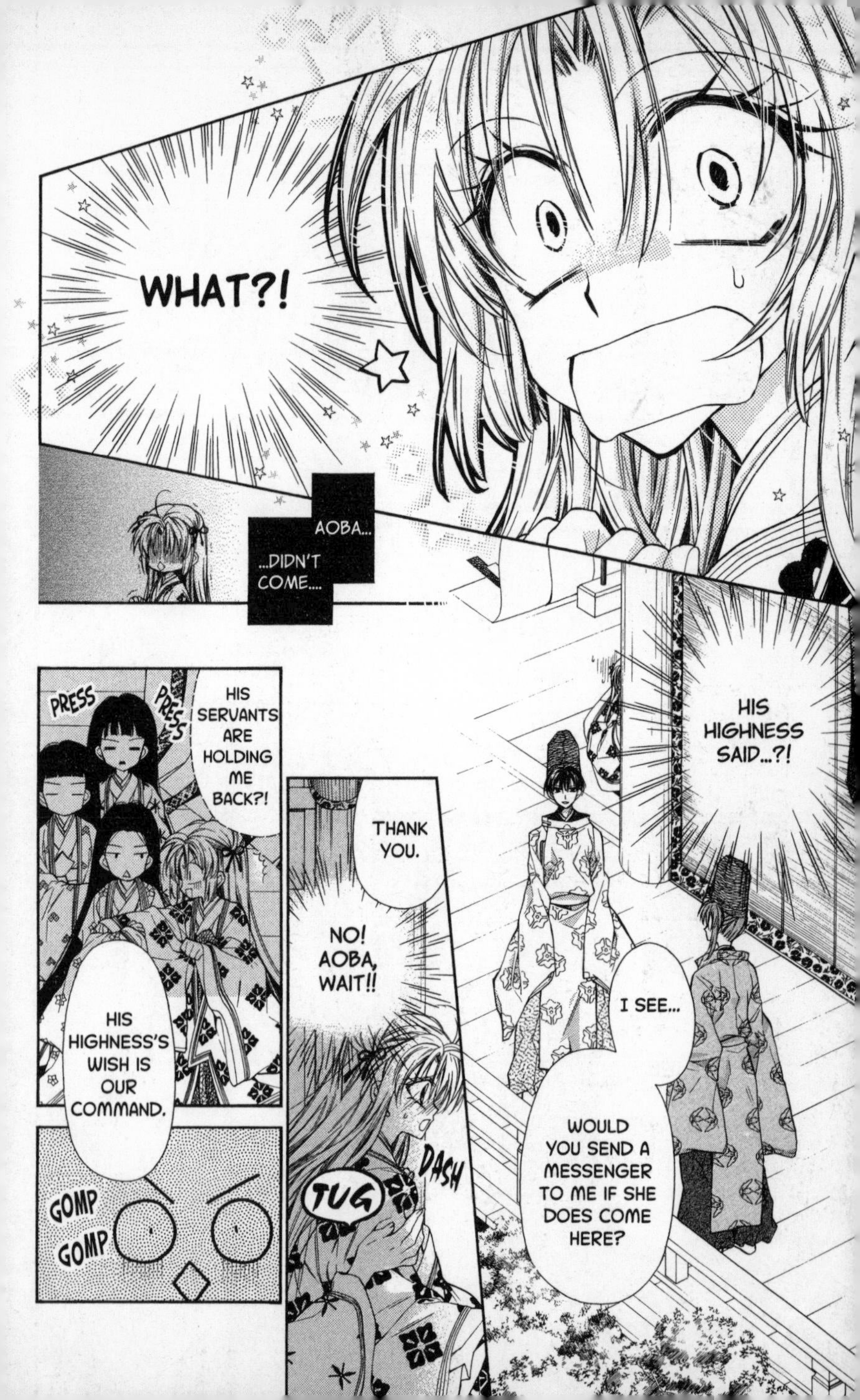
WHAT?!
AOBA...
...DIDN'T COME....
HIS HIGHNESS SAID...?!
I SEE...
WOULD YOU SEND A MESSENGER TO ME IF SHE DOES COME HERE?
THANK YOU.
NO! AOBA, WAIT!!
DASH
TUG
PRESS
PRESS
HIS SERVANTS ARE HOLDING ME BACK?!
HIS HIGHNESS'S WISH IS OUR COMMAND.
GOMP
GOMP

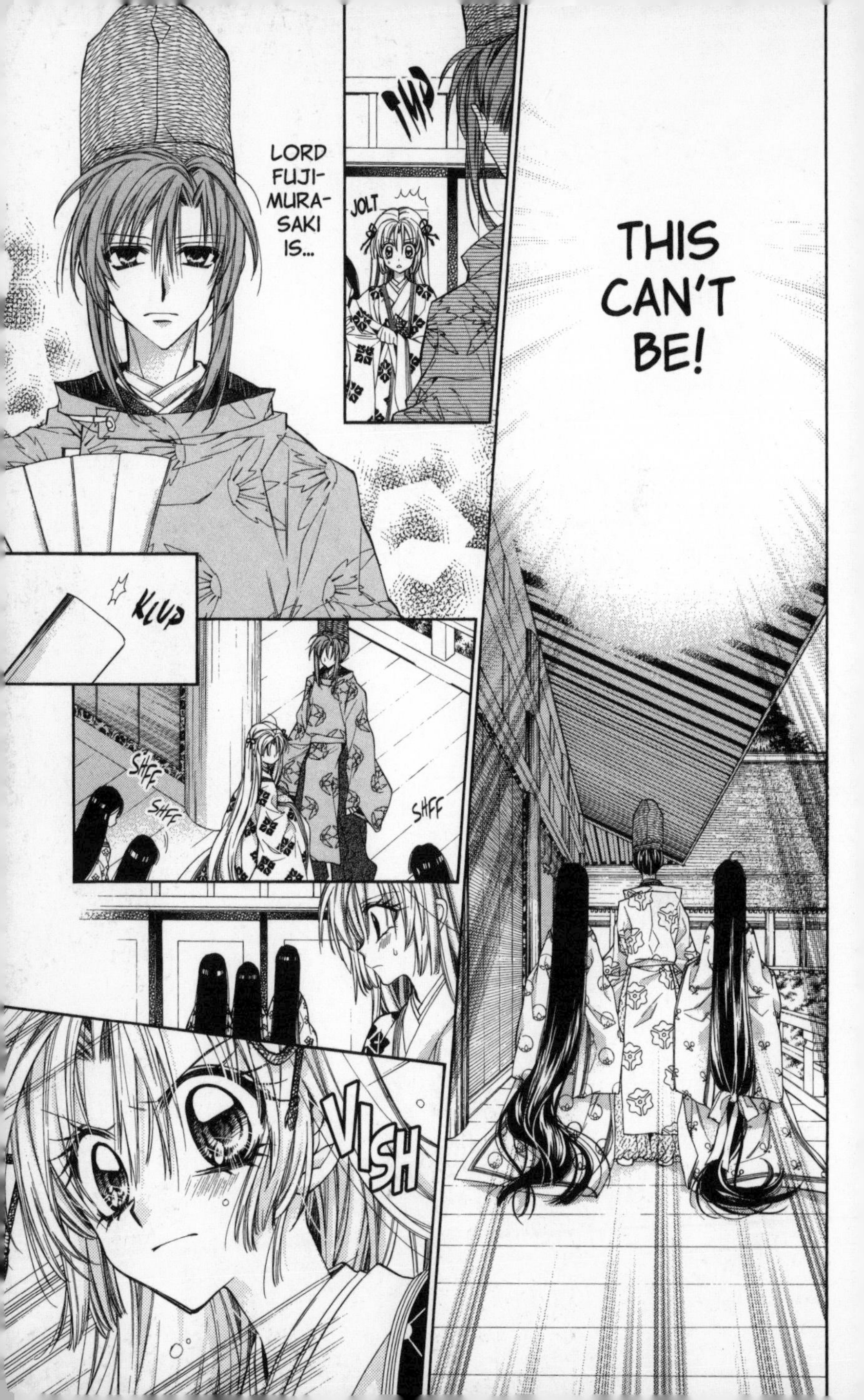
THIS CAN'T BE!
TMP
JOLT
LORD FUJI-MURA-SAKI IS...
KLUP
SHFF
SHFF
SHFF
VISH

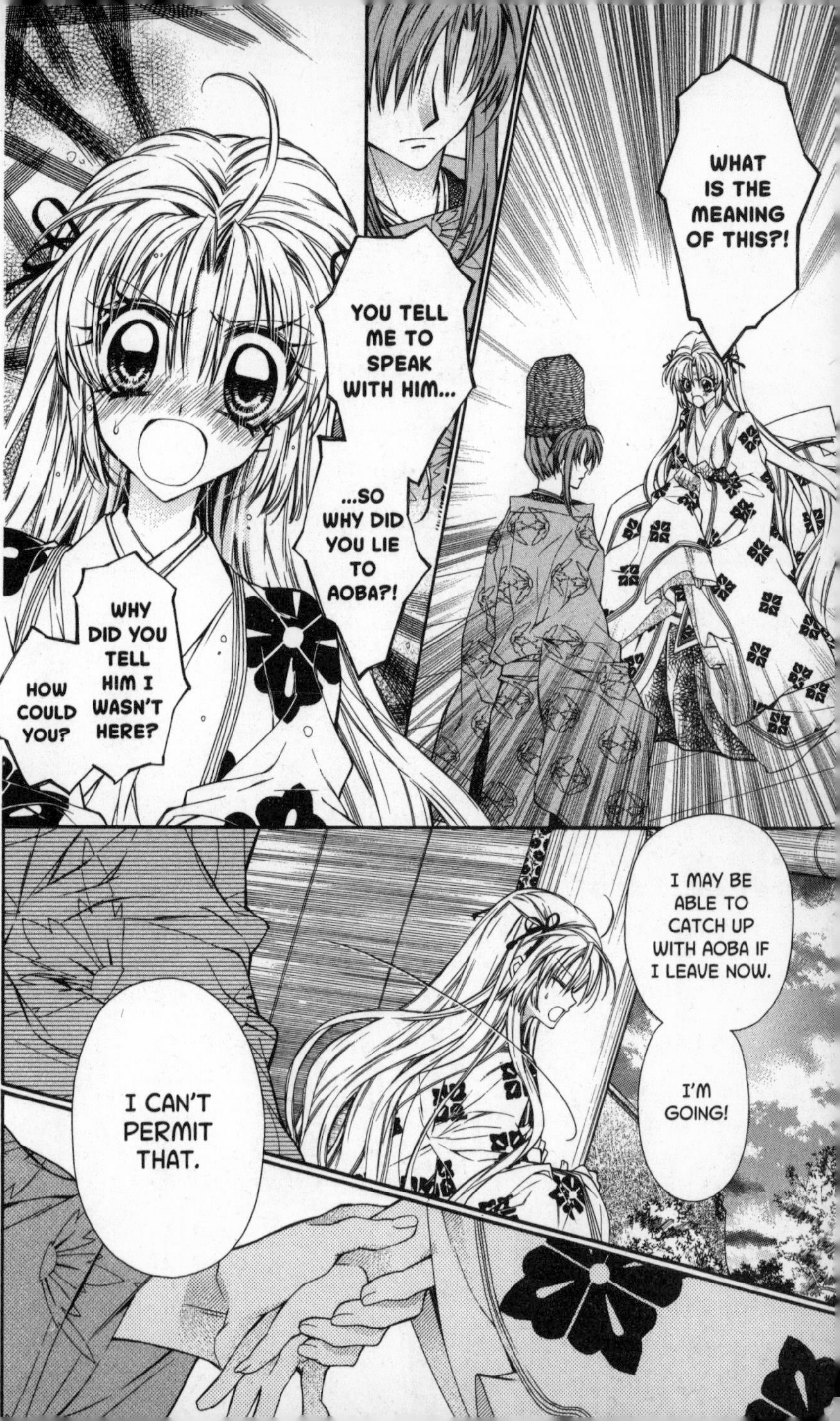
WHAT IS THE MEANING OF THIS?!
YOU TELL ME TO SPEAK WITH HIM...
...SO WHY DID YOU LIE TO AOBA?!
WHY DID YOU TELL HIM I WASN'T HERE?
HOW COULD YOU?
I MAY BE ABLE TO CATCH UP WITH AOBA IF I LEAVE NOW.
I'M GOING!
I CAN'T PERMIT THAT.

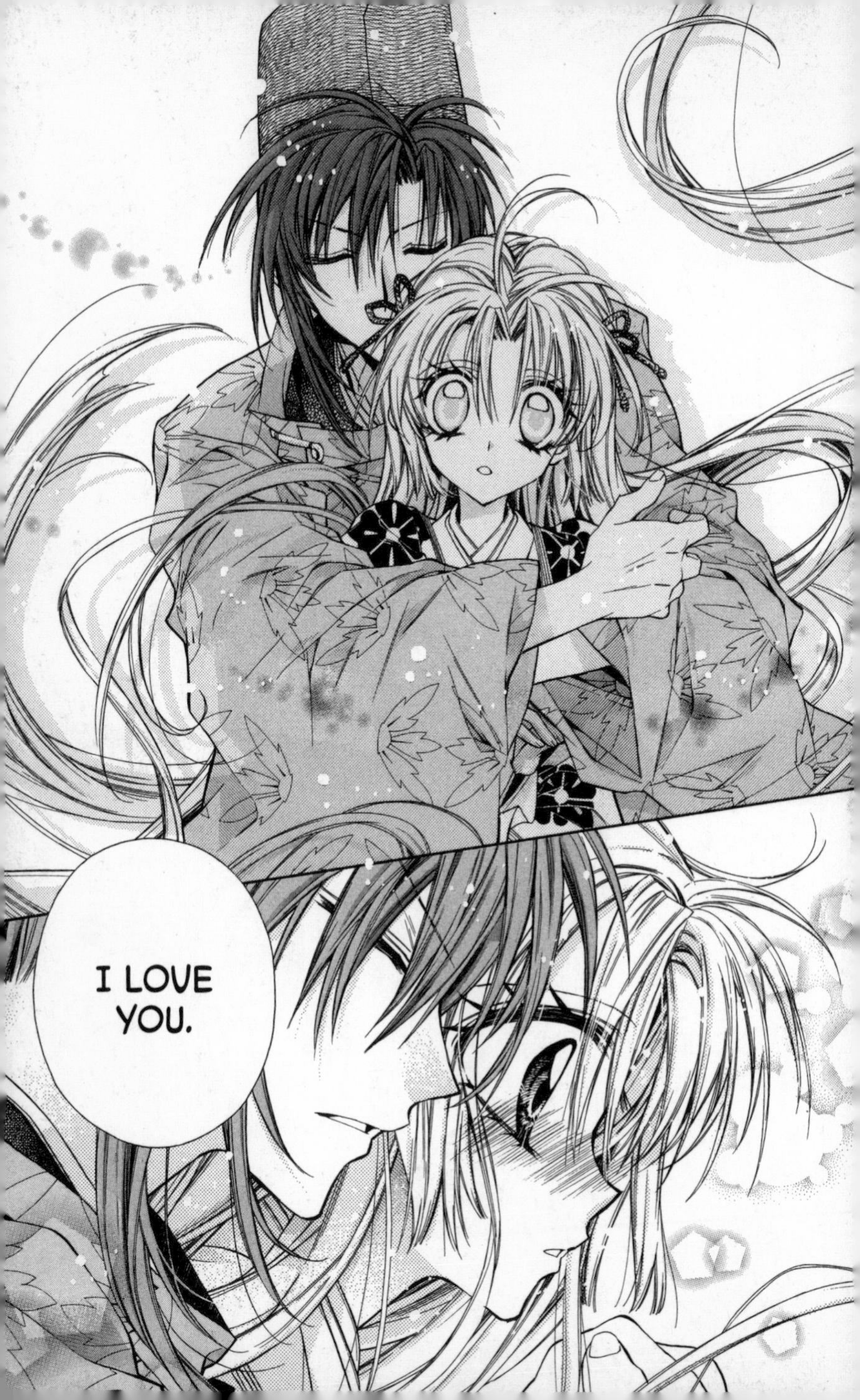
I LOVE YOU.

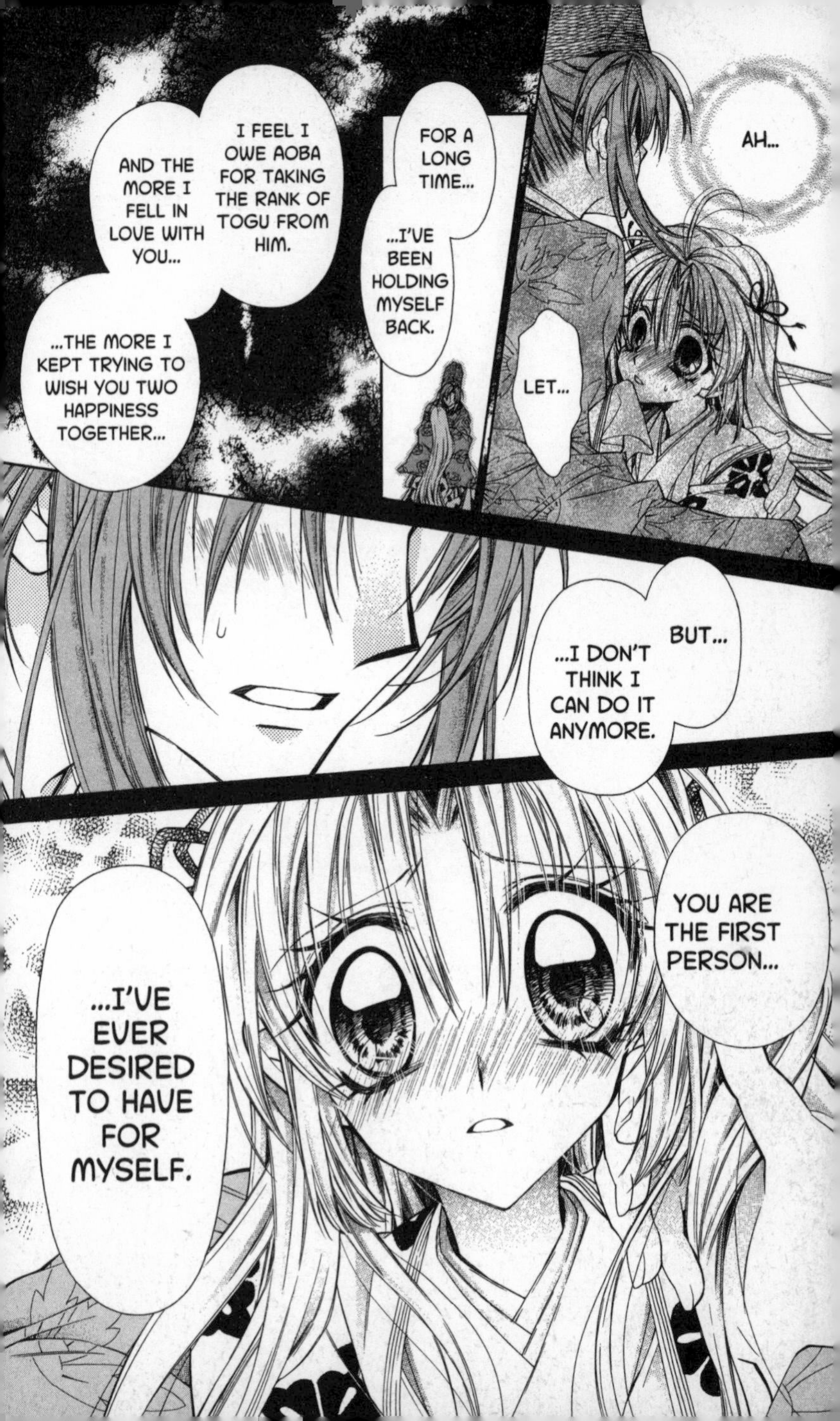
AH...
LET...
FOR A LONG TIME...
...I'VE BEEN HOLDING MYSELF BACK.
I FEEL I OWE AOBA FOR TAKING THE RANK OF TOGU FROM HIM.
AND THE MORE I FELL IN LOVE WITH YOU...
...THE MORE I KEPT TRYING TO WISH YOU TWO HAPPINESS TOGETHER...
BUT...
...I DON'T THINK I CAN DO IT ANYMORE.
YOU ARE THE FIRST PERSON...
...I'VE EVER DESIRED TO HAVE FOR MYSELF.

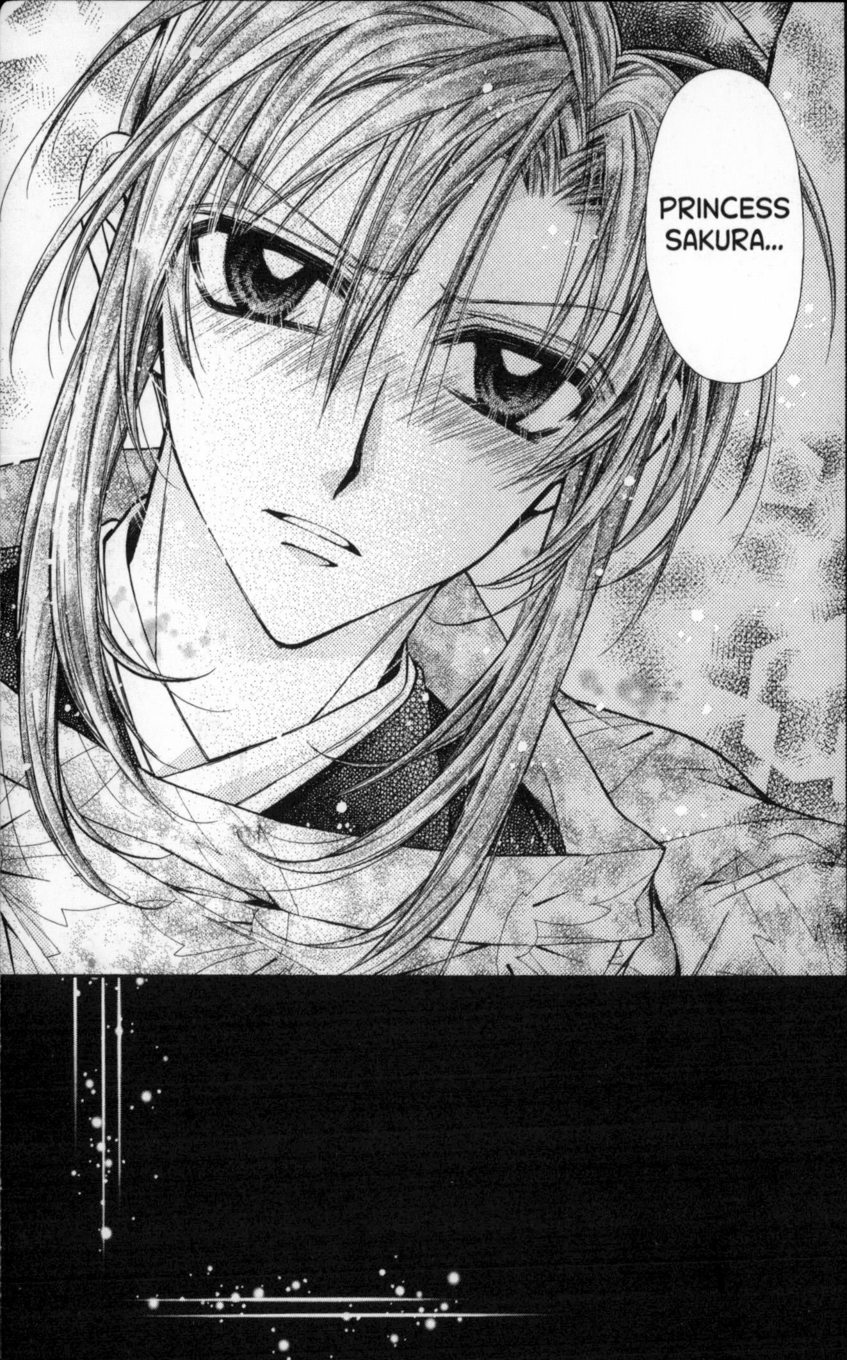
PRINCESS SAKURA...

SAKURA HIME: THE LEGEND OF PRINCESS SAKURA VOL. 8/END

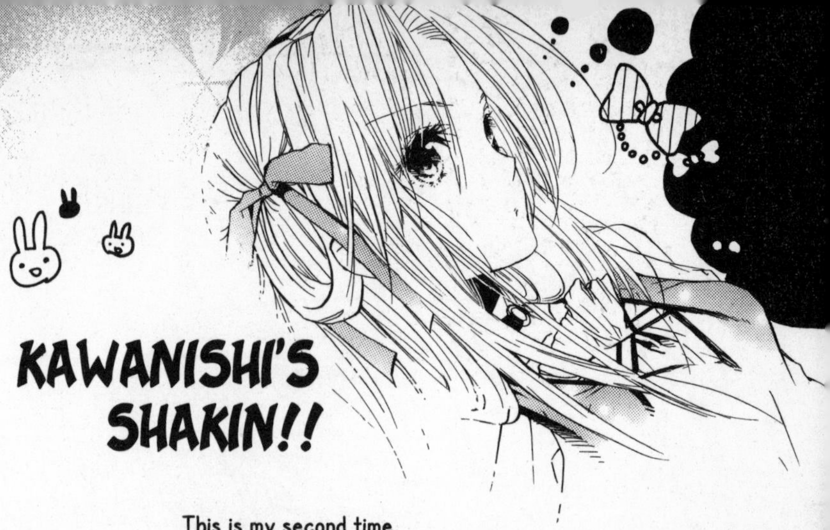

KAWANISHI'S SHAKIN!!

This is my second time. I'm Moe Kawanishi, an assistant. I paste screentones and whatnot.

YURI HIME: THE LEGEND OF PRINCESS YURI!!

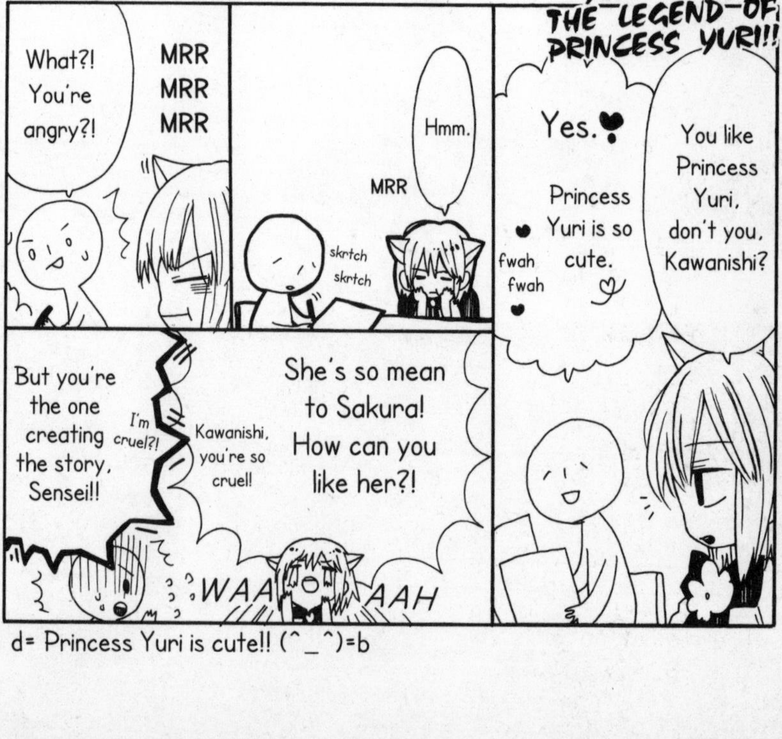

You like Princess Yuri, don't you, Kawanishi?
Yes. Princess Yuri is so cute.
fwah fwah
Hmm.
MRR
skrtch skrtch
MRR MRR MRR
What?! You're angry?!
She's so mean to Sakura! How can you like her?!
Kawanishi, you're so cruel!
WAAAAH
I'm cruel?!
But you're the one creating the story, Sensei!!

d= Princess Yuri is cute!! (^_^)=b

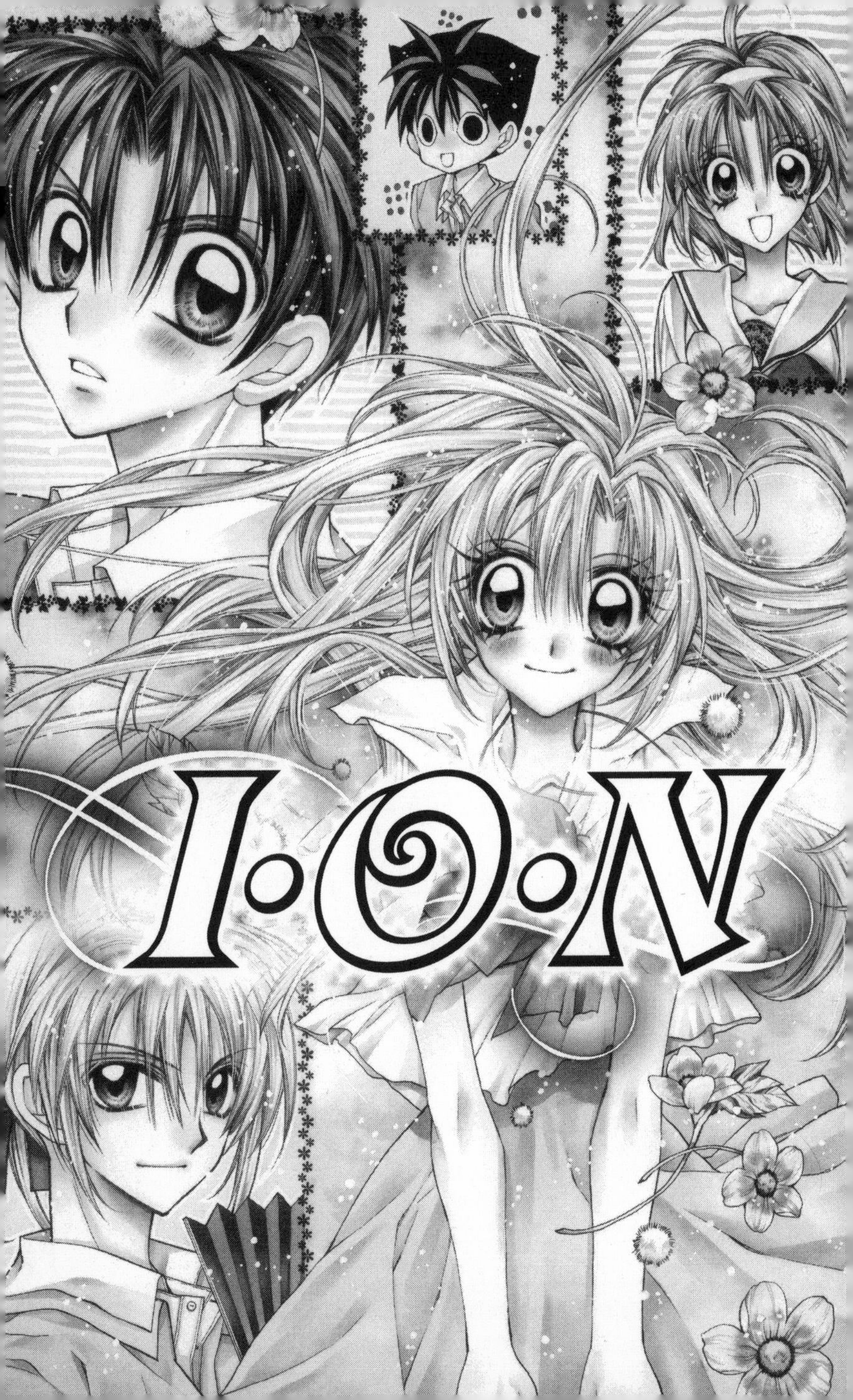
I.O.N

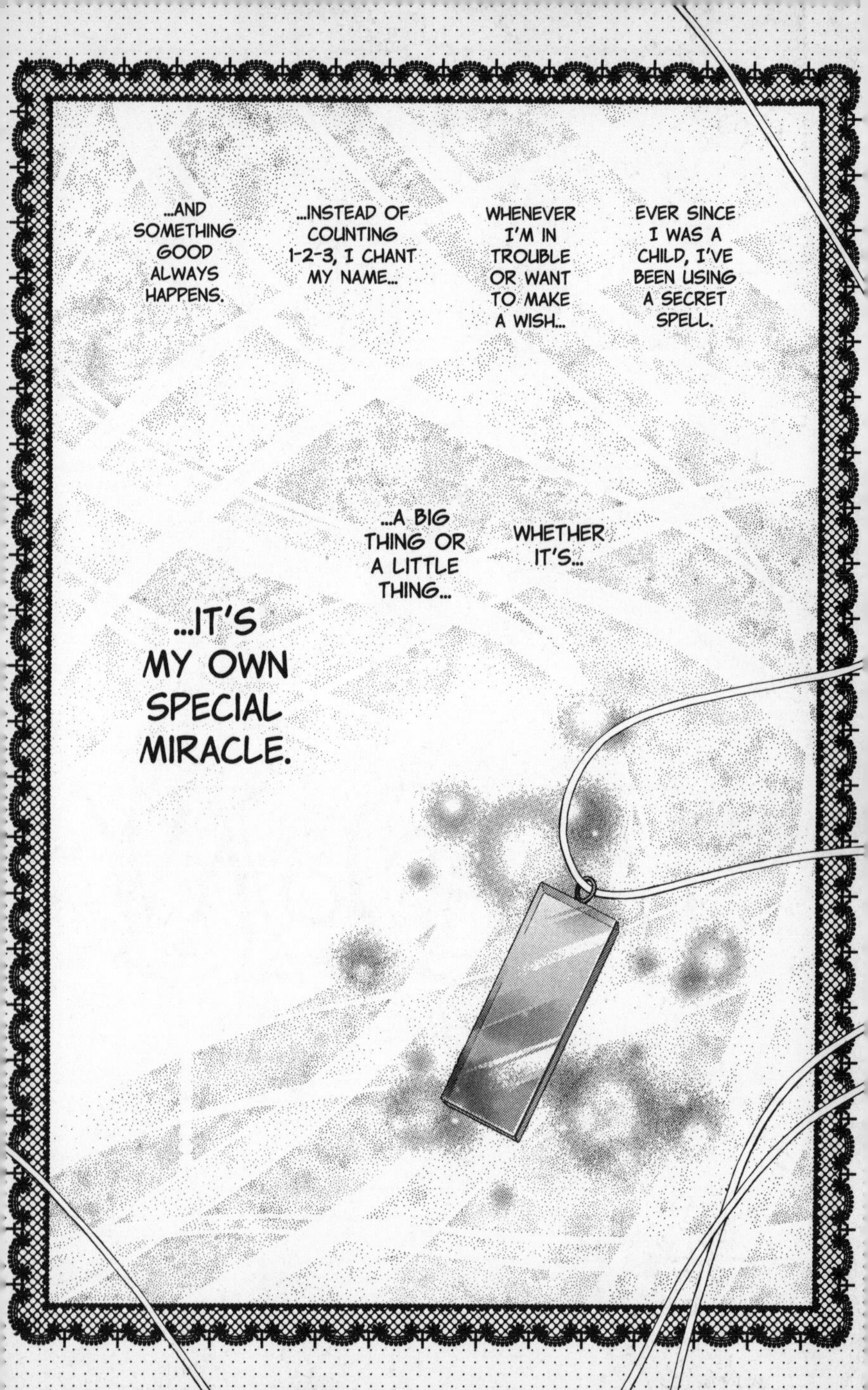
EVER SINCE I WAS A CHILD, I'VE BEEN USING A SECRET SPELL.
WHENEVER I'M IN TROUBLE OR WANT TO MAKE A WISH...
...INSTEAD OF COUNTING 1-2-3, I CHANT MY NAME...
...AND SOMETHING GOOD ALWAYS HAPPENS.
WHETHER IT'S...
...A BIG THING OR A LITTLE THING...
...IT'S MY OWN SPECIAL MIRACLE.

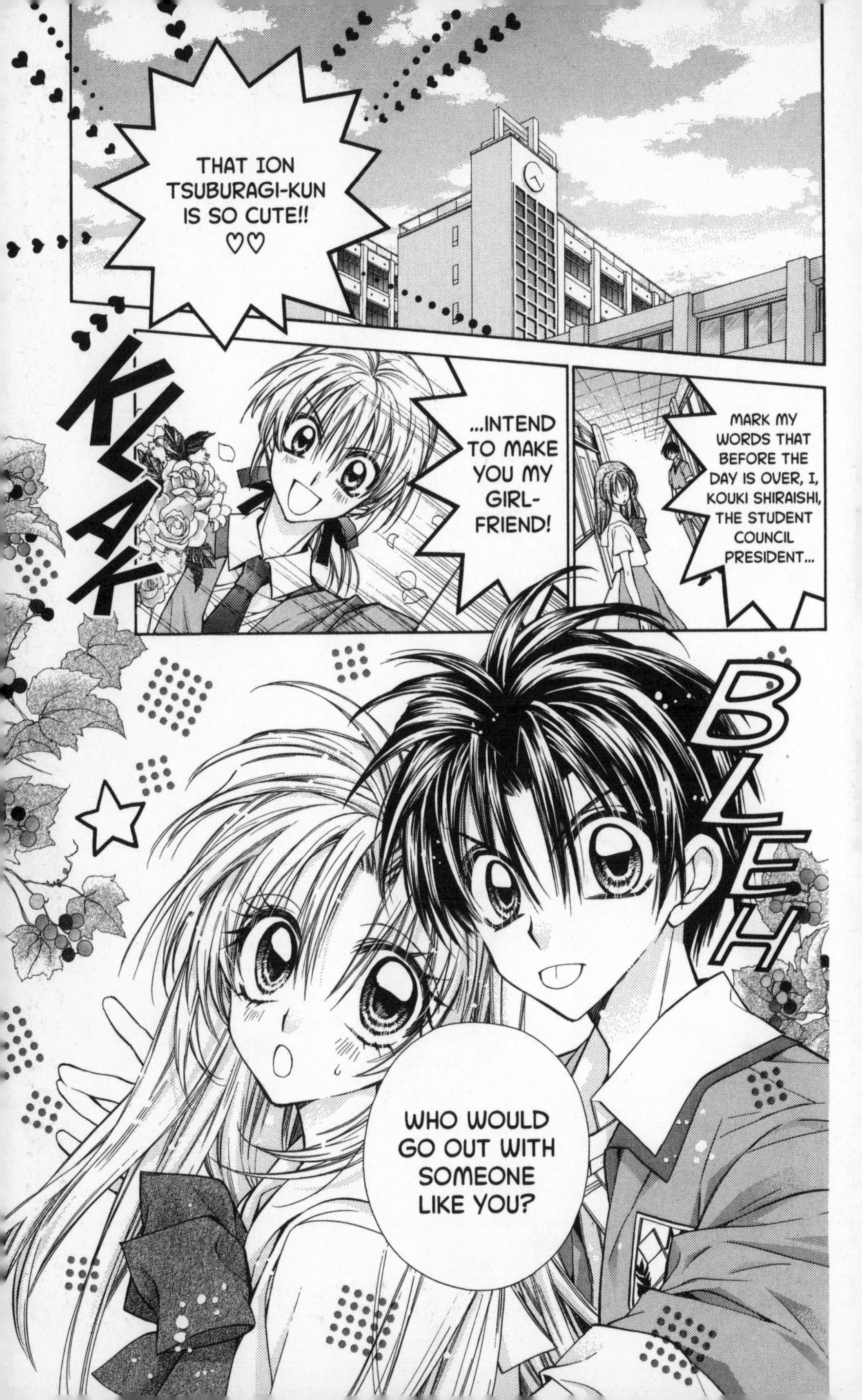
THAT ION TSUBURAGI-KUN IS SO CUTE!! ♡♡
MARK MY WORDS THAT BEFORE THE DAY IS OVER, I, KOUKI SHIRAISHI, THE STUDENT COUNCIL PRESIDENT...
...INTEND TO MAKE YOU MY GIRL-FRIEND!
KLAK
BLEH
WHO WOULD GO OUT WITH SOMEONE LIKE YOU?

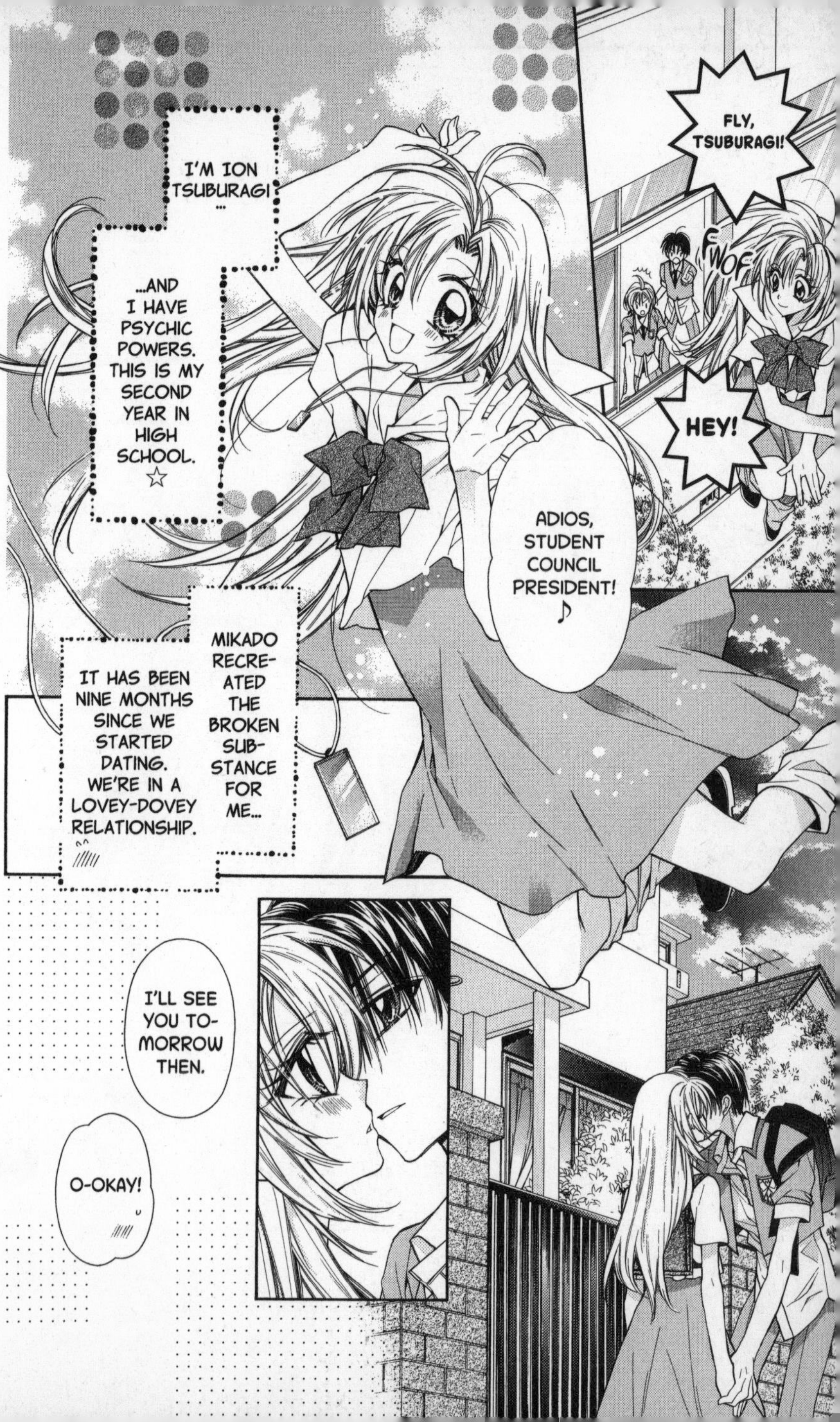
FLY, TSUBURAGI!
FWOF
HEY!
I'M ION TSUBURAGI...
...AND I HAVE PSYCHIC POWERS. THIS IS MY SECOND YEAR IN HIGH SCHOOL. ☆
ADIOS, STUDENT COUNCIL PRESIDENT! ♪
MIKADO RECRE-ATED THE BROKEN SUB-STANCE FOR ME...
IT HAS BEEN NINE MONTHS SINCE WE STARTED DATING. WE'RE IN A LOVEY-DOVEY RELATIONSHIP.
I'LL SEE YOU TO-MORROW THEN.
O-OKAY!

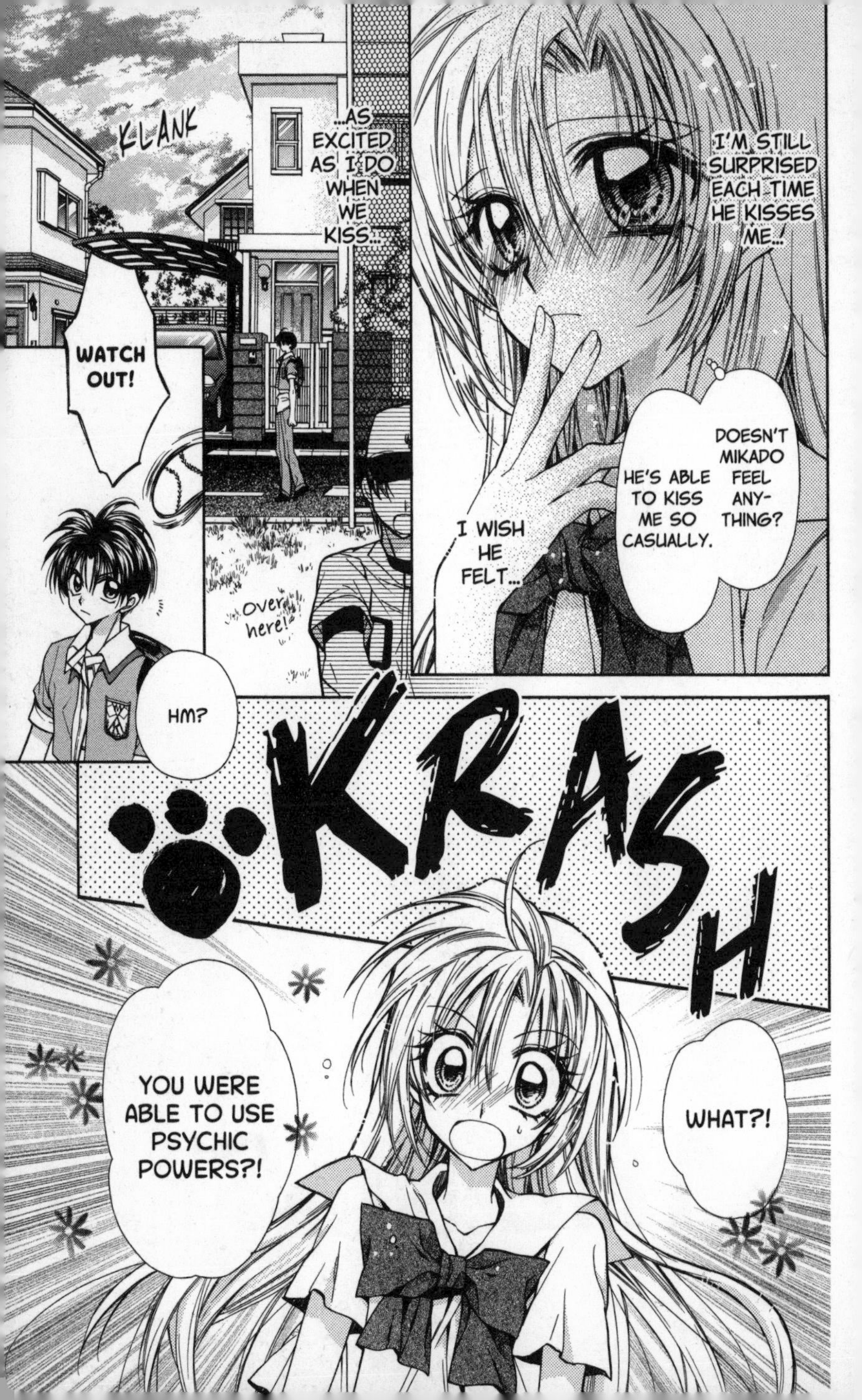
I'M STILL SURPRISED EACH TIME HE KISSES ME..
DOESN'T MIKADO FEEL ANYTHING?
HE'S ABLE TO KISS ME SO CASUALLY.
I WISH HE FELT...
...AS EXCITED AS I DO WHEN WE KISS...
KLANK
WATCH OUT!
Over here!
HM?
KRASH
WHAT?!
YOU WERE ABLE TO USE PSYCHIC POWERS?!

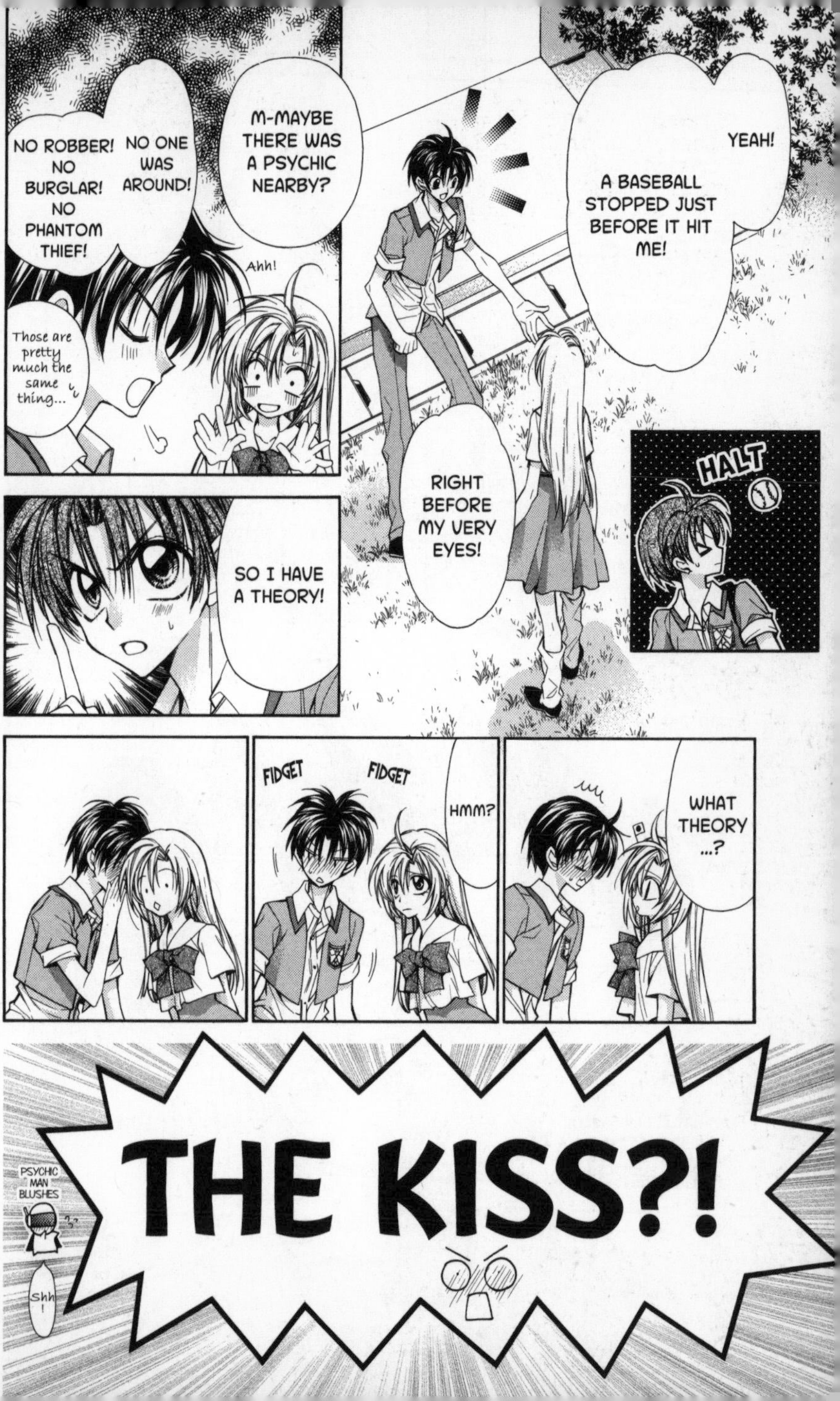
YEAH!
A BASEBALL STOPPED JUST BEFORE IT HIT ME!
RIGHT BEFORE MY VERY EYES!
HALT
M-MAYBE THERE WAS A PSYCHIC NEARBY?
Ahh!
NO ONE WAS AROUND!
NO ROBBER! NO BURGLAR! NO PHANTOM THIEF!
Those are pretty much the same thing...
SO I HAVE A THEORY!
WHAT THEORY ...?
HMM?
FIDGET
FIDGET
THE KISS?!
PSYCHIC MAN BLUSHES
Shh!

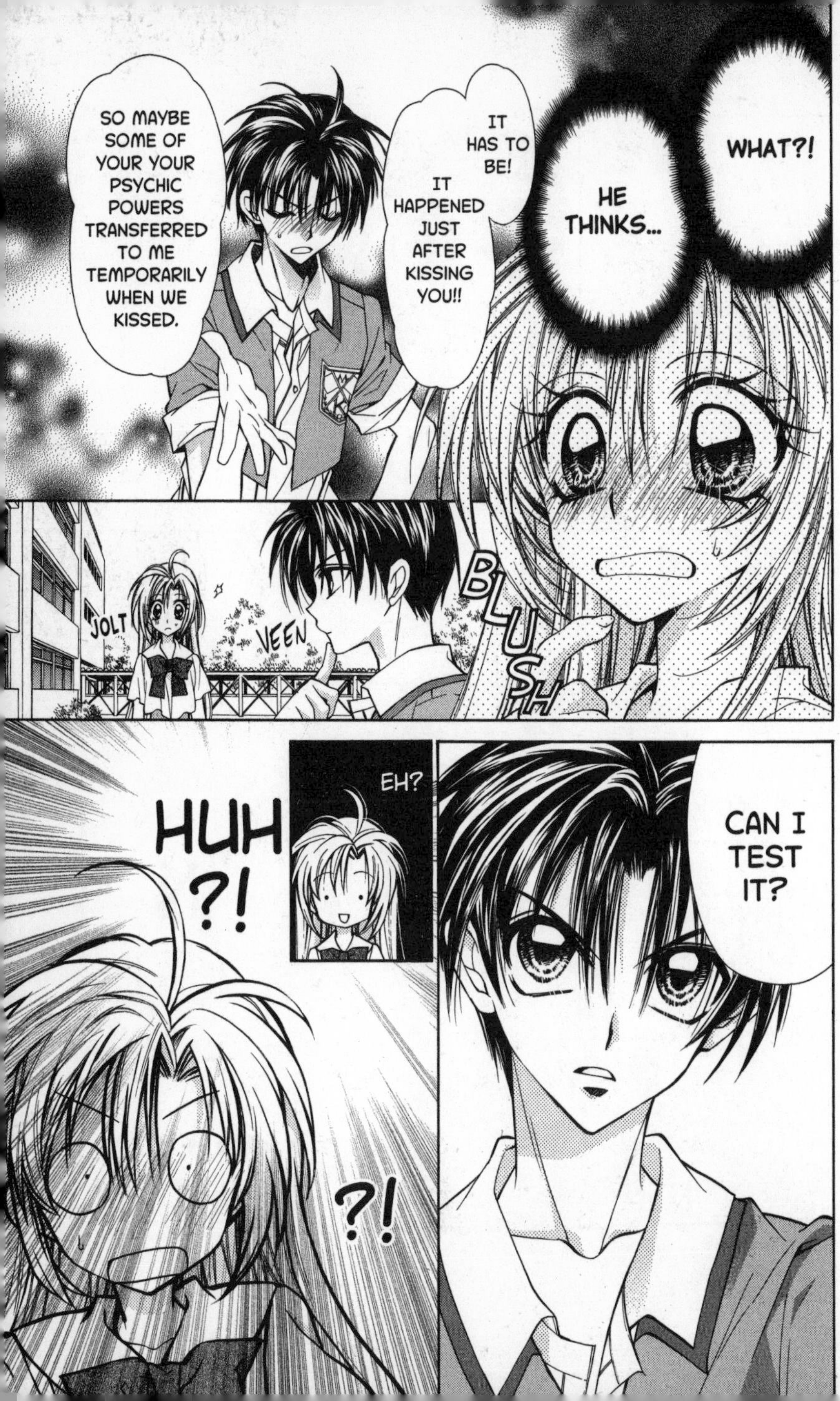
WHAT?!
HE THINKS...
BLUSH
IT HAS TO BE!
IT HAPPENED JUST AFTER KISSING YOU!!
SO MAYBE SOME OF YOUR YOUR PSYCHIC POWERS TRANSFERRED TO ME TEMPORARILY WHEN WE KISSED.
VEEN
JOLT
CAN I TEST IT?
EH?
HUH ?!
?!

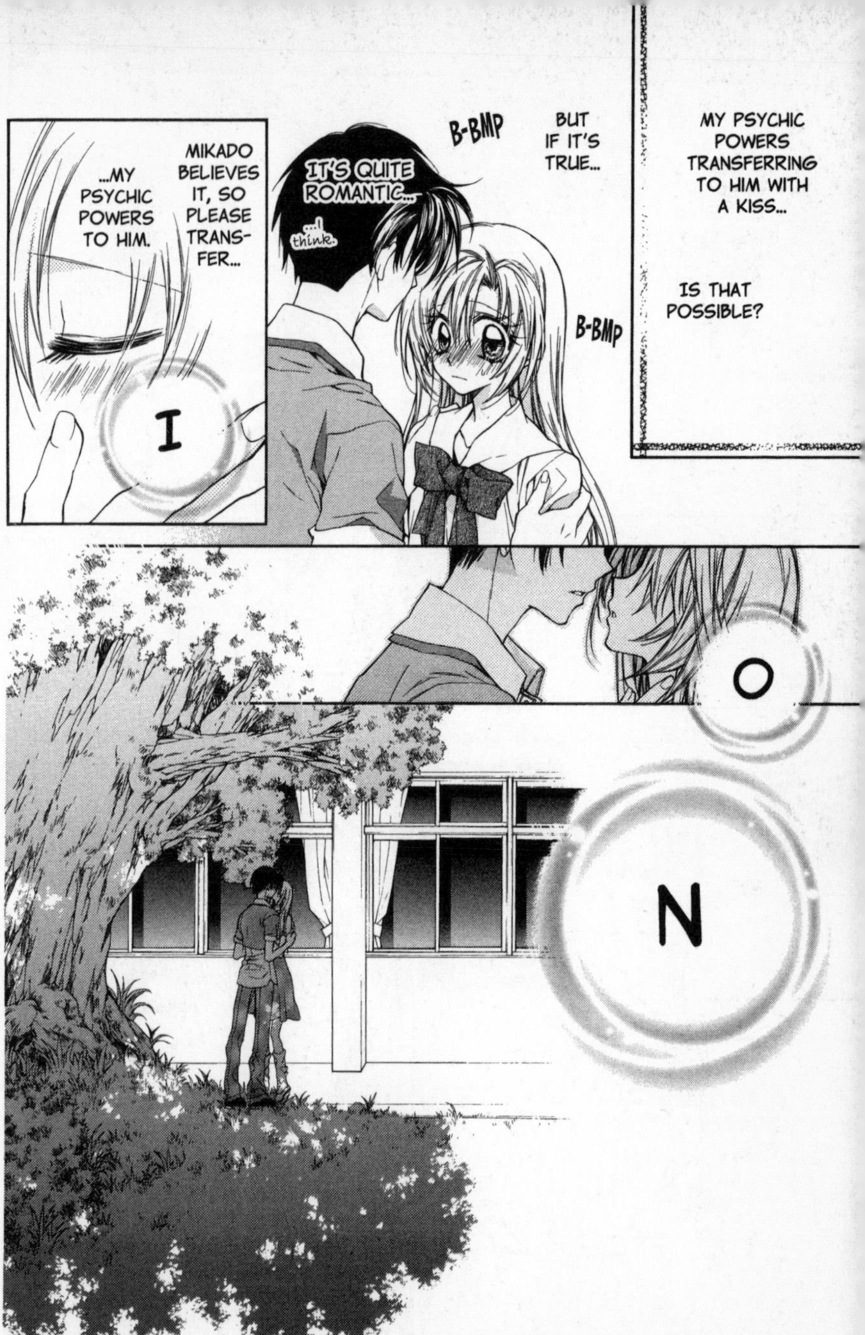
MY PSYCHIC POWERS TRANSFERRING TO HIM WITH A KISS...
IS THAT POSSIBLE?
B-BMP
BUT IF IT'S TRUE...
IT'S QUITE ROMANTIC...
...I think.
B-BMP
MIKADO BELIEVES IT, SO PLEASE TRANS-FER...
...MY PSYCHIC POWERS TO HIM.
I
O
N

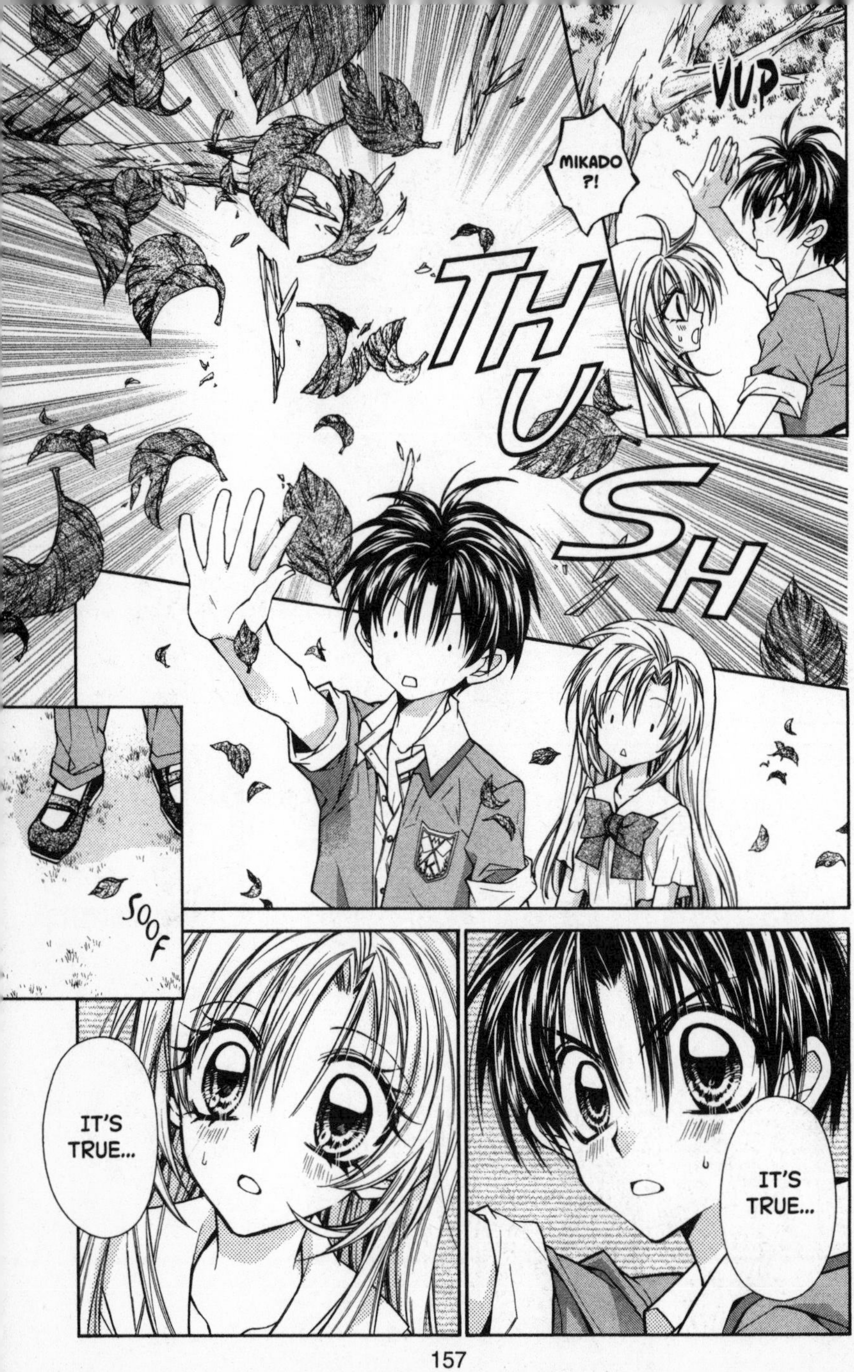
VUP
MIKADO ?!
THUSH
SOOF
IT'S TRUE...
IT'S TRUE...

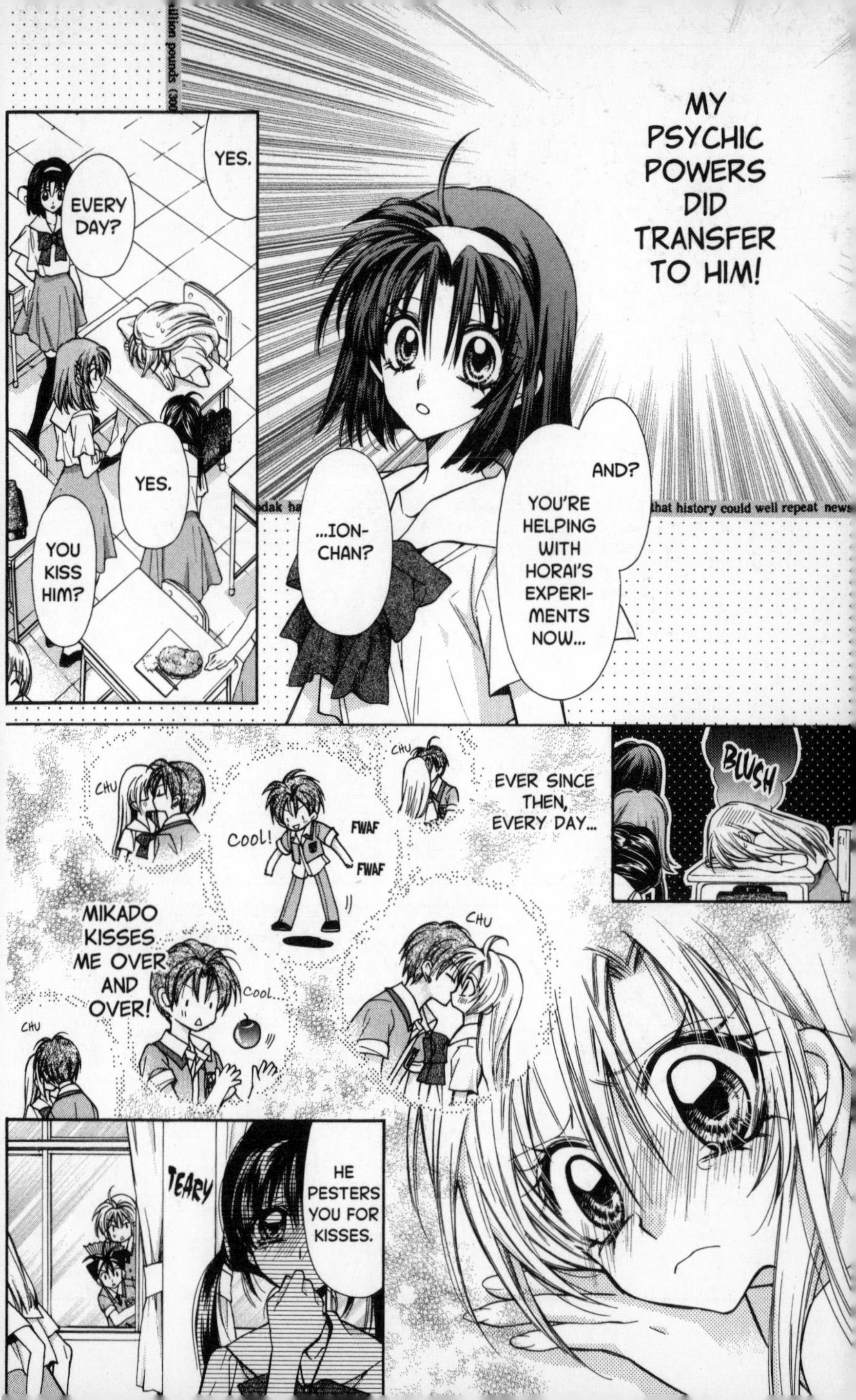
MY PSYCHIC POWERS DID TRANSFER TO HIM!
that history could well repeat news
AND? YOU'RE HELPING WITH HORAI'S EXPERIMENTS NOW...
...ION-CHAN?
YES.
EVERY DAY?
YES.
YOU KISS HIM?
BLUSH
EVER SINCE THEN, EVERY DAY...
CHU
FWAF
FWAF
COOL!
CHU
MIKADO KISSES ME OVER AND OVER!
CHU
COOL...
CHU
HE PESTERS YOU FOR KISSES.
TEARY

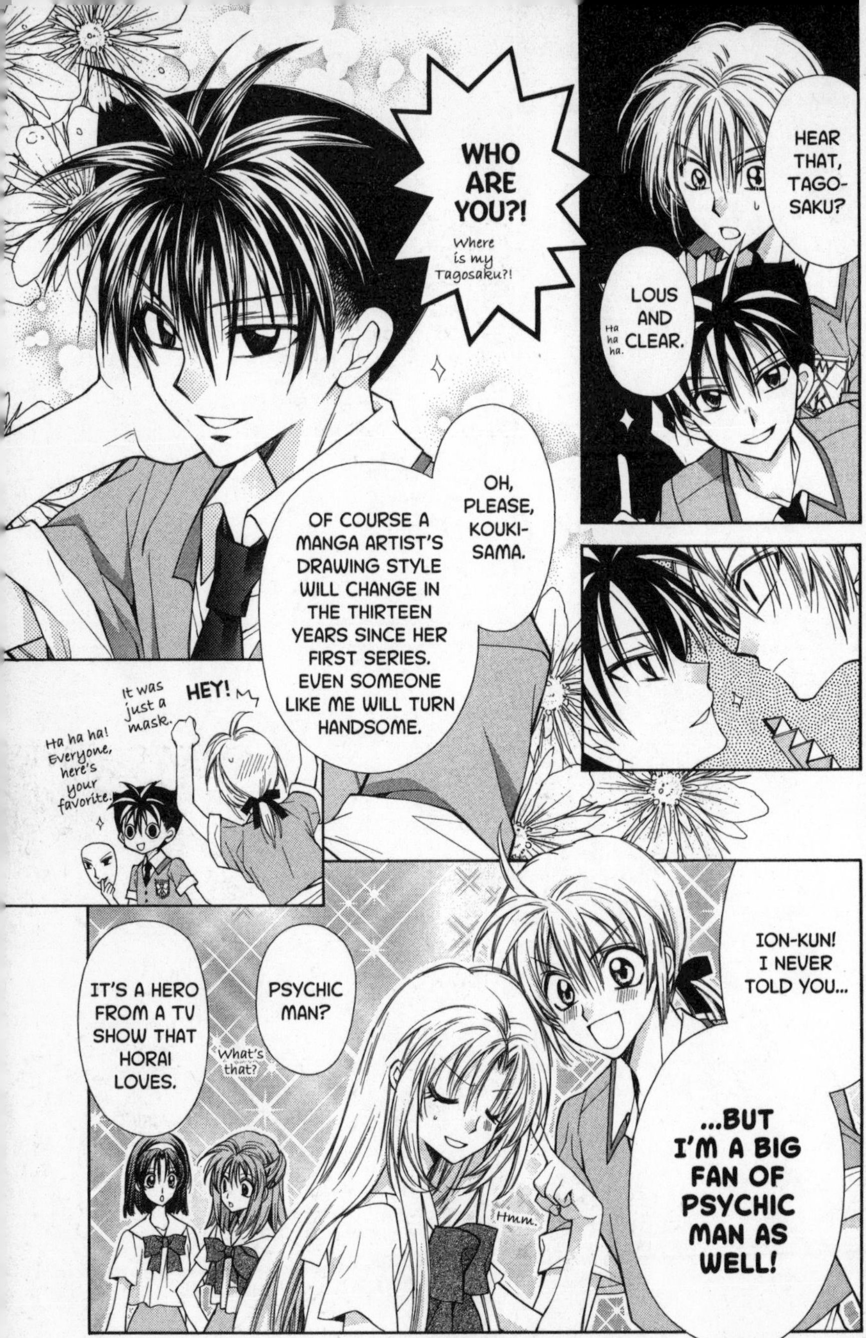
HEAR THAT, TAGO-SAKU?
LOUS AND CLEAR.
Ha ha ha.
WHO ARE YOU?!
Where is my Tagosaku?!
OH, PLEASE, KOUKI-SAMA.
OF COURSE A MANGA ARTIST'S DRAWING STYLE WILL CHANGE IN THE THIRTEEN YEARS SINCE HER FIRST SERIES. EVEN SOMEONE LIKE ME WILL TURN HANDSOME.
HEY!
It was just a mask.
Ha ha ha! Everyone, here's your favorite.
ION-KUN! I NEVER TOLD YOU...
...BUT I'M A BIG FAN OF PSYCHIC MAN AS WELL!
Hmm.
PSYCHIC MAN?
What's that?
IT'S A HERO FROM A TV SHOW THAT HORAI LOVES.

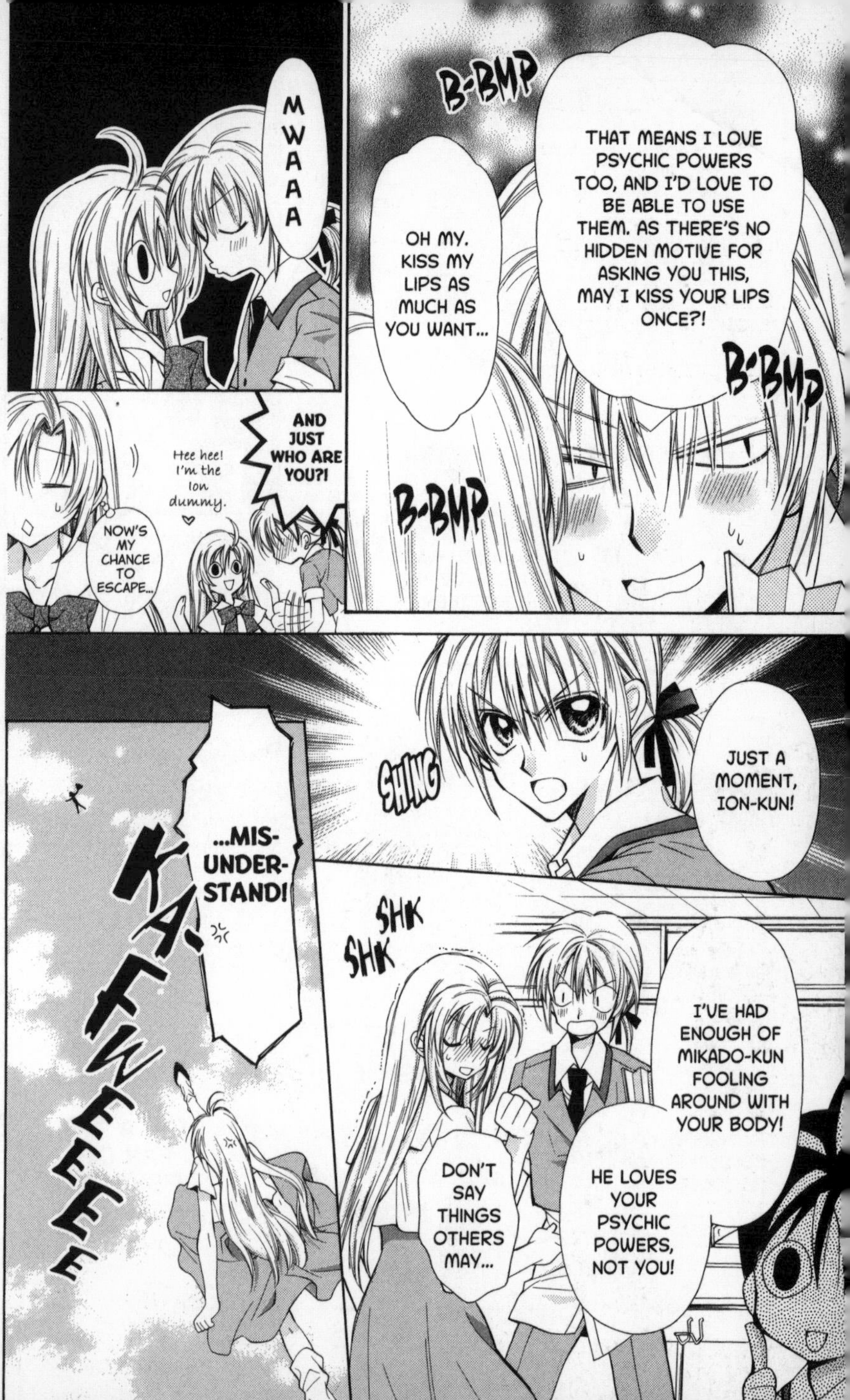
B-BMP
THAT MEANS I LOVE PSYCHIC POWERS TOO, AND I'D LOVE TO BE ABLE TO USE THEM. AS THERE'S NO HIDDEN MOTIVE FOR ASKING YOU THIS, MAY I KISS YOUR LIPS ONCE?!
OH MY. KISS MY LIPS AS MUCH AS YOU WANT...
B-BMP
B-BMP
MWAAAA
AND JUST WHO ARE YOU?!
Hee hee! I'm the Ion dummy.
NOW'S MY CHANCE TO ESCAPE...
SHING
JUST A MOMENT, ION-KUN!
SHK
SHK
I'VE HAD ENOUGH OF MIKADO-KUN FOOLING AROUND WITH YOUR BODY!
HE LOVES YOUR PSYCHIC POWERS, NOT YOU!
DON'T SAY THINGS OTHERS MAY...
...MIS-UNDER-STAND!
KA-FWEEEEE

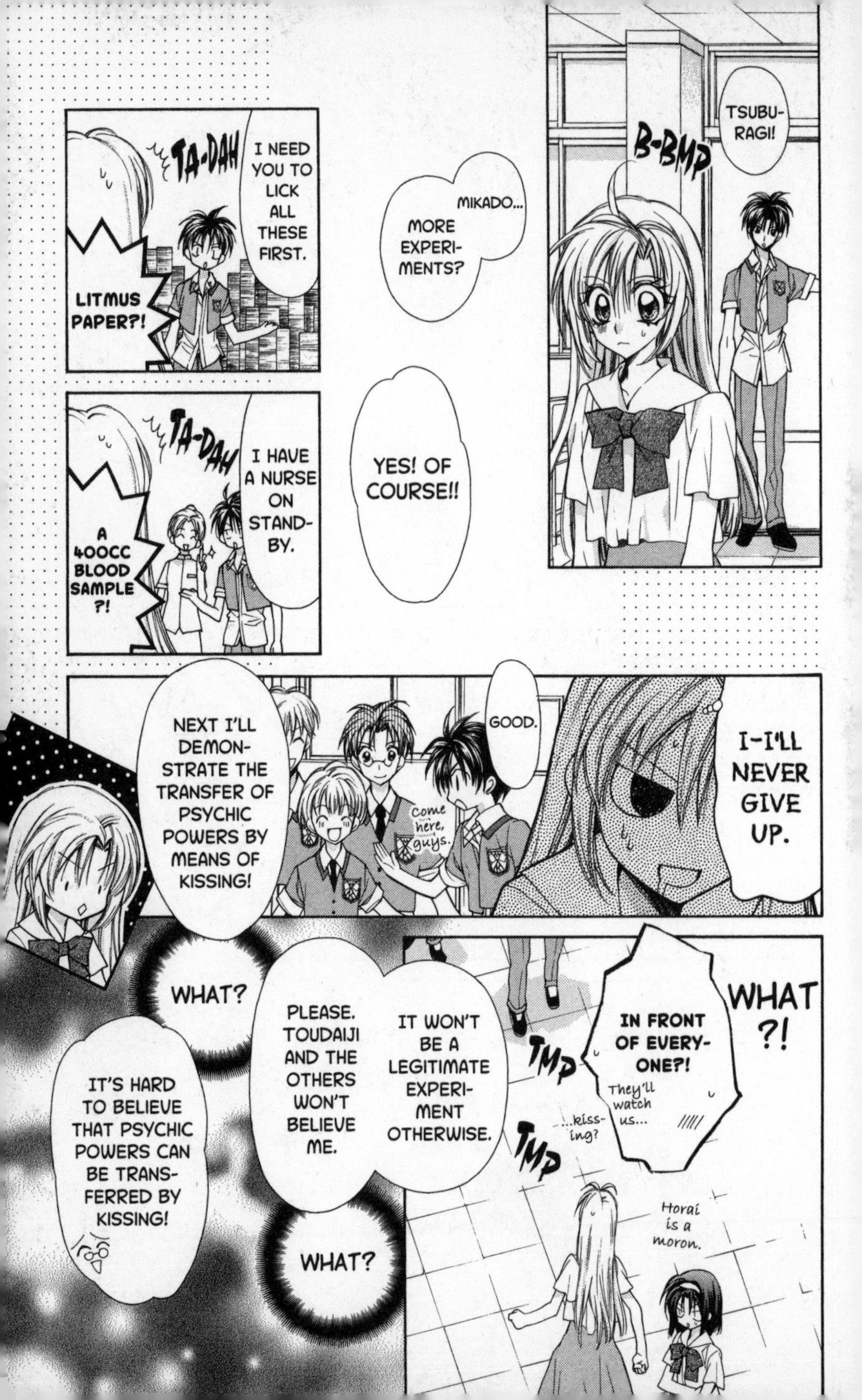

TSUBU-RAGI!
B-BMP
MIKADO... MORE EXPERI-MENTS?
YES! OF COURSE!!
I NEED YOU TO LICK ALL THESE FIRST.
TA-DAH
LITMUS PAPER?!
I HAVE A NURSE ON STAND-BY.
TA-DAH
A 400CC BLOOD SAMPLE ?!
I-I'LL NEVER GIVE UP.
GOOD.
Come here, guys.
NEXT I'LL DEMON-STRATE THE TRANSFER OF PSYCHIC POWERS BY MEANS OF KISSING!
WHAT ?!
IN FRONT OF EVERY-ONE?!
They'll watch us...
TMP
TMP
...kiss-ing?
Horai is a moron.
WHAT?
IT WON'T BE A LEGITIMATE EXPERI-MENT OTHERWISE.
PLEASE. TOUDAIJI AND THE OTHERS WON'T BELIEVE ME.
IT'S HARD TO BELIEVE THAT PSYCHIC POWERS CAN BE TRANS-FERRED BY KISSING!
WHAT?

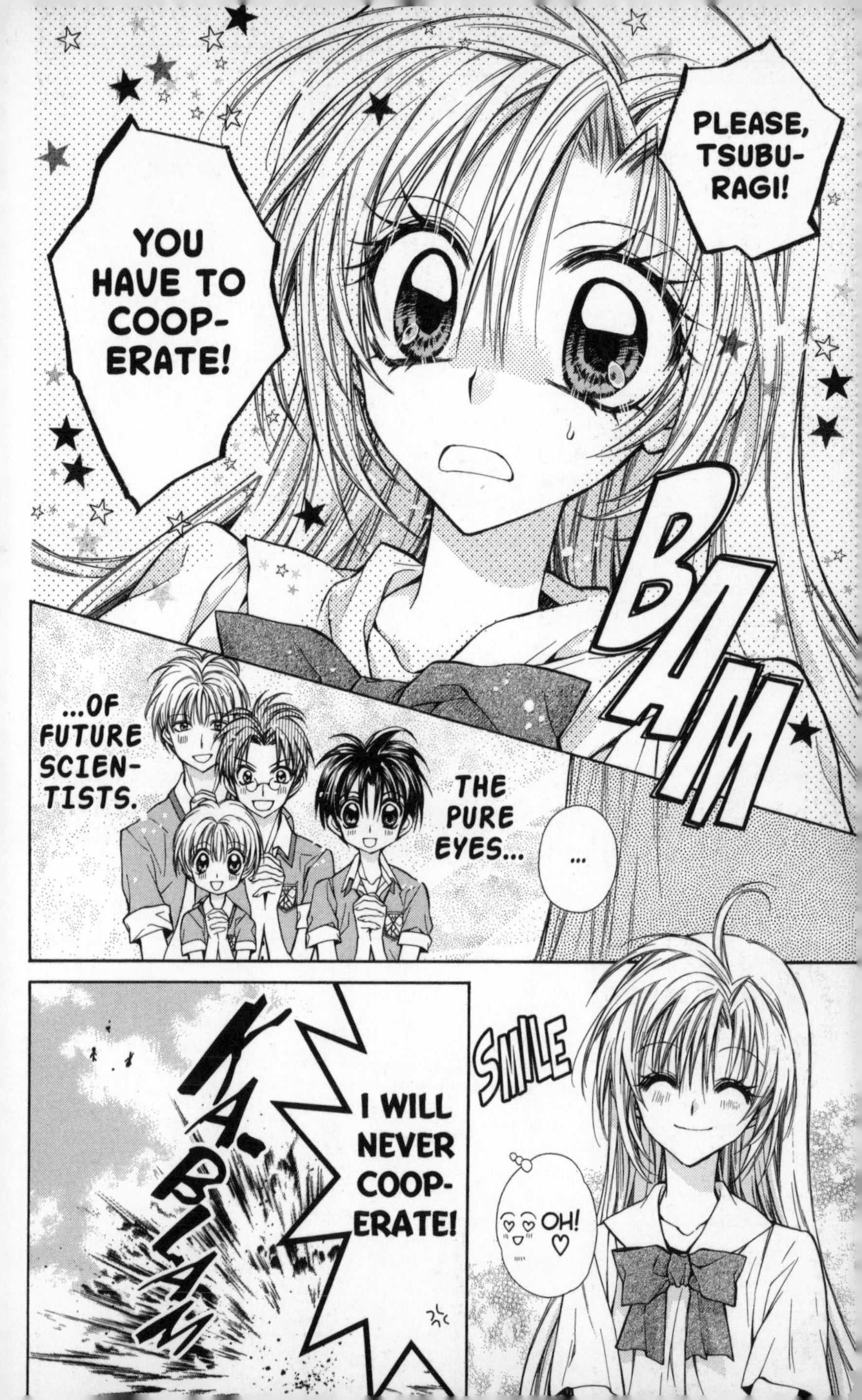
PLEASE, TSUBU-RAGI!
YOU HAVE TO COOP-ERATE!
BAM
...
THE PURE EYES...
...OF FUTURE SCIEN-TISTS.
SMILE
OH!
I WILL NEVER COOP-ERATE!
KA-BLAM

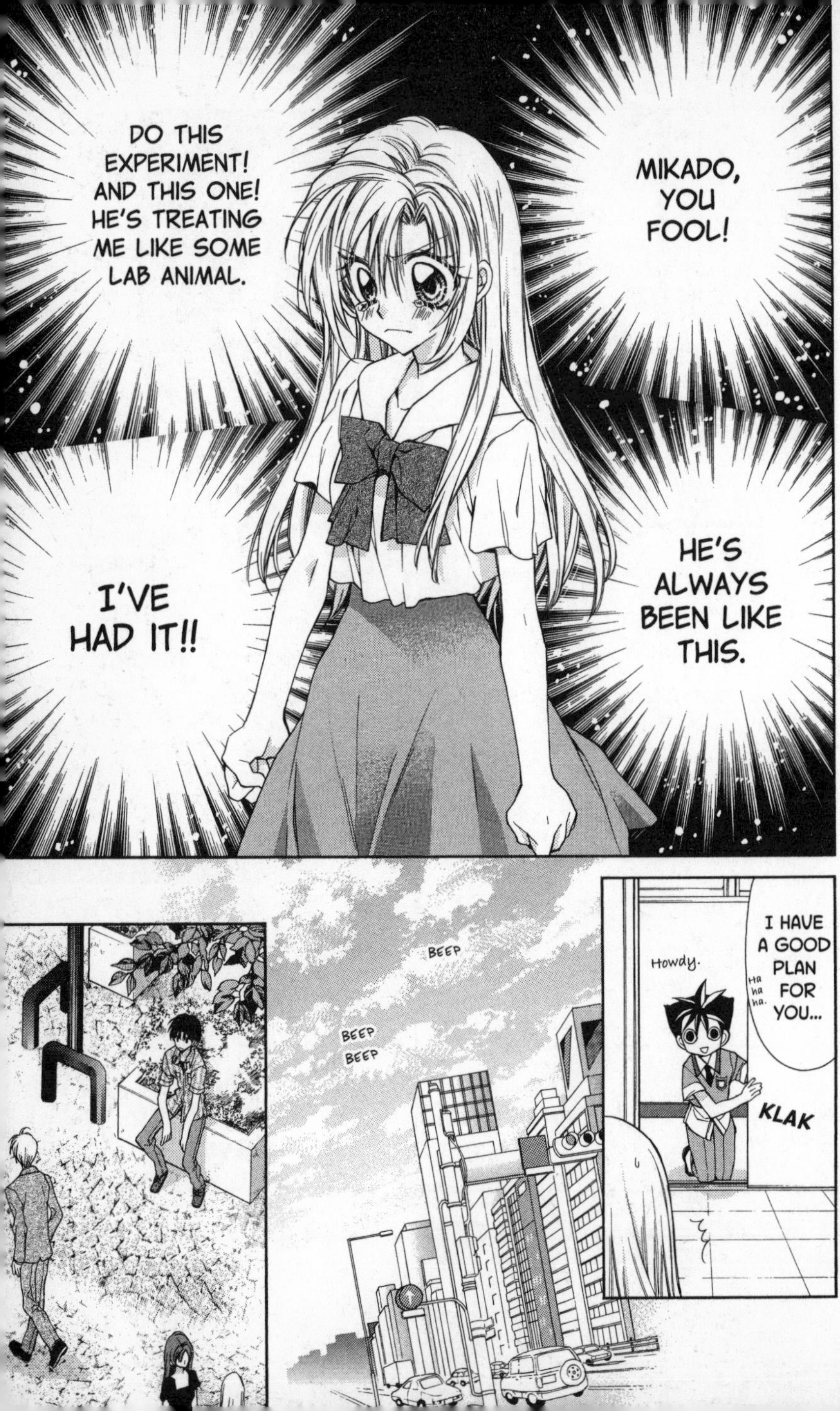
MIKADO, YOU FOOL!
DO THIS EXPERIMENT! AND THIS ONE! HE'S TREATING ME LIKE SOME LAB ANIMAL.
HE'S ALWAYS BEEN LIKE THIS.
I'VE HAD IT!!
I HAVE A GOOD PLAN FOR YOU...
Ha ha ha.
Howdy.
KLAK
BEEP
BEEP BEEP

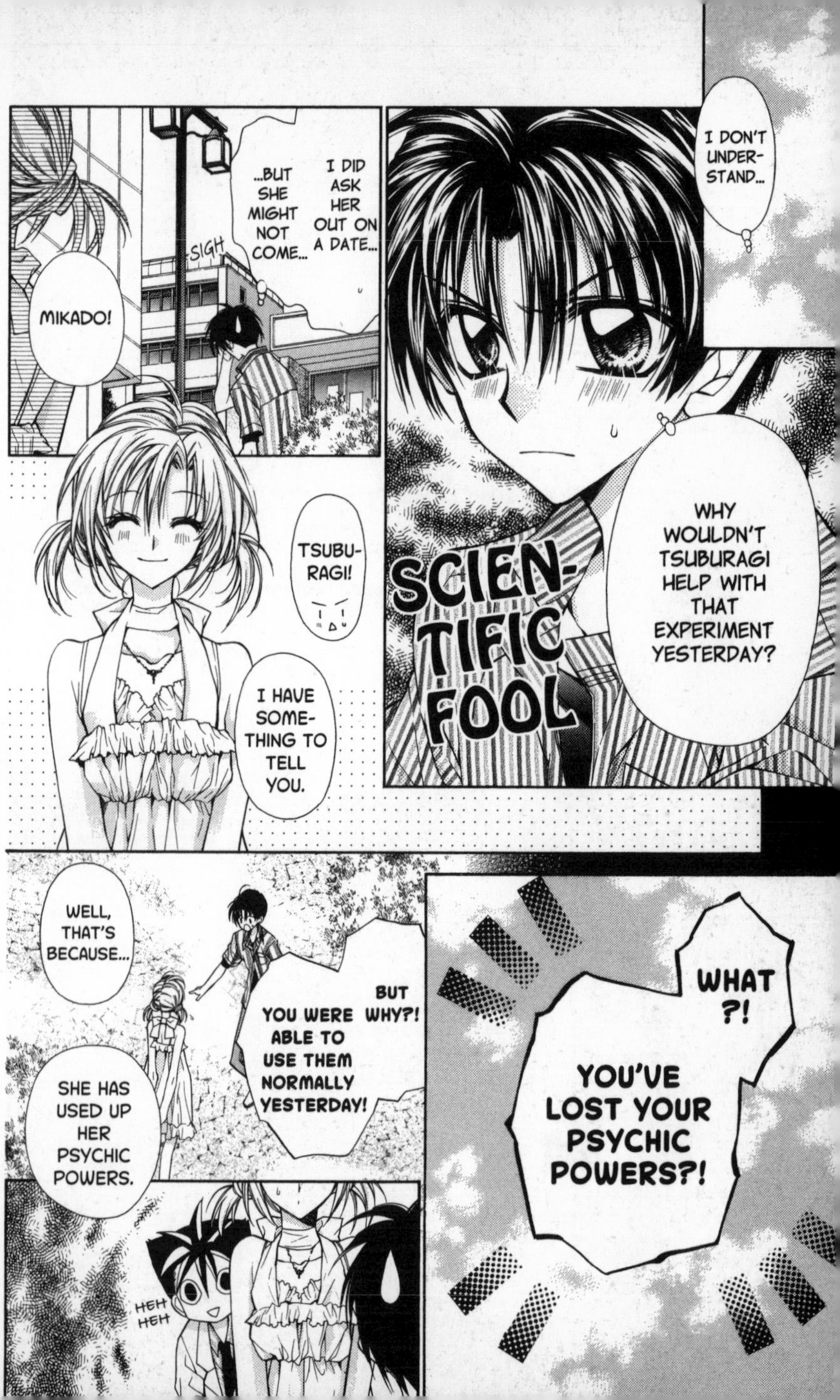
I DON'T UNDERSTAND...
WHY WOULDN'T TSUBURAGI HELP WITH THAT EXPERIMENT YESTERDAY?
SCIEN-TIFIC FOOL
I DID ASK HER OUT ON A DATE...
...BUT SHE MIGHT NOT COME...
SIGH
MIKADO!
TSUBU-RAGI!
I HAVE SOME-THING TO TELL YOU.
WHAT?!
YOU'VE LOST YOUR PSYCHIC POWERS?!
BUT WHY?!
YOU WERE ABLE TO USE THEM NORMALLY YESTERDAY!
WELL, THAT'S BECAUSE...
SHE HAS USED UP HER PSYCHIC POWERS.
HEH HEH

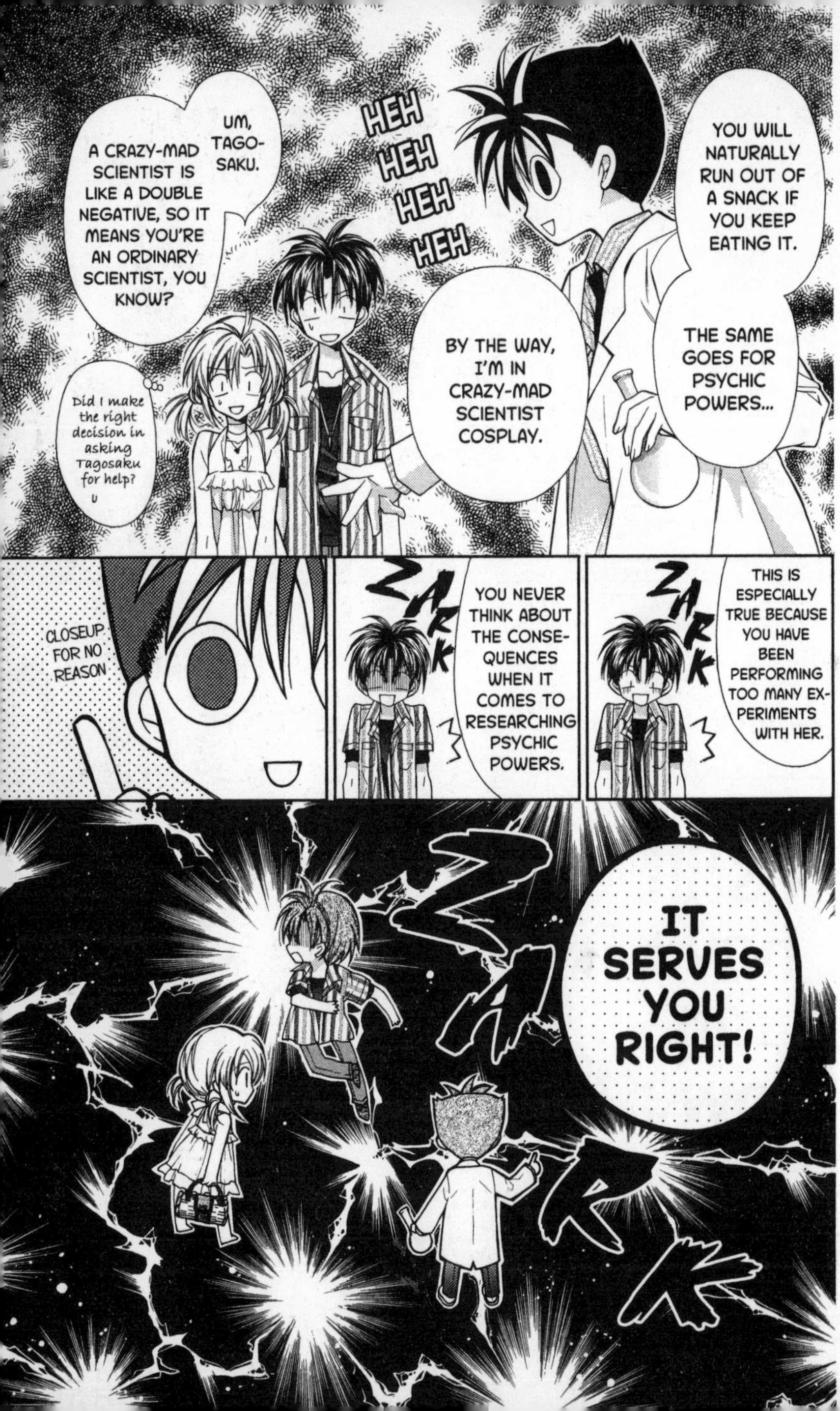
YOU WILL NATURALLY RUN OUT OF A SNACK IF YOU KEEP EATING IT.
THE SAME GOES FOR PSYCHIC POWERS...
HEH HEH HEH HEH
BY THE WAY, I'M IN CRAZY-MAD SCIENTIST COSPLAY.
UM, TAGO-SAKU.
A CRAZY-MAD SCIENTIST IS LIKE A DOUBLE NEGATIVE, SO IT MEANS YOU'RE AN ORDINARY SCIENTIST, YOU KNOW?
Did I make the right decision in asking Tagosaku for help?
ZARK
THIS IS ESPECIALLY TRUE BECAUSE YOU HAVE BEEN PERFORMING TOO MANY EX-PERIMENTS WITH HER.
ZARK
YOU NEVER THINK ABOUT THE CONSE-QUENCES WHEN IT COMES TO RESEARCHING PSYCHIC POWERS.
CLOSEUP FOR NO REASON
IT SERVES YOU RIGHT!
ZARK

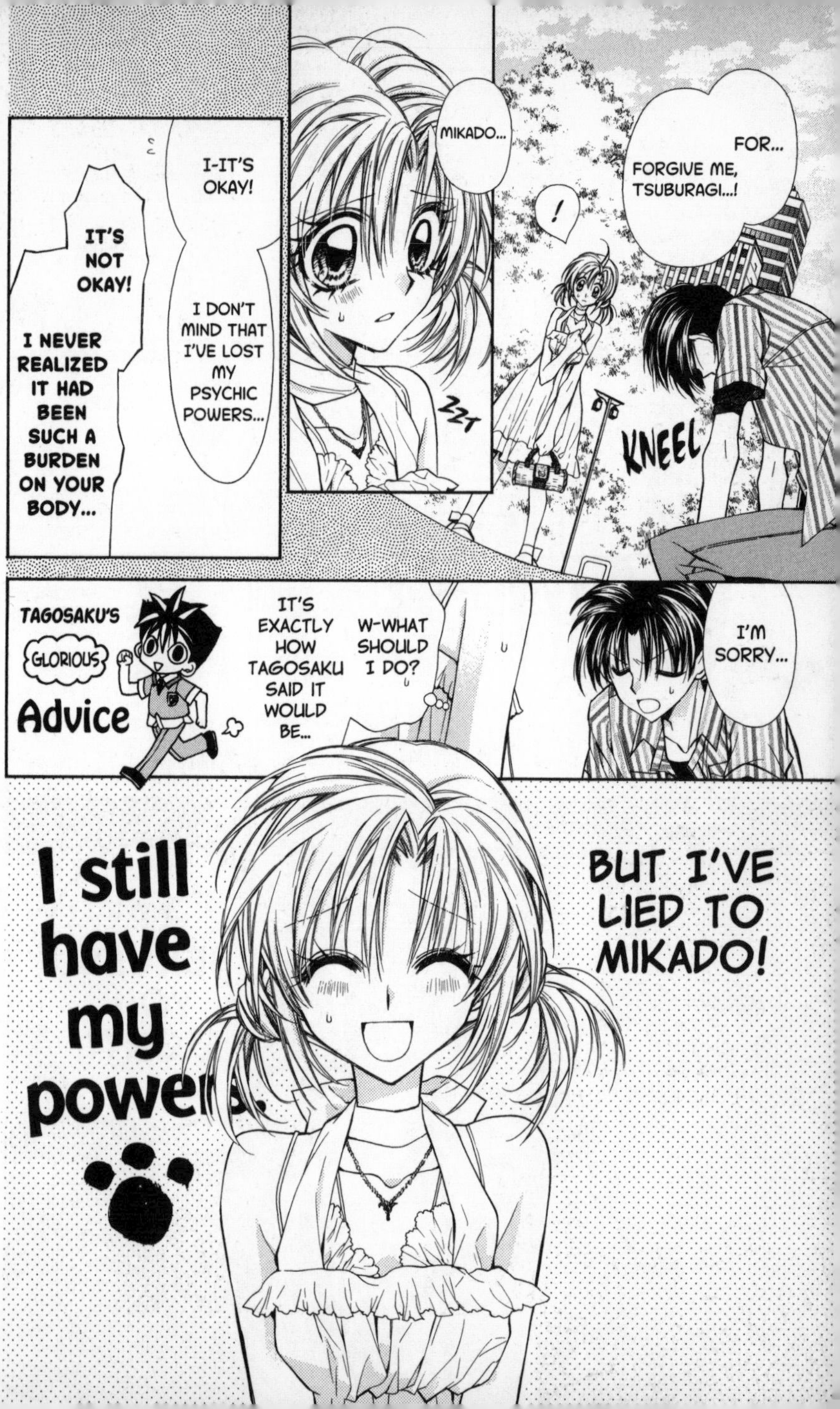
FOR...
FORGIVE ME, TSUBURAGI...!
!
KNEEL
MIKADO...
ZZT
I-IT'S OKAY!
I DON'T MIND THAT I'VE LOST MY PSYCHIC POWERS...
IT'S NOT OKAY!
I NEVER REALIZED IT HAD BEEN SUCH A BURDEN ON YOUR BODY...
I'M SORRY...
W-WHAT SHOULD I DO?
IT'S EXACTLY HOW TAGOSAKU SAID IT WOULD BE...
TAGOSAKU'S GLORIOUS Advice
BUT I'VE LIED TO MIKADO!
I still have my powers.

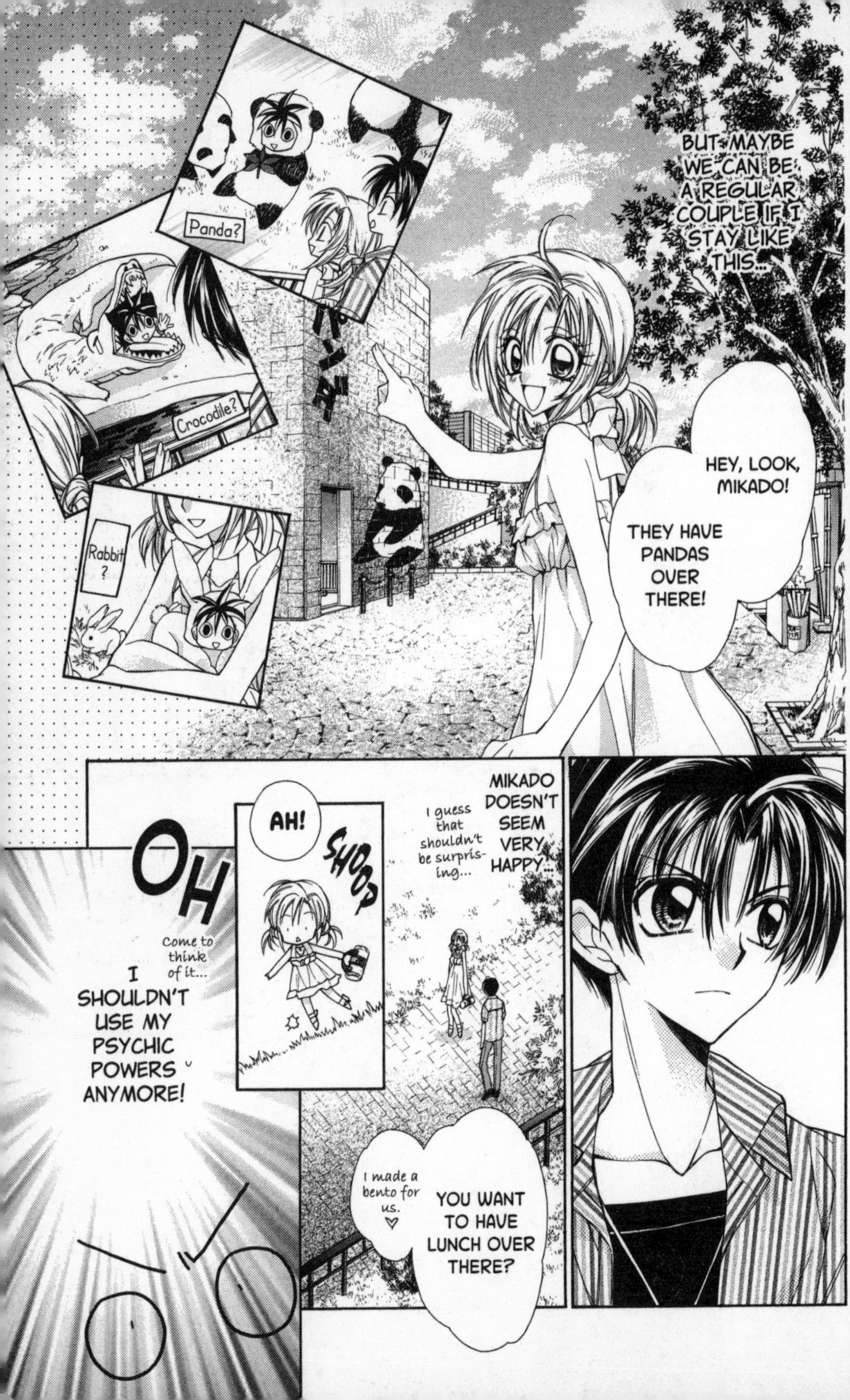
BUT MAYBE WE CAN BE A REGULAR COUPLE IF I STAY LIKE THIS...
HEY, LOOK, MIKADO!
THEY HAVE PANDAS OVER THERE!
Panda?
Crocodile?
Rabbit ?
MIKADO DOESN'T SEEM VERY HAPPY...
I guess that shouldn't be surprising...
YOU WANT TO HAVE LUNCH OVER THERE?
I made a bento for us. ♡
AH!
SHOOP
OH
Come to think of it...
I SHOULDN'T USE MY PSYCHIC POWERS ANYMORE!

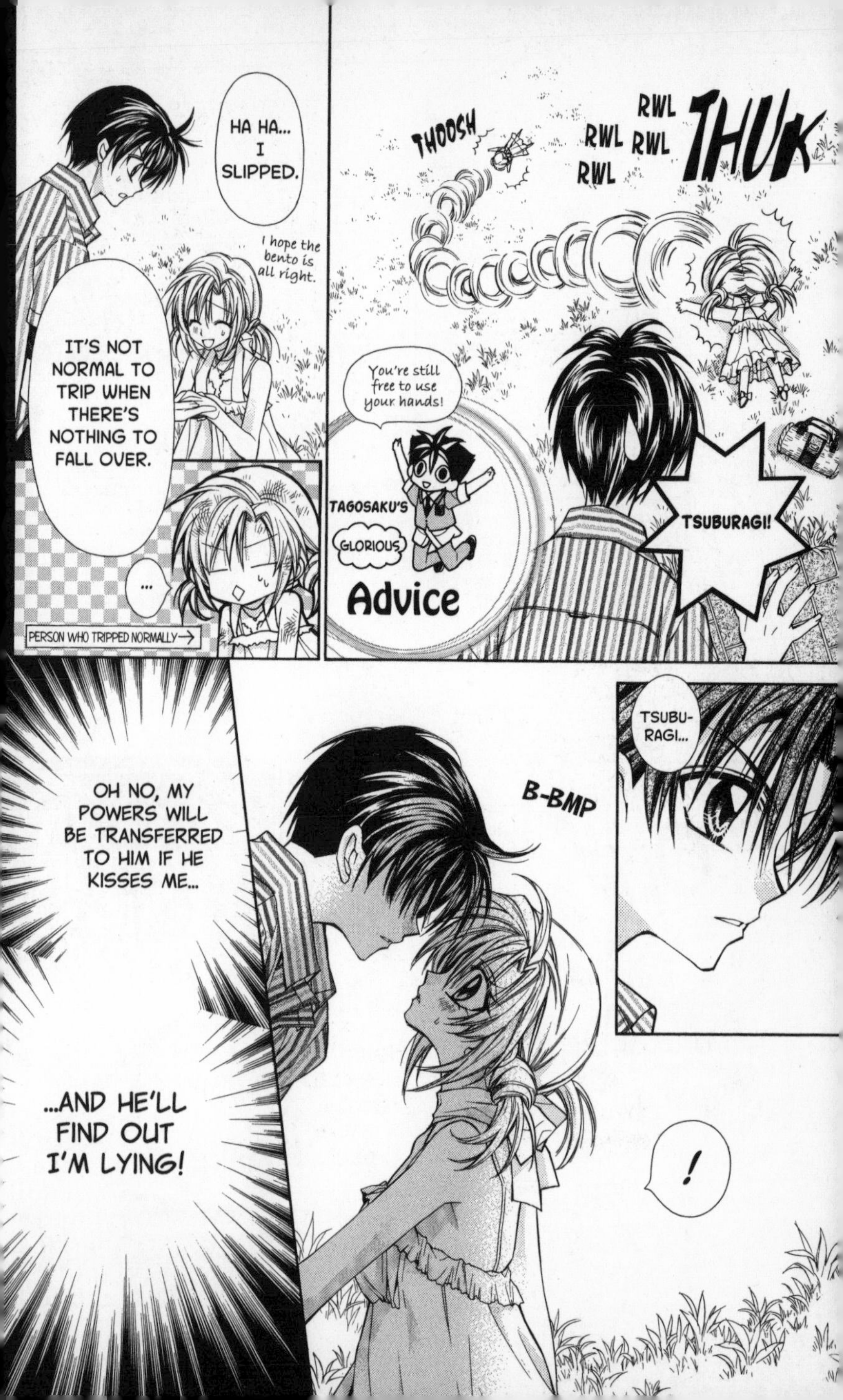
THUK
RWL RWL RWL RWL
THOOSH
TSUBURAGI!
You're still free to use your hands!
TAGOSAKU'S GLORIOUS Advice
HA HA... I SLIPPED.
I hope the bento is all right.
IT'S NOT NORMAL TO TRIP WHEN THERE'S NOTHING TO FALL OVER.
...
PERSON WHO TRIPPED NORMALLY→
TSUBU-RAGI...
B-BMP
!
OH NO, MY POWERS WILL BE TRANSFERRED TO HIM IF HE KISSES ME...
...AND HE'LL FIND OUT I'M LYING!

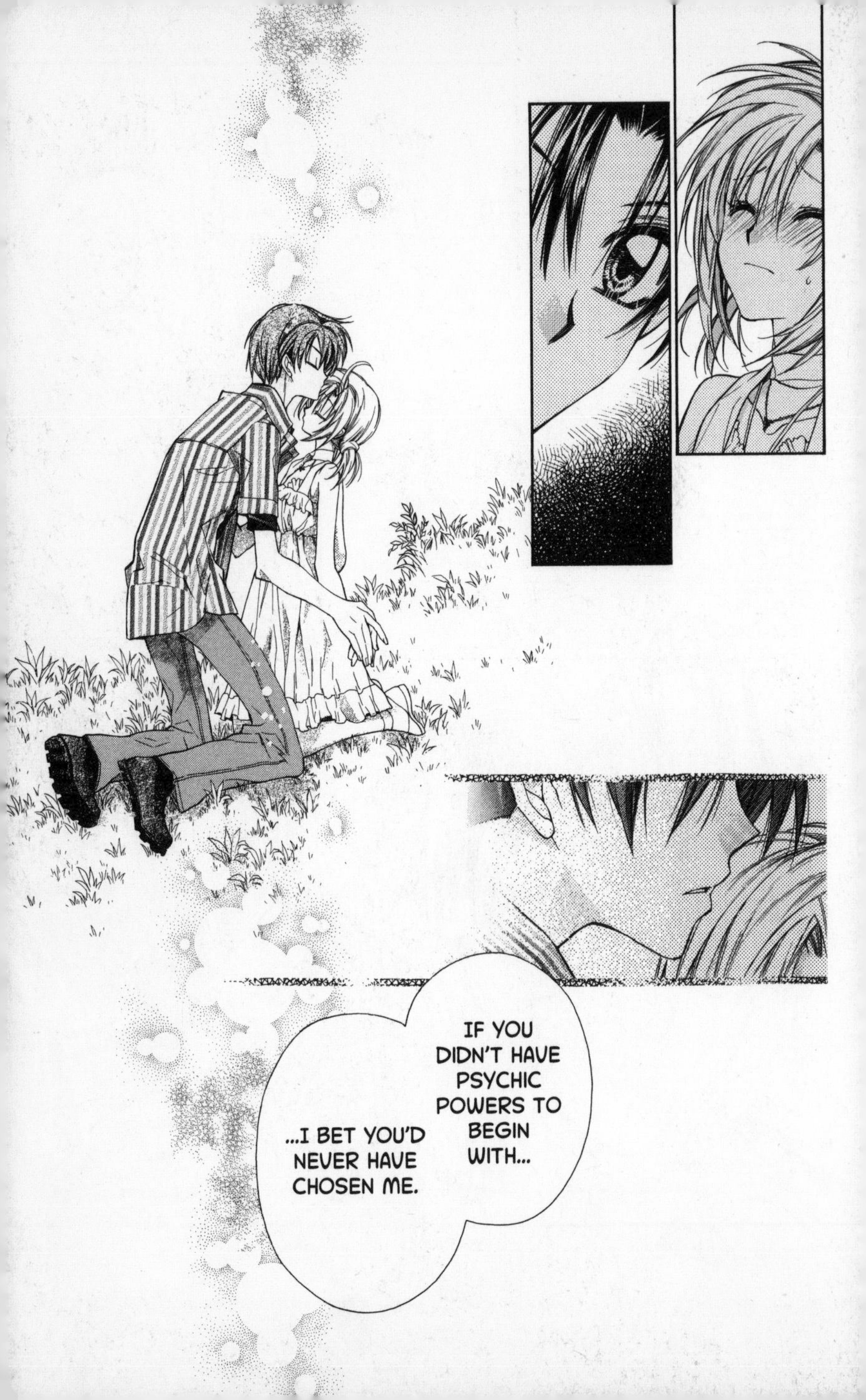
IF YOU DIDN'T HAVE PSYCHIC POWERS TO BEGIN WITH...
...I BET YOU'D NEVER HAVE CHOSEN ME.

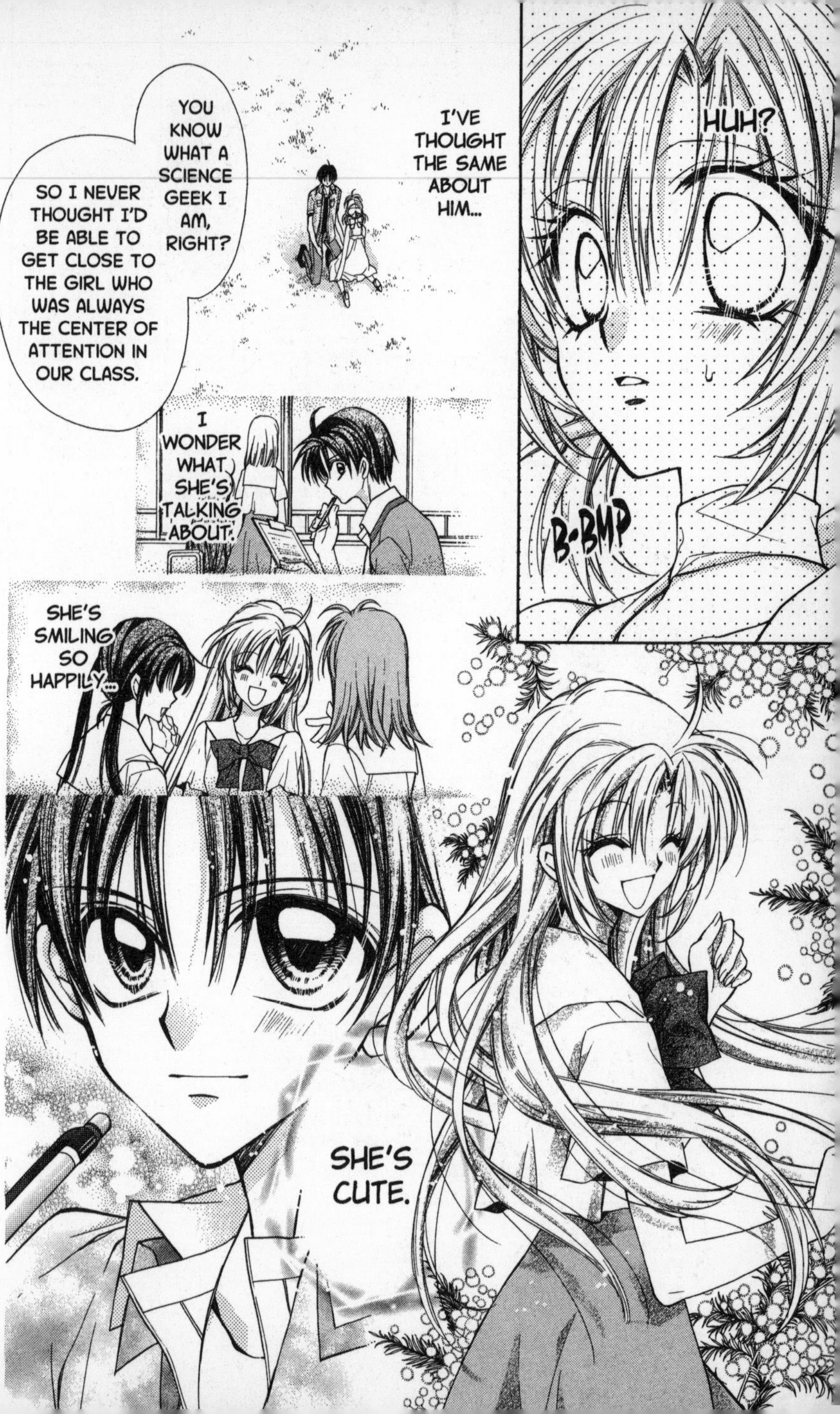
HUH?
B-BMP
I'VE THOUGHT THE SAME ABOUT HIM...
YOU KNOW WHAT A SCIENCE GEEK I AM, RIGHT?
SO I NEVER THOUGHT I'D BE ABLE TO GET CLOSE TO THE GIRL WHO WAS ALWAYS THE CENTER OF ATTENTION IN OUR CLASS.
I WONDER WHAT SHE'S TALKING ABOUT.
SHE'S SMILING SO HAPPILY...
SHE'S CUTE.

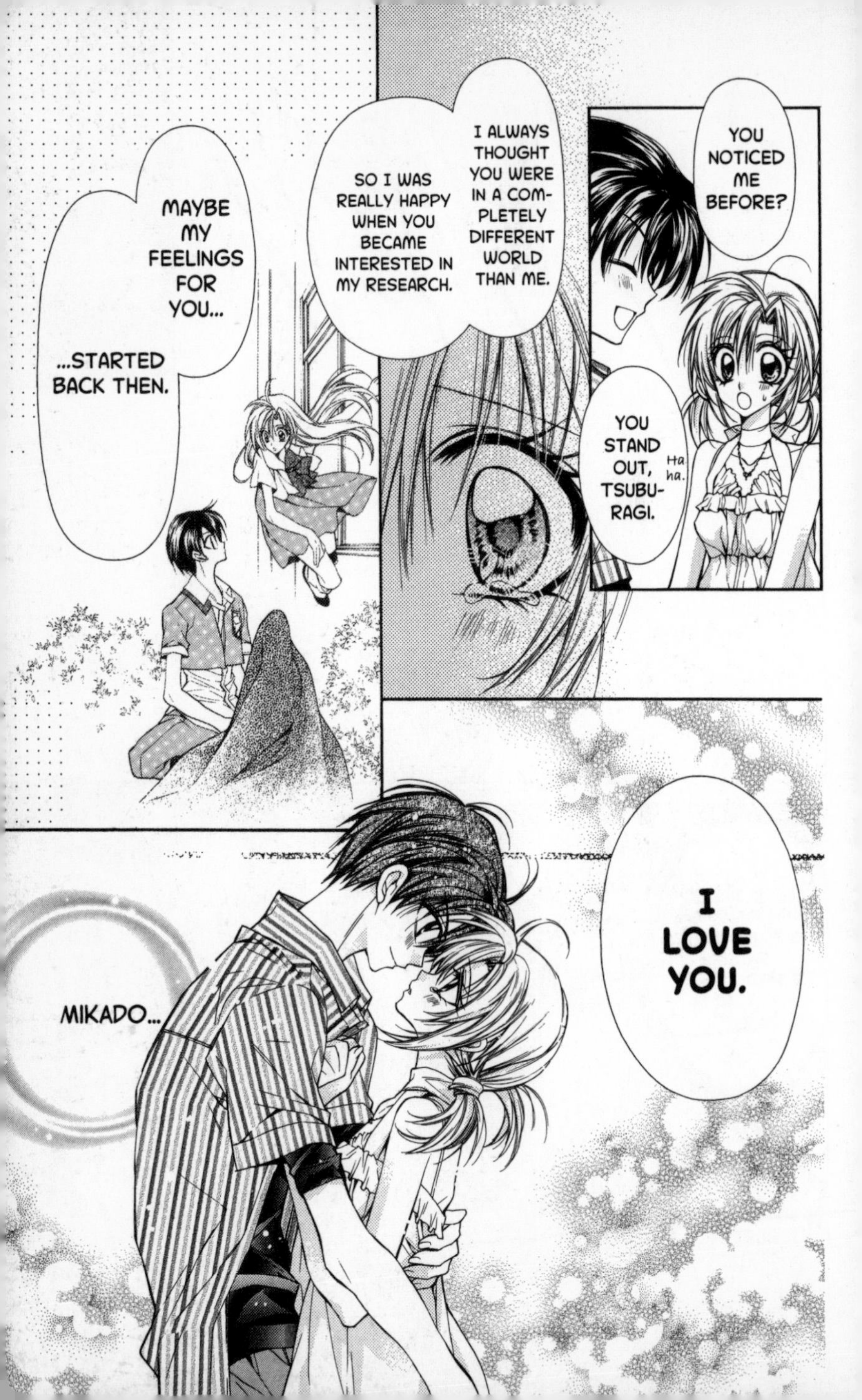

YOU NOTICED ME BEFORE?
YOU STAND OUT, TSUBURAGI.
Ha ha.
I ALWAYS THOUGHT YOU WERE IN A COMPLETELY DIFFERENT WORLD THAN ME.
SO I WAS REALLY HAPPY WHEN YOU BECAME INTERESTED IN MY RESEARCH.
MAYBE MY FEELINGS FOR YOU...
...STARTED BACK THEN.
I LOVE YOU.
MIKADO...

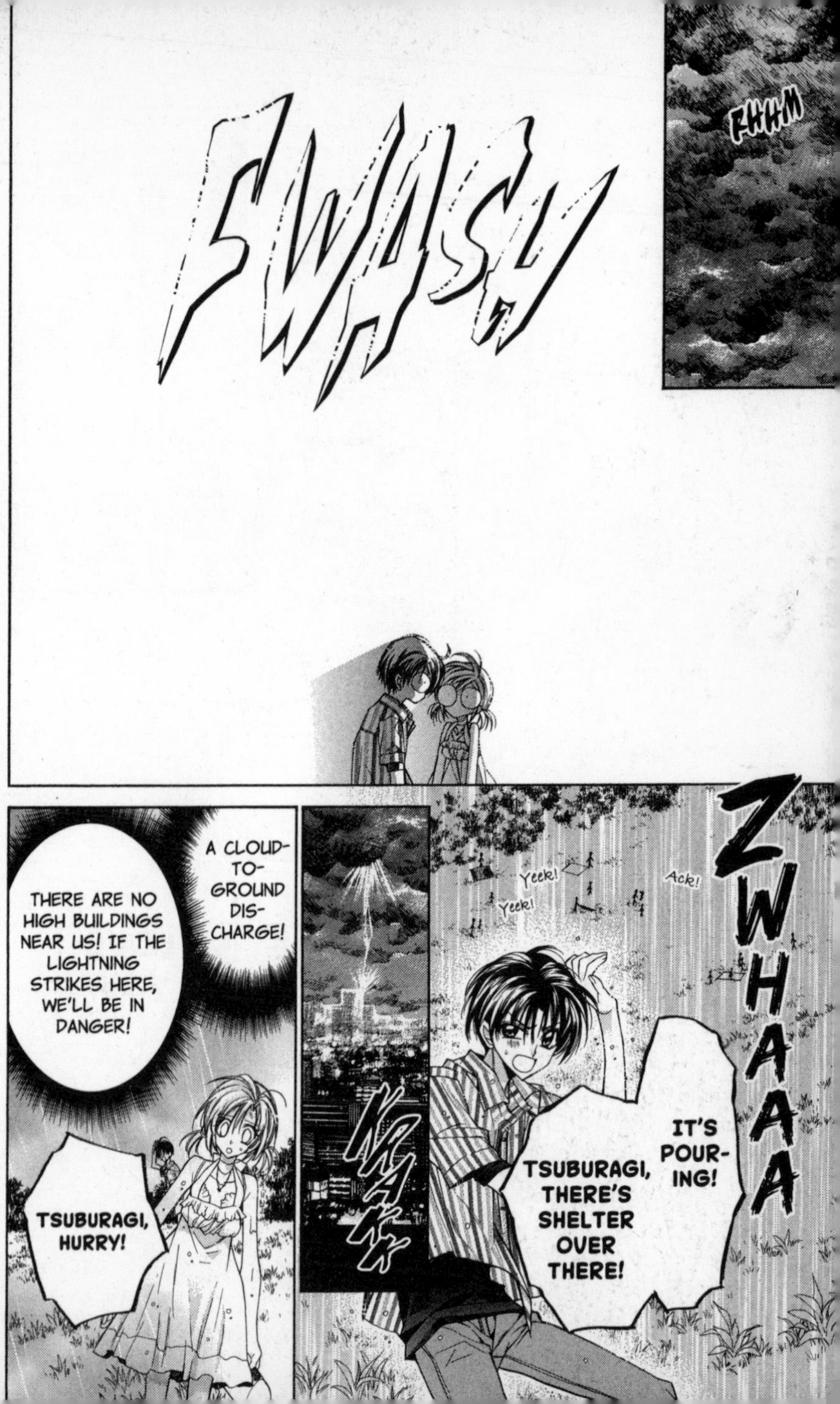
RHHM
SWASH
ZWHAAA
Ack!
Yeek!
Yeek!
IT'S POURING!
TSUBURAGI, THERE'S SHELTER OVER THERE!
A CLOUD-TO-GROUND DISCHARGE!
THERE ARE NO HIGH BUILDINGS NEAR US! IF THE LIGHTNING STRIKES HERE, WE'LL BE IN DANGER!
TSUBURAGI, HURRY!

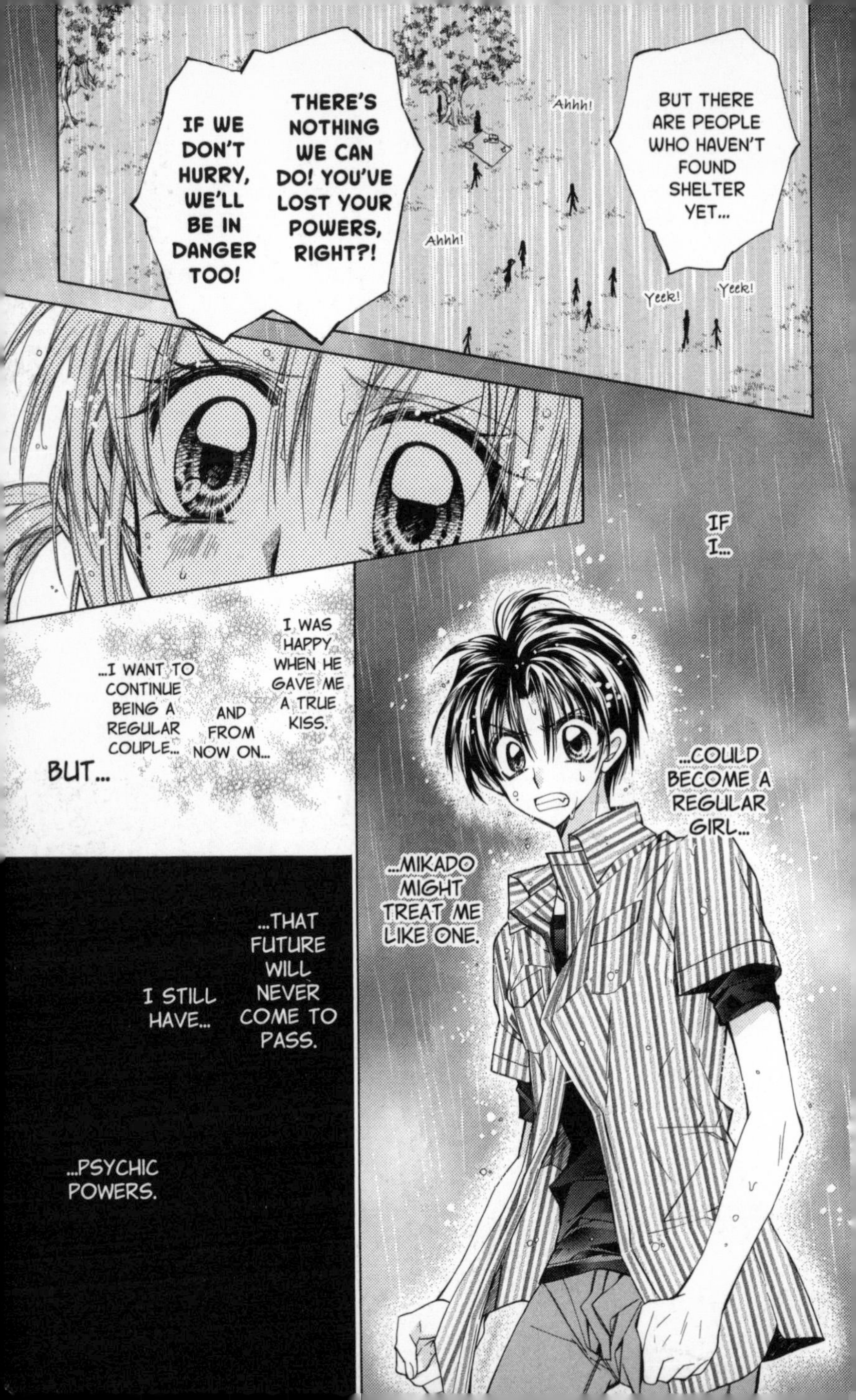
BUT THERE ARE PEOPLE WHO HAVEN'T FOUND SHELTER YET...
Ahhh!
Yeek!
Yeek!
Ahhh!
THERE'S NOTHING WE CAN DO! YOU'VE LOST YOUR POWERS, RIGHT?!
IF WE DON'T HURRY, WE'LL BE IN DANGER TOO!
IF I...
...COULD BECOME A REGULAR GIRL...
...MIKADO MIGHT TREAT ME LIKE ONE.
I WAS HAPPY WHEN HE GAVE ME A TRUE KISS.
AND FROM NOW ON...
...I WANT TO CONTINUE BEING A REGULAR COUPLE...
BUT...
...THAT FUTURE WILL NEVER COME TO PASS.
I STILL HAVE...
...PSYCHIC POWERS.

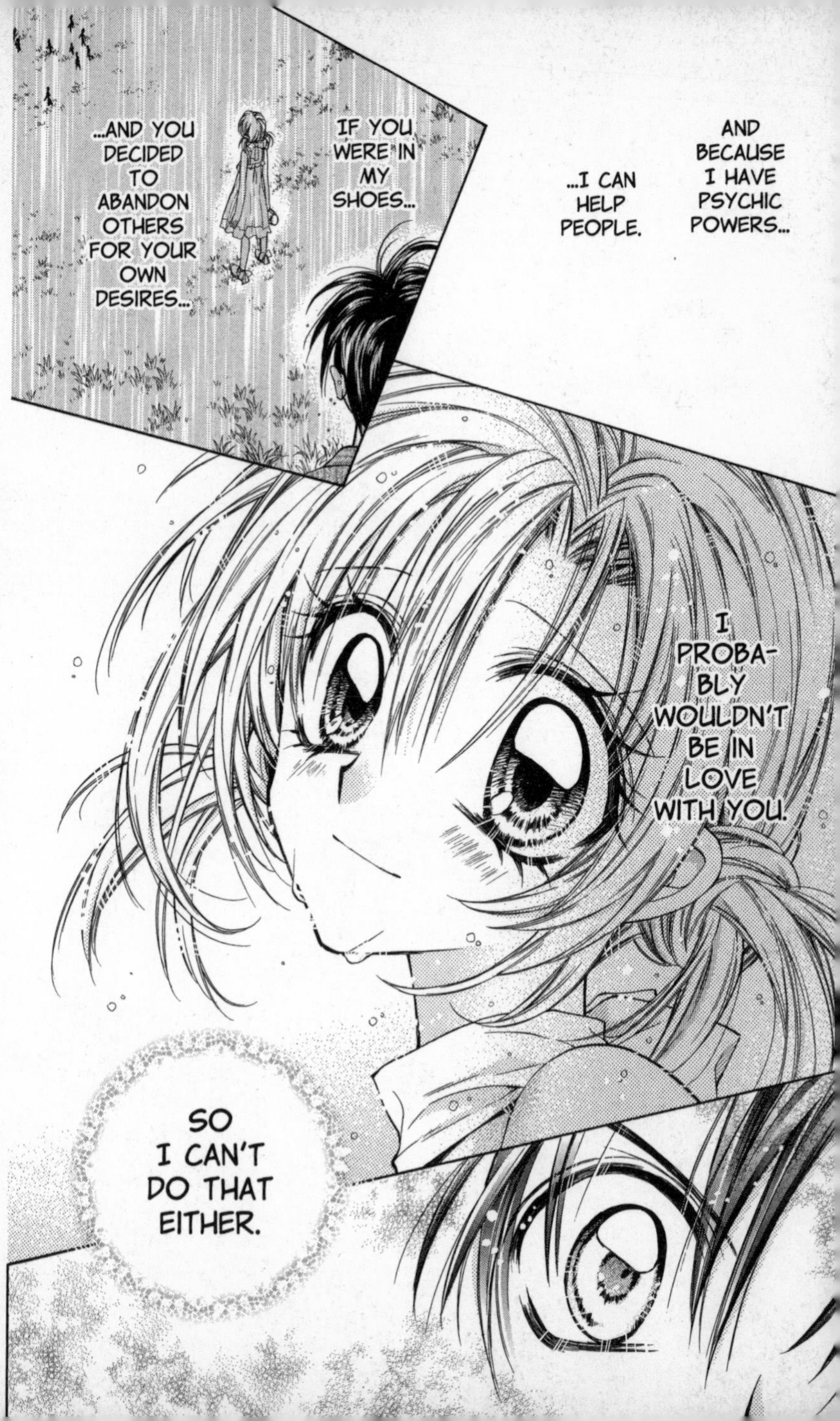
AND BECAUSE I HAVE PSYCHIC POWERS...
...I CAN HELP PEOPLE.
IF YOU WERE IN MY SHOES...
...AND YOU DECIDED TO ABANDON OTHERS FOR YOUR OWN DESIRES...
I PROBABLY WOULDN'T BE IN LOVE WITH YOU.
SO I CAN'T DO THAT EITHER.

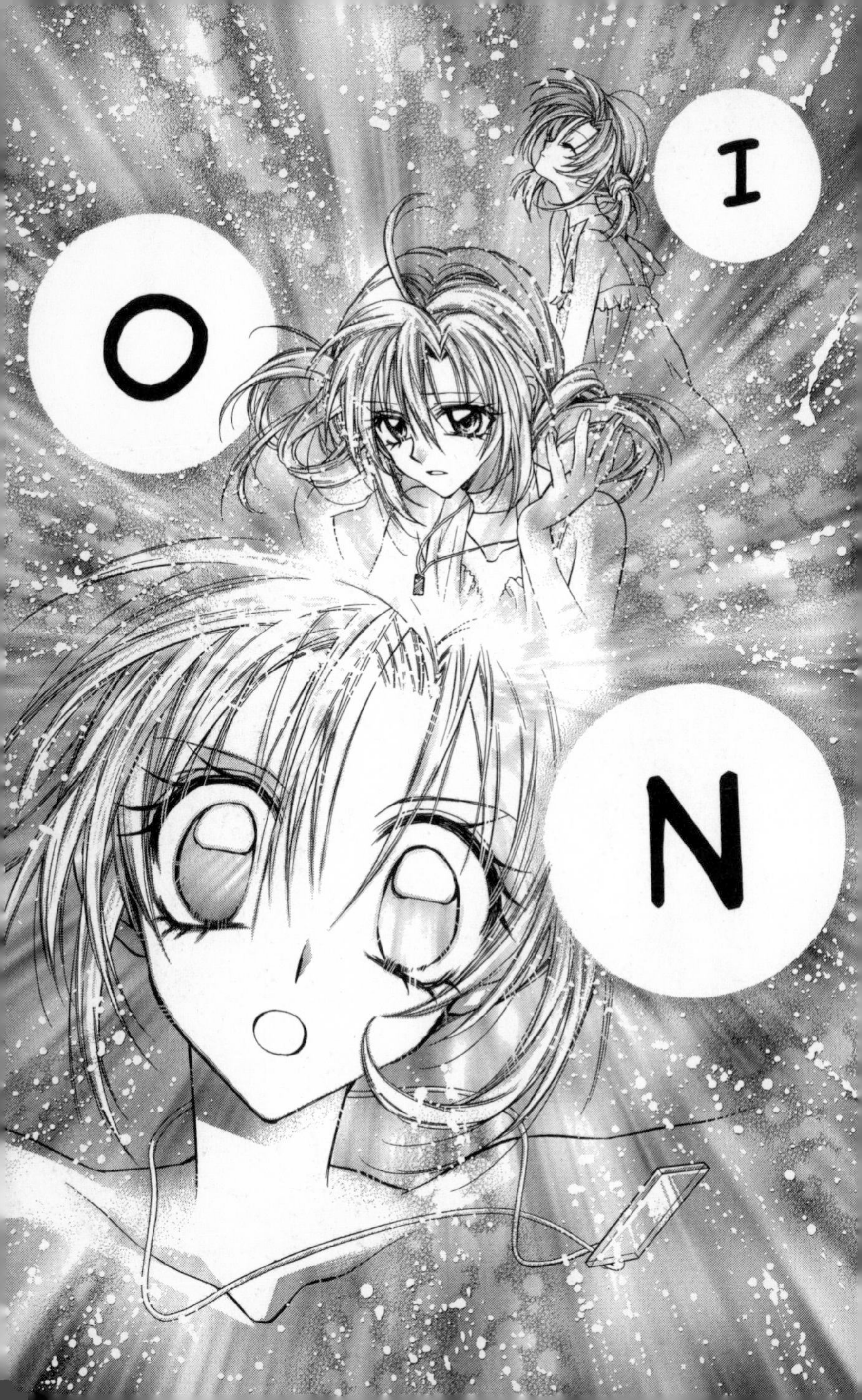
I
O
N

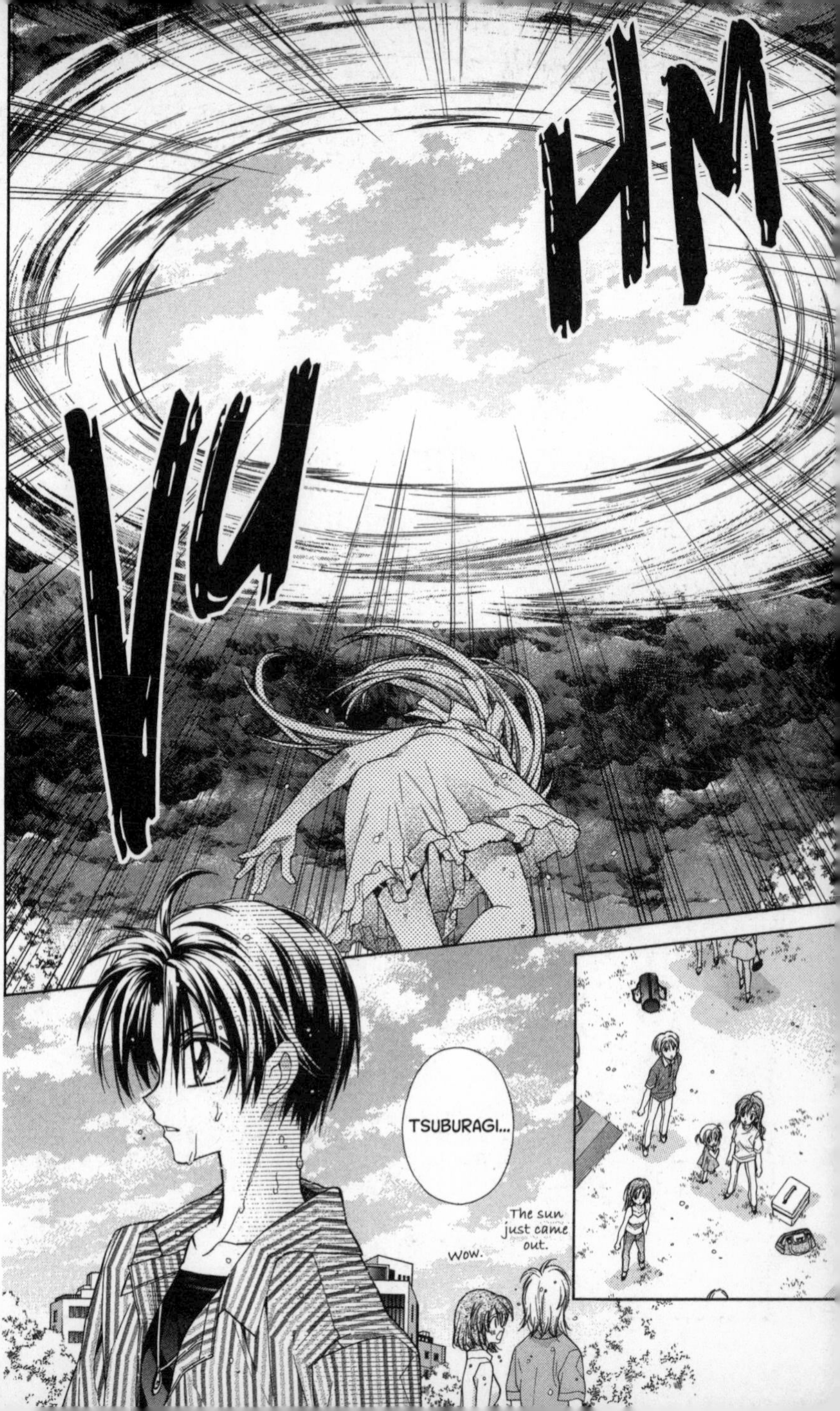
VUHM
TSUBURAGI...
The sun just came out.
Wow.

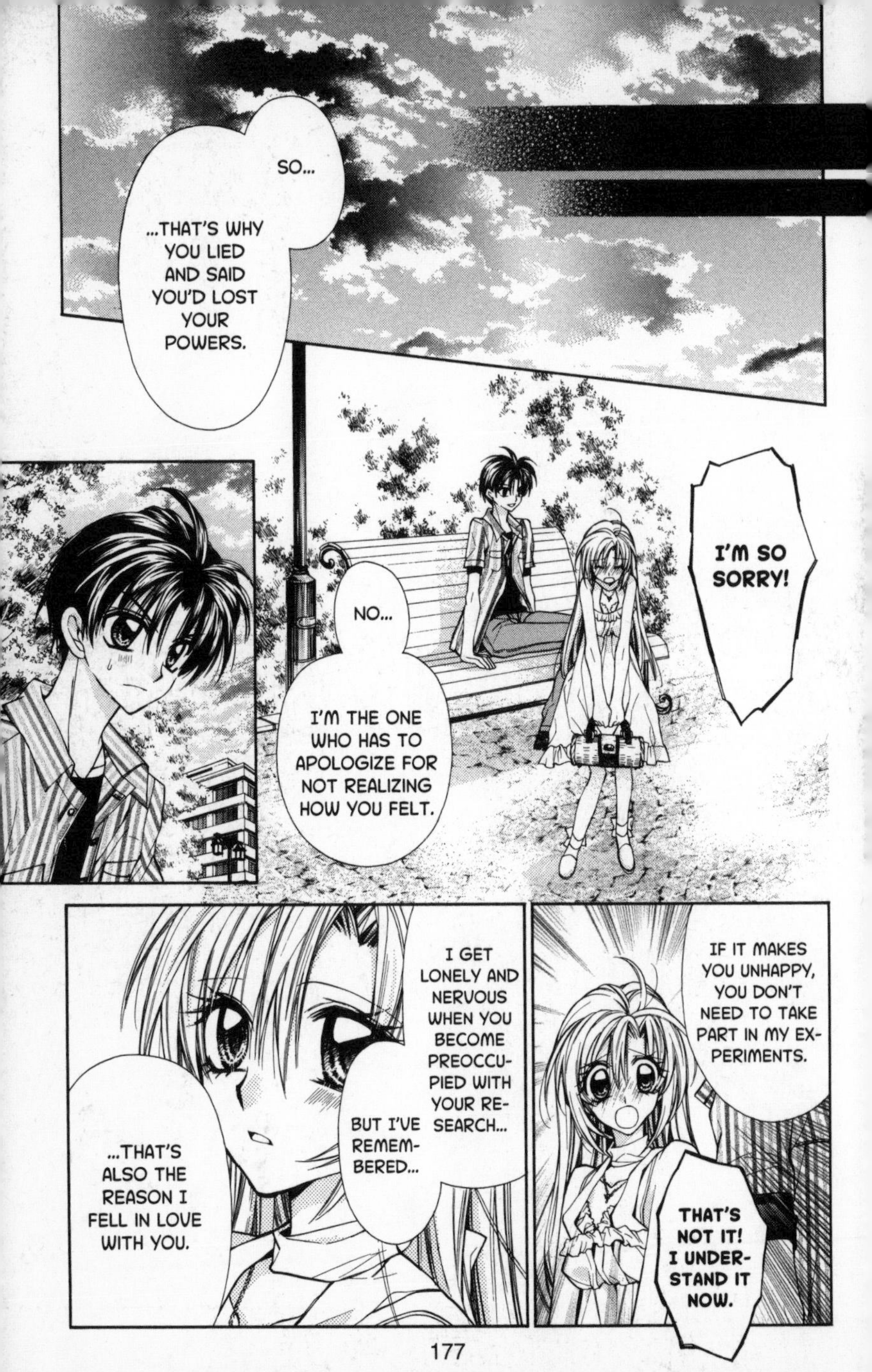
SO...
...THAT'S WHY YOU LIED AND SAID YOU'D LOST YOUR POWERS.
I'M SO SORRY!
NO...
I'M THE ONE WHO HAS TO APOLOGIZE FOR NOT REALIZING HOW YOU FELT.
IF IT MAKES YOU UNHAPPY, YOU DON'T NEED TO TAKE PART IN MY EX-PERIMENTS.
THAT'S NOT IT! I UNDER-STAND IT NOW.
I GET LONELY AND NERVOUS WHEN YOU BECOME PREOCCU-PIED WITH YOUR RE-SEARCH...
BUT I'VE REMEM-BERED...
...THAT'S ALSO THE REASON I FELL IN LOVE WITH YOU.

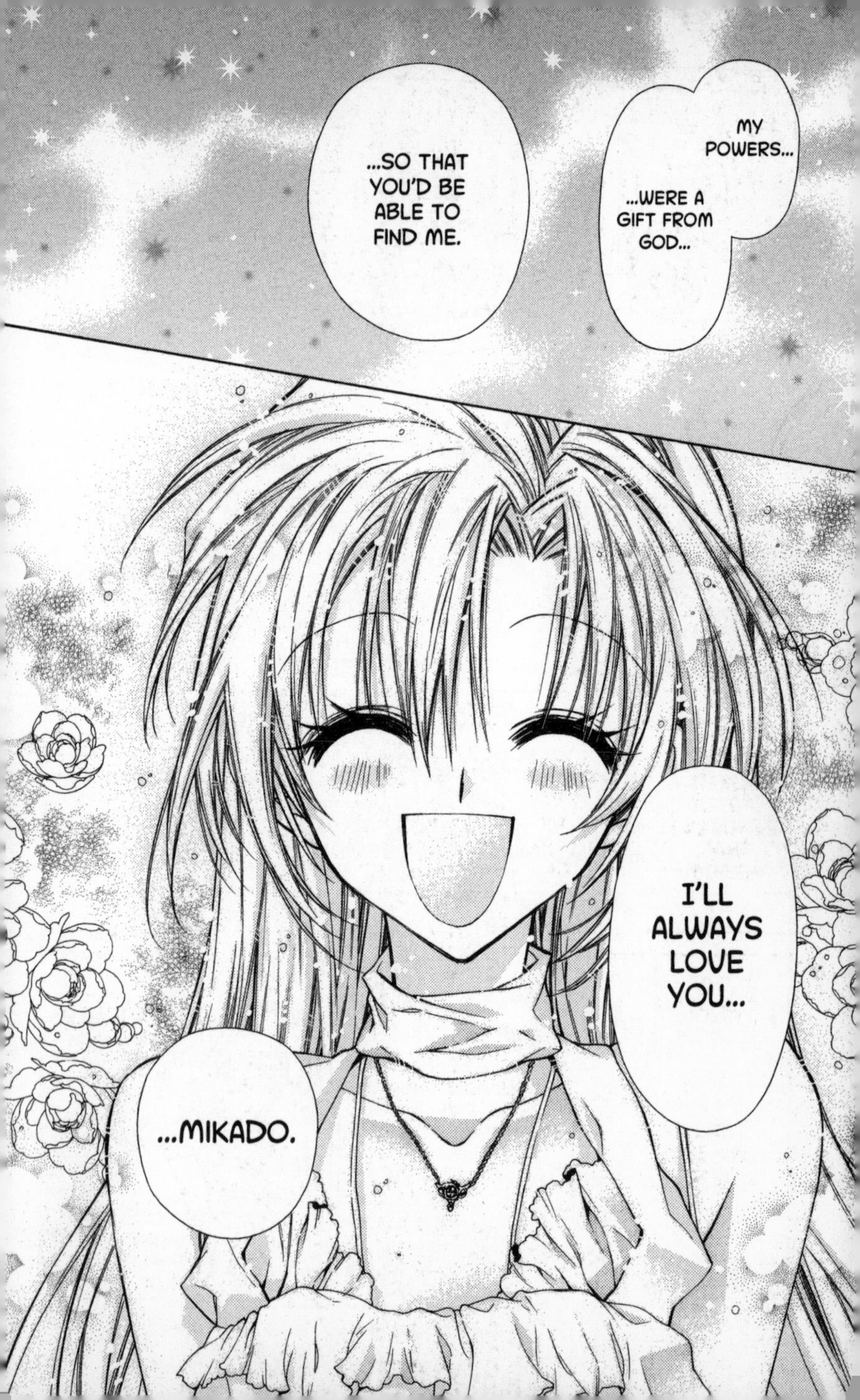
MY POWERS... ...WERE A GIFT FROM GOD...
...SO THAT YOU'D BE ABLE TO FIND ME.
I'LL ALWAYS LOVE YOU...
...MIKADO.

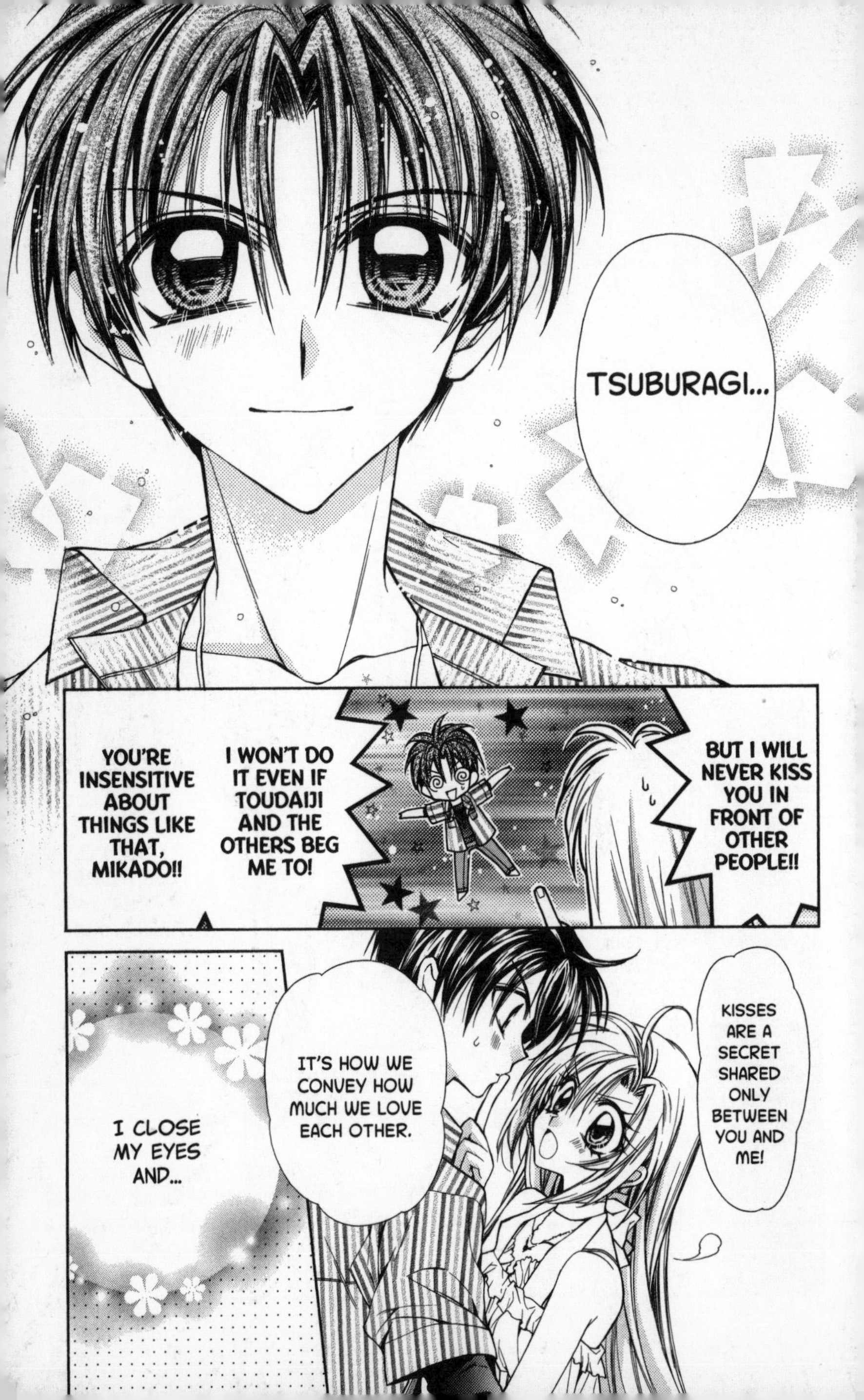
TSUBURAGI...
BUT I WILL NEVER KISS YOU IN FRONT OF OTHER PEOPLE!!
I WON'T DO IT EVEN IF TOUDAIJI AND THE OTHERS BEG ME TO!
YOU'RE INSENSITIVE ABOUT THINGS LIKE THAT, MIKADO!!
KISSES ARE A SECRET SHARED ONLY BETWEEN YOU AND ME!
IT'S HOW WE CONVEY HOW MUCH WE LOVE EACH OTHER.
I CLOSE MY EYES AND...

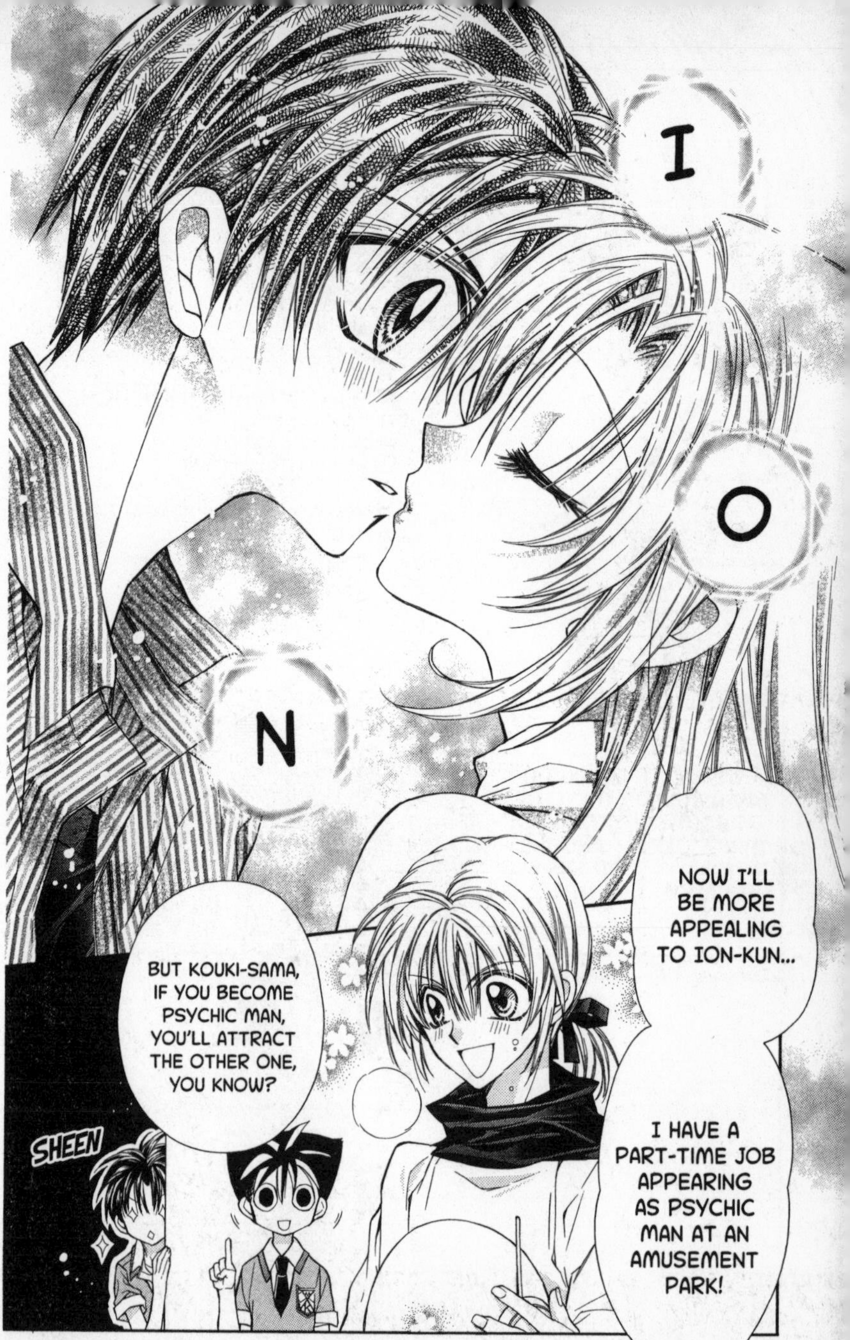
I
O
N
NOW I'LL BE MORE APPEALING TO ION-KUN...
I HAVE A PART-TIME JOB APPEARING AS PSYCHIC MAN AT AN AMUSEMENT PARK!
BUT KOUKI-SAMA, IF YOU BECOME PSYCHIC MAN, YOU'LL ATTRACT THE OTHER ONE, YOU KNOW?
SHEEN

I • O • N/END

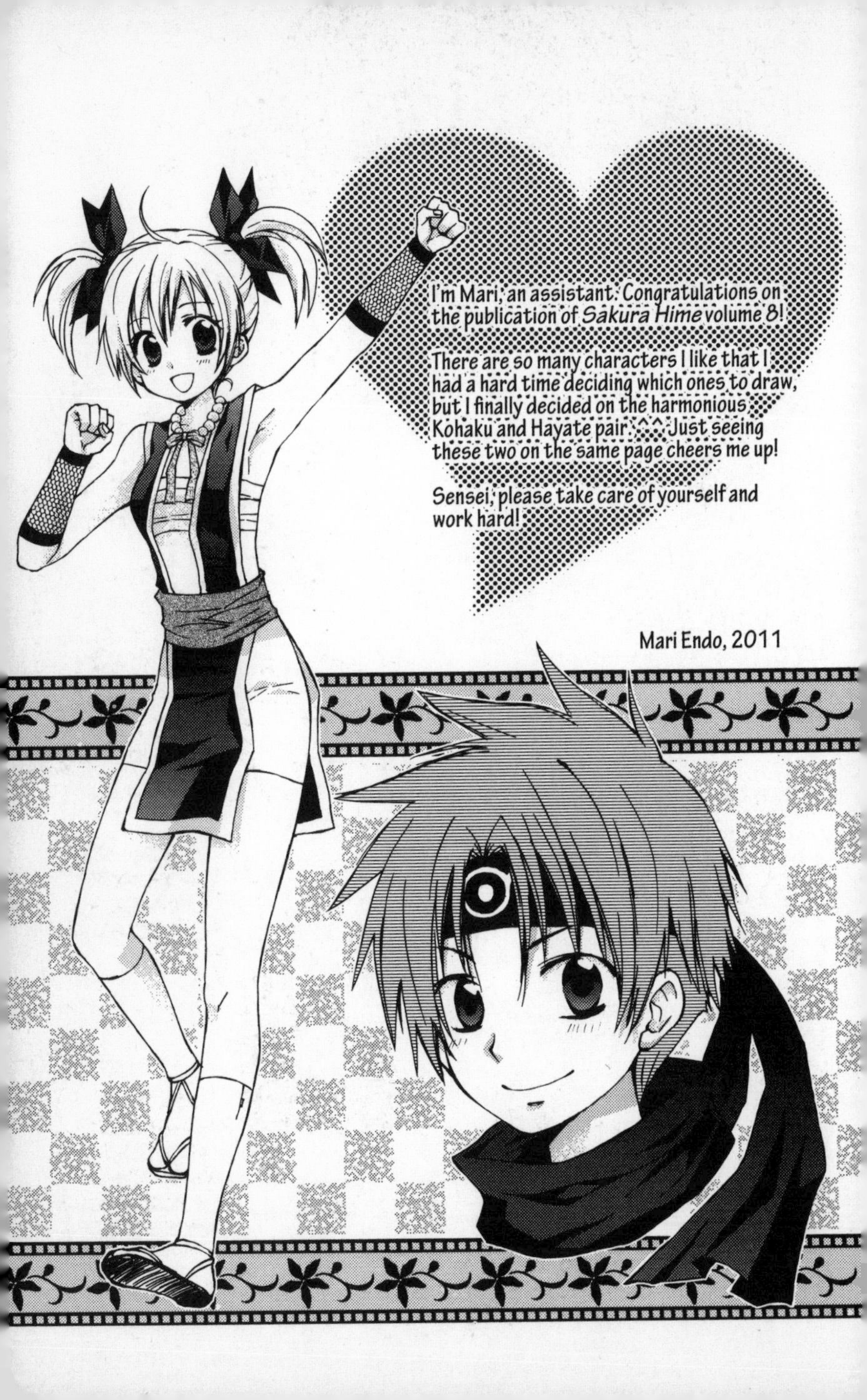
I'm Mari, an assistant. Congratulations on the publication of *Sakura Hime* volume 8!
There are so many characters I like that I had a hard time deciding which ones to draw, but I finally decided on the harmonious Kohaku and Hayate pair. ^^ Just seeing these two on the same page cheers me up!
Sensei, please take care of yourself and work hard!
Mari Endo, 2011

...revious volume, this one is filled with
...edy. Princess Yuri, the new character, is
...girly. I found myself being overwhelmed
...hen I created her. I enjoyed working on
...ut I wondered if it was all right to include
...his in the midst of a serious battle. The
...tionships are taking sharp turns now, so
...rward to the next volume as well.

...ura began her manga career in 1996 when
...es debuted in *Ribon* magazine. She gained
...e 1997 publication of *I·O·N*, and ever since
...nemura has been a major force in shojo
...popular series *Kamikaze Kaito Jeanne*,
...r *Kyoko*, *Full Moon*, and *The Gentlemen's*
...th *Kamikaze Kaito Jeanne* and *Full Moon*
...pted into animated TV series.

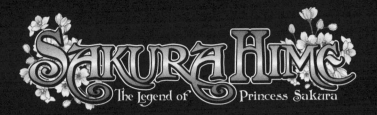

Sakura Hime: The Legend of Princess Sakura

Sakura Hime: The Legend of Princess Sakura
Volume 8
Shojo Beat Edition

STORY AND ART BY
Arina Tanemura

Translation & Adaptation/Tetsuichiro Miyaki
Touch-up Art & Lettering/Inori Fukuda Trant
Design/Sam Elzway
Editor/Nancy Thistlethwaite

Printed in the U.S.A.

Published by VIZ Media, LLC
P.O. Box 77010
San Francisco, CA 94107

10 9 8 7 6 5 4 3 2 1
First printing, June 2012

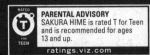

SURPRISE!

You may be reading the wrong way!

It's true: In keeping with the original Japanese comic format, this book reads from right to left—so action, sound effects, and word balloons are completely reversed. This preserves the orientation of the original artwork—plus, it's fun! Check out the diagram shown here to get the hang of things, and then turn to the other side of the book to get started!

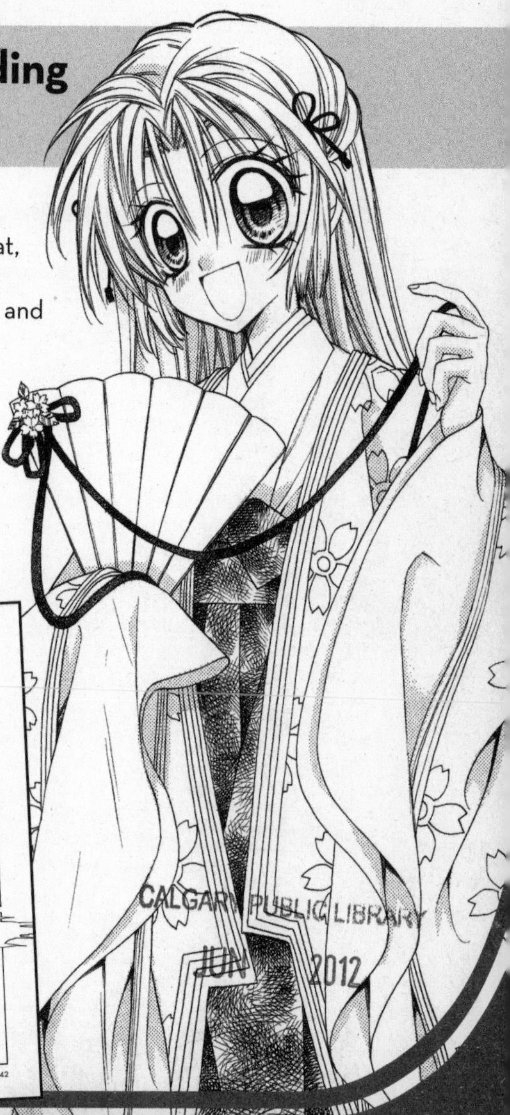

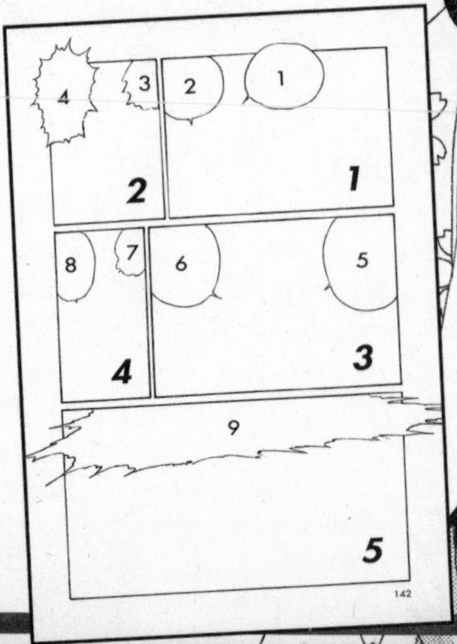
1
2
1
3
4
2
5
6
3
7
8
4
9
5
142